IN
CASTLE
AND
COURT HOUSE

RAMSAY COLLES.

(From the painting by Mr. J. Colin Forbes, R.C.A)

IN CASTLE AND COURT HOUSE

BEING REMINISCENCES OF 30 YEARS IN IRELAND

BY

RAMSAY COLLES

"The world's a stage," a stage without a light,
Whereon the actors blindly grope their way;
Happy are they whom Fortune guides aright:
For them she doth not, sorry is the play!

LONDON
T. WERNER LAURIE
CLIFFORD'S INN

To
J. E. EVANS-JACKSON
("ONE OF THE BEST. THERE ARE VERY
FEW OF US LEFT")

Contents

Contents

List of Illustrations

In Castle and Court House

CHAPTER I

CHARLES STEWART PARNELL'S LAST FIGHT

Parnell's Last Fight—Election in Carlow—The Priest:
In Politics—Hammond *v.* Kettle—I am Presiding
Officer—Sworn in at Carlow—Drive to Clonegall—
Midnight Visitors—A Personating Agent—Scenes in
Polling Booth—Illiterates Innumerable—I Frustrate
the Game—Expostulation—A Drive to Carlow—Our
Armed Guard—Result of Election—Parnell's Atti-
tude—His Return to Dublin—My Sonnet to Him—
His Death—Father Skerrett.

An unknown Greek philosopher remarked " Know
Thyself "; the modern philosopher says: " Let the
Public Know! " Acting on this excellent advice, I
proceed, as is now fashionable, to jot down what I
remember, before I am fifty, and have possibly
forgotten these " Footnotes to History."

My entry into public life commenced with my
being appointed Presiding officer at Clonegall, Co.
Carlow, when the struggle commenced between
Parnell's nominee, the late Mr Andrew Kettle, and

11

the late Mr Thomas Hammond, who had the support of the Priests.

It will be remembered that in 1891, Parnell's private life had been very dramatically exposed to the public gaze, and the Irish Priesthood saw their chance to free themselves from his autocratic rule, and threw themselves into the arena with a zest which eventually secured for the Church the victory; their war-cry being, " Purity in private as in public life."

In working to this end the priests fought to the death. They knew no such terms as compromise. I myself heard a young priest in the main street of Carlow, say to a voter, " You must either vote for this (holding out a crucifix) and Hammond, or vote for the Devil and Parnell." Such tactics employed by their spiritual guides had, of course, an immense weight with an ignorant and superstitious peasantry.

I was sworn in at 3 o'clock on Monday, 6th July, 1891, by Mr John Alexander, the Sheriff, and drove to Clonegall, and was put up at a small house for the night.

As my clerk, who accompanied me, was a thirsty soul, and as I was myself very dubious as to the resources of Clonegall, I purchased a couple of bottles of whisky, and lucky it was that I did so, for when, in order to be fresh for the duties of the morrow, I retired early to bed, I was so mercilessly persecuted by midnight visitors in the shape of agile agitators " from whom is derived the verb to flee," that in despair I arose, poured all the whisky into the wash basin, and proceeded to soak my pyjamas in the pure spirit!

I then wrung the garments out thoroughly, into the basin, and putting them on, sprang into bed, with the happy result of a total rout of the foe and the sleep of the just for myself!

When my clerk, who had slept at the house of the local clergyman, a teetotaller, turned up in the morning at 7 o'clock, I was still asleep. As the polling booth had to open at 8, he awoke me, and I explained the reason of the heavy aroma of alcohol in the room. Looking into the basin, he said, " Begorra! some poor fellah might like to have that, I'll just cork what remains of the blessed liquor up again." I expostulated in vain. He reminded me that when a big whisky fire at Roe's Distillery took place in Dublin, the crowd in the street drank the ignited fluid as it poured down the channels, taking their shoes off to serve them as drinking vessels. " I'll just put the bottle in my outside pocket," he said, " and some poor fellah 'll be glad enough to steal it out of it! " This was exactly what happened that very night in the crowded streets of Carlow.

Polling commenced sharp at 8 o'clock, many men hanging around for the polling booth to open. I shall not give the names of the personating agents, but one of them was a priest. As a resident in Dublin, and knowing little or nothing of Carlow, I was astonished at the number of illiterates.

In order to make my statement clear to the general reader, I must explain the method of procedure.

13

In Castle and Court House

If Pat Murphy, on being handed his voting paper, says he cannot read or write, the Presiding Officer fills a form of solemn declaration to that effect, and having read it aloud to him, witnesses Murphy's mark on the form. Murphy then declares aloud that he votes either for Hammond or Kettle, as the case may be; but the ballot being no longer secret, the personating agents know how he votes, and the priest being a personating agent, becomes aware that Pat has done as he was told to do.

As nearly every voter in the district appeared to be illiterate, I became suspicious, and after a little reflection, I handed the next illiterate his voting paper upside down. He confirmed my suspicions by turning it round, the while declaring himself unable to read! This was too much for me. I said to him " Are you prepared to make a solemn declaration that you can neither read nor write ? "

" I am, sir," he replied.

A happy thought struck me, " Are you prepared to take your *oath* that you can neither read nor write ? "

He hesitated. I continued, " See here," I said, producing the familiar, so-called " Swearing Book " (a New Testament with a cross painted on it in white enamel). " Are you prepared to kiss that Book ? " handing it to him, and pointing to the cross ; " are you prepared to kiss *that* and swear that you cannot read ? Remember there is such a thing as perjury, and that you can be severely punished for swearing what is false !"

Charles Stewart Parnell's Last Fight

The priest here sought to interfere. He saw that things were looking very blue. He could absolve Pat for making a solemn declaration which, though it was false, his spiritual adviser approved of his making; he could not shield poor Pat from the punishment the law awards to perjurers.

I silenced his Reverence by holding up my hand, while I continued, addressing the voter:

"Why did you turn that paper round?"

"Och, shure! I was only twisting it," said Pat.

"Well," I said, "either swear that you can't read, or 'twist' into that corner (pointing to it) where you will find a pencil, and put your mark against the name of the candidate for whom you intend to vote. Then fold the paper in two, and put it into this box," pointing to the ballot-box, which stood on the table; "and remember the ballot is secret."

From this time on, my course was clear. In only one case, from that hour, about 2 o'clock, until the polling booth closed at 8 p.m., did anyone take the oath. One and all of the so-called illiterates were eager to make the solemn declaration, but shirked the consequences of the oath.

The priest expostulated, but I was firm.

"Reverend Sir," I said, "You must really keep quiet. I will take the consequences of my conduct, and if you interfere with me any more, I shall, with great reluctance, have you removed."

This had the desired effect, and I parted the best of friends with all present. Later I wrote to Mr

15

In Castle and Court House

A. J. Balfour, who was then Chief Secretary for Ireland, on this subject.

At twenty minutes past eight that evening all Clonegall had assembled to see us depart. First an Irish jaunting car with four armed policemen. Then the ballot-box placed in a conspicuous position on the well of the car, with my clerk on one side with a policeman, and a policeman with me on the other side. Then a third car, like the car in front, with four policemen, and in this order we drove along the country roads, on a lovely July night, with the golden sickle of a new moon on high; drove between hedgerows which were prodigal homes of unmarketable beauty, and which glistened with the shaken silver of a recent summer shower. Carlow was reached at five minutes to eleven, and the ballot-box handed over to be dealt with by those to whom the counting of the votes had been entrusted. Our task was ended.

The result of the poll was declared at 1.20 next day, in favour of Hammond. Parnell was very cool. He spoke, as usual, with much deliberation, and even with the defeat at Kilkenny fresh in his memory, declared that this was not the end. Parnell was always a speaker who impressed me as one who thought first and spoke afterwards. He did not merely talk for the sake of talking. His voice had a fine, sonorous ring in it, and carried conviction with it. We returned by the same train to Dublin. Parnell hardly spoke a word all the way. As a proof of the kindliness of the man, I may mention the fact that the first thing he did on reaching Dublin, was to drive to a private hospital in Harcourt Street to inquire about one of his followers who had been injured at the previous Election in Kilkenny.

Although nominally a Conservative, I had great sympathy with Charles Stewart Parnell, especially in his struggle against the interference of the priests in politics, and I addressed the following sonnet to him, submitting it first to that severe critic, Dr George Sigerson, who approved of it, and gratified me by saying that he considered it very good.

To Charles Stewart Parnell, M.P.

He is not vanquish'd who renews the fight,
　And open-breasted bids the foe again
　Defiance, while alert he waits the rain
Of blows that fall, and, meeting might with might,
Is conscious of his strength, as of his right.
　He is not vanquish'd who erect doth stand,
　And holdeth fortune in his own right hand,
With face uplifted and with eyes alight.

Nay, rather, though his foes plant many a blow,
　And mock his silence with untimely mirth;
　Tho' marr'd his visage be beyond recall—
Yea, though his blood should as a river flow—
　Hail him we victor, who from every fall
　Riseth, Antæus-like, from Mother Earth!

The polling day in Clonegall was the 7th July, 1891, and on the 7th October, exactly three months later, Charles Stewart Parnell was dead! Dead? Has anyone who has seen Charles Stewart Parnell alive seen him after death? The Rev. Father Skerret, a dignitary of the Roman Catholic Church, assured me that he did his best, as a Priest, to see the corpse, but was refused. Father Skerret impressed me as being a lover of truth. He died very suddenly himself. On the last occasion on which I saw him, an occasion made memorable to me by a disgraceful assault upon myself, the story of which I tell later, he said, " I declare solemnly that though I have searched high and low, I have never met anyone, man or woman, even his nearest and dearest, who saw the dead Parnell."

There we may leave the matter. We may not agree with his methods. As William Ernest Henley pointed out, in that brilliant but short-lived paper *The Scot's Observer*, Parnell had all the qualifications to militate against his being a Leader of the Irish Parliamentary Party. He was a Landowner, a Protestant, and a Gentleman, and surely when we look at

" The apes whose ancestors were men,"

we must solemnly admit this statement.

He was a man, take him for all in all;
We ne'er shall look upon his like again.

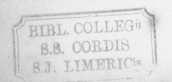

CHAPTER II

THE IRISH LITERARY MOVEMENT

Irish Literary Movement—Sir Walter Besant and " The
Author "—The Poets and Poetry of Young Ireland—
A Literary Pilgrimage—Miss Katharine Tynan—W.
B. Yeats—Rev. Father Russell, S.J.—Rosa Mulholland
(Lady Gilbert)—John O'Leary the Fenian Leader—
Some Visitors to Whitehall—George Pellew—Some
American Writers—Richard Ashe King—Anecdote of
James Payn—Dr Douglas Hyde—" A. E." Russell—
Charlotte Grace O'Brien—Dr Sigerson.

I SANDWICH between the description of Parnell's last
fight, and my account of Lecky's candidature for the
representation of T. C. D. in Parliament, an account
of some of the representatives of literature in Ireland
at a time when many who are now well known were
starting their careers.

When " The Author " was founded by Sir Walter
Besant in July, 1890, he wrote to me, asking me to
contribute an article on "Literature in Ireland." I
did so to the best of my ability, but like many another
well meant effort, my attempt to catalogue the names
of my contemporaries was not altogether well
received. This was not my fault, for the article was
mutilated in an extraordinary manner, not, I am
certain by Sir Walter; and, as an instance of the

19

In Castle and Court House

stupidity with which the excisions were made, I may point to the fact that my references to a young and rising poet who had fully justified the praise with which his work was greeted (Mr W. B. Yeats), were cut completely out.

Professor Dowden had laughingly remarked, on his deciding to decline the offer of the Chair of Literature in an American University: "I suppose I make take out a perpetuity in Mount Jerome now." Mount Jerome is the Protestant burial ground, and I had used Dowden's remark without acknowledging its source, and was naturally accused of bad taste in consequence. These were some of the troubles that afflicted the just, but I was not much worried by the strictures passed upon me, for I was conscious of the fact that I never spoke a word or wrote a line with the object of paining anyone. Swinburne paid me the compliment of writing to me, " I am sure you cannot have written anything to offend a sensible reader." I mention this lest there should be anything in this book that may be mis-interpreted.

The Irish Literary Movement, as it has since been called, was started about 1886. Poets who have since won world-wide reputations, were then either writing verses for circulation amongst their friends, or sending the poems to " The Irish Fireside," edited, I believe, by Miss Rose Kavanagh, a charming young woman, herself a writer of graceful verse, who, alas! was laid in a few years in an early grave, the victim of consumption.

An attempt had been made, in 1886, to resusci-

20

The Irish Literary Movement

tate "The Dublin University Magazine," which was
in 1840 a publication of which Ireland might be
proud; and to this later issue, contributions were
sent by all who aspired to be literary. Mr Yeats
sent some of his earlier work to this magazine, and
in it appeared his finest dramatic poem, "Mosada."

Those were the days when pilgrimages were made,
every Sunday, to Whitehall, Clondalkin, where Miss
Katharine Tynan (now Mrs H. A. Hinkson) lived
in a delightful old farmhouse. Miss Tynan, who
has since contributed very largely both in prose and
verse, to the delight of her readers, had at that time
only a slender little volume bearing her name:
"Louise de la Vallière." It was, however, a little
book full of promise, and was followed by another
in which a great advance in her art was discernible,
"Shamrocks," for which I suggested the motto
chosen from a poem by Richard Hengist Horne,
"'Tis always morning somewhere in the world."

At the time of which I write, there was no steam-
tram to help pilgrims on their way to this literary
Mecca. Four miles, at least, of country road had to
be walked or cycled, but to young hearts full of
enthusiasm, young heads full of glorious projects,
and to the springy step of youth, what are four
miles? I used to think it was most appropriate that
the glass panels of the hall door at Whitehall were
couleur de rose, for the young writer's view of her
friends was always "kindly Irish of the Irish,"
making the most of their virtues, and quite blind to
their faults, whatever they might be.

21

In Castle and Court House

In the delightful low, thatched farmhouse under the Dublin Mountains, with its tangled orchard at the back, its garden with a sundial, its labyrinth of little flower-beds with box borders, and its great walnut tree, all sorts and conditions of men and women might be met. Here a Protestant Home Ruler hob-a-nobbed fraternally with an enthusiastic Conservative, or a Fenian leader. All politics were forgotten as well as were all creeds. Here I met, amongst others, Father Russell of the Society of Jesus, Editor of " The Irish Monthly," an old established and ably conducted magazine, in which the literary tone predominated. To this magazine Oscar Wilde contributed some of his earlier verses; for it M. E. Francis (Mrs Blundell) wrote her first novel " Whither? " and some of her best work. Father Russell, a brother of Lord Russell of Killowen, has a fine catholic taste in literature, and " The Irish Monthly " represented some of the best productions of the literary party in Ireland. Miss Tynan, of course, was a contributor, as were also Miss Rosa Mulholland, now Lady Gilbert, Miss Ellen O'Leary, sister of John O'Leary (the old Fenian chief) and Miss Dora Sigerson (now Mrs Clement Shorter) and her sister Hester (now Mrs Piatt).

Not the least noticeable person in Whitehall was Miss Tynan's father, a fine old man, not unlike Walter Savage Landor in that old lion's most combative moods. Mr Tynan expressed himself in vigorous terms, and always won an audience who listened to him with more than ordinary pleasure.

The Irish Literary Movement

" Amongst the guests star-scattered o'er the grass "
on the afternoon of a summer's day, I found Miss
Frances Wynne, the author of a very beautiful little
book of verse, entitled " Whisper." Yeats also was
there and recited to me on the road home his musical
verses on the old fisherman, with its refrain—

" When I was a boy with never a crack in my heart."

Frederick Gregg, now an author and journalist in
New York, was a constant visitor, as were also W. S.
Pyper and Pococke, who wrote a clever parody on
Browning, and was joint author with my old schoolfellow, Henry Stewart Macran, of a paper entitled
Signs of the Times, which, though it did not
contain a word of sense, was read before the Philosophical Society in T.C.D., and gained the Gold
Medal for composition; a medal which the authors
refused, under the circumstances, to accept. Macran
is now a Fellow of T.C.D., and the author of an
important work on Greek music. Few men combine,
as does Macran, a knowledge of Greek and Music.

It is to Miss Tynan that I owe my knowledge of
George Pellew, of Katonah, New York. He was
then collecting the materials of his book " In Castle
and Cabin, or Talks in Ireland in 1887," which on
its appearance Lord Morley of Blackburn declared
in " The Nineteenth Century," to be one of the most
important contributions towards the solution af the
Irish problem.

A mad dog was in the neighbourhood of Clondalkin at the time and many people carried revolvers.

Pellew had to pass through a lonely stretch of road
to reach "Belgard" where Sir Henry Hayes
Laurence, Bart., a descendant of the great Indian
hero, lived, and on whom he proposed to call, but
he refused the loan of any weapon whatsoever.
Pellew and I were driven into Dublin that evening
and spent the greater part of the night at the
Imperial Hotel, discussing literature. I remember
he was enthusiastic about Wilfrid Scawen Blunt's
"Love Sonnets of Proteus," and he was the only
man I ever met, save Mr Watts-Dunton who appreciated the poems of Ebenezer Jones, the author of
"Studies in Sensation and Event." I can hear him,
after this lapse of time, reciting "When the World is
Burning," a truly extraordinary poem which, like
Wordsworth's Lucy

> There were none to praise
> And very few to love.

Pellew it was who sent me novels by Edgar
Saltus, whose work I collected with enthusiasm, and
on whom, years after, I wrote an article in *The
Westminster Review*, gaining a letter thereby from
Saltus, signed "Yours attentively." Pellew also
called my attention to the verse of Edgar Fawcett,
especially to a poem entitled "Dei Gratia." He
gave me an introduction to Thomas Sergeant Perry,
of Boston, author of "From Opitz to Lessing"; "A
Study in Neo-Classicism"; "The Evolution of the
Snob"; and a Study of "Greek Literature," an
exhaustive treatise on the subject. Mrs Perry is an
artist and the author of some beautiful translations

from the Greek Anthology entitled "From the Garden of Hellas." She published anonymously a charming little volume of poems, "The Heart of the Weed," a title explained by a quotation from James Russell Lowell, "to win the secret of the weed's plain heart." This little book contains a sonnet on Swinburne's poems to children, a copy of which I sent to the author of "A Dark Month."

Another friend I owe to Pellew was Richard Hovey, the American poet, author of some beautiful verse. But I must reserve my recollections of American poets for the section to be devoted to Walt Whitman and other representatives of literature in America.

I have always admired Miss Katharine Tynan's poems. One of her poems contributed to "The Dublin University Magazine," she has, I believe, never reprinted, but the following, which I quote from memory is, I think, exquisite in many of its expressions; for instance, "Her eyes are starring the happy shadows."

O my swallows! hasten up from the South,
For young May walks knee-deep in the Irish meadows,
And living gold is her hair, and the breath of her mouth
Is delight, and her eyes are starring the happy shadows.
The honey-heart of the cowslip lies at her feet,
The faint fresh buds of the hawthorn trail o'er her bosom,
And the garment that covers her, fragrant and sweet,
Is the mingled rose and snow of the apple blossom.

In another poem which won my admiration she writes of the dawn—

All the East, a rose uncurled,
Grows golden at the heart.

25

In Castle and Court House

There is nothing from " the gossamer spun on the dewy lea " to the " dawn's rose leaves shed on a yellow sea " that she has not rendered dearer to us by virtue of poetic association.

Mr H. A. Hinkson, a distinguished graduate of T.C.D., I also met at Whitehall. He is the author of one or two law books and of many capital novels, and is a Prince of Good Fellows. He married Miss Tynan in 1892.

Another writer I met at Whitehall was Mr Richard Ashe King, author of " The Wearing of the Green." I am indebted to him for the following story told him by James Payn, the novelist. It appears that Payn received a letter from an unknown person praising his works. " I liked to hear my books called ' works '," said Payn, " and I replied. He wrote me again, and I wrote in return a jocose letter. He replied in like terms. I again wrote telling him a funny story. He sent me a funny story. I capped it, and in a short time I got a Roland for my Oliver. I got a rather blue story in his next, and I wrote him one to match it, finally I got an indignant letter, commencing ' Sir, are you aware that I am a woman! ' I often," said Payn, " blush under the bedclothes when I think of the stories I told that woman! "

Others who used to visit Whitehall were: Dr Douglas Hyde, very learned in the Irish tongue, of which he compiled a dictionary; George Russell, the poet, better known as " A. E.," the author of much mystical verse; Dr Sigerson, who wrote on many subjects, including poets and poetry; Edwin

The Irish Literary Movement

Hamilton, the Aristophanes of Ireland; Mr James Bowker, an official in the G.P.O., a lover of old books and a contributor to " The Irish Monthly "; and Charles Johnson and his sister, the son and daughter of that fine old fire-eater, Johnson of Bally-kilbeg. I have also a dim recollection of a very charming personality, that of the late Charlotte Grace O'Brien, daughter of Smith O'Brien, the Irish rebel, whose statue, arrayed in a perfect frock coat, ornaments an approach to O'Connell Bridge.

CHAPTER III

LECKY'S CANDIDATURE FOR T.C.D.

W. E. H. Lecky the great Historian—Michael Hickie, a
well-known Dublin Bookseller—An Amusing Inci-
dent—Vacancy in Parliamentary Representation of
T.C.D. — Electioneering Arguments — Professor
Mahaffy's Comment—My Lucky Discovery—Lecky's
Early Book—" The Religious Tendencies of the
Age "—*Irish Times v. Dublin Daily Express*—Lecky
and the Church—Extracts from a very scarce Book—
Lecky on Christianity—The Church Militant—My
Interview with Lecky—Why I hold Unpublished
Letters—His Triumphant Return for T.C.D.—His
Personal Kindness to Myself.

THE first time I saw W. E. H. Lecky, the historian,
was in 1891, in a second-hand book shop kept by
one Michael Hickie. I remember Lecky, " angular
and profound," with his hands clasped behind him,
gazing at the titles of books far beyond the range
of my vision. He seemed to my fancy—let me say
it with all reverence for a great man and a great
writer—like an inspired giraffe browsing upon the
foliage on the topmost boughs of the tree of knowledge! Hickie stood in the centre of his shop piled
up with stacks of books on every subject. A man

came in with a volume he had picked up off the improvised shelf outside the shop, and asked:

"What do you want for that?"

It was a shabby looking copy of the Bible.

Hickie pulled his beard meditatively, and said "one shilling."

"It's not worth a shilling," said the man, emphatically, "I'll give you sixpence for it."

Upon this Hickie awoke, and shouted "Get out of my shop! Any man who says that the word of God is not worth a shilling won't stop here!"

Hickie was not religious, he told me afterwards that he had mistaken Lecky for a clergyman!

When, in the latter part of 1895, a vacancy was created in the Parliamentary representation of Dublin University by the Right Hon. David Plunket being raised to the Upper House as Lord Rathmore, the candidates were George Wright, Q.C., and Lecky. The fight raged hot, for both were well known men, the one on account of his personality, and his skill and eminence as a lawyer, the other on account of his world-wide celebrity as an historian. All's fair in love and war, and it is not surprising that Lecky's opponents used as a weapon against him his heterodox opinions as expressed in his works, especially in "The Rise of Rationalism in Europe," and "History of European Morals."

A very large number of the electors were clergymen, and it was held that if by any possibility they were ignorant of Lecky's works, they should be made aware of his having called an unfortunate class of women, " The High Priestesses of Purity "; and consequently everything was done that could be done, to intensify his supposed hostile attitude towards Christianity in general, and the Church in particular. He was branded not alone as an agnostic, but as an out and out atheist, and the simple, kindly-hearted gentleman was painted as a very devil incarnate.

Elections in Ireland are perhaps no worse than in England, but the absurdity of the arguments on both sides may be gauged from the fact that one of Mr Lecky's supporters wrote to the daily papers pointing out that Lecky paid pew rent! This was followed by a letter from an opponent who demonstrated clearly that the historian, notwithstanding his payment of pew rent, never went to church. Another correspondent rushed into print stating that he knew for a fact that Mr George Wright was a devout attendant every Sunday at such and such a church! Finally Professor Mahaffy wittily remarked that the electors were called upon to face the problem as to whether they would prefer to support a candidate who paid pew rent but did not go to church, or a candidate who went regularly to church, but did not pay pew rent.

However laughable, at this time and distance, such arguments may appear to be, there is no doubt whatever that heavy artillery was being used against Lecky, the weapons being somewhat antiquated and, as students of American history may remember, the ammunition consisted of theology as it did actually consist on one occasion in the American War of Watt's hymn books. After all, orthodoxy carries weight, and the church which, as I shall prove, leant towards Lecky's side, began to have doubts about the wisdom of its choice.

At this critical time I was, one Saturday, wandering along the quays in Dublin (almost as famous as those in Paris, and for the same reason) in search of old books. Seeing me passing, and knowing my keen interest in such things, a second-hand bookseller, Mr George Webb, of 5, Crampton Quay, asked me in to see a book by Lecky. I entered the shop in a most sceptical mood, for I had studied Lecky's books, including his " Leaders of Public Opinion in Ireland "; judge then my astonishment when Mr Webb produced a little volume bound in blue cloth, entitled " The Religious Tendencies of the Age," published by Messrs Otley and Saunders in 1860. The book did not bear the author's name on the title page, and there was no reference to previous work by the same hand in its 320 pages, but an advertisement at the end of the volume stated that by the same author was written " Leaders of Public Opinion in Ireland."

In addition to the book, which I eagerly acquired, was an autograph letter from the author, written from 14, Onslow Gardens, his residence in London, and addressed to a correspondent in Dublin, in which Mr Lecky evidently replied to a question with regard to his authorship, by admitting the fact.

Never did I pay fifteen shillings more willingly than to Mr Webb, the bookseller, on that occasion! I now possessed materials from which to manufacture a bomb to throw into the camp of the enemy!

The Irish Times, the most powerful organ in Ireland, and a supporter of Lecky, was then edited by the late Mr Scott. "Promising Scott" he was, called, because he had a habit of promising anything; and such I found him to be when later I called upon him. *The Dublin Daily Express* was owned by my friend, James Poole Maunsell, who died all too soon. I had been connected, off and on, with the *Express* as a reviewer, occasional leader writer, etc., and accordingly to the *Express* I went, and saw the late Dr Patton, who at once saw the force of my argument, and, he having promised me the space I required, I repaired to the offices of *The Irish Times* and saw Mr Scott, who promised me the same amount of space—a full column.

The result of my perusal of " The Religious Tendencies of the Age" appeared on the following Monday morning, when my full column appeared in *The Dublin Daily Express*, and not one word was to be found in *The Irish Times!* The immediate effect of my signed letter on the subject of the contents of the book, was the trebling of the circulation of the *Express*, which was quoted by all the papers in the kingdom, and was made much use of by Lecky's committee.

Readers of Mrs Lecky's beautiful life of her husband, may wonder that there is no reference to

RAMSAY COLLES (1896).

these matters to be found in her pages. The fact is that when Mrs Lecky was advertising for letters written by the great historian, I was in Germany, and my attention not being drawn to the advertisement, I did not forward the letters written to me by Mr Lecky, to his biographer for inspection. Readers of that life will remember that Lecky intended to enter the Church, and only abandoned the idea after devoting some years to the study of theology. The tone, therefore, of " The Religious Tendencies of the Age," his first book, is not to be wondered at.

As the book had so great an effect in connection with Dublin University Election, and as it has been quite out of print for years, and is indeed very scarce, the following quotation may not be out of place, and may give the reader an idea of the contents, as well as a picture of what Lecky considered the profession which he intended to follow to be—

" The position," he wrote, " of the Protestant clergyman is, in theory at least, one of the most beautiful that can be conceived. It forms, as Goethe remarked, the one idyll of modern civilisation. Our reformers, by abolishing compulsory celibacy would remove religion from an unamiable and comparatively unproductive isolation and transfuse it through society as an ameliorating and harmonizing influence. They would blend it with every scene of domestic joy, with the ineffable love, and the open sympathy, and the unclouded confidence of the family circle, with the ringing laugh of children and the soaring hopes of youth. They would exhibit in a single man the model christian and the model citizen; the lights of heaven and of earth mingling and intensifying each other. He who aspires to so high a position should seek, in every way to make religion in his person attractive, and to gain the respect and the affection of those around him. Youth should find him a participator in its pleasures, and a cordial sympathiser with its hopes; manhood, a sagacious counsellor in secular matters as well as in religion; age, a patient listener and an unwearied minister to its wants. He should endeavour, by varied studies, by the cultivation of every grace, by the ascendancy in society as would secure a respectful attention to his statements. If he has wit, it should coruscate with a bright, though innocuous flame. If he possesses conversational powers he should employ them in allaying discord and promoting charity and adorning truth. In the pulpit he should make his many studies converge to a single object, deriving illustrations from the most varied sources, culling pregnant thoughts from the most dissimilar writers, borrowing examples from every page of history and biography. Untenable arguments and exaggerated assertions should find no place in his discourses. Virulent controversy should never be introduced into his pulpit. He should combat error by the enforcement of truth, and dwell rather on doctrines that are generally admitted than on those that are questioned. Above

34

all, he should represent Christianity as an ennobling and harmonizing principle, promoting human happiness and developing human capacities, a principle designed to reform society, not to subvert it, and to purify the enjoyments of life, not to destroy them."

Such, I wrote in my letter to the *Express*, is the picture drawn by Mr Lecky of the modern " man of God," and who shall say that his brush is tinged with either agnosticism or atheism?

" There lives no record of reply," to quote Tennyson's " In Memoriam," and I drove my argument home with but one more extract with which I shall trouble my readers, an extract trebly valuable at the time, as can be readily understood, for I alone possessed the book, and I alone could quote from it!

In reference to a future life, the so-called atheist had written—

" But as finite things can never satisfy the longing of man after the infinite, as a canker lurks in every pleasure, and time withers life's noblest works, as imagination creates aspirations for higher existences and more perfect forms of enjoyment than earth can afford, there is an object of ambition offered to us grander than any of those things that are seen, a state of life is revealed where the capacities of man may be developed to the fullest extent, where his affections may find worthy objects, his intellect an ample range, his hopes a full completion. This life is supplemented by death; earth is made the portal to heaven, and ambition finds in the future world its noblest and its final object."

The effect of my letter, which contained other extracts, and closed with the words, " I have dwelt thus long on this book, because it exhibits an attitude towards Christianity on the part of the great historian with which his opponents do not credit him," was undoubtedly very great, and I was much gratified by a letter of thanks from Mr Lecky, in which he pathetically refers to the fact that the book was published so long ago as 1860. "Who would have thought," he wrote, "that a book dead and buried so long should arise from the tomb to confront me now," and concluded by inviting me to call to see him at a private hotel in Molesworth Street.

I had received another letter on the same subject. This was from a high dignitary of the Church, and an old friend of mine, also asking me to call. I did so, and was much amused to find the Church was largely represented on the occasion. I laughingly inquired of my friend why he had summoned a spirit like myself to face such an assembly, and the reply was that the Church, as represented by those present, had read the letter in the *Express* with much satisfaction, but were anxious, if possible, that I should prove from " The Religious Tendencies of the Age " that Lecky believed in the Divinity of Christ.

Remembering the sentence given above, " Untenable arguments and exaggerated assertions should find no place in the discourses of the clergy," I felt at once the difficulty of such a task, but promised to do my best, with which unsatisfactory assurance I left my audience, happy in the main, and, on dipping

Lecky's Candidature for T.C.D.

further into the book, managed to write a second
letter, which occupied two columns in *The Daily
Express*, besides appearing in *The Belfast Newsletter* and *The Cork Constitution*.

In the meantime *The Irish Times* remained silent
on the subject, and aroused the ire of its opponent,
which had the following:—

"THE UNIVERSITY ELECTION

It is only right to state that the complete refutation of Mr Lecky's critics, supplied in Mr Ramsay
Colles's extracts from Mr Lecky's 'Religious
Tendencies of the Age,' was deliberately withheld
from the readers of a newspaper purporting to
support Mr Wright. This is a fair sample of the
way in which Mr Lecky's opponents are economising
truth to serve their own ends."

I called to see Mr Lecky on the afternoon of
Friday, 29th November, and found him as serene
as if no storm were sweeping around him. He asked
me where I had found the book, and thanked me
most graciously for the good use I had made of
it. I felt sorry to be worrying him on the afternoon
of a busy day, and said so, but he replied that his
speech made during the day had not wearied him
in the least, though he had been frequently interrupted. He said, "I take a pleasure in the exuberance of youth." I thought of his reference to the
"ringing laughter of children" in the little book.
He referred to his forthcoming "Liberty and
Democracy," which reminded me of a promise made

to a friend, and I asked him to sign for me one or two copies of his little volume of poems; which he asked me to leave with him for the purpose. These he kindly signed and sent me.

He sat in a low armchair, his massive head swaying occasionally from side to side, and his hands clasped in front of him. I did not stay long, for he had a public dinner to attend in an hour or so, a function at which I also had to be present. I said in leaving, " I feel certain of your success, Mr Lecky! " but he merely replied " Thank you," and added " and thank you for all you have done in the matter."

Lecky's return as representative of T.C.D. was received with great enthusiasm, and how ably and energetically he acted in that capacity is a matter of history. He never forgot the humble but effective part I played at that period of his career, and when, many years later, I was a candidate for a commissionership in West Africa, he was one of my most ardent supporters; and it was through his influence that I was appointed in 1896 a Justice of the Peace for the Borough of Dublin. I may add that, notwithstanding the machinations of many enemies, political and social, I still retain my Commission of the Peace.

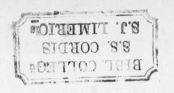

CHAPTER IV

SOCIAL LIFE IN DUBLIN

The Two Sections of Society in Düblin—Castle *v.* Mansion House—Sir George Moyers—Same Division in Literary as in Social Life—People *v.* Professors— Thomas Moore Centenary—Amusing Incidents—Tercentenary of T.C.D.—Aloofness of "the Silent Sister"—Some Young Poets—A Don's Luncheon Party—The Poet and the Bee—Lionel Johnson—W. A. Craig—What happened at "The Professor's Love Story"—The Corinthian Club—Some Members— Martin Harvey and Edward Terry—Miss Irene Vanbrugh—Chancellor Tisdall—Shakespeare and Bacon— George Alexander—W. S. Penley—A Unique Recitation—The Scientific Beggar Man.

SOCIETY in Dublin may be said to be divided into two sections composed of those who attend receptions at the Mansion House and those who go to Drawing Rooms at Dublin Castle. Very few, indeed, are those who go to functions at both. This used not to be so. At one time it was customary for the Lord Lieutenant to be present at civic banquets given by the Lord Mayor, and for the Lord Mayor of Dublin to attend His Excellency's levees and be present at St Patrick's ball, given on the 17th March in each year.

39

All this, however, is changed, owing chiefly to
"the great divide" made by the political feeling
which has been allowed to create distrust on both
sides, and has fixed such an immeasurable gulf
between the Castle and the Mansion House;
between the Representative of the Crown and
Representative of the City, as is not likely to be
bridged over in our time.

Sir George Moyers, LL.D., when Lord Mayor of
Dublin in 1881, entertained the Lord Lieutenant and
Countess Cowper. This was the last occasion on
which the representatives of the sovereign were
received at the Mansion House.

This division of the body Social in Dublin is also
seen in the cleft between the representatives of the
Literary Movement in younger Ireland, and those
who represent the traditions of Trinity College.
Never, indeed, has there been a popular movement
in connection with the literary life of Ireland, that
has had the whole-hearted sympathy of those connected with Dublin University. As an example, I
may point to the Thomas Moore Centenary, which
got no countenance from T.C.D., though Oliver
Wendell Holmes, from the far United States, sent a
poem specially written for the occasion, and Moore's
genius received recognition from all parts of the
world. This spirit of aloofness from the life of the
people is the great mistake made by "the Silent
Sister."

In all great popular movements there are bound
to be mistakes and *fiascoes*, and the Moore Cen-

tenary was not without its laughable incidents; the
chief of which was that the late Dennis Florence
MacCarthy, himself a gifted translator of Calderon,
and a poet whose verses on " Waiting for the May "
are as musical as any in our language, was no after-
dinner speaker, and although expected to deliver an
oration, could get no further than " Ladies and
Gentleman," despite which fact, the oration duly
appeared in the morrow's papers! Another whim-
sical occurrence was that the laurel wreath designed
for MacCarthy's brows, when placed upon his head,
fell down to his shoulders, making a necklet instead
of a crown!

The Centenary committee would have been worthy
of all admiration and true applause, if the result of
its labours had been the removal of a hideous statue
to Moore, which stands in College Street. Professor
Dowden had a good humoured jest on this, and said
that the new one to take its place should represent
the Muse giving a sound castigation to " Our
Western Bul-Bul, half Cupid, half Tom-Tit " for his
many peccadillos.

Be that as it may, Moore was a true singer, his
songs are singable, and although Professor Yelverton Tyrrell in his admirable book on " Latin Poetry "
has likened his work to Horace at its worst, and has
laughed at—

> Fill the bumper fair;
>   Every drop we sprinkle,
> From the brow of care,
>   Wipes away a wrinkle,

there are still left some to whom Wendell Holmes's

poem on the Centenary will appeal. I quote from
memory a couple of stanzas, as the poem has not
been reprinted.

> She is seated before the Clementi piano;
>   There were six of us then—there are two of us now.
> She is singing, the girl with the silver soprano,
>   How the Lord of the Valley was false to his vow.
> " Let Erin remember," the echoes are calling,
>   Through the Vale of Avoca the waters are rolled,
> The Exile laments while the night-dews are falling—
>   The Morning of Life dawns again as of old.

But if T.C.D. was indifferent to a popular movement like the Moore Centenary, the vast body of the
people were equally indifferent to subjects which
greatly moved the University, as, for instance, the
Tercentenary Celebrations, which were strictly
academic in tone and environment, and of which the
most noteworthy were, a garden party given in the
Fellows' garden, when a mulberry tree was planted
by Miss Salmon, daughter of the Provost; the performance in the Leinster Hall of an ode specially
composed for the occasion by Sir Robert Stewart,
and the production of a play by Undergraduates at
the Gaiety Theatre.

But though the University, as a body, remained
indifferent to the Irish Literary Movement,
individual professors took a kindly interest in some
of the youthful poets. Thus I met two of these
young men at luncheon one Sunday. For policy's
sake I shall call them Bates and Thompson. I
arrived earlier than the bards and was shown into the
Professor's study. I found him busy reading the

Social Life in Dublin

poems of Bates. He handed me a volume by Thompson, and said:

" I think it would be well if you memorised a line or so, to fire off at the author, during luncheon. I am choosing a line from Bates, with the same view."

The line I chose was

" How much of pain it takes to purify the world."

The day was an unclouded one in July, and when we reached the dining-room with its French windows opening on the garden full of summer spice and humming air, I wondered if I had chosen my quotation wisely. The Professor got in his quotation very aptly and I was in despair. However, Providence came to my aid. A blundering bee came buzzing in and, taking Thompson's nose for a red, red rose, which it closely resembled, was brushed away, only to return and bury its sting in the poet's preface! Then there was a hub-bub, and blue-bags and other forms of consolation were administered. " When the tumult dwindled to a calm," I quietly observed, " How much of pain it takes to purify the world."

Poets are strange things whom we must not judge harshly. One of the poets I met at this period was the late Lionel Johnson, author of " The Art of Thomas Hardy." I was introduced to him by a local bard, W. A. Craig, who wrote a volume of ballads and poems, and of whom more anon. We dined at the hotel, and repaired to the Gaiety Theatre, where we were shown into a small box.

43

Johnson, who was quite sober, was no sooner seated than he went to sleep, and snored very loudly. In order to smother the sound I pulled one of the curtains which draped the box around him. This only intensified the mystery, and we were, in consequence, the observed of all observers. The play was "The Professor's Love Story," and to the fact that the stage was strewn with hay, and its aroma filling the house, I attribute Johnson's somnolescence.

The box was a small one and just held three, but such was Craig's courtesy that he invited a lady to join us. This lady was surprised on seeing the snoring bard. Craig said, apologetically,

" He's a very nice fellow when he's awake."

" Oh, don't waken him on any account," cried the lady, as she took my seat in front, and I prepared to gaze at the back of her head during the rest of the performance.

While I stood with my back to the door I felt an inrush of cold air and, turning round, saw the door quickly close. Thinking someone had made a mistake, I faced about and once more gazed at the coiffure of the lady in front of me. Once again an inrush of cold air, and again a sudden closing of the door. This time I did not turn round. When the door opened again, I saw a man I had never seen before, and whispered, " Do you know anyone here ? " He did not reply, but kept pushing past me. I repeated my query, but he remained silent, and pushed more vigorously, whereupon I smote him, and he fell into the passage. Craig, hearing the commotion, turned as he fell, and cried " Oh my God, my guest, Jack Moloney," or some such a name. We, of course, rushed to the prostrate figure and lifted him in, whereupon Craig, with superfluous politeness, formally introduced us! Then followed mutual recriminations, apologies and regrets, and in the end we all went to supper, and parted the best of friends.

Craig was Treasurer to the Corinthian Club, a club run on much the same lines as the Savage. It was founded by Sir Charles Cameron, C.B., the City Analyst, who is, I believe, also a member of the Savage Club. The Corinthians make a point of entertaining people of note who visit Dublin. The membership is large and includes such citizens as Mr Justice Ross, Sir Andrew Reed, Sir George Moyers, and Sir John Ross of Bladenburg.

The guests have been many, and have included men and women of all ranks and professions. On one occasion an invitation to supper for Saturday night had been sent to Mr Martin Harvey who was at the Theatre Royal, and to Mr Edward Terry who was at the Gaiety. Both the distinguished actors declined, on the plea that they were leaving for England on the night of the proposed supper, but they accepted an invitation to luncheon which was substituted for supper.

As a rule the menus were adorned with verses written by the members, and Craig's, I remember, were exceedingly appropriate. They included the

45

following, which I quote, as indeed I do throughout this book, from memory—

> For when " Sweet Lavender " perfumed the air,
> We knew that Edward Terry must be there;
> A compliment we also wished to pay
> To Martin Harvey and his tragic play,
> And found this luncheon was " The Only Way."

Miss Irene Vanbrugh made a fascinating speech at the Corinthians, when she was a guest at a luncheon given in her honour. If ever women sit in Parliament, Miss Irene Vanbrugh should lead the Opposition.

An amusing incident at the Club luncheon referred to, was the recital by the Rev. Chancellor Tisdall of a poem on the Shakespeare-Bacon controversy, written by Sir Francis Brady. Chancellor Tisdall was a picturesque figure, and he recited with vigour the following lines from the poem—

> " If Shakespeare had eaten of rashers well-dressed,
>   Then a glass of 'John Jameson' taken,
>   We all would have said that his plays, at their best,
>   Were largely indebted to *Bacon*.
>   'Tis the banner of Matterson flies o'er the world——"

Here the elocutionist was interrupted by shouts of laughter, caused by the fact that he alone was ignorant of the fact that his *vis-a-vis* at the luncheon table was Mr Matterson, head of the celebrated firm of bacon curers of Limerick!

On one occasion Mr George Alexander and Mr W. S. Penley were both playing at Dublin, and were both invited to supper by the Corinthian Club. Mr Alexander accepted. Mr Penley, for some reason or other declined, and gave a supper himself at a well-known restaurant. I attended both functions, and when I was the guest of Penley, I asked the impersonator of "Charley's Aunt" if I might recite. Everyone was disgusted, and Penley gave a very reluctant consent. I recited the following lines by my friend Edwin Hamilton—

> " 'Twas a scientific beggar-man who said,
>   ' Of starvation I am very nearly dead;
>   Grant a cube of butter, please,
>   And a cylinder of cheese,
>   And a parallelopipedon of bread.' "

and then sat down.

"Have you forgotten the rest?" asked the chairman.

"There is no more," I replied.

Never was the conclusion of a recitation received with such rapturous applause and with such evident relief!

CHAPTER V

QUEEN VICTORIA'S VISIT

In March, 1900, Queen Victoria paid her memorable
visit to Ireland. The announcement of the Queen's
approaching visit was made at a Reception given at
Dublin Castle on the 16th, a Reception which took
the place of St. Patrick's Ball, which is usually given
annually on the 17th of March. The reason for
this change I forget, although I was present on the
occasion.

My recollection of that particular night is very
vivid on account of a singular misfortune that befel
me. On account of my not having grown thinner
during the twelve months preceding, I had sent my

Court suit to my tailors to be, if possible, enlarged, and had promised to call and have it tried on. I forgot all about my promise, and on the afternoon of the Reception I was particularly busy, so I did not call, but sent for the suit in which I arrayed myself in due course, and set out for the function in the best conveyance I could procure, a heavy brougham of the old type, drawn by two horses. Not being a Cabinet Minister, I had the usual weary wait in a long line of vehicles, and as I neared the Lower Castle Yard I thought I would look out of the window and see how matters were progressing. With considerable exertion I managed to open the window, and in doing so, heard a sound as of ripping of stitches giving way! My suspicions were, alas! confirmed when I sat down and found nothing between myself and the carriage cushions.

"Here's a how-do-ye-do!" said I to myself, as I endeavoured ineffectually to discover if the "rent" were as great as that attributed to Cassius. The friend who accompanied me, an Army Captain, endeavoured to console me by saying it was "all right" and he would get me "pinned up" if I drove back to the Club. Seeing that there was nothing for it, I consented, stipulating, however, that the gallant Captain was to wait until the entrance to the Castle was reached, and then leave me to my fate. This he declined to do, and accordingly we got out of line and drove to the Club, where my garments were pinned together, including the tails of my coat, and we returned in time to arrive at the tail end of the long line of carriages. With the skilful manipulation of my hat, which I held behind me with both hands I bowed to Their Excellencies, Lord and Lady Cadogan, and passed on, but I could not help reflecting that my condition was representative of the condition of the country generally! Of a land of old renown, of which the inhabitants claim to be the descendants of kings, while they themselves are content to career about in battered hats and with no seats in their nether garments!

Of course, Queen Victoria's visit was the cause of not a little political agitation. In the City Hall long and loud were the debates as to whether or not an address of welcome should be presented to Her Majesty, and I am glad to say that my old friend Sir Thomas Devereux Pile, Bart., then Lord Mayor of Dublin carried the day and duly read the address to the Queen.

One of the most active of the agitators at this period was Miss Maud Gonne, " a daughter of the gods, divinely tall and most divinely fair." I met Miss Gonne some years earlier in the studio of Miss Sarah Purser, A.R.H.A., who painted a portrait of Miss Gonne and of Mr Michael Davitt, M.P. I also sat, at her request, to Miss Purser, and as the hour at which I did so came between those of the other two sitters, I used to complain of being placed between Beauty and the Beast.

Miss Gonne was at this time publishing statements in two papers, one published in Paris, called *L'Irelande Libre*; the other published in Dublin

Photo, Chancellor.]

MISS MAUD GONNE.

and entitled *The United Irishman*. She wrote for the French paper, articles which were translated for the Irish one. In one of these articles she stated that the Irish soldiers ordered to the front in the South African War were put on board the transports with manacled wrists. I took exception to such statements, and even went so far as to state in print in a paper of which I was then proprietor and editor, that she was a liar. This led to much unpleasantness, as will be seen.

The Queen arrived on Wednesday, the 4th of March, and entered the city about one o'clock. I spent the Saturday following in acting as one of the stewards in the Phœnix Park, when Her Majesty inspected some 50,000 children, and on Monday I invited several people to view, from the windows of my office, the Royal procession, as it passed through Grafton Street.

At about half past one o'clock I found a man waiting to see me. He had on a top coat, and had his arms folded in quite a Napoleonic fashion. I asked him what he wanted. He replied by asking me if I were Mr Ramsay Colles. On my saying "Yes," he struck my silk hat off my head, saying "then take that." I was completely surprised, but I at once grappled with him and found that the stick he carried was a South African jambok (made of hide) and that therefore I could not break it. There were round the walls of my office a number of short swords which I had purchased at a sale. I took off my frock coat and placed it and my silk hat in a place

51

of safety, locked the door, and offering one of the swords to the man, I said, "defend yourself, or you will not leave this place alive!" He made no offer of resistance, whereupon I assumed the airs of a maniac, and chased him round and round the board-room table which stood in the centre of the large room. Finally he tripped over something and fell, and I said to him, "If Her Majesty were not passing through this street under these very windows, I would throw you out of them." I then opened the door, and said, "Get out." He said "I won't." I settled the matter by taking him by the back of the neck and handing him over to the constable on duty at the corner of the street. He was taken to the police station and brought up before Mr Byrne, a divisional magistrate, by whom he was fined one pound or fourteen days, and ordered to find two sureties of five pounds each to keep the peace towards me. This he refused to do, and was sentenced to another fourteen days, exclaiming as he left the dock, "I'll not enter into any bail to keep the peace towards Mr Colles."

The report of this case caused some agitation, and a body of men entitled "The Old Guards' Union," sent me a report of the proceedings of their august corporation, in the course of which it was resolved that I should be summarily dealt with for having slandered a lady. I replied in my paper that I cared little for either the Old Guards' Union or the Blackguards' Union, and if any of their number visited my office they might bring the City Ambulance with them as I should give them Colles's fracture, referring thereby to the double fracture of the radius known by that name. I was visited by some of these "boys" a little later. One evening, when talking in my office to a friend, a man shuffled in and asked random questions about the paper and some of its contents, and pretended to look over the file. My friend being suspicious, suddenly opened the office door and three men who were waiting outside cleared off at once, only to be hastily followed by the one in the office.

It is not astonishing that under these circumstances that Mr John Mallon, J.P., Assistant-Commissioner of Police wrote to me, warning me to carry firearms, and telling me that "Miss Gonne has landed; she carries a dog whip." Mr Mallon also added that I was shadowed by the police. In reply I wrote:

"DEAR MR MALLON,—Thanks for your letter. Did you ever in your youth read a little book called 'A Kiss for a Blow'? There is no knowing what may happen to Miss Gonne if she hits me."

I called to see Mr Mallon, whose name is well known in connection with the Phœnix Park murders, the story of which he told in his book "Kilmainham Memories." All the time I was seated with Mr Mallon, police constables kept coming into the room and saluting and then stating such a fact as "Her Majesty is just past the South Circular Road now," and Mr Mallon would look at his watch and take a note of the fact. At last he said, with a sigh, " I wish to God she was out of the country."

" Why? " I asked, " do you fear any trouble? "

" No, no," he replied, " but I've got some information that Maud Gonne intends to make herself a nuisance by organising a row of some kind or another."

I was much interested, and doubly so when Mr Mallon said, on parting, " and, of course, you know that Miss Gonne has £300 a year pension."

I did *not* know, but thought it would do some good to call public attention to the fact, which I did in the next issue of my paper, *The Irish Figaro*, printing on the poster " Maud Gonne's Pension." In the paper I pointed out that Miss Gonne, if she continued to agitate as she was then doing, ought to drop her pension. The result was that Miss Gonne took an action against me for criminal libel.

The action was based, not on what I had written in the paper, but solely on the contents of the poster. The case presented one curious feature, viz., that the Crown Prosecutor, Mr J. H. Campbell, K.C., M.P., instead of prosecuting me, was defending me! Of course the National Press commented on the fact. The case was heard by Mr Swifte in the Southern Police Court. When Miss Gonne appeared leaning on the arm of the late John O'Leary, the old Fenian leader, she was loudly cheered, whilst I was greeted with hisses!

There is no use in raking up the ashes of the dead unhappy past, but in order to understand my case, I may refer to the fact that Miss Gonne's language with regard to Queen Victoria was in the very worst of bad taste, and the lengths to which her absurd opinions drove her can be seen in the fact, that she, the daughter of a Colonel in the British Army, wrote advising the Irish soldiers in South Africa to shoot their officers.

Sergeant Dodd, Q.C., now Mr Justice Dodd, and the late John F. Taylor, Q.C., appeared for Miss Gonne. Mr Campbell (ex-Solicitor General for Ireland), made an eloquent and able defence, but Mr Swifte had no option but to return the case for trial, my own bail being accepted.

If I could have stated from whom I got the information, there would have been much foment, and I deemed it best to be silent. In certain quarters I asked for assistance, and even went so far as to beg that a question might be asked in the House, but I was told not to harass the Government, who had decided not to prosecute. Under these circumstances, and as I had no personal grudge whatever against Miss Gonne, whom I had met in social circles in Dublin, on several occasions, I followed the advice of my Counsel, and apologised. On my way back from Court, where we appeared before the late Sir Frederick Falkiner, now succeeded as Recorder of Dublin by that very able lawyer, Mr Thomas L. O'Shaughnessy, K.C., I told my friend Mr J. F. Taylor, Miss Gonne's Counsel, that I would apologise to her not alone in the *Figaro* itself, but also on the offending poster, which accordingly was done.

In Castle and Court House

My friends rallied round me, a subscription list was opened and a handsome sum subscribed to pay my law expenses, and relieve me of what I described at the time as " an all-Gonne feeling."

I have never seen Miss Gonne since I sat opposite to her at the Solicitor's table in Green Street Court House, but I learnt that the reason why she took this action, was because Michael Davitt accused her of being a spy. I never deemed her to be a spy. My belief was that a special grant was made to her and her sister as daughters of a distinguished officer, who had died very suddenly of scarlatina by being housed in insanitary barracks at Kilmainham, but I never had an opportunity to explain this to my fair prosecutor, who has been designated " The Irish Joan of Arc." All I can say is that if Joan of Arc was half as beautiful as Miss Maud Gonne, no man could possibly have been found willing to burn her!

CHAPTER VI

SOME ACTORS AND ACTRESSES

Mrs Brown-Potter and Kyrle-Bellew—I appear with Mrs
Brown-Potter in " La Dame Aux Camelias "—
" Armand has Won! " — " There's Gold! Gold!!
Gold!!! "—Consternation of Kyrle Bellew—No
Gold!—Sir Frederick Falkiner's " At Home "—Mr
Hugh Fleming—" Mr and Mrs Brown-Potter! "—
Mrs Brown-Potter as an After-dinner Speaker—
Amateur Actors—I appear as "My Blue-eyed Boy"—
The Hero and the Lancet—Sir Henry Irving—T.C.D.
Historical Society's Banquet—" My dear fellow-
worker Ellen Terry "—Anecdote of Irving—John
Fergus O'Hea—Herman Vezin—Romola Tynte—The
Split Infinitives—Sir Herbert Tree—May Fortescue—
Helen Ferrers—Bram Stoker—Frankfort Moore—
Surgeon Parke.

I HAVE had the pleasure of meeting many actors and
actresses, not a few of whom I count among my very
good friends. In connection with the Corinthian
Club I have already mentioned some notable names.

I sometimes amuse myself startling people by
telling them that I have appeared on the stage with
Mrs Brown-Potter!

The facts are these: When Mrs Brown-Potter
and Kyrle Bellew were playing at the Theatre Royal,
Dublin, in " La Dame Aux Camelias "; they wanted

two or three ladies and gentlemen in evening dress
to walk on the stage in the gambling scene. All
that these amateur actors and actresses had to do,
was to watch the play at the tables and pretend to
play, and for this purpose they were provided with
imitation banknotes and gold coin. At a certain
cue they were to cry out " Armand has Won! " and
when supper was announced, to say " Ah, Supper! "

Wilfred Cotton, whose name is familiar as late
manager for Forbes Robertson, and whose wife, Ada
Reeve, is even better known in the theatrical world
than he is himself; was then the Resident Manager
of the Theatre Royal. He did not think a rehearsal
necessary, but introduced the amateurs to Mr Mus-
grave's manager, who was running the company, and
he, considering the few words that had to be spoken,
contented himself with giving verbal instructions.
All went well. " Armand has Won! " was given at
the proper time, as was also " Ah, Supper! "; but
to the annoyance of Kyrle Bellew, all the amateurs
cleared off to " supper," leaving the gold and notes
with which they had been provided, on the gaming
tables in full view of the audience!

Those who remember " La Dame Aux Camelias,"
will recollect that the heroine returns almost immediately to the front to be pelted by the hero with
gold, who, as he flings it in handfuls at her, cries
" There's Gold! Gold!! Gold!!! " Mr Kyrle Bellew
had little or no gold to fling, and asked hurriedly for
it. I had all my coins to hand him, and had noticed
that little heaps of sovereigns had been left on the

tables, but did not dare to touch them, lest the audience should notice the fact, and take me for a thief! The last time I had the pleasure of a chat with Kyrle Bellew was in the Lyric Theatre when my friend Baroness Orczy's play "The Sin of William Jackson" was produced.

The Recorder of Dublin, at that time Sir Frederick Falkiner, gave an "At Home" for Mrs Brown-Potter. Mr Hugh Fleming, her advance manager, will forgive me for recalling the amusing incident which occurred on that occasion, when the servant, noticing the attention paid by Mr Fleming to Mrs Brown-Potter as she entered, flung open the drawing-room door with the announcement "Mr and Mrs Brown-Potter!"

Mrs Brown-Potter is one of the most beautiful of women, and most versatile and graceful of actresses. I am glad to think that through my suggestion she was asked quite recently by Mr Evans-Jackson, Honorary Secretary of the Imperial Industries Club, to respond to the toast of "The Ladies." Her speech was so remarkably fine, and the delivery so admirable, that I will be forgiven for quoting the most noticeable passage in it. "We women occupy a great place in the field of work to-day. We go shoulder to shoulder with men; you cannot better yourselves without helping us; you cannot help us without bettering yourselves. I know and feel our power, our influence increases with yours. It matters really not much whether you agree to let us cast a paper into a ballot-box or not, without voting we influence politics, science, and art. Who trains and develops the future statesman, scientist, artist, and merchant prince—the future unknown ruler?—his Mother; who stimulates the man within his own home and inspires him to plant the flag of his ambition on some high hill in life?—his Sweetheart; who helps the man perplexed and worried with the stress and cares of life?—his Wife; who delights and charms existence for the old, and makes him prize the evening of his life?—his Daughter. Men and women go hand in hand and heart to heart through this life—we have gained through our work a position of great importance in the world of toilers which no one can take away."

Apropos of amateur actors, I once played the part of the hero of Jerome K. Jerome's pretty little curtain raiser " Sunset," under somewhat trying circumstances.

The heroine was a very charming young girl, since happily married, but at that time engaged to a very jealous young man, a medical student. As readers of " Sunset " will remember, the heroine sinks into an armchair, exclaiming:

" He is coming, my own dear love, my Blue-eyed Boy, my King, my Darling" !

This was the cue for my appearance! The first night of the performance I merely played in the same manner as that in which Miss—— and I had rehearsed it. But I had to moderate the Blue-eyed Boy's transports at meeting his Beloved on all later occasions, for the medical student, who was an

Photo, Huber, Edinburgh.

MRS. BROWN=POTTER.

athletic youth, watched the proceedings on the stage from the wings with a " lancet " in his hand, prepared to let out the hero's gore if he should exhibit any symptoms of warm bloodedness! The play ran for three nights, and at the closing performance the heroine had to make love to a very nervous hero!

One of the best amateur performances I ever saw in my life, was that of " The Ballad-Monger," given by a very youthful company of amateurs at " Winstead," Upper Rathmines, when Professor Dowden lived there. Some of my readers may care to see the following which I wrote on the occasion—

> The " Ballad-Monger " once I saw them play
>   (That merry, youthful company I knew);
>   The starving poet weighed a ton or two,
> And poor Loyse wept like a rainy day
> When he would supplicate the stars, and pray
>   To them for bread, as he was wont to do.
> The fair Juliette, with hair of ebon hue,
> The king, the page, the barber—all were gay.
> And as I gazed I yearned that I might see
>   What Fate for each might in the future hold.
> Shall Gringoire win as fair a maid? Shall she
>   Homage receive from poet half as bold?
> Who'll shave the barber? Who will Juliette gain?
> The Sphinx is silent, and I ask in vain!

I met Sir Henry Irving on many occasions, the last being at the Inaugural Supper of the College Historical Society, given at the Shelbourne Hotel on 22nd November, 1894. He was the guest of the evening, and attended the function after appearing in " Nance Oldfield " and " The Bells " and was very warmly received. His health was proposed by the late Senior Fellow, Dr George Ferdinand Shaw, and, in responding, Irving paid a graceful compliment to his " dear fellow-worker, Ellen Terry." Mr Richard Tweedy contributed a recitation to which Irving listened with evident pleasure.

My friend, John Fergus O'Hea, the artist, told me a rather amusing story of Irving.

When Irving paid his first visit to Ireland, he was called upon by O'Hea who wished to make some lightning sketches of the great actor. Having made a few thumbnail portraits, O'Hea said:

" May I ask, Mr Irving, if you can give me a photograph? It may assist me in completing these sketches."

" Certainly," replied Irving, producing a couple of dozen photographs of himself, " you can have which you like."

O'Hea chose a photograph, and then as he was taking leave, said, " Will you add to your kindness, Mr Irving, by signing this photograph?"

" With pleasure," said Irving, and, taking up a pen he wrote across the foot of the photograph:

" To my very dear friend—" he paused, and turning to O'Hea, asked in the charming manner, which all lovers of Irving will recall with a sigh, " What name did you say?"

I saw that grand old man, Herman Vezin first, when many years ago he appeared at a recital given by him and Miss Romola Tynte. I must say I greatly admired Miss Tynte's recitations. And her portrait by Sant inspired the following sonnet

addressed to her, and published in *The Dublin
Evening Mail* in 1887, when I was twenty-five—

O flower-like form! fairer than fairest flowers—
  A Dante's rose aflame with Heaven's clear light—
Thou glowest, star-like, tremulously bright,
Breathing effulgence on the soul's dark hours;
E'en brightening with thy light the cloud that lowers,
  And hides from human eyes life's utmost bound;

For when thou standest with mild beauty crown'd.
Under no weight the spirit longer cowers,
But turneth, like the sunflower, to the sun—
  The sun: the Truth: to which the soul aspires.
So shall it be—until all days be done—
  When Beauty speaks—when, as by lightning's fires,
We see that Truth and Beauty are as one—
To move the soul up never-ending gyres!

I wrote a dramatic poem for Miss Romola Tynte,
which Herman Vezin wrote her was very good, and
advised her to recite it, saying "I would do it if
I were you."

Never have I heard any recitation to equal in
force and fidelity, Herman Vezin's recital of Edgar
Allan Poe's "The Raven," which was the interpreta-
tion by a magician of the work of an artist in words.
The last time I met the great actor was at the now
defunct Pharos Club when Lady Warwick and other
advocates of so-called "Rational Dress" for women
were present. I asked Vezin "Why, what brings you
here?" He replied, "To see the Split Infinitives!"

Sir Herbert Tree and Lady Tree I have met at
Professor Dowden's. Mr Beerbohm Tree, as he was
then, appeared with Julia Neilson in "The Dancing

Girl." Miss Neilson won all hearts by her beauty
and her impersonation of the heroine. Mr Tree as
his scapegrace the duke, was most impressive,
especially in the final act before the play was altered
to suit the playgoers who want a happy ending, and
I was particularly struck by Mrs Tree's quiet force-
fulness as Sybil the cripple girl. Another actor who
won not a little praise for his dignified conduct on
the stage, was Sir Herbert's bull-dog, now deceased.

I wrote a leading article in *The Dublin Evening
Mail* on the performance, and had a letter from Mr
Beerbohm Tree thanking me for my appreciation of
the play. This letter I showed to the Editor of
the paper referred to, whereupon he sent me one of
his inimitable sketches showing Tree on one side and
myself on the other of the following duologue—

> Says Ramsay C. to Beerbohm Tree,
> "Your acting doth o'erpower me."
> Says Beerbohm Tree to Ramsay C.,
> "You are a critic, Sir, I see."

Tears of appreciation were falling from my eyes,
which Tree was depicted as catching in his hat!

At Dr John Knott's I met the Garthornes and
Miss Helen Ferrers, the gifted sister of that charming actress, Miss May Fortescue, whom I first met
at Mrs Orr William's house at Blackrock. Miss
Fortescue made a decided hit in the dramatic version
of Ouida's "Moths," in which Miss Ferrers appeared
as the Countess. Mrs Knott's sisters were married
to Mr Bram Stoker (for many years Sir Henry
Irving's manager, and eventually his biographer), and

Some Actors and Actresses

Mr Frankfort Moore, the author of many delightful novels. Mr Bram Stoker's " Dracula " and other weird tales are very powerful.

With this connection with the stage it is not surprising that Mrs Knott frequently entertained leading actors and actresses as well as the representatives of other professions, for Dr John Knott is a specialist, of whom more anon; and it was in 34, York Street, that I was introduced to the late Surgeon Parke, of South African fame, to whom a monument was erected in the grounds of Leinster House. Surgeon Parke was a very remarkable man who died quite young, the result of an arduous life in a very trying climate. His book on Stanley's work has had a big circulation. His sister is married to Mr Herbert Malley, the well-known solicitor. On one occasion someone looking at Mrs Malley, asked me, " Is she a professional beauty? " " No," I replied, " Mrs Malley is content to be an amateur."

Another representative of the stage whom I met was the beautiful and gifted Lily Hanbury (Mrs Herbert Guedalla), whom I had the pleasure of taking in to supper on an occasion when the late Provost of T.C.D., Dr Edward Salmon, the great mathematician, took in Mrs Tree. Miss Hanbury, I remember, talked chiefly of Canada, under the impression that I had been there. I never have!

CHAPTER VII

LAW AND SOME LAWYERS

THERE are very few eminent representatives of the law in Dublin whom I have not met inside the Courts, if not outside. Lord Ashbourne, Lord Chancellor for Ireland, 1885-1892, 1895-1906, married a Miss Colles, herself the daughter of a lawyer, the late H. J. Cope Colles, Principal Taxing

66

Master for Ireland. The late Judge, Sir Edmund Bewley married her sister. Their brother, John Mayne Colles, LL.D., J.P., Registrar in Lunacy, edited a very interesting diary kept by his grand-father, John Mayne, in 1814, and is author of one or two legal handbooks. Mr Lecky, the historian, gave me a letter to Sir Edward Carson when I was appli-cant for a Commissionership in Western Africa, a post for which I was recommended by, amongst other lawyers, Mr J. H. M. Campbell, K.C., M.P., ex-Solicitor General for Ireland, and Mr John Gordon, K.C., M.P., South Londonderry.

I have always had a great respect for the law, and a great reverence for lawyers, although some of the incidents in my career may seem to prove the con-trary, as, for instance, my conduct in connection with the Dublin Boundaries Bill of 1900. The facts are these. The Act of 1874, section 12, lays it down that every spirit dealer must have his license renewed at a licensing petty sessions. Now the Boundaries Bill detaches Clontarf and Drumcondra (two suburbs of Dublin) from the County for all criminal and civil business and expressly declares that County Dublin Magistrates shall cease to have jurisdiction. Under an Act of George III. the Dublin City magistrates received more than usual powers, and the area of their jurisdiction was defined. Clontarf and Drum-condra were not included, and the Boundaries Bill, which was, I believe, framed by the then Attorney-General for Ireland, Sir John Atkinson (now Baron Atkinson, K.C., P.C., Lord of Appeal), did not clear the matter up. Hence the crux; the tangle which I resolved to set straight.

Under the Boundaries Act, the County magistrates were unable to sit at Drumcondra, and, of course, the Divisional magistrates refused to go outside their recognised sphere of jurisdiction. There was nothing for me to do but to go as a borough magistrate and hold Petty Sessions in the neglected area!

Accordingly, on the morning of Friday, 18th January, 1901, I appeared at the small Court House at Drumcondra, on one of the windows of which had been pasted the following:—

" NOTICE.—Drumcondra Petty Sessions will not be held here in future for the hearing of cases which have arisen since the 14th inst. Cases arising in the Drumcondra Petty Sessions District, County Dublin, will be heard at the Gymnasium, Claremont, Glasnevin, on 17th January, 1901.

H. DUFFY, Clerk of the Petty Sessions."

Entering the Court House I asked to see the Petty Sessions Clerk, to whom I presented the great Parchment Document issued in February, 1896 (just five years earlier) when Her Majesty's Commission of the Peace had been assigned to me. Mr Duffy was dumfounded! He had never anticipated such a turn of events. While very respectful, he declined to produce the Petty Sessions Book, and remained as far in the background as possible.

The legal gentlemen present were the late E. A.

Law and Some Lawyers

Ennis, a barrister (instructed by Messrs Ennis and Machen), and two well-known solicitors, each with a large practice, Mr James Brady, T.C., and the late Michael Hanmore. But, strange to say, there were no persons present to represent the prosecutors! The Royal Irish Constabulary, who are usually very much in evidence at such proceedings, were conspicuous by their absence! Only one sergeant—and he in what may be styled " undress " uniform—after first casting furtive glances from outside the door and windows of the Court, at last entered with a tread as noiseless as one on the track of a burglar.

Thus, as *The Dublin Evening Telegraph* wittily put it, there was presented, perhaps for the first time in the history of Ireland, the spectacle of a Court with a magistrate eager to dispense justice, advocates armed *cap-a-pie*, panting to enter the lists for their clients, but no police constable willing to prosecute, not even deigning to put his foot inside the Court.

I shall not weary my readers with an account of the proceedings, which were very amusing and lasted for over an hour, but will content myself with an extract from Mr Ennis's speech, in the course of which he said:—

" We have been invited to nothing less than a burlesque here to-day. The action of the authorities was like that of a person who put an advertisement into a newspaper, ' Lodgings to Let,' and then when someone went down to engage the lodgings they found that the bill had disappeared off the window. Evidently law is to be administered no longer in

Drumcondra, and the inhabitants of the district will find themselves face to face with the fact that 'the enterprising burglar' who loves to hear 'the little brook a-gurgling, or listen to the pleasant village chime,' may burgle with impunity; the cut-throat pursue unmolested his career in crime, and the coster indulge without molestation in his favourite pastime of jumping on his mother." Mr Ennis also referred, in mock grandiloquent language, to what he facetiously called " The *lapsus linguæ* of the law! "

The Dublin Boundaries Bill had been advocated by the Lord Mayor, Sir Thomas Devereux Pile, Bart., and Mr Ennis's remarks included one to the effect that Lord Mayor Pile might be censured and opposed on account of attaching to the City of Dublin a new area in which crime can be committed with impunity! Ennis—familiarly known as Gasparo Ennis—had a pretty wit. Addressing the Bench, he said:

" You give me one pound costs against Constable O'Shea, your Worship? "

His Worship—Certainly.

Mr Ennis (to Sergeant Joyce)—What is the name of the new Inspector General?

Sergeant Joyce—Colonel Neville Chamberlain.

Mr Ennis—I'll apply to him for this money if Constable O'Shea does not pay up.

The proceedings ended by my endorsing the summonses on which defendants attended; " No appearance, costs awarded 20s."; thus giving costs against the Crown! The matter was ended, months

later by a Proclamation by the Lord Lieutenant,
Earl Cadogan, K.G., including the disputed areas
within the new area. What Sir John Atkinson or
Sir Patrick Coll, chief crown solicitor for Ireland,
thought of the affair, I never ascertained, but Sir
Thomas Pile told me, with a smile, that he thought
I ought to be transported.

Gasparo Ennis's love of a practical joke got me
into trouble with the late Michael Hanmore. Ennis
produced a letter from Mr Spencer Lyttleton, at one
time secretary to Mr W. E. Gladstone, in which it
was stated that Mr Gladstone was glad to hear that
Mr Philip Keogh, B.L. was engaged on a life of
Mr Hanmore, but that with regard to the book
being dedicated to him (W.E.G.) he preferred to
leave the matter to his own discretion. Hanmore
took an action for libel and, of course, I had no
defence, but he eventually forgave me for my part
in the matter, and was quite friendly when he
appeared at Drumcondra on the unique occasion to
which I have referred.

Years later I created a precedent in English law
which is frequently cited; and will be found in the
" Yearly Practice."

In 1904 I was receiver for the Debenture Holders
of Chic Limited, and in order to keep the paper
going I assigned to the Printers, the Robinson
Printing Company, of Brighton, a portion of the book
debts. To this action the Debenture Holders, Mr
William O'Malley, M.P., and Mr John Cansfield,
then Manager of Pearkes Limited, objected. An

action was taken by Robinson against Chic and came before Mr Justice Warrington, who said I had far exceeded my powers as Receiver, and held that " the Receiver had no power to give a charge or lien on the Company's property."

The Robinson Printing Company appealed, and on 24th November, 1904, the case came before Lord Justice Vaughan Williams, Lord Justice Romer and Lord Justice Cozens-Hardy, who sent the case for re-trial, with the result that Mr Justice Warrington gave judgment in favour of the Plaintiffs, as reported in nearly a column of *The Times*, 17th April, 1905. In delivering judgment with personal liability against the defendants, I was (I presume inadvertently) referred to as " the Defendant, Colles," and accordingly, I wrote to *The Times* from The Royal Colonial Institute of which I was at the time a Fellow:—

" My attention has been drawn to a statement in your issue of the 17th inst., in which I am referred to in the above trial (Robinson *v.* Chic) by Mr Justice Warrington as ' the Defendant, Colles.' As his Lordship's judgment was given with costs and personal liability against the defendants, I shall be much obliged by your insertion of my statement to the effect that I was no party to the trial. My acts as Receiver for the Debenture Holders were ratified by the decision of the learned judge, which creates a very important precedent in law."

This letter was given a conspicuous position in *The Times*.

RIGHT HON. EDWARD GIBSON, LORD ASHBOURNE, P.C.,
Lord High Chancellor of Ireland, 1885-6, 1886-1892, 1895-1906.

Law and Some Lawyers

This has, I fear, been a dull chapter, but, after all, it is not every man who has driven a coach-and-four through an Act of Parliament and created a precedent in English Law.

Apropos of the law, I once had the pleasure of discovering in the original MS. " The Laws of England " of Henry de Bracton, translated word for w rd and line for line by Richard Colles, who was called to the English Bar in 1842, and died Sheriff of Castlemaine, Victoria, in 1883. This volume I had strongly bound, and I then presented it to the Royal Irish Academy, of which I was at the time a Member, and in the library of which it now reposes.

When a boy at Bective College, a school referred to by Thackeray in his " Irish Sketch Book " as one in which there were more prizes given than there were pupils, I was ground in English Literature by Mr John Ross (now Mr Justice Ross) who had a very brilliant career at T.C.D., and has had the almost unprecedented good fortune of being made a judge at forty years of age. Mr Seymour Bushe, K.C., and Mr Richard Meredith (now the Master of the Rolls) acted as my counsel on more than one occasion. Mr T. M. Healy, M.P., has also appeared on my behalf, and won my case for me. One of the most brilliant lawyers I ever met was Constantine Molloy, Q.C., a criminal lawyer of remarkable acumen. Molloy was a friend of Neilson Hancock, Clerk of the Crown and Hanaper, a post ably filled later by J. Nugent Lentaigne. Hancock's sister married Professor James Thompson, a brother of

Lord Kelvin.   I knew Hancock's nephew, **W. J.**
Hancock, who used, when we were boys, to tell
me stories of his illustrious uncle's doings.   Young
Hancock went to Perth, Western Australia.   He
was a remarkable boy, perhaps the most remarkable
I ever met, save only young Bell, the inventor of
the Edison-Bell phonograph.

I must not forget my friend George Dames
Burtchaell, who is a specialist in Genealogies and
Registrar of the Office of Arms, Ireland, and Inspector of Historical MSS., and Athlone Pursuivant, and
has more than once been summoned before the Committee of Privileges of the House of Lords in cases
of disputed titles, notably in the late case of the
Claims of the Countess of Yarborough and the
Countess of Powis to the Baronies of Fauconberg,
Darcy de Knayth and Mcinill.   Burtchaell was
successful as to the first two Baronies, and consequently the Barony of Fauconberg was allowed to
the Countess of Yarborough and the Barony of
Darcy de Knayth to the Countess of Powis.
George Dames Burtchaell was also engaged
in the case of the claim of Lord Mowbray
Segrave and Stourton to the Earldom of
Norfolk, created in 1312.   This was not successful,
but the main point at issue has not been decided.
These are the only two instances of a member of the
Irish Bar only being engaged in purely English
cases.

CHAPTER VIII

ALGERNON CHARLES SWINBURNE

Algernon Charles Swinburne—Ralph Waldo Emerson—
William Wordsworth—My Visit to the Lake Dis-
trict—Keswick—I stay in Coleridge's Cottage next
Greta Hall—I wind Wordsworth's Clock!—Canon
Rawnsley—Mrs Lynn Linton—" Her Autobiography
of Christopher Kirkland "—Robert Southey—Gras-
mere—I sleep all night at the foot of Wordsworth's
Grave—Professor Dowden on " Intimations of
Immortality " — Thomas Gray — Swinburne and
Wordsworth.

In his " English Traits," Ralph Waldo Emerson in
describing his visit to Walter Savage Landor, wrote
" He pestered me with Southey, but who is
Southey? " This statement so roused Swinburne's
ire that he referred to Emerson as an " impudent and
foulmouthed Yankee Philosophaster." Although I
trust I have never been guilty of being impudent or
foulmouthed, I must confess that in my sixteenth and
seventeenth years I " pestered " a great many people
with Swinburne. Until 1878, or thereabouts, my
" great poet " was Wordsworth, and I diligently read
all the Lake Poets and studied the writings of De

Quincey. So great was my enthusiasm that I paid a visit to Lake Land, tramping over the whole of that beautiful country on foot.

In order to more closely follow the career of Wordsworth, I, in my enthusiasm first visited Cockermouth, the birthplace of the poet, and then repaired to Keswick, where I had the happiness to stay for a week under the hospitable roof of Miss Christopherson who resided in the cottage next to, and in the same grounds as Southey's house, Greta Hall. In this cottage Samuel Taylor Coleridge lived for some time. It was the residence of Southey's model landlord. Miss Christopherson had purchased at a sale a large grandfather's clock, once the property of Wordsworth, and this clock she, to my great delight, permitted me to wind! It was one of the old-fashioned kind which told the day of the week and of the month, and the changes of the moon.

During my short sojourn in Keswick, I had the pleasure of being introduced to the Rev. Canon Rawnsley, who has written well and wisely on the Lake Poets, and is a poet himself of no mean powers, his forte being " the weaving of the sonnet." Canon Rawnsley is related to the Tennysons, and is thus a link between two Poets Laureate. Mrs Lynn Linton was expected to arrive shortly, but I could not await the day of her arrival and did not see her, though later she invited me to what she facetiously called her " mansion in the skies," referring thereby to her flat in Queen Anne's Mansions. I bought in Keswick a three volume copy of " The Autobiography

Algernon Charles Swinburne

of Christopher Kirkland," in which those who read between the lines discover the autobiography of Mrs Lynn Linton, and I had one or two letters from her during my stay in her beloved Keswick. On a Sunday I walked beside the Greta and attended the church in which Lough's monument of Southey recalls a great and gracious memory to his forgetful country; and heard Canon Rawnsley preach. I visited the graveyard at the side of the church and read on the tomb in which Southey's ashes repose, the injunction—

> Not to the grave, not to the grave,
> My soul descend to contemplate
> The form that once was dear.

I was young and impressionable, and I must confess I burst into tears, for Southey, thanks to my friend Edward Dowden, is to me no mere name. He is a living presence, and this humble tribute to the fine monograph on Southey in "The Englishmen of Letters" series, is the lowest stone on the cairn of praise erected by many readers, the apex being the judgment pronounced by Sir Henry Taylor, who knew and loved Southey, and who said of Professor Dowden's book that for him it made Southey live once more. Higher praise than this could not be given.

But I could not stay long in Keswick, and one evening in July I determined to push on to Grasmere. I started at 8 p.m., and walked along the dusty road

through the beautiful Vale of St. John, looking out
for the cottage described by De Quincey, who gives
a humorous account of seeing at midnight in
December, when the frost was keen as it can be in
the Lake District, a mammoth in shirt-sleeves sitting
smoking in the front garden! When I visited the
district the mammoth, no doubt, had long ago
departed to those regions where the good mammoths
go, and I passed his cottage as silent as my shadow
cast by the full moon.

Walking beside the shore of Lake Thirlmere, I
came upon a group of workmen whose daily work
was, like old Kaspar's, done; and who were enjoying
their pipes before turning in. They were engaged,
I learned, on the works, just then in full swing, for
the carrying of the waters of Thirlmere to Manchester. I was invited by the foreman to inspect
some of the machinery, and I readily consented to
do so, though it was nearly eleven o'clock, and when,
having followed the many windings of the tunnel
into which I was taken, and having listened to
elaborate descriptions of the machinery employed,
I emerged a wearied though a wiser man, I found
it was midnight.

I had intended to put up at the Old Swan Inn,
about a mile nearer Grasmere, but when I reached
it, the Inn was closed and evidently untenanted.
This was the Inn, it will be remembered, at which
Scott used to call daily for a glass of beer, when
staying with Wordsworth, who was a teetotaller, and
how the Inn-keeper disconcerted Scott by inquiring

one day as he passed with his host, whether he would
have his glass as usual! I also was disconcerted to
find the Inn closed, but I pushed on into Grasmere
passing the little church on my right and walked up
to the door of the modern hotel, the Rothsay. It
also was closed. They keep early hours in Lake
Land.

> Not a twinkle from the fly,
> Not a glimmer from the worm.
>
> .   .   .   .
>
> Windows fast and obdurate!
>   How the garden grudged me grass!
> Where I stood the iron gate
>   Ground its teeth to let me pass!

I did not like to be selfish. There was evidently
no hall porter, and I did not wish to disturb the rest
of the sojourners in the hotel. There was also another
good reason for my not applying my hand to the
knocker or the bell, and that was a huge mastiff who,
unlike the gate, "ground its teeth" but would *not*
"let me pass." Every movement I made was to
the accompaniment of a growl from this Cerberus.
I therefore beat a retreat without enquiring with
Coleridge "What is it ails the mastiff bitch?" I
was like Browning's serenader at the villa—

> " So wore night; the East was grey,
>   White the broad-faced hemlock flowers :
> There would be another day.
>   'Ere its first of heavy hours
> Found me, I had passed away."

Passed away, but not to any great distance. I had

marked the church and the churchyard as I passed
them, and I opened the little wooden gate and went
to the church door, but it was, as I expected, locked.
Then I explored the churchyard with the view of
finding a resting-place, but there was none. I had
a warm cloak in the double strap which held the
tramp's outfit on my back, and wrapping this about
me, I made my lodging on the cold, cold ground,
agreeably cold on this lovely July night; and with
the light of the moon overhead and the music of the
river Rotha in my ear, wearied with my tramp from
Keswick, I slept soundly.

I awoke at about six o'clock and glancing round,
the first object that met my eyes was a tombstone
bearing the name "William Wordsworth." Rising,
I sat on the low stone wall that runs round the
churchyard, and read also by the increasing sunlight,
the familiar name of Hartley Coleridge and also that
of Jane Clough, the mother, I believe, of Arthur
Hugh Clough. This incident was referred to by
H. A. Hinkson, Barrister and Novelist, in a skit he
published at the time of the T.C.D. Tercentenary,
and was pointed out to me before I met Mr Hinkson.
Referring to those who visited Professor Dowden's
house on Sunday afternoons, he says "those who
assemble there include all kind of students of English
literature, from the youth who has just discovered
that there is a difference in style between the work
of Tennyson and that of Browning, to the enthusiast
who sought inspiration by sleeping on the grave of
Wordsworth." When I mentioned to Professor

Algernon Charles Swinburne

Dowden the fact that I had slept at the foot of Wordsworth's grave, he enquired with all the gravity of the true humorist: " Had you any Intimations of Immortality '? "

Years after, when I edited the poems of Hartley Coleridge for Messrs Routledge, my knowledge of the Lake District proved of immense value to me, for I knew every inch of the ground. I ascended Skiddaw when in Keswick, and admired the Cockshot Woods praised by Gray, who was, as Mr Edmund Gosse pointed out, the pioneer in praise of the Lake District. In his admirable volume " English Literature in the Eighteenth Century," my friend Thomas Sergeant Perry clearly proved how up to Gray's time, any great elevation was always looked on in poetry as " horrid." Gray loved the mountains with all the love which Wordsworth afterwards displayed, and was the first to praise their grandeur, and make the reader of poetry have a true sense of their sublimity.

My readers will naturally ask what has all this to do with Swinburne? The link it must be confessed is slight. I began with the intention of devoting the chapter to Swinburne, but the reference to Wordsworth led me off on a side track. Swinburne, it must be remembered, was a Wordsworthian all his life, and his tributes to Wordsworth in prose and verse are many, ranging from the reference to him in the sonnet on Thomas Carlyle's " two venemous volumes of Reminiscences," in which he is referred to as—

In Castle and Court House

" One whose clear spirit like an angel hung
Between the mountains, hallowed by his love,
And the sky, stainless as his soul, above : "

to the famous essay on Wordsworth and Byron which
appeared in " The Nineteenth Century," and is
reprinted in the " Miscellanies."

In the Life of the author of a little book very
popular in my childhood, entitled " Amy Herbert,
or the Happy Home," we are told that the writer
accompanied Lady Jane Swinburne and Algernon,
then a little boy, to call on Wordsworth. The old
poet received his visitors courteously and, patting
Algernon on the head, enquired if he knew any of
his poems. Yes, Algernon knew several of them,
including " We are seven," and " The Pet Lamb."
Wordsworth was pleased, and remarked that a knowledge of his poems would not do the boy any harm.
So far as his readers are aware, a knowledge of
Wordsworth had no ill effect on Swinburne, who
praised Wordsworth with a poet's discernment in the
essay referred to, pointing out the Æschylean quality
of such verses as those on Peele Castle with their
" trampling waves " as a phrase worthy of him who
wrote—

ποντίων τε κυμάτων ἀνήριθμον γέλασμα

and praising in glowing language the beauty of such
lines as—

" She is known to every star
And every wind that blows,"

from that otherwise prosaic poem " The Thorn."

Algernon Charles Swinburne

Swinburne cannot be discussed in this chapter, but must be referred to in the next. My readers must be content to accept, so far as this chapter is concerned, the lines of Landor—

> " Pass me. I only am the rind
> To the rich fruit that you will find,
> My friends, in every leaf behind."

CHAPTER IX

A. C. SWINBURNE (CONTINUED)

The Warden of Alexandra College—Rev. R. Perceval
Graves—Professor Mahaffy—Dr W. J. Chetwode
Crawley—The Life of Sir William Rowan Hamilton—
Professor Mahaffy on Old Age—Swinburne's Prose
and Poetry—" Under the Microscope "—I write to
Swinburne—His Letters to me—A Forgotten Poem
by Swinburne—Richard Herne Shepherd—Swin-
burne's " Cleopatra "—Swinburne and the Irish
Unionist Alliance—A Quick-change Artist!

THE first person I ever met who knew Swinburne
personally was the Warden of Alexandra College,
Dublin, the Rev. R. Perceval Graves, who wrote the
" Life of Sir William Rowan Hamilton." When that
book was first published I met one Sunday afternoon
Professor John Pentland Mahaffy whose fame is
world-wide as a scholar, and in particular in connection with his books on Greece. We met as we had
done before, at the house of that genial member of
the Senate of T.C.D., Dr W. J. Chetwode Crawley,
11, Merrion Square, at one time the residence of
the Lord High Chancellor of Ireland, Lord Ash-

bourne who, on several occasions held levees there. Professor Mahaffy praised the book but laughingly said in the course of his remarks, " Graves has no sense of humour, he writes for instance, ' Hamilton was not much of a poet, but on one occasion after a very tempestuous crossing from Holyhead to Dublin, he threw off the following sonnet '! "

Knowing Dr Chetwode Crawley's love of humour, I said " *A propos* of ' throwing off,' I have been reading some of Milton's prose works."

" Are they worth reading? " asked Mahaffy.

" Oh, yes," I said, " I think they are, for instance he says, *a propos* of your remarks, ' there are some people full of such a queasy spirit of luke-warmness that they would give a vomit to God Himself!' "

Crawley was amused when I added that Mr Alfred Austin, the Poet Laureate had a sonnet written on a cross-channel steamer, in which he exclaims:

" England, I *reach* forth my soul to thy shores."

It was on that occasion when discussing old age in general, and " De Senectute " in particular, that Professor Mahaffy said:

" The most marvellous old man I ever met was after the siege of Paris. It was at a civic banquet given to celebrate our deliverance from having to eat cats and dogs and rats and mice. He was one hundred and eight and as gay as a lark! A marvellous man! But I am sorry to say there were some very wicked French actresses present, and he went away with the worst of them, and was found dead in his bed next morning!"

"Well," I said, "the moral is, I suppose, ' beware of wicked French actresses!'"

"Ah, yes!" said Mahaffy, gravely, "when you are *a hundred and eight*."

Professor Mahaffy, it will be remembered, does not confine his attention to Greece, he is also the author of a charming book on "The Principles of the Art of Conversation," a delightful volume dedicated to the Marchioness of Zetland.

The Rev. Perceval Graves was a picturesque figure. He also was a Wordsworthian, and knew Wordsworth personally, as readers of Alexander Grossart's edition of the prose works of Wordsworth are aware. I first met Dr Graves at Professor Dowden's house, "Winstead," Upper Rathmines, when the visitors included a son of Louis von Ranke, the great historian.

At that time the poems and prose of Swinburne were to me "a wonder and a wild delight." His " Study of Shakespeare," the first volume of his prose which I read, seemed eloquent as a poet's appreciation of a poet, and the grand chorus in " Atalanta in Calydon " haunted me with the magnificence of its music, while the " Erectheus " was full of the sounds of battle and of a breaking sea. I read every scrap of printed matter to which Swinburne's name was attached, and as I had not the means to purchase everything, I transcribed from volumes in Trinity College Library, or in the National Library of

Ireland, all his fugitive contributions to *The Athenæum*, *The Spectator*, and other papers, besides his articles on Marlowe and Beaumont and Fletcher, which appeared in the " Encyclopædia Britannica." Thus I possess at the present moment, the work of my youth, in the shape of a MS. volume of Swinburne which Mr Watts-Dunton has told me is unique. The contents include transcriptions of Swinburne's letters to Lord Houghton and to Sir Henry Taylor, and also a poem which appeared in " The Contemporary Review," a most amusing parody of Tennyson's " Despair," entitled " Disgust."

As time rolled on I acquired copies of " Once a Week " containing Swinburne's short prose story " Dead Love " with the illustration by M. J. Lawless and the first edition of " Bloody Son " which appeared later under the title of " Fratricide " in the first series of " Poems and Ballads." Thus I became word-perfect in Swinburne's poetry and prose, and have frequently been complimented by Mr Watts-Dunton on the fact that I have so faithfully memorised long passages from both.

In 1886, when I was twenty-four, I became much interested in a controversy which had aroused bad blood as early as 1872, that which arose out of the publication of Robert Buchanan's " The Fleshly School of Poetry," and Swinburne's reply, entitled " Under the Microscope." I found that the latter was completely out of print, and it struck me that I ought to suggest to Swinburne to reprint it. Accordingly I wrote in November, 1886, to the poet, care of his publishers, Messrs Chatto and Windus, and received in reply a postcard on which Swinburne wrote that he would very much like to see a copy of the pamphlet in question. I happened to mention this fact to Professor Dowden, whose Sunday afternoon receptions found me a frequent visitor at "Winstead," Temple Road, Upper Rathmines, where he then lived, and he, with the ready kindliness which is one of his leading characteristics, offered to lend me a copy of the pamphlet. Having secured this, I wrote to Swinburne on the subject, and he replied, saying that his friends had often advised him to reprint the pamphlet, at the same time cutting away the merely ephemeral passages of satire or controversy.

My readers will naturally ask, "Where are these letters?" My reply is that my good friend Mr Watts-Dunton, who has seen the letters and finds them quite worthy of printing, in face of his public announcement that no letters of Swinburne are to be printed, cannot see his way to allow me to print them, a decision he told me, caused him not a little regret. Mr Watts-Dunton is Swinburne's sole executor and even if I could rebel against his decision I would not do so, for his unfailing kindness to me on many occasions is counted amongst the most pleasurable experiences of my life.

I have, however, received his permission to give the gist of the letters, though not their *ipsissima verba*.

Swinburne's wishes with regard to the pamphlet

Algernon Charles Swinburne

made me very enthusiastic, and I wrote offering to transcribe it and prepare it for the press. This offer Swinburne accepted in the most gracious way, and I spent my evenings for nearly three weeks busily engaged in making a clear and faithful transcription of the little book from cover to cover, and when completed, I sent it off to "The Pines" with a letter expressing the pleasure it had given me to meet his wishes, and taking the opportunity to ask one or two questions in connection with passages and references in his poems which had puzzled me.

One of my questions was as to the identity of the persons referred to in the following verses—

> There lived a singer in France of old
>   By the tideless, dolorous Midland Sea;
> In a land of sand and ruin and gold
>   There shone one woman, and none but she.

Another inquiry was as to where I should find the verses addressed by Landor to Victor Hugo, to which reference is made in a footnote in "Essays and Studies."

In his reply, Swinburne, after thanking me for the MS., which arrived safely, told me that the "Singer in France" and the lady, were Rudel and the lady of Tripoli, whom, he pointed out had been the subject of one of Robert Browning's shorter lyrics; and he informed me that Landor's lines to Hugo are on page 160 of his "Heroic Idylls," and added: "Lest you should not have the book by you, I transcribe them for you separately." This he did, and I give

the lines here with the words he wrote under
them—

.VICTOR HUGO

Whether a poet yet is left
  In France, I know not—and who knows?
But Hugo, of his home bereft,
  In quiet Jersey finds repose.
Honour to him who dares to utter
  A word of truth in writ or speech;
In Hugo's land the brave but mutter
  Half one, in dread whose ear it reach.

Under these lines Swinburne wrote—

" Written by Walter Savage Landor, *æt.* 88,
  and transcribed for Ramsay Colles by
  Algernon Charles Swinburne."

The letter which contained these lines, which were
clearly written on one side of a sheet of notepaper,
concluded as follows, and I feel sure I shall be forgiven for the pride with which I transcribe them :—

"And now, having replied to your various
queries, let me thank you again very cordially for the
great trouble you have taken and the great obligation
you have conferred on,—Yours very sincerely,
                          A. C. SWINBURNE."

During later years whenever a passage in his
writings puzzled me, I ventured to write to the poet,

and always received a courteous answer, generally
by return post. With Mr Andrew Lang I admire
the verses on Cleopatra which appeared in an early
issue of the " Cornhill Magazine," and I suggested
to Swinburne to reprint them, but he replied that
they were scribbled off to accompany Mr Frederick
Sandys' " noble design," which had been used as a
frontispiece to the " Cornhill," and added that he had
written another set of verses to serve as an illustration to the same artist's " Gentle Spring," which was
printed in the " Royal Academy Catalogue." This
was fresh news to me. I turned to R. Herne
Shepherd's Bibliography of Swinburne and failed to
find any reference to these verses, and wrote to Mr
Shepherd, telling him. He replied he had looked
up the lines in the catalogue, and transcribed them
for me.

The verses on Cleopatra were not reprinted
because George Meredith had protested against their
re-appearance, saying that they were a travesty of
Swinburne's worst style. Nevertheless, they contain
some memorable and haunting lines as, for instance,
the following—

> She holds her future close, her lips
>   Hold fast the face of things to be;
> Actium, and sound of war that dips
>   Down the blown valleys of the sea,
> Far sails that flee, and storms of ships.

The poem was prefaced by a clipping from the
first sketch of " Chastelard," which was never pub-

lished, the lines being attributed to "T. Hayman,
Fall of Anthony, 1655."

> "Her beauty might outface the jealous hours,
> Turn shame to love and pain to a tender sleep,
> And the strong nerve of hate to sloth and tears;
> Make Spring rebellious in the sides of frost,
> Thrust out lank Winter with hot August growths,
> Compel sweet blood into the husks of death,
> And from strange beasts enforce harsh courtesy."

The poem of "Gentle Spring," being buried in
the Catalogue of the Exhibition of the Royal
Academy of Arts for 1865 (page 20), I transcribe for
the delectation of those to whom every scrap of
Swinburne's verse gives pleasure—

> O virgin mother of gentle days and nights,
> Spring of fresh buds and Spring of swift delights,
> Come, with lips kiss'd of many an amorous hour,
> Come, with hands heavy from the fervent flower,
> The fleet first flower that feels the wind and sighs,
> The tenderer leaf that draws the sun and dies;
> Light butterflies, like flowers alive in the air,
> Circling and crowning thy delicious hair,
> And many a fruitful flower and floral fruit
> Born of thy breath and fragrant from thy foot.
> Thee, mother, all things born desire, and thee,
> Earth, and the fruitless hollows of the sea
> Praise, and thy tender winds of ungrown wing
> Fill heaven with murmurs of the sudden Spring.

In 1893, when Gladstone's Home Rule Bill roused
into being at the call of Mr Culverwell, F.T.C.D.,
one of the strongest political organizations in Ireland,
The Irish Unionist Alliance, Swinburne was

appealed to for a poem, and wrote his " A Song for Unionists." In the MS. which I saw, were the lines—

> See the ravens flock to feast
> Dark as robe or creed of priest.

It was pointed out to the poet that on a great political question like Home Rule or Unity, the people should be united, and that the reference to priesthood in these lines might lead to disagreement and possibly disintegration of an otherwise united body, and he was asked to substitute another line, which he did by return post, as follows—

> See the ravens flock to feast
> Dense as round some death-struck beast,

a reading which was adhered to on the appearance of the poem in the collected edition of 1904.

CHAPTER X

A. C. SWINBURNE (CONCLUDED)

Walt Whitman—W. M. Rossetti—I try to raise Subscription in Ireland for Whitman—Correspondence with Good Gray Poet — Swinburne's Earlier and Later Criticism of Walt Whitman—" Under the Microscope "—" Whitmania " — " The Damnedest Simulacrum "—Lillah Cabot Perry—Her " Heart of the Weed "—John Addington Symonds—The King's Inns, Dublin—Mr Thomas Wright—I call on Swinburne and Watts-Dunton — The Pines, Putney Hill —Mr Alfred Noyes.

LOOKING back at my life I appear in 1886 to have had more time at my command than I have ever had since. I had purchased early in 1879, or thereabouts, John Camden Hotten's edition of a selection from Walt Whitman, with a Preface by Mr W. M. Rossetti. In some way, possibly by lending it, I lost this book, and, on trying to get another copy, I found it was out of print. I at once wrote to Messrs Chatto and Windus and communicated with Mr Rossetti, with the gratifying result that a new and handsome edition in buckram was issued, the publishers, in acknowledgment of my suggestion, sending me a copy.

Mr Rossetti was the soul of courtesy and wrote

me several kindly letters on the subject, in his beautiful handwriting, expressing his old admiration for the author of " Leaves of Grass." I had heard that Walt Whitman was very ill and in lack of money, and I wrote to him to Mickle Street, Camden, New Jersey, suggesting the raising of a subscription in Ireland. He replied:

" DEAR FRIEND,—I shall gladly accept anything which you and my Irish friends care to give. Take leisure and time about it, and let it be large or small, or nought at all, if Destiny so decide. (Professor Edward Dowden must not be approached, as he has already been most generous.)   I was out for two hours to-day in the sunny mid-day hours, and enjoyed them much,—   WALT WHITMAN."

I wrote to many of my friends on the subject, but got no response. This disheartened me, and in the end I had to content myself with sending the poet £2, and telling him I would make the sum an annual subscription. To this he would not consent, and sent me for the money his two volumes, " Leaves of Grass" and " Two Rivulets," each copy being signed. Until his death I sent the £2, and at last, having many copies of his books, I sold the auto-graphed volumes to the National Library of Ireland, on the shelves of which they now repose under the guardianship of that true lover of books, Mr Thomas W. Lyster, M.A., the Librarian, whose name is familiar to all students of German literature in con-nection with his admirable translation of Duntzer's

" Life of Goethe." I also sold to the then Provost of T.C.D., Dr Jellett, copies of " Leaves of Grass " and " Specimen Days."

When I wrote to Swinburne about the reprint of " Under the Microscope," I ventured to ask him if his opinion of Whitman was as high as when he addressed the American poet in " Songs before Sunrise "—

> Send but a song oversea for us,
>   Heart of their hearts who are free.
> Heart of their singer to be for us
>   More than our singing can be;
> Ours in the tempest at error,
> With no light but the twilight of terror;
>   Send us a song oversea!
> Sweet-smelling of pine leaves and grasses,
>   And blown as a tree through and through
> With the winds of the keen mountain passes,
>   And tender as sun-smitten dew;
> Sharp-tongued as the winter that shakes
> The wastes of your limitless lakes;
>   Wide-eyed as the sea-line's blue.

Swinburne replied that he still genuinely admired Walt Whitman's best earlier work, but that his indiscriminate admirers had made him " sick of the man's very name," and, he added, " I doubt whether posterity will have patience to pick out his plums from such a mass of indigestible dough."

In my " first fine careless rapture " I had communicated to Whitman the fact that Swinburne contemplated reprinting " Under the Microscope," in which much praise had been bestowed on Walt, who was compared to William Blake, and whose work-

manship was accepted without demur. Walt
Whitman wrote me asking me to send him on the
article when it appeared, and enclosed in his letter
a card in black and silver admitting the bearer to
his Lecture on the Death of Abraham Lincoln.

When the article appeared in the " Fortnightly,"
entitled " Whitmania," I saw at once that I must not
grieve the " good gray poet " by sending it to him,
especially as I was the innocent cause of its having
been written, but he insisted, and Mr Horace
Traubel tells us that Whitman on reading it contented himself by asking those present, if Swinburne
were " not the damnedest simulacrum," and there, so
far as Walt was concerned, the matter ended.

Not so in England, where John Addington
Symonds rushed into print in defence of Whitman,
noting especially the fact that in the verses quoted
from " Songs before Sunrise," Walt Whitman is
designated a " Singer." This he undoubtedly was,
as well as being one of the most ardent among
liberators of the human spirit from the shackles of
conventionality.

Addington Symonds did not clinch his argument
by referring to the footnote on page 21 of " Essays
and Studies," in which, while expatiating on Victor
Hugo's " L'Année Terrible," Swinburne designates
Whitman " The greatest of American voices," and
in concluding calls him " The first poet of American
democracy." Surely higher praise than this no man
could ask for or expect!

In the year referred to appeared a little volume

of poems entitled " The Heart of the Weed," with
no author's name, but to explain the title, a quotation
from James Russell Lowell " to win the secret of the
weed's plain heart." This little book, the contents
of which are far above the average output of poetry,
was written by the wife of my friend Thomas Sergeant Perry. Mrs Perry later did more justice to her
muse in her perfect translations from the Greek
Anthology, which were issued under the title of
" From the Garden of Hellas." One of the poems
in " The Heart of the Weed " was " On Swinburne's
' Poems to a Child,' " a sonnet which I forwarded to
Swinburne, but which he did not acknowledge. I
learned later that his letter to me was insufficiently
addressed, and was returned to him. I give the
sonnet here by kind permission of the authoress,
Lillah Cabot Perry—

> You sing of passion, freedom, of the sea,
> All mighty themes to touch the hearts of men,
> Yet scarce are past the fire and whirlwind, when
> We hear a still, small voice, and lovingly
> You lull the babe upon its mother's knee,
> Songs mingling with its dreams. Her bosom then
> Thrills to the echo of each note again
> That sings all childhood's joy and mystery.
> Small flower-like faces look out from your rhyme,
> And there among them smile my very own;
> Sweet children's voices from your measures ring
> Like shaken silver bells in liquid chime—
> I hear my darlings', yet not theirs alone
> Since for all childhood through all time you sing.

When I was a student in Dublin I spent the
greater part of my time reading in the delightful

ALGERNON CHARLES SWINBURNE.

library of King's Inns, Henrietta Street, where, in a quiet recess, partitioned off from the rest of the room, furnished with "storied windows richly dight" shedding upon me and my book at sunset all the colours which Keats declared were thrown by the full moon upon the kneeling heroine of "St Agnes' Eve," I could scarcely realise that I was buried in "the dusty purlieus of the law." Consulting the Library Catalogue one afternoon, I discovered that the Benchers took as little interest in Swinburne as one Gamaliel is reported to have cared for the study of Sociology. I hastened to the genial librarian, my old friend James McIvor, and laid the matter before him, and having by his advice filled the necessary space in the Suggestion Book, a complete edition of Swinburne's works was ordered forthwith, and now adorns the shelves of the Library.

Living, as I did, far from London, I had not the opportunity to see Swinburne, which I might have had, had I been resident in London. From time to time I received postcards or letters from him, one of the former I find states in reply to an enquiry regarding a sentence in "A Study of Shakespeare" that "the greatest living humorist in 1880" was, in the writer's opinion Thomas Carlyle, and on another postcard I am referred to the "Agricola" of Tacitus for the allusion made in the concluding stanza of the memorial verses on the death of John William Inchbold in the third series of "Poems and Ballads."

In 1902 I left Ireland and came to London, en

route for Western Africa. I did not get further than London, for reasons which will be found in a later chapter. In August, 1903, I contributed an article on Mr Swinburne's early dramas and poems to " The Gentleman's Magazine," a copy of which I left with my card at " The Pines," Putney Hill, a delightfully situated residence which has been fully described in his graphic manner by Mr James Douglas of *The Star* newspaper, in his fine volume on the life-work of our greatest living critic (and as Swinburne himself declared, possibly the greatest of all time), Mr Theodore Watts-Dunton. Both Swinburne and Watts-Dunton happened, as I learnt afterwards to be away at the time, I believe at Lancing. I called again, a little later, and found that the two poets were still away from home, and had to content myself by taking Swinburne's favourite walk up Putney Hill to Wimbledon, a walk described by Mr Watts-Dunton in the new edition, published with an illustration, of the little volume of " Selections from Poems of Swinburne."

A little later when I edited the poems of Thomas Lovell Beddoes for the excellent " Muses' Library " series of Messrs Routledge, I sent Swinburne and Mr Watts-Dunton copies of the little book, receiving gracious acknowledgments from both, and Mr Thomas Wright to whom we are indebted for lives of Pater, Edward FitzGerald, Burnaby and Sir Richard Burton, told me that calling at " The Pines " about this time, his hosts mentioned my name, and expressed some interest in my work.

Algernon Charles Swinburne

After sending a copy of the complete poetical works of George Darley in the same Library, the pleasurable task of editing which had been undertaken by me at the suggestion of Professor Dowden, I received from both Swinburne and Watts-Dunton (as well as from other recognised leaders in literature), letters full of generous praise, which gratified me greatly, coupled as they were with an invitation to call as soon as convenient, and suggesting the following Sunday afternoon. Luckily I was able to avail myself of the kindness thus extended, and four o'clock on a beautiful afternoon in May found me at " The Pines."

I was shown into a room richly furnished with Chinese carved cabinets and rare old furniture, the walls being covered with oil paintings, some of them evidently the work of Dante Gabriel Rossetti. Through the window could be seen a garden of larger dimensions than one is accustomed to in London, where every foot of ground is precious, having in the centre of a grassy mound a classical draped female figure in either stone or stucco. This statue, I learned later, had been in D. G. Rossetti's garden.

Mr Watts-Dunton was the first to greet me, and a little later Mr Swinburne glided in. Both poets shook hands, Mr Watts-Dunton with vigour, but Swinburne's hand lay in mine with the pressure of a butterfly. The thought that flashed through me that second was, that the hand I held had once lain in that of Walter Savage Landor, a writer who was,

In Castle and Court House

indeed " In holiest age our mightiest mind," and whose great qualities as poet and prose writer have been magnificently celebrated by Swinburne in poems written in English, Latin, and Greek. Mr Watts-Dunton, on the contrary, holds that Landor in striving to realise the characters of other men and to utter their thoughts, as he did in " The Imaginary Conversations," neglected to utter his own, and thereby swamped his own originality with a much poorer substitute, a fact to be deplored. " Landor," said Mr Watts-Dunton, " boasted that he would sup late, but that the guests would be few and select, I am afraid that Landor will never sup at all."

As I am not one of those who jot down other men's utterances in order to make " copy " of them, I fear there is little I can record here of our conversation.

I noted that Swinburne's eyes kindled when I mentioned the works of Robert Landor, whose " Impious Feast " and " Faith's Fraud " and " The Ferryman " I possess in copies which at one time belonged to Anthony Trollope. Swinburne praised another play by Robert Landor, " The Earl of Brecon," a drama in which we see (in the words of Sir Henry Taylor) " persons impassioned, not passions personified." Thinking Swinburne would be interested I presented him with a copy of " Under the Microscope," in the American edition published by Thomas B. Mosher, of Portland, Maine. Although he had gained nothing from a pecuniary

Algernon Charles Swinburne

point of view, from this edition, he was pleased with
the format of the book which is beautifully turned
out.

Since that memorable evening in May, I have
had the honour and pleasure of dining many times
at " The Pines " with both poets, and have partaken
of afternoon tea on Sundays. Owing to Swinburne's
deafness, not a little of what I said had to be communicated through Mr Watts-Dunton, who also took
a kindly interest in any subject which I broached,
particularly in a volume of selections from living
poets which I contemplated compiling, and to which
both my hosts readily promised to contribute, Mr
Watts-Dunton telling me I would get them all save
George Meredith, which proved to be the case, Mr
Meredith writing me on his last birthday thanking
me for copies of Hartley Coleridge, Beddoes, and
Darley which I had edited, but firmly stating that
he would not allow me to include any of his poems
in the projected volume. Mr Watts-Dunton was
interested in the fact that I admired the writings of
Ebenezer Jones, the author of " Studies in Sensation
and Event," on whom he contributed three letters
to *The Athenæum* some years ago, and whom
he knew personally, and whose brother, Sumner
Jones, called on him. Mr Alfred Noyes, whose epic
on Drake is one of the finest poetic utterances of late
years, had been dining at " The Pines " a few days
earlier, and when I referred to his " Lines for a
Seventieth Birthday " and declared my humble
opinion that these verses were the only ones written

103

worthy of their subject, Mr Watts-Dunton (Mr Swinburne was not present) said that he quite agreed with me.

Alas! for all lovers of song, the great singer was not to see another birthday. I happened to be in the office of *The Sunday Times* when the news of his death arrived, and Mr Leonard Rees, the Editor, turning to me, said "We look to you for a special article." I had no materials and wrote simply from memory and my knowledge of the dead poet's writings, and in closing my chapter of Remembrance can only quote his own lines on Victor Hugo:

Return! We dare not, as we fain
  Would cry from hearts that yearn.
Love dares not bid its dead again
            Return.

Oh, hearts that burn and yearn,
  As fires fast fettered strain and burn,
Bow down, lie still, and learn.
The heart that eased all hearts of pain
  No funeral rites in-urn,
Its echoes, while the stars remain,
            Return.

CHAPTER XI

In 1730, or thereabouts, one William Colles of
Kilkenny, having invented machinery for the sawing
of marble by water power, took a perpetual lease
of the marble quarries in Ireland, and erected the
mills which are still worked by his descendant, my
cousin Mr Richard Colles, J.P.

The first time I remember hearing the name Oscar
Wilde, was in connection with these mills. It was
asserted that owing to the Æsthetic Movement
inaugurated by Wilde who advocated the substitution of oaken mantelpieces for marble ones, that the
mills in Kilkenny must be, if the Movement was con-

tinued, shut down, and the branch of the Colles family which ran them, in consequence, be ruined!

With the selfishness of seventeen, having another career in prospect, I did not trouble much about this outlook, and it did not prevent my taking the keenest interest in Oscar Wilde's Poems, which were published by David Bogue about 1882. I remember with what keen delight I read such verse as—

> And many an Afghan chief, who lies
> Beneath his cool pomegranate trees,
> Clutches his sword in fierce surmise
> When on the mountain-side he sees
> The fleet-foot Marri scout, who comes
> To tell how he hath heard afar
> The measured roll of English drums
> Beat at the gate of Kandahar.

Years later, when I met Wilde, I suggested to him the substitution of the word " British " for " English " drums, on account of the onomatopœia, the fine roll of " R's " to correspond with the roll of drums. He said he thought there were quite enough " R's " in the line already.

The first time I met Oscar Wilde was when he had just returned from lecturing in America. It will be remembered that the D'Oyly Carte Opera Company preceded him everywhere throughout the United States, playing " Patience " with its attitudinising figure of Bunthorne the poet. Wilde did not seem to have troubled himself about the matter. At the luncheon table of my friend, who

lived in a pleasant detached house in the Green
Lane district of Clontarf, not far from where Brian
Boru was defeated, he spoke of his American
tour, and smiled when he was reminded that
he had been "disappointed" with the Atlantic.
He spoke of Mrs Langtry having had her photograph taken "with the Falls of Niagara as a kind of
unpretentious background," and incidentally referred
to the American girl as being "a delicious oasis of
unreasonableness in a desert of commonsense."
After he had gone, my host, a well-known Dublin
solicitor, who has long been dead, told me that Wilde
had asked, concerning me, "who is that interesting
young fellow?" an inquiry which greatly gratified
the young fellow in question.

Years later, about 1893, or thereabouts, I was
shown by Professor Dowden a head in red chalk
which he had purchased as a portrait of Oscar Wilde
when a boy. I asked and obtained permission to
have it photographed, and had three platinatypes
done by Mr Louis Werner, of Grafton Street. Wilde
was then living in 16, Tite Street, Chelsea, and no
doubt often saw—

> The Thames nocturne of blue and gold
> Change to a harmony in grey;
> A boat with ochre-coloured hay
> Drop from the wharf.

He had sent me his plays published at the Bodley
Head by Mr John Lane, who, if I remember aright,
had just then severed partnership with Mr Elkin

Mathews, and was ushering newly discovered poets into print with a rapidity that threatened to make England once more " a nest of singing birds."

The poems included " The Sphinx," as well as his better known work, and the play " Salomé." He gave me these poems in recognition of the fact that I had sent him Mr W. Carew Hazlitt's interesting collection of the Essays of Thomas Griffiths Wainwright, the murderer, once the friend or acquaintance of Charles Lamb, Thomas Noon Talfourd and other notable men of his day, and whose work had once or twice been mistaken for that of Elia. Wilde, it will be remembered, wrote an article in " The Fortnightly " on the subject, entitled " Pen, Pencil, and Poison," a phrase he found in Swinburne's " Study of William Blake," in which the author said of Wainwright, " with pen, with palate, or with poison his hand was no mean craftsman's."

About the same time I had drawn his attention to " Mary Magdalen," by Edgar Saltus, a copy of which had been sent me from America by George Pellew, and which was eventually published in this country by Harper's, under the title of " Mary of Magdala." Wilde's study of the prophet John bears a close resemblance to that of Saltus, and the two studies are worth comparing.

Having secured my photographs, I sent them to Wilde, asking him to enrich them with his autograph. He replied that I really must not ask him to do so. That they were far too ugly, and returned them unsigned, accompanied by a signed photograph of

THE BARONESS DE BAZUS
(better known as "Frank Leslie.")

himself by Ellis and Walery taken very recently, and
showing him standing upright, with his right hand
buried just above the top button of his overcoat
which had an ucstrakhan collar and which bore a
carnation in the left buttonhole. This was the last
time I heard from him. A little later came the great
tragedy in his life, and in common with many of his
admirers, I turned away from him, and feminine influence being very strong in my life at the moment, I
burned his letters and all the photographs in my
possession, only one of the three done of the picture
escaping the holocaust by my having presented it to
Professor Dowden! The original chalk head, I may
mention, was done by Henry O'Neill, a well-known
portrait painter in his day, to whom Wilde paid a
kindly tribute in one of his letters to me.

That I was not alone in my sudden change from
admiration to revulsion is proved by the fact that
when my friend Mr H. A. Hinkson collected " Poems
by Graduates of T.C.D.," which were published by
Mr Elkin Mathews in 1895, the book fell dead,
simply because it contained poems by Oscar Wilde.

When in 1904 " De Profundis " was published, I
was deeply touched, and wrote to Mr Robert Ross,
the Editor of the book, expressing my contrition for
burning the dead man's letters, and heartily congratulating him on the great work he was doing for his
memory, by clearing off his debts, and getting his
bankruptcy annulled. Mr Ross has added to the
indebtedness to him of all admirers of Wilde by the
monumental edition of Wilde's books which he has

had issued by Messrs Methuen. It is to be hoped that a popular edition of Oscar Wilde's plays and poems will soon be published. An edition in one volume would certainly sell. Thanks to the staunch support of Mr George Alexander the poet's name has been restored to the playbills, and " The Importance of Being Earnest " has had a long run at the St James's Theatre.

Wilde borrowed very largely from the French, but his plays, nevertheless, contain not a little that is deliciously original. In " A Woman of No Importance," for instance, we are told that the Peerage is " the best thing in fiction that the English have ever done." That " American dry-goods " are American novels! and there are dozens of others equally good.

The author of " Oscar Wilde: The Story of an Unhappy Friendship " took me to see Mrs Frank Leslie, at one time Mrs Willy Wilde, and now that she has retired into private life, known by her title of the Baroness de Bazus.

We found the Baroness, who was merely flitting through London, en route for Paris, deeply engaged in reading the poems of Joaquin Miller in a six volume edition with which the poet had just presented her. Naturally, the conversation turned on the " Songs of the Sierras," and other poems by the poet of the West, and I was delighted to get news of the fine old author and to hear the Baroness read aloud his striking poem " Columbus " with its refrain " Sail on! Sail on!! Sail on!!! " I had long admired

Oscar Wilde and Others

Joaquin Miller's poetry and in order to prove to the Baroness that my admiration was genuine, I recited his verses entitled " Jewess," which is not the only poem of the author's I have memorised. As some of my readers may not be familiar with it, I give it here—

> My dark-browed daughter of the sun,
>   Dear Bedouin of the desert sands,
>   Sad daughter of the ravished lands,
> Of savage Sinai, Babylon—
>   O Egypt-eyed, thou art to me
>   A God-encompassed mystery!
>
> I see sad Hagar in thine eyes,
>   The obelisks, the pyramids,
>   Lie hid beneath thy drooping lids.
> The tawny Nile of Moses lies
>   Portrayed in thy strange people's force
>   And solemn mystery of source.
>
> The black abundance of thy hair
>   Falls like some twilight sad of June
>   Above the dying afternoon,
> And mourns thy people's mute despair.
>   The large solemnity of night,
>   O Israel, is in thy sight.
>
> Then come where stars of freedom spill
>   Their splendour, Jewess. In this land
>   The broad hollow of God's hand
> That held you ever, outholds still.
>   And whether you be right or nay,
>   'Tis God's, not Russia's, here to say.

Some reference was made to " Speranza," Lady Wilde, and to Irish poets in general, and I mentioned George Darley, and incidentally said that when I discovered the cemetery in which he was buried, I

III

visited the grave, and finding it much neglected, I called the attention of a member of Darley's family to the fact, with the gratifying result that the superintendent wrote me " It looks as if the grave belonged to somebody now." The Baroness said that the grave of " Speranza " was in a shockingly neglected condition.

So ended my interview with this very remarkable woman who took over her dead husband's business, which by his premature death he left buried in debt, assumed by law the name of " Frank Leslie," and not alone cleared off all the debts, but ran " Leslie's Home Journal," until its name was familiar all over the world, by reason of its gigantic circulation, and then retired with a huge fortune, to be courted and honoured by all who love the best in journalism and literature.

The Baroness has wonderfully beautiful eyes—large, grey, melting, and sympathetic; her figure is perfect, and her carriage enhances it. She has the bright clear complexion that comes of exercise and health; and luxuriant hair of a very light colour. Her voice is delightful. She is frankly feminine in her manner, showing her gentle breeding to the tips of her aristocratic fingers. If one did not know, one would say that she had never known a moment of work or worry in her life.

Every summer she enjoys a European holiday, and invariably, in London, Paris, Madrid, and the fashionable watering places on the Continent, she is fêted, admired and interviewed by the newspapers even more than when she is at home—for in Europe it is vacation in earnest for her. From the Government of Venezuela she has received the distinguished and beautiful decoration of " El Busto del Libertador," bestowed by the South American Republic upon " those who have rendered service in the cause of humanity, progress and civilisation," and she has also a French decoration, bestowed by the martyred President Carnot, and the decoration of Saint Catherine as well.

How has she done it all? By a bold and decisive mind, the audacity of genius, tireless energy and the perfection of physique. The child Miriam Florence Folline was a fragile creature, a delicate Huguenot exotic in the French quarter of New Orleans. The woman Baroness de Bazus is the perfection of physical development. By the exercise of all her faculties, physical and mental, she has kept her whole nature in perfect equilibrium. Her handwriting is characteristic, the characters large, the strokes firm with a notable upward impulse, regular, connected, and flowing. And she has never lost an intellectual opportunity. She speaks English, French, Spanish, and Italian with fluent perfection, besides understanding Latin. She has read much and seen more, and welded into her own originality her studies and reflections and experiences. Much as she owes to nature, she owes more to herself. She proves that genius is a capacity for hard work; that significant success comes like the onward-creeping dawn, and is no blast of heat-lightning. Whatever she has done, too, she has done as a woman in a womanly way. She has found her sex has rights enough when it wants to employ them.

Her *salon* is one of the institutions of New York. She is the Mme. Adam of New York. At them are to be met all sorts of people worth knowing, and very few that are not distinguished for something or other. She gives her invitations on the famous receipt of Mrs Jeune. " Millions for amusement; not one line for tribute! " Plenty of society people are to be found at her *salon*, but they are all some-bodies outside the drawing-room.

She is great as a hostess, full of sympathy and tact and bonhomie. She has a large fund of good stories, and doesn't have to go outside her own experience for their subjects.

One of the most fascinating women I have ever met is Mrs Irene Osgood, author of " To a Nun Confess'd," and " Servitude." I met her at a fashionable West End Hotel, and having shown an interest in her books, she kindly invited me to visit her in her beautiful home, Guilsborough Hall, which is her own property and lies in a very pretty country between Rugby and Northampton. It is the Hall of an ancient and picturesque village, where there are many cottages with thatched roofs, and where there is an old Jacobean grammar school, built and endowed by the Langham family.

When Irene Osgood acquired the place a few years ago, Guilsborough Hall, which had long been occupied by the Countess Spencer, to whom a memorial stands in the adjoining parish church; was a dilapidated manor-house in a wilderness of laurel bushes.

To-day, Guilsborough Hall is one of the most beautiful houses in the Midlands, and the gardens which surround it are the admiration of all the authorities on artistic gardening. These gardens were designed and carried out by the fair owner, whose taste and discernment in their construction proves that she is an artist in more walks of life than one.

A pretty fancy is shown by Mrs Osgood in her all-white garden, which for simplicity and beauty is unrivalled, every shrub and flower being pure white.

I recall many talks with this young and gifted woman in the exquisite Adams room which forms part of her private suite, and which she designates the music room. She is by no means a mere woman of letters, for she was, until she met with many nasty accidents in the field, an enthusiastic rider to hounds, and her taste in dress is perfect as her form.

Her books have had a phenomenal sale, especially "Servitude," which deals with Christian slavery in Algiers before the victory of Lord Exmouth, and "To a Nun Confess'd," has run through many editions.

One of the greatest charms of Irene Osgood is her voice. It reminded me of Walt Whitman's beautiful lines—

" Surely whoever speaks to me in the right voice
Him or her I shall follow, as the water follows the moon,
Anywhere around the globe."

In Castle and Court House

I can hear it now, as she tells me about "Full Free," a novel she has projected dealing with the negro question in the West Indies. "I have always," she said, "taken a particular interest in black folk, because, as perhaps you know, I come from a line of Virginia planters, who owned slaves before the war. The horrible things that were of such common occurrence in the West Indies were unheard of in Virginia, and I shall be able to draw some comparisons from what my people have told me, which will not be very flattering to the West Indian planters. Our slaves were devoted to us, my mother has often told me, and during the war showed the greatest affection and loyalty to their masters."

I remember also much about another new book, to be called "Where Pharoah Dreams." This book, Irene Osgood wrote in Helouan, near Cairo. It is to be illustrated by W. Gordon Mein, and published in the United States.

Amongst personal items Mrs Osgood told me that she was born on a plantation in Old Virginia. Her father's people were from Normandy, one of her ancestors, Baron Jean de Belot, having left France for political reasons, and on account of being a Huguenot. Baron de Belot traced his history from much earlier times, it being on record that one of the members of his family officiated in the private chapel of Louis XI.

I was particularly delighted with Irene Osgood's love and protection of wild birds. Hundreds of nesting boxes are to be seen in the trees in the park,

IRENE OSGOOD.

and trays of food are outside most of the bedroom windows, with saucers of water for the birds to either drink or bathe in. And the birds are not ungrateful, for morning and evening the whole place is filled with the music of their songs.

That Irene Osgood is a good business woman and no dreamer, is proved by the huge run she has erected for prize poultry on the borders of the park; and here may be seen fowls of all plumage, many of them first prize winners in all parts of the country. Walter Savage Landor prided himself on the number of trees he had planted at Llanthony, rightly deeming that he had done a patriotic act thereby. I can imagine the delight he would have expressed had he seen the plantation of fine young trees with which Irene Osgood has enriched Guilsborough Hall.

It is an ideal home for an artist and poetess. And those who read Irene Osgood's books, or have the privilege of seeing her, will not refuse her either title.

CHAPTER XII

EDWARD DOWDEN

Professor Edward Dowden—His "Life of Percy Bysshe Shelley"—Matthew Arnold's Criticism—The Ways of Dowden like those of Providence—William Watson on Shelley and Harriett Westbrook—Professor Dowden and Walt Whitman—Dowden the Poet—His French and German Studies—President of the English Goethe Society—Visitors to "Winstead"—Montagu Griffin—J. J. Piatt—Lord Tennyson and George Darley.

I HAVE already made many references to Professor Edward Dowden, whom I shall always deem it an honour to "count upon my list of friends." I have had the pleasure of knowing Dowden for nearly a quarter of a century. He is, as many of my readers are aware, Professor of English Literature and Oratory in the University of Dublin, and is the author of "Shakspere: His Mind and Art," "Studies in Literature, 1798-1877," "Transcripts and Studies," and other critical essays. He is also the author of the only reliable "Life of Shelley," having compiled the two volumes from the original documents submitted to him by the poet's son, the late Sir Percy Florence Shelley, and his wife Lady Shelley.

Edward Dowden

Professor Dowden, with important documentary evidence before him, wrote with the cool critical acumen which distinguishes him, and while wishing to deal as gently as possible with the memory of Harriett Westbrook, Shelley's first wife, he was obliged, in justice to the poet, to make a reflection on her character, but at the same time he gave, in a footnote, a reference to the files of *The Times* newspaper, in corroboration of his judgment. This reference the critics, one and all, ignored, even Matthew Arnold, who in his later essays, appears to have lost all his former clearness of vision, going so far as to write that the ways of Professor Dowden resembled those of Providence, in that they were inscrutable. Mr William Watson, who had addressed a sonnet to Dowden on his " Life of Shelley," made the same error with regard to Harriett in his " Epigrams on Life, Art, and Nature."

> A great star stooped from heaven and loved a flower
> Grown in earth's garden, loved it for an hour.
> Let those who mark his progress through the spheres
> Refuse not to a ruined rosebud—tears.

Harriett was far from being " a ruined rosebud." Professor Dowden replied in " Last Words on Shelley " in his " Transcripts and Studies " and effectually silenced his critics.

Dowden's published work covers a wide area and exhibits a wonderful catholicity in literary appreciation. He was one of the very first to recognise the significance of the advent of Walt Whitman; while his sympathy with the " barbaric yawp " of the American did not prevent his being sensitive to the beauty of Walter Pater's delicate sentimentalism, as displayed in such dicta as that " life should be lived as delicately as one may pluck a flower." He has noted with a keen eye the opposed mental attitudes of Tennyson and Browning, and has interpreted their messages to their age with singular clearness and truth. He has taught many to feel and understand the moral significance and the value of the work of George Eliot. He has traced the influence on English literature of the various movements on the Continent of Europe, such as the transcendental movement, and the scientific. Nor has he confined his studies to English alone. In his earliest essays he drew attention to the grandeur of the poetry of Victor Hugo, and that of Leconte de Lisle, and Lamennais and Edgar Quinet found in him a delicately true interpreter. He has contributed a noteworthy volume on French Literature to Heinemann's " Literatures of the World," edited by Mr Edmund Gosse.

To be thoroughly acquainted with Professor Dowden's studies in literature is to be possessed of much more than mere knowledge of the subjects treated in his books. It is to have as constant companion and friend, one whose ethical teaching is of the highest value, whose spiritual vision is clear, and one who is ever ready to point to the sources from which he himself derives much of the wisdom and strength which he is desirous his pupil should possess. It

Edward Dowden

is as an interpreter that Professor Dowden stands pre-eminent. He has seized the best that has been said in the English tongue and so treated it that truths hidden in the occult utterances of the poet, or rendered obscure by being " embodied in a tale " acquire their due potentiality. Shakespeare, though lovingly commented on by such writers as Coleridge, Lamb, and Landor, has in Dowden a rare and delicately true exponent, and one whom I firmly believe has penetrated more deeply into the mind of the great interpreter of life than any of the writers named. He has in " Shakspere: His Mind and Art " contributed not alone an invaluable volume to modern criticism, but has distinctly made an addition to previous conceptions of the mind of the Master.

It is in this book that the reader comes upon such a sentence as the following:—" Even though death end all, these things at least *are*—beauty and force, purity, sin, and love, and anguish and joy. These things are, and therefore life cannot be a little idle whirl of dust." Such a sentence as this cannot but have a moral effect. It is one of those " antidotes of medicated music " of which the poet writes, " answering for mankind's forlornest uses." Professor Dowden has often played the part he assigns in his essay on " Victorian Literature " to Browning, whose poetry he declares to be " a galvanic battery for the use of spiritual paralytics." " Which of us," he asks, " does not need at times that virtue should pass into him from a stronger human soul? To touch the singing robes of the author of ' Rabbi Ben

Ezra' and 'Prospice,' and 'The Grammarian's Funeral,' is to feel an influx of new strength. We gain from Mr Browning, each in his degree, some of that moral ardour and spiritual faith and vigour of human sympathy which make interesting to him all the commonplace, confused, and ugly portions of life . . . ." Consciously or unconsciously such has been Professor Dowden's own rôle as a teacher. To read his books is to gain new strength and courage to endure, and we come at length to acknowledge that to be weak is to be miserable. He has, as it were, hearkened to all the prophets of the time, and when any had an authentic word of the Lord to deliver, be he Tennyson or Whitman, Browning or George Eliot, that word has gained a larger audience by being caught up and conveyed to those who had at first paid but little heed to the cry of " Blessed be ye " or of " Woe unto you." I have not dwelt on Professor Dowden's books as text-books; no doubt as such they have their value. " The true question to ask about any book," said a librarian once, " is ' has it helped any human soul? ' " Were such a question addressed to me regarding " Studies in Literature " or other works by Professor Dowden, I would gladly acknowledge the great help I have derived from them, and I am certain I am not alone in my experience.

In his latest volume " Essays Modern and Elizabethan," Dowden includes a study of Goethe's " West-Eastern Divan," with translations into English verse of Goethe's poems, translations which

Edward Dowden

bear testimony alike to his ability as a translator and to his gifts as a poet. For Dowden is a poet, and as such is recognised by the more discerning of those who have read his volume of Poems, published in 1876. This volume could only have been written by one who was essentially a poet, and proves that had the author chosen to seek solely the reputation of a poet, he could easily have taken a high place as a singer. Here is a fine specimen of his workmanship—

BURDENS.

Are sorrows hard to bear—the ruin
  Of flowers, the rotting of red fruit,
A love's decease, a life's undoing,
  And summer slain, and song-birds mute,
And skies of snow and bitter air?
These things, you deem, are hard to bear.

But ah, the burden, the delight
  Of dreadful joys! Noon opening wide,
Golden and great; the gulfs of night,
  Fair deaths, and rent veils cast aside,
Strong soul to strong soul rendered up,
And silence filling like a cup.

As the book is completely out of print I may give this magnificent passage on Nature's need of Man—

O now I guess why you have summoned me,
Headlands and heights, to your companionship;
Confess that I this day am needful to you!
The heavens were loaded with great light, the winds
Brought you calm summer from a hundred fields,
All night the stars had pricked you to desire,
The imminent joy at its full season flowered,

In Castle and Court House

There was a consummation, the broad wave
Toppled and fell. And had ye voice for this?
Sufficient song to unburden the urged breast?
A pastoral pipe to play, a lyre to touch?
The brightening glory of the heath and gorse
Could not appease your passion, nor the cry
Of this wild bird that flits from bush to bush.
Me therefore you required, a voice for song,
A pastoral pipe to play, a lyre to touch.
I recognise your bliss to find me here:
The sky at morning when the sun upleaps
Demands her atom of intense melody,
Her point of quivering passion and delight,
And will not let the lark's heart be at ease.
Take me, the brain with various' subtile fold,
The breast that knows swift joy, the vocal lips;
I yield you here the cunning instrument
Between your knees; now let the plectrum fall!

Not Wordsworth in his most ecstatic mood in
communing with Nature could have surpassed the
passage about the lark, either in emotion or expression. One more specimen of Professor Dowden's
poetical work, and I leave Dowden the poet for my
readers to seek and enjoy, but as they may experience some difficulty in obtaining the volume I give
the following noble sonnet on—

BROTHER DEATH.

When thou would'st have me go with thee, O Death,
Over the utmost verge, to the dim place,
Practise upon me with no amorous grace
Of fawning lips, and words of delicate breath,
And curious music thy lute uttereth;
Nor think for me there must be sought-out ways
Of cloud and terror; have we many days

PROFESSOR DOWDEN, LL.D., D.C.L.

Edward Dowden

Sojourned together, and is this thy faith?
Nay, be there plainness 'twixt us; come to me
Even as thou art, O brother of my soul;
Hold thy hand out and I will place mine there;
I trust thy mouth's inscrutable irony,
And dare to lay my forehead where the whole
Shadow lies deep of the purpureal hair.

Professor Dowden is President of the English Goethe Society, and his essays include several thoughtful and penetrative studies of the work and wisdom of the author of " Faust." That on the correspondence of Goethe and Schiller is particularly attractive.

Dowden's humour is of a rare and elusive kind, as, for instance, when he writes on " The Text of Wordsworth's Poems." "Wordsworth's omissions, made for the sake of avoiding the merely trivial, literal, matter of fact, accidental, or grotesque, are numerous, and some of these are sufficiently well known. Simon Lee, during two and twenty years stood before the reader in that 'long blue livery coat '—

'That's fair behind and fair before,'

and which is only faintly referred to after 1815; during several years more he remained bereft of his right eye; *finally the eye was restored to him, but the lustre of his livery was dimmed.*"

At "Winstead" I met many notable men and women, some of whom I have already mentioned, as, for instance, Perceval Graves, the author of the " Life of Sir William Rowan Hamilton," the great

125

mathematician; Charles Dickens, Jr., Bettina Walker, the enthusiastic pianist, who knew Liszt, and had had lessons from Henselt; Sir Herbert and Lady Tree, Sir Henry Irving; Miss May Fortescue; Miss Ellen Terry; Professor Thomas Arnold, father of Mrs Humphry Ward; W. Macneile Dixon, who is now a Professor of English Literature in Glasgow University; and two poets who had not at the time published a volume of verse, W. B. Yeats and William Watson.

In 1887, as well I remember, Watson's " Words-worth's Grave " was published. The little volume of " Epigrams," published by a firm in Liverpool, having proceeded it. I reviewed the book in *The Dublin Evening Mail*, and, while I could not but delight in its judicious praise of Wordsworth, I demurred at the tone adopted towards William Morris, who was referred to as displaying—

" The scholar's, not the child's, simplicity."

Watson complained of my review as being the only jarring note in a chorus of praise.

Yeats' first book I had the pleasure of subscribing for. It contained " Mosada," a dramatic poem of much promise, and one which his later work has not surpassed.

In 1893 I suggested to Messrs Macmillan that they should get Professor Dowden to make a selec-tion from Southey's poems and include them in their well-known " Golden Treasury " series, with those of Wordsworth, Keats, Shelley, and Coleridge.

Edward Dowden

This was done and the copy of the book which I possess contains an inscription by the Editor, "To Ramsay Colles, who kindly suggested this little book, from Edward Dowden." No man has rendered so signal a service to the memory of Robert Southey as has Edward Dowden. His monograph on Southey is one of the best in the "English Men of Letters" series, and he has in addition, edited the correspondence of Southey with Caroline Bowles, who became Southey's second wife.

No matter how much we depreciate Southey to-day, there is no doubt that he deeply impressed such men as Walter Savage Landor and Sir Henry Taylor. The former addressed some of his finest verse to one whom he deemed "poet, soldier, saint," and Taylor declared that though the admirers of Southey were few—

"The womb of time is big with devotees."

Possibly; but if such was the case, they were, alas! all still-born. One of the most interesting men I met at Dowden's was Montagu Griffin, a nephew of Canon Griffin, of Mill Street, Cork. Griffin was a great admirer of Dowden's poetry, and wrote poetry himself, of excellent quality. Another poet whom I met was J. J. Piatt, at one time U.S. Consul in Dublin, author of "A Dream of Church Windows," and I also met his gifted wife who is, I believe, known as the Elizabeth Barrett Browning of America. Dom Piatt, a son of the poets, was assistant to the Consul, then the Hon. Joshua Wilbour, when I left Dublin in 1902. Mr Dom Piatt married a poetess in the person of Miss Hester Sigerson, a daughter of Dr George Sigerson and sister of Mrs Clement Shorter.

Professor Dowden suggested to me the publication of a complete edition of the poems of George Darley, an Irish poet, the friend of Charles Lamb, and a contributor to " The London Magazine."   Messrs Routledge kindly consenting, I procured, at not a little expense, the plays and poems of Darley, some of which I purchased through Messrs Ellis of Bond Street, and others through a publisher in Liverpool. I applied to Canon Livingstone, the Hon. Mrs Livingstone, and Miss Evelyn Darley, with the result that the complete poetical works of Darley can now be purchased for one shilling net; and I have had the gratification of a public acknowledgment from Professor Saintsbury, in the third volume of his " History of English Prosdy."   I dedicated the volume, which had given me much pleasure to compile, to Dowden.   Amongst my purchases in this connection was a copy of Darley's " Thomas à Becket " presented by the author to " Alfred Tennyson, Esq.," Lord Tennyson, the late Laureate's son, kindly replied to one or two queries, and when I told him about this book, said he would like to possess it in case I should at any time wish to part with it.   I am glad to say that it is still in my possession.

CHAPTER XIII

SOME DUBLIN CHARACTERS

DUBLIN is full of people with strongly marked person-
alities. People who are not satisfied to be like
others, but prefer to be themselves alone. If a
visitor travels to Ireland via Holyhead and Kingstown, by the fine boats of the City of Dublin Steam
Packet Co., he will, on landing at Kingstown, strike
a well-known personality in the newsvendor " Sir "
Davy Stephens, who was knighted many years ago
by Lord Spencer, popularly known as " the Red
Earl," on account of his fine tawny beard. Lord
Spencer was Lord Lieutenant of Ireland at the time
(1882), and the legend is that as Davy Stephens on
bended knee presented Her Majesty's representative
with copies of the Irish daily papers, the " Red
Earl " smote him on the shoulder, and jocularly
exclaimed " Arise, Sir Davy Stephens! " " Sir " Davy

Stephens had only to take out letters patent to be a true knight, but he preferred, like the Irishman he is, a joke to remain a joke, showing thereby a true sense of humour. "Sir" Davy attends the Derby every year, and annually calls upon his many friends, including the writer.

It is ten to one that the first car driver one strikes on visiting Ireland is as truly a born humorist as was Mark Twain. Sir George Moyers was fond of telling a good story about a jarvey who used to drive him to Glenageary at night when by any chance he missed the last train from Westland Row. One cold night, or rather morning, Sir George having paid the fare, handed the jarvey a glass of whisky, and on being handed back the empty glass, said "Well, Pat, isn't that good whisky?" "Begorrah, yer honour," said honest Pat, "I forgot to taste it!" Another jarvey on being asked the same question, replied, "Faith it's made *a new man* of me, and shure *he's* thirsty, too!"

One of the most amusing characters in Dublin was Dicky Borne, a diminutive barrister and Justice of the Peace. Dicky used to sit on the bench at Rathfarnham Petty Sessions. One day a delinquent was brought before him, who was noticeable chiefly for his very red nose. "What is this case, Borne?" asked a brother magistrate, "Another case of *damnosa hereditas*," replied Dicky, as he took a pinch of snuff.

A very pompous individual, whom we shall call "Jones" was fond of airing his views. His Majesty

Some Dublin Characters

King Edward had laid the foundation stone of a public building—I think that of the King's and Queen's College of Physicians—when I met Jones and said to him, " Well, Mr Jones, I saw you at the ceremony yesterday.   What did you think of the King? " Jones pressed the finger tips of one hand against those of the other, and replied with characteristic pomposity:

" Oh! he's quite the gentleman, you know, quite the gentleman."

Another noted character in Dublin was the late Michael Doyle, manager of the Gaiety Theatre, a trusted servant and friend of Mr Michael Gunn, who was long associated with Mr D'Oyly Carte.   Doyle was a very laconic individual.   He reminded me of the twin brothers in one of Edgar Saltus's novels, who were blessed with the gift of taciturnity and were known in consequence as " Dry " and " Extra Mumm."   My friend, Mr James Glover, the well-known composer and musical director at Drury Lane, and ex-Mayor of Bexhill-on-Sea, years ago called at the Gaiety Theatre, and asked for Mr Doyle.

" I'm Mr Doyle," said Michael.

" My name," said Glover, sticking his glass more firmly in his eye, " is Mackey Glover."

" I can't help that," said the imperturable Doyle!

One of the many rôles I have filled was that of sub-manager of the Ulster Bank, College Green, Dublin.   I was at the same time attached, in a nominal way, to *The Dublin Evening Mail*, writing

In Castle and Court House

dramatic notes and notices of the Opera. In this
way I came into personal contact with Mr Doyle
who at first was icy in his manner but gradually
thawed as time went on. I found he appreciated a
little attention and therefore from time to time sent
him copies of the magazines and books which I
reviewed.

One day I found I had no books by me, and therefore wrote a line to Messrs Hodges Figgis and Co.,
Booksellers to the University, saying " Please give
bearer a two-shilling novel." This note I handed to
the bank porter with another addressed to the
manager of the Gaiety Theatre, asking for a couple
of stalls, instructing the porter to take the parcel he
got from Hodges Figgis on to the theatre and hand
it in with my letter to Mr Doyle. The porter did as
he was instructed, and in due course I got my pass.
Judge my surprise, however, when at the end of
the month I got included in my bill from the bookseller an item " twelve novels at two shillings each,
£1 4s." As I had not mentioned title or author, the
firm had kindly sent me a dozen from which to
select, and James had delivered the lot to Mr
Doyle!

I have to plead guilty to rather a heartless joke
in connection with Michael Doyle, with whom I
never was on really friendly terms, and whom I
always addressed as " Dear Sir " save on one occasion. The occasion arose out of the fact that I had
promised to try to secure a box at the Gaiety for some
friends, and on the very morning of the day on which

my application should be made, I saw with consternation in a morning paper: " Sudden death of Mr Michael Doyle."

Officials in Irish banks are not overburdened by the amount of their salaries, and three guineas are three guineas, and represented a sum of money I had no inclination to spend on this particular evening's amusement. At first I thought the theatre might be closed. No such luck! It was to be closed on the day of the funeral. " Dead men tell no tales," said I, as I penned a request for a box in the following terms—

" MY DEAR DOYLE,—I am coming down to-night. Keep the omnibus box for me, like a good chap,— Your old friend,— RAMSAY COLLES."

This I sent off early in the day, and received in due course a voucher for Box A, a fact on which I congratulated myself, for had I not saved three guineas? Three weeks later I received a letter in an envelope edged with black. " Hello," I mused, " Who's dead? " The letter ran—

" GAIETY THEATRE, DUBLIN."

" DEAR SIR,—As a personal friend of the late Mr Michael Doyle you will, no doubt, be pleased to subscribe to the funds for a fitting memorial to him, etc.— (signed) CHARLES HYLAND."

Doyle was succeeded as manager of the Gaiety by one of the most popular men in Dublin, the writer of the letter just quoted. I never referred to my application for a box on the day of Doyle's death to Hyland, as I thought the matter too delicate, but I feel certain Hyland knew what he was about when he sent me that order for Box A!

A keen lover of reform, and, with all respect (and indeed, admiration), a watch-dog for abuses is Major Gamble, R.N., who has for many years been, in his own words, "first grave-digger" at Mount Jerome Cemetery. In other words Major Gamble is at the head of affairs in connection with the Protestant Burial Ground in South Dublin. I at one time cherished the hope that he would see that I was myself "buried respectable" but, having joined the Cremation Society of England, even that slight link between Ireland and me has been severed, and Matthew Arnold's lines have been realised—

> Men dig graves with bitter tears
> For their dead hopes!

Major Gamble is an ardent enthusiast in all matters of social reform. He keeps a keen eye on human affairs, in addition to watching "o'er man's mortality," and the vast majority of reforms in Dublin have been owing to his initiative. In order to relieve the monotony of living in a house surrounded by graves, he has had erected in the picturesque neighbourhood of Brittas a compact dwelling made of corrugated iron, and I have had the pleasure of fishing with him in the little lake close to his house among the Dublin Mountains, and of drawing the net which annually clears the waters of destructive perch.

Some Dublin Characters

Major Gamble had, years ago, a chaplain at Mount Jerome who was a poet of rare gifts, as the following specimen of his verse will prove—

O, had I a Lumpty-tum, Umpty-tum to,
  In the land of the Olive and Fig,
I would sing of my Lumpty-tum Umpty to you,
  And play on my Thing-um-a-jig.

And if in the Lumpty-tum battle I fall,
  A Lumpty-tum's all that I crave;
O, bury me deep in the What-ye-may-call,
  And plant Thing-um-bobs over my grave!

Major Gamble has an able lieutenant in my old friend Simon Maddock, who is the happy possessor of a tenor voice of rare quality, and whose sunny disposition cannot be affected by worms or graves or epitaphs.

One of the most picturesque figures in Dublin is the erect and soldier-like one of John O'Duffy, L.D.S., R.C.S.I. A pioneer in his profession, Mr O'Duffy was one of the founders of the Dental Institute, and has for years been calling public attention to a crying evil, and one which has of recent years received the serious consideration it deserves. More than half a century has elapsed since John O'Duffy pointed out the national calamity which must follow the general neglect of the teeth. It required a national calamity to rouse the nation to a sense of the gravity of his words. The war in South Africa proved the truth of his dictum that an army marches on its stomach and fights with its teeth. O'Duffy on one occasion won a bet by running blindfold

from Nelson's Pillar in Sackville Street to the
Wellington Monument in the Phœnix Park, touching
all the public buildings on his way to and from. He
started at one o'clock in the morning and finished
two hours later, covering the distance, some six
miles, in wonderful time considering that he was
temporarily deprived of his eyesight.

I am glad that when I lived in Dublin, Percy
French resided there also. His "Chuckles in
Chalk" are now familiar to London audiences, but
at the time to which I refer he was only commencing
his career of crime in conjunction with the Rev.
Houston Collisson, Mus. D., with whom he perpe-
trated a comic opera on the subject of Freeny, a
highway robber, who had been—

> Brought up on the strictest plan—
> That's why he became a highwayman.

One of the best bits in the opera was the exclama-
tion by the highwayman after he had deprived his
victims of all their valuables—

> Ye got off very well;
> I'd have fleeced ye far more if I kept a hotel!

I suggested to the collaborators, through Mr
Whitbread the genial manager of the Queen's
Theatre, that an opera on the subject of Strongbow
would prove a success if closed with a tableau of
Maclis's great picture, "The Marriage of Strongbow
and Eva." French and Collisson took my advice
and produced "Strongbow up to Date," with strik-

ing success. French made a speech at the fall of the curtain on the first night, asking those present to come again and bring their " relatives and friends," not necessarily the same persons!

Encouraged by French and Collisson's success, Alfred Smyth, F.R.G.S., the author of " Sir Dunstan's Daughter," and other entertaining volumes of verse, and the late Edgar Little produced " The Warlock," a very able piece of work. There was a strange resemblance between the libretto of " The Warlock " and Sidney Grundy's libretto to " Haddon Hall," produced about the same time. In fact, so close was the resemblance that Alfred Smyth, got the passages printed in parallel lines, and sent them to Grundy for an explanation. Sydney Grundy replied " This is very interesting, but you've forgotten one point of resemblance, my private secretary's name is Smith."

Percy French's songs are very popular, particularly " Mat Hannigan's Aunt," which to me has always been reminiscent of " Martin Hannigan's Aunt," by Lever. Much of his published fun is buried in the files of " The Irish Jarvey " and in back numbers of " The Irish Cyclist." He told me on one occasion that he was staying in the country at a house where the landlady professed to give bed and board for twenty-five shillings a week. " I assure you," said French, gravely " I was there a week before I discovered which was the bed and which was the board."

CHAPTER XIV

PUBLIC ENTERTAINERS

THE first public entertainer I had the good fortune to see was Valentine Vousden the ventriloquist and variety artist whom all old Dubliners will remember. Vousden used to sing a song about the Irish jaunting car, in the character of the driver. One verse of it ran something like the following—

> Do ye want a car, yer honour? —
> Och, shure, here's the wan for you:
> A rale Irish jaunting-car,
> And it's painted green and blue.

The rest of the song was devoted to the glories of being " rowled out to Sandymount " " to pick cockles on the strand," or driving to " the strawberry beds and back to town again."

Vousden went through one or two fortunes. The

138

last time I saw him was in January, 1900, when on the invitation of the Guardians, I visited the North Dublin Union with Mr T. W. Russell, M.P. Vousden was an inmate, and a very cheerful one, and I was able to shake hands with a man who had delighted me when I was a child.

Another public entertainer, and one who had a world-wide reputation was Charles Duval who used to appear annually at the Rotunda in Dublin. The Rotunda Buildings include a Chapel of Ease, a Lying-in Hospital, a Rink, and halls which are devoted to concerts and political and religious meetings. One evening I sat in the gallery listening to Duval reciting the plot of a pseudo play which he did very rapidly and which ran something like the following—

"The Piratical Pirate of the Precipitous Precipice, or The Premediated Prey of Proud Power and the Prodigiously Proper Plight of the Preponderous Plunderer of Patagonian Proportions. Children and nurses may witness this play as the plot is not taken from the French." A little later he appeared in a monologue as the lodging-house slavey, blackening a boot and alternately brushing the boot and the wig which he wore to represent the slavey's hair.

Boy-like I was listening intently when a country man sitting beside me, who had also been listening with marked gravity, whispered to me, " An' whin, may I ax, does Misther Parnell come on?"

Parnell was addressing a political meeting in another part of the Rotunda!

In Castle and Court House

Public attention had recently been directed, through a libel action to Mlle Marie Greville whose name was long associated with the late M. Guibal. This extraordinary man at one time essayed to teach me French, a task in which he was not very successful, which was my fault, not his. He gave up giving lessons in French about 1880, and left Dublin, only to reappear a few years later as " a dealer in magic and spells," accompanied by Miss Marie Greville, who with closed eyes and to all appearance in a trance, walked about the room, thought-reading.

I went to see Guibal in his new rôle, and was welcomed by him at the entrance to the hall in which his performances took place. He greeted me, I thought, rather effusively, even for a Frenchman; clapping me on the back and patting me on the shoulder. I discovered the secret of this demonstration of affection on his part on taking off my top-coat, for, as I removed my gloves and put them in one of my outer pockets, I found in it a lady's gold watch! My first impulse was to return it. My second was to spoil Guibal's game. I did neither. I was loyal to him, and, when having borrowed a small gold watch, he sent it flying through the air and declared it had settled in my pocket, I assumed an air of innocent surprise, and, after a diligent search through all my pockets, I produced the watch to the great delight and astonishment of the audience.

Guibal asked me to write some verses for publication, addressed to Mlle Greville. I wrote the following—

Public Entertainers

As, clad in white, thou walk'st 'mid silence deep,
  With loosen'd hair and ever closèd eyes,
  Methinks thou comest in no meaner guise
Than Shakespeare's queen who wandered in her sleep,
Telling the secret that she fain would keep
  Unto the listening air.   Or Elaine pale
  The Lily Maid who down the stream did sail
'Neath autumn skies to sound of sickles' sweep.

Thou seemest these; nor less than these art thou:
  A spirit regal and, as these are, bright,
Bearing thy queenship written on thy brow,
  Crowned with beauty, clad about with light.
Thy soul upon thy lips and in thy glance,
O daughter worthy of great Húgo's France!

It is strange that after long years an absurd story should have been revived that Guibal was shot dead in South America by Mlle Greville!

Other public entertainers I remember were the Kennedy family, all of whom perished in a theatre fire at Nice.   They used to sing songs in Scottish dialect with infinite humour.

The prince of public entertainers is, of course, the unrivalled George Grossmith, who used to appear at the Antient Concert Rooms in Dublin at least once a year.   I had a visiting card printed bearing the legend—

JAMES BERRY,
Public Executioner.

Sheriffs Attended.

In Castle and Court House

This card I sent to Mr Grossmith's retiring room in the interval between the first and second part of his programme, with a request for an interview. He at once appeared and smilingly asked, glancing at the card, "does this mean come and have a *chop* with me?" I apologised and said I wanted his autograph for a richly bound volume of his autobiography, entitled "A Society Clown," which it was intended to sell at a charity bazaar. He immediately signed the book for me. Mr Grossmith, whenever I met him on later occasions said he had never forgotten this incident.

Percy French, whom I have already mentioned, is in his own line inimitable. His entertainments given with Harrison Hill were capital. Some of French's songs deserve to be better known. His " The Night that Miss Cooney Eloped," for instance, with the statement that the sweep with whom Miss Cooney eloped moved in the best society.

> " As a sweep he might go
> To their houses, you know,
> But was only admitted as such."

French, in his amusing lectures on Dublin, was a capital entertainer. He hit off Dubliners in a wonderful way. A very respectable man who sells whips to the carmen at the corner of the Provost's house is a well-known figure in Dublin. " No one," said French, "appears to know who he is. Some says that he is a gentleman in disguise, all I can say is that if this is the case, the disguise is very complete."

One of the most fascinating of public entertainers,

Public Entertainers

if not indeed the most fascinating I have ever seen, was Miss Adelaide Detchon. No pen and ink description of her could possibly convey any idea of her charm and grace. She used to recite poems—chiefly American—and her recital of Tennyson's "Blow, Bugle, Blow" was exquisite in its delicate beauty.

My friend Charles Collette is too well known in England to be more than merely mentioned here. It may be news to some that Charles Collette is not alone a comedian of world-wide repute, but also a poet of the deepest dye, as the following lines prove—

> " When the monolith nods in its lair,
>   And the butterfly chirps to the drone;
> When asbestos has buried his care
>   'Neath the oval philosopher's stone.
>
> Oh, then wreathe the daffodil's song
>   Round the walrus's pale dappled brow,
> While whispering whortles all throng
>   To the honey-flecked juniper bough.
>
> And if the weird plethora's mate
>   Should creep to the cacophone's niece,
> Then tortuous woodbines are straight,
>   And the dawn of the dodo is peace.
>
> Opodeldoc is melting to curd,
>   And far on the Caspian Sea
> The pale crescent moon may be heard
>   In her hundred and third apogee.
>
> Loud sings the mohurram in glee,
>   And his saraband waves up aloft,
> *Si Tityre tu patulæ*
>   *Recubans sub tegmine,*—Soft!

In Castle and Court House

Do you think there is sense in my lay?
Do you think there is wisdom in me?
If you do—and you do, I daresay,—
WHY THEN, WHAT AN ASS YOU MUST BE!"

The first public reciter I ever heard was Professor David Charles Bell, author of "Bell's Standard Elocutionist," a very popular book. Professor Bell's son is associated with Edison in the Edison-Bell phonograph. Bell's "Elocutionist" was, to a certain extent, superseded by an excellent volume compiled by the Rev. John A. Jennings, whose recitals in public were always well attended. Sir Henry Taylor deplored the neglect of the art of reading aloud. In our own day the strictures of *Mr Punch* on the attitudinising of the reciter has led to a still greater neglect of oratory or declamation.

Among lecturers, Sir Robert Ball, the Astronomer Royal, is one of the most successful. His lectures on astronomy are always popular, and he makes them a skilful mixture of the mirthful and the marvellous. One of Sir Robert's stories is that some years ago he was invited to stay with friends in the country. At the last moment they wrote apologising for not meeting him at the railway station, which for some reason or other they could not do. Sir Robert, on his arrival, looked in every direction for the carriage which was to convey him to his friend's house. At last the coachman approached him and apologised for not having done so earlier, saying, "I was told, sir, to look for a distinguished-looking gentleman."

144

Public Entertainers

Sir Robert, after a lecture on the stars delivered before a provincial audience, turned to a lad near him (who happened to be my nephew, Robert Beare, now, alas, gone where there is none) and inquired, " How do you spell Orion? " " O'Ryan," replied young Beare, " from the Irishman who discovered it! "

Professor Mahaffy makes an excellent lecturer. On one occasion I found my name on a list of lecturers between those of Professor Mahaffy and Professor Greville Cole, a fact of which I am naturally proud.

I was engaged to lecture on Swinburne at the Assembly Rooms in Cork, by the Cork Literary and Scientific Association. By a curious error I missed my train and the next train from Dublin did not arrive in Cork until ten minutes after the lecture was announced to commence! There was no help for it. I wired Mr Stoney, the secretary, and donned evening dress in my compartment as the train approached Cork. It was raining heavily and the month was November, " the dreariest month of the year." I flung my bag on a jaunting car, and drove rapidly to the Assembly Rooms. As I got off the car, my foot slipped in the darkness and my bag fell, opening as it did so, and the contents, including my books and clothes, were in an instant smothered in mud! My chagrin can easily be imagined as I groped about, aided by the driver, in search of studs or tooth brush! One MS. volume to this day bears stains of mud on its cover acquired that night!

The lecture was not a success, though my audience was a most patient one, and of the thousand persons of which it was originally composed, at least seven hundred heard me through.

My reason for thinking the lecture was not a success arose from the fact that a man on whom I called next day and asked if he had been to the Assembly Rooms, replied that he had not, but that his wife and daughter who had been there had told him that it was the " rottenest " lecture they had ever heard! Not having been to the lecture he did not guess he was speaking to the lecturer!

Since that evil day I have delivered lectures on literary subjects in London with gratifying success, on one occasion being asked to fill the place of Mr G. K. Chesterton at a dinner of the Poets' Club. Of course, I could not fill Mr Chesterton's place, but I spoke for three-quarters of an hour, extempore, on the relations of Science and Poetry, and by this means succeeded in distracting the attention of the audience from the fact of his absence, to the evident satisfaction of the excellent chairman, Mr Henry Simpson, the President, and, I believe, the founder of the Club.

CHAPTER XV

THE name Colles is closely associated with surgery
—ever since Abraham Colles described the double
fracture of the radius, now known as " Colles'
fracture." Abraham Colles was twice President of
the Royal College of Surgeons, Ireland. His life
has been written in a special memoir prefixed to a
selection from his works made by Dr Robert M'Don-
nell for the New Sydenham Society, and his name
appears in the Dictionary of National Biography.
He was Regius Professor of Surgery in Trinity
College, Dublin, and Surgeon-in-Ordinary to the
Queen in Ireland. Abraham Colles was twice
offered a baronetcy but declined the honour on the
ground that he wished to distribute his money

equally among his children. He was a friend of Charles Lever, and his name occurs twice in " Harry Lorrequer."

William Colles, son of Abraham, held both his father's appointments. He also was President of the Royal College of Surgeons, and his portrait by Osborne hangs in the same room as that of a full length portrait of his father by Martin Creegan, President of the Royal Irish Academy. A marble bust, by Foley, of Abraham Colles is in the entrance hall of the College.

Of William Colles, Sir Thomas Myles, himself a Past President, is fond of telling a good story. It appears that when Sir Thomas was a student, an abnormal case of tumour puzzled the class, and the lecturers also. The class were all in readiness, note-books out, pencils sharpened. Breathless attention as the Regius Professor entered the room and approached the patient. Colles looked attentively at the tumour, and to the astonishment of everyone present declared it to be " one of them lumps! " That was all that could be got out of him!

Of Professor John Mallet Purser, an amusing story is told by Dr Fitzgibbon. It was a *viva voce* examination, and the serum of a frog had been put on the slide of a microscope for the examination of the student who was to declare what it was. The first student successfully pronounced it to be " the blood of a frog." On leaving the room he managed to convey the information to a fellow student, who was far from bright. Purser had in the meantime removed the slide and substituted one bearing a drop of his own blood. The student was asked to pronounce, and declared that the object was " blood." He was then asked " What kind of blood? " to which he replied, " I think, sir, it's the blood of a reptile! "

My friends in Dublin included the coroner, Dr Joseph Kenny, who was at one time mixed up with the Home Rule Party, and his brother Robert, who was a bit of a wag. He also was a medical man, and was popularly known as Doctor Bob.

I was a Fellow of the Royal Zoological Society of Dublin, a body I joined on the invitation of Professor D. J. Cunningham, M.D., late of Edinburgh. Doctor Bob and I were one day inspecting some new cages supplied to the Gardens by Messrs Kennan and Sons (whose premises in Fishamble Street, by the way, were once occupied by Handel). As Kenny and I were looking at the cages, in which three or four small kangaroos had temporarily been placed, a man inquired " An', may I ax, sir, what may them animals be? " Doctor Bob at once replied, glancing at the label on the cages, " So far as I can see they're Kennan and Sons! "

A propos of the Zoo, on one occasion the Gardens required some expenditure of money, and Judge Ross being Chairman of the Committee, repaired to the Bank of Ireland where the account of the Society was kept, to ask Mr Macmorragh Murphy, the Secretary of the Bank, for a little temporary overdraft until the subscriptions came in at the beginning of the new year. The Bank Secretary naturally inquired what collateral security the Zoological

In Castle and Court House

Society proposed to offer, to which His Honour Judge Ross replied, " Simple deposit of two Royal Bengal Tigers and a Boa Constrictor! "

A sad fate was that of Maurice Henry Collis, of the Meath Hospital, who was known as Battersby Collis, on account of a remarkable operation he performed on the late Mr Battersby. That estimable gentleman was a well-known auctioneer and land-agent, and one of the most respected citizens of Dublin. He suffered from an osseous growth on his face, a growth which finally began to impinge on one of his eyes and threatened to close it. He consulted Collis who got an ivory mallet and a chisel specially made for the purpose, and by these means removed the ossified obstruction. Collis, whose career has been noticed in " The History of the Meath Hospital," written by Sir Lambert Hepenstall Ormsby, M.D., died while still a young man. During an operation he was performing he punctured his hand with a spicula of diseased bone, and died of blood poisoning. Half Dublin attended his funeral.

The profession of medicine does not lend itself much to humorous treatment, so I may be forgiven for telling the following in connection with a well-known medical man in Dublin who was several times married. On the occasion of the funeral of, I think, the doctor's third wife, one of his professional brethren arrived too late to follow the hearse from the residence, and, being anxious to catch up to the other carriages, he asked the old butler, who had been for years with the family, in which direction the

funeral had gone, to which query the butler, without
a moment's hesitation replied, " Well, sir, *he generally takes them* " (meaning the various wives) " up
by the South Circular Road."

My own acquaintance with medical men from a
professional standpoint has, unfortunately, been
extensive. I was condemned to death by seven fully
qualified M.D.'s so long ago as 1890, and was told
by more than one man eminent in his profession, that
I had not more than twelve months to live! I was
trying to get my life insured, and had some difficulty
in getting my desire fulfilled. One man told me my
heart (the organ that troubled me) would burst.
Finally the late Sir George Porter passed me as a
good life, and I have now the melancholy satisfaction
of having outlived all the wiseacres who condemned
me to death!

I have already mentioned the name of Dr John
Knott, the brain specialist who often amused me with
stories about the profession. Dr Knott, Mr Bram
Stoker, and Mr Frankfort Moore married sisters,
the Misses Balcombe. One of Knott's stories was
to the effect that a Liverpool man arriving in Dublin,
had a serious affection of the brain. A great surgeon,
now deceased, was called in and being an advocate
of the knife insisted on the operation known as
trepanning, *i.e.*, cutting through the skull a circular
hole in order to discover if possible, the cause of the
disease. Knott demurred, but the great man had his
way. The patient died, and his widow was furious
that she had not been consulted. The great man
was called to account by his peers at the College of

Surgeons, and being nervous of the issue he wrote
to Knott as follows:

" DEAR KNOTT,—Please send me a note stating
why we trephined in that Liverpool case. Let your
answer be very scientific and very long."

I suppress the name for obvious reasons, though
there is little need to do so.

My friend Dr Ernest Harris had a curious experience on one occasion. He was staying at an hotel
on the coast near Dublin and was called up at
two o'clock one morning by the Irish night porter
who, knocking loudly at the bedroom door awakened
him and shouted, "Doctor, doctor, you're wanted at
wanst, come at wanst for the luv av' Heaven.
You're wanted be 47."

Dr Harris hastily donned some clothes and
hastened to the door indicated. Here he found a
lady whom he recognised as staying at the hotel,
having met her and her daughter several times at
the table d'hôte. The younger lady was lying in bed,
and the elder at once appealed to Dr Harris, saying
" Oh, doctor, doctor, what can be the matter with
my poor darling?" Harris was much disconcerted,
but being one of the most courteous of men, he
replied:

" I'm very sorry, but I really don't know."

" You don't know!" almost shrieked the distracted
mother, while two chambermaids opened their eyes
in astonishment at the idea of a doctor not being
able at a glance to diagnose any ailment.

" No," replied Harris, suavely, " possibly she's
taken something that's disagreed with her."

"Perhaps its poison!" wailed the mother, "save her, doctor, save her!"

"I'm sorry I can't do anything for her, madam," said Dr Harris.

"Oh, don't say that, doctor, don't say that," cried the lady, while over the patient's face stole the semblance of a smile.

"Calm yourself, dear lady," said Harris, "and send for a medical man, that is my advice."

"But you're a doctor, are you not?" asked the lady, much surprised.

"Yes, I am," replied Dr Harris, "I'm a Doctor of Laws!"

This is the story, but it has been stated that the elder lady having heard that Dr Harris remarked that a woman's beauty consisted in her hair, had determined that he should see that the golden wealth on her daughter's head was genuine, and hearing Harris addressed as "Doctor" had devised a scheme by means of which she could display these tresses for the admiration of a young, good-looking, and, at that time, unmarried man! But the looked-for engagement, like the lady's hair, did not come off! Dr Ernest Harris, far from being a medical man, is a well-known Solicitor, and Director of the Theatre Royal, of which my old friend and schoolfellow, Frederick Mouillot, is another. It is to Mouillot and David Telford, of Craig, Gardner and Co., that Dublin owes the existence of this fine theatre, which is second only to Drury Lane in seating accommodation and stage appointments.

CHAPTER XVI

MUSICIANS I HAVE MET

Dublin a Musical City—Sir Robert Stewart and his
    Successor—Dr James C. Culwick—One Way to
    Criticise Opera!—Herr Theodore Werner—Dr Annie
    W. Patterson, the Originator of the *Feis Ceoil*—Mr
    Swift McNeill, M.P.—Caught at the Catch Club—
    John Hemsley—Mme. Adelaide Mullen and Mr Henry
    Beaumont—" The Spectre's Bride "—Mme. Georgina
    Burns—Mrs Power O'Donoghue—Dr Hans Richter—
    Sir George Grove—Rev. R. H. Haweis—Mrs Page
    Thrower.

DUBLIN, it is well known, is a city in which good
music is not alone thoroughly appreciated, but it is
one in which I have been told by many musicians,
the audiences at opera, concert, or recital, display
keen discernment.

One of the ablest exponents of music, and an
eminent composer, was the late Sir Robert Stewart,
organist of the Chapel Royal. Sir Robert Stewart
was the chief music critic on *The Dublin Daily
Express*, and his articles on grand opera were very
much admired. After Sir Robert's death there was
some difficulty experienced in filling his post on the

Express. One man who was appointed, *pro tem.*, was such an admirer of Stewart's articles that he followed his leader too slavishly. For instance, Stewart on one occasion wrote a sentence something like this: "How can Signor Arditi imagine that he can dispense with the second trombone in Act II? This is an insult to an audience possessed of any knowledge of Wagner's work," etc. The new critic who criticised the same opera after Sir Robert's death, had the same fault to find, the absence of the second trombone. But alas! for the critic, the second trombone was not absent on the occasion! The writer had looked up the files of the *Express* and transcribed Sir Robert's criticism.

Sir Robert Stewart was succeeded as organist of the Chapel Royal by the late James C. Culwick, Mus. Doc., the composer of "The Legend of Staufenberg," in which, when performed at the Antient Concert Rooms, I had the pleasure of hearing Madame Clara Samuel. Dr Culwick in buying some old books discovered a score of Handel's in the parchment covering of one of them. When a performance of Culwick's works was given in the theatre of Trinity College, Dublin, in recognition of his assistance during the Tercentenary Celebrations, he included in the programme one of his songs, "Forsaken," of which I wrote the words, which are as follows—

Oh, what to me the bursting bud and harmony of Spring,
If not for you the blossoms blow, for you the throstles
    sing?

In Castle and Court House

The sweetest song, the fairest flower, is neither sweet
    nor fair,
If you no more are by my side with me the joy to share.
Can Summer be what Summer was in sunny hours gone by,
When longest days were short to me, for you were ever
    nigh?
No joy the brightest day can bring, no peace the fairest
    scene—
They bring but back the memory of that which once hath
    been.
Sad, sad to me the Autumn hues, and desolate the ways
Where by the stream at eve we went to dream of golden
    days;
Those days, alas! that find me now as you I ne'er had
    known—
Alone I breast the winter winds—I live and die alone!

Culwick's composition was a little too heavy for
these simple words, but I was deeply gratified by
the fact that the song was sung by Mrs Culwick with
a violin obligato specially composed for the occasion
by Herr Theodore Werner.

A lady who started a great movement in Ireland
is Annie W. Patterson, Doctor of Music. Miss
Patterson (I shall not sink the sex in the degree)
originated the Feis Ceoil which has become a recognised institution in Ireland. The Committee give
prizes for musical compositions varying from operas,
or operettas, to pianoforte solos and songs. The
organisation of this great movement for the
encouragement of musical talent, is now quite a
complex affair, as every village in Ireland is
embraced in the scheme. To Dr Annie Patterson
the honour belongs of starting the Feis Ceoil. The
first meeting in connection with the scheme when

projected by her, being held in Dr Sigerson's drawing-room.

The Catch Club in Dublin is an old and famous institution. The membership is composed largely of the Vicars-Choral of St. Patrick's Cathedral. I have frequently been the guest of one or other member of the club at their pleasant dinners, which are, as may be supposed, enlivened by song. Being all loyal Britishers, it is a custom at the Catch Club to sing the National Anthem at the dinners after the loyal toast. Judge my surprise when on one occasion during the singing of this item, a protest was raised by Mr Swift McNeill, Nationalist M.P., who indignantly left the room, followed by his reluctant and astonished host! I was the guest that night of the late John Hemsley, a Vicar-choral of St. Patrick's, who will long be remembered in Dublin on account, not alone of his wonderfully sweet alto, but also for his sweetness of disposition. Hemsley was an Englishman, and his indignation knew no bounds and he implored me to give publicity to the affair, which I did in a leading article in *The Dublin Evening Mail*, entitled, " Caught at the Catch Club," in which I called attention to the fact that the Club was composed of loyalists and gentlemen (a phrase used by the *Freeman's Journal* to which organ Swift McNeill had appealed), but that occasionally they entertained people who were neither.

One of the members of the Catch Club, and one of the finest bassos the world had ever heard was my dear old friend Ben Mullen, whose son of the same name was my companion at Bective College, and is now Curator of Pendlebury Museum, near Manchester. A daughter of the grand old basso, Mme Adelaide Mullen, is well known in London, not alone as a Cantatrice, but also as " Wilton King," the composer of some beautiful songs, notably one with the refrain " For the Hearts in good old Ireland are the Hearts that don't forget." Miss Mullen has been for many years the happy wife of Harry Beaumont the able exponent of leading parts in the old Carl Rosa Opera Company during Rosa's life, and later in the Arthur Rowsby and National Opera Companies, and, if I mistake not, in the Moody-Manners also. Some humorous comments were made when Miss Adelaide Mullen and Mr Henry Beaumont on the eve of their marriage, took the leading parts in " The Spectre's Bride," at a performance given by the Trinity College Choral Society. Beaumont certainly looked far from being a spectre!

Among musicians I have known I can count Mme. Georgina Burns. She had a marvellous voice and told me that when she appeared in Sir Julius Benedict's opera, " The Lily of Killarney," the aged composer, who was blind, was, by request, led up to the young girl (as Madame Burns was then), in order to congratulate her on her performance. Georgina Burns married Leslie Crotty, a fine baritone, who used to make one of the most vigorous *Escamillos* I have ever heard in " Carmen."

Musicians I Have Met

Another musician well known not alone in Dublin, but in London and New York, was Dr Power O'Donoghue, whose wife, and now, alas! widow, Nannie Power O'Donoghue is famous as a horse-woman, having won the brush from the Empress of Austria when her late Majesty visited Ireland; and, as the author of "Grandfather's Hunter," "Ladies on Horseback," and other works of fiction or of reference. At the O'Donoghue's pleasant gather-ings in quiet Peter's Place all the most noted musicians who visited Dublin might be seen. Dr O'Donoghue was a prince of good fellows, and few could match him at telling funny stories and whimsi-cal anecdotes, while Mrs O'Donoghue made an ideal hostess. Occasionally when pressed by their guests to sing, their voices might be heard in an unaccom-panied duet, such as " I Saw from the Beach."

There are a few leading musicians I have not met, from Mme. Patti down. Looking over my diaries I note such names as Albani; Nikita, the Russian Nightingale; Decca; Guilia Ravogli; an ideal " Carmen," and a magnificent exponent in " Orfeo "; Lablache; Zelie de Lussan; a delightful Juliet in Gounod's " Romeo "; Alice Gomez, praised by Haweis; Madame Clara Butt; Ada Crossley; Minnie Hauk; Olitzka; Miss Percival Allen; Medora Henson; Mme. Fanny Moody; Aurelie Revy; and many other queens of song. I have met from time to time Charles Santley, whose gifts have rightly been recognised in a knighthood; Mr Joseph O'Mara; Sir Arthur Sullivan; David Bishpam;

Kennerly Rumford; Edward Lloyd, and Pierpoint Mr Charles Manners and I attended the same college "grinder" and sat side by side for some months. I can claim an old acquaintanceship with Barton McGuckin, who took the leading parts in the old Carl Rosa for years; and with Snazelle, of whom the same may be said. Few that heard Snazelle in those days as "Mephistophiles" can forget his voice, which, strange to say, is to-day as strong as ever.

When Dr Hans Richter visited Dublin to conduct the series of Wagner's works produced through the untiring energy of Mrs Page-Thrower, I had the pleasure of meeting the great conductor at the Provost's house. I have been praised for my criticism of music by no less an authority than Sir George Grove, and have been complimented by R. H. Haweis, the author of "Music and Morals," in a letter which it took me weeks to decipher!

In local musicians Dublin is rich while she can claim such composers as Signor Esposito and Dr José and such executants as a Walter Bapty, a Melfort D'Alton, and a Charles Kelly. As I have left Ireland some years I do not know whether she still possesses Mrs Scott-ffenell, and Miss Lucy Ashton Hackett. I hope she does.

I have had the pleasure of hearing words of my own composing twice encored when sung by Miss Helen Brooks, to whom the song had been dedicated by the composer of the music, my cousin, Alexander Colles, and with these words I close a very egotistical

chapter, contenting myself by stating that the verses
were written in my teens.

In the Springtime's early beauty,
In the morning's primal hue,
When the earth is ever fairest
And the skies are ever blue;
In the Springtime of our being,
When no sorrows mar the brow,
Will you love me now, my darling?
Will you love me, love me now?

In the noontide's golden glories,
In the glow of Summer's prime,
Ere we reach the Autumn langour
In the onward march of time;
When at the soul's meridian,
Which we ne'er can reach again,
Will you love me then, my darling?
Will you love me, love me then?

In the sad and solemn twilight,
Ere the night shall end our day;
In the dark and weary winter,
Ere our lives shall pass away.
When Death comes slowly, surely,
As he cometh to all men,
Will you love me then, my darling?
Will you love me, love me then?

CHAPTER XVII

NOCTES AMBROSIANÆ

A Mild Symposium—Some of the Company—" Dying all
over the Shop "—The Imperturbability of Waiters—
" Any smaller change, Sir ? "—Irish Stew—A Theory
on Heredity—Mahaffy on Cleopatra's Twins—Edwin
Hamilton on Sheep-dip—The Value of Shorn Lambs—
The " Noiseless Tenor "—Judge Madden and the
American Lady—" Dutch William " and " The Diary
of Master William Silence "—Colquhoun and The
Great Bed of Ware.

I HAD a habit when living in Dublin, of giving what
my friend Professor Louis Claude Purser, F.T.C.D.
called a symposium, but which I designated by the
more prosaic title of " a whiff and a whisky." This
consisted of gathering a few male friends into my
study in No. 6, Warwick Terrace, Leeson Park ;
and discussing with them all manner of things, while
on a side table reposed a jar of whisky, or, as Sir
John T. Gilbert, the historian, termed it, " The
Spirit of the Nation," a bottle of brandy, some
syphons of mineral waters, a jug containing a sample
of water from the river Vartry, and a tray filled with
cherry pipes and churchwardens, and a jar of
tobacco.

Noctes Ambrosianæ

I say these things "reposed" but occasionally their repose was rudely broken, for, as a wit remarked, "whisky improves with age, but we won't let it."

Let me see if I can recall the past, and bring before my readers a true picture of one of these "parties in a parlour." My parties consisted at one time, or another, of such men as George Dames Burtchaell, Barrister-at-Law, and Assistant Ulster King of Arms, Robert Yelverton Tyrrell, ex-Regius Professor of Greek in T.C.D., J. R. Clegg, Editor of *The Dublin Evening Mail*, Professor Dowden, Edwin Hamilton, the Aristophanes of Ireland, J. Moody Lowry, of the Vice-Chancellor's Court, a Barrister, and author of "The Keys' 'At Home,'" and other humorous verse; Percy French, James Poole Maunsell, proprietor of *The Dublin Daily Express*, Signor Esposito the Composer, the Rt. Hon. W. F. Bailey, at that time of the Irish Land Commission, George Kelly, B.L., who was known as "the man who knew everything," W. A. Craig, the Poet, John B. Healy, now the Editor of *The Irish Times*, Dr A. J. Callaghan, the able Secretary of the Royal Irish Steam Packet Co., H. S. Macran, F.T.C.D., F. St. John Morrow, B.L., now Secretary to Sir Edward Carson, M.P., Signor Negroni, the Composer; E. Haviland Burke, M.P., a grand-nephew of Edmund Burke, and many others whose names I cannot at the moment recall.

The proceedings were undoubtedly cheerful, for we were all younger than we are now, but never hilarious, for not even the most youthful person present belonged even remotely to the crowd—

"That crashed the glass and beat the floor"

nay, rather to the goodly company of those pictured by Tennyson in "In Memoriam" who held debate—

> "On mind and art,
> And labour, and the changing mart,
> And all the framework of the land."

I remember Burtchaell remarking one night— "Strange death reported in the papers this morning: 'Died suddenly at 101, 102, 103, 104, and 105, Great Snook Street, John Smith, aged 80.'"

"Ah," said Hamilton, "another case of 'dying all over the shop,' I suppose."

Colquhoun, a well-known member of the City and County Conservative Club told us that he had had a rough time when getting examined in connection with a life-annuity.

"The doctor," he said, "asked me at least fifty questions. Had I had this disease; had I had that disease, until he tired me out. At last he said, 'I have only one more question to ask you, Mr Colquhoun, what do you usually drink?'"

"And what did you reply?" I queried.

"Oh," said Colquhoun, "I simply said 'whatever you're taking yourself, doctor.'"

Someone having told a story of having played a practical joke on a waiter, Hamilton said, "I never do that. It always ends in failure. I once gave a city waiter, as if in ignorance, a brass trouser button in payment of drinks for a party, and he drew my attention to it on the salver by asking ' Any smaller change, sir? ' "

" But, surely," I asked, " country waiters are vulnerable? "

" No," replied Hamilton, " once in the heart of the country, I entered a small inn on a July day and found the coffee-room swarming with blue-bottle flies. I turned to the waiter and asked, ' What are the flies a dozen? ' and I assure you he replied with the utmost gravity, ' Sure, sir, it's by the pound we sell them.' "

Clegg one night recited some verses he had written on " Irish Stew," which I thought very good, and give a few lines from memory here, reminding my readers of Moore's reference to the time—

> " When Malachi wore *the Collar of Gold*
> Which he won from the proud invader."

" This is only a preliminary," said Clegg, " as the alligator said to the soldier, when he swallowed his knapsack "—

In ould ancient days, faith! the dish was a sneezer—
  'Twas full of men's hands of a deep bloody red,
Skulls, cross-bows, and long-bows, and grand harps of
    Tara,
  And slices of Malachi's *gold-collared head*.

It was on one of these occasions that I introduced to Hamilton my friend John O'Duffy, and I remember when they were parting O'Duffy's making an inquiry as to Hamilton's age, and when he learned what it was, exclaiming—" Why, I might be your father! "

" Well, perhaps you are," said Hamilton, unable to resist giving utterance to one of the best impromptus I ever heard in my life, " perhaps you are, good night."

Someone started the subject of heredity and I told those present of Mahaffy's statement to me: " if you have a good strain you intensify the good strain, and if you have a bad strain you intensify the bad strain. Look at Cleopatra: she represented the fourth generation of brothers and sisters who intermarried."

" And yet she had beauty? " I queried.

" Oh, yes; we have historic evidence that she was beautiful."

" But had she health and strength? " I asked.

" She must have had," replied Mahaffy, " she had twins! "

It was Mahaffy who, when asked for a definition of " an Irish bull," replied " an Irish bull, my dear sir, is pregnant with wit."

Edwin Hamilton told us how having attended an auction of goods left in railway carriages, a watch chain was put up for sale, but failed to attract any bid until someone called out, " Put up a watch with it," which, being done, the chains were sold rapidly. Later, umbrellas, rugs, hats, and a variety of other articles came under the hammer. At last a quantity of sheep-dip was put up, but attracted no buyers, until Hamilton called out, " Put up a sheep with it! "

Noctes Ambrosianæ

Someone referred to the " Carols of Cockayne," by
Henry S. Leigh, and a member of the Savage Club
told us that one night a man whom we shall call
Lowe made himself so objectionable that he silenced
the whole room, all the members present being
anxious that he should, like a clock, run down by his
own weight.   Henry S. Leigh, with the view of
accelerating his departure, said—

> We've heard, in language highly spiced,
> That Lowe does not believe in Christ;
> But what we really want to know,
> Is whether Christ believes in Lowe!

This led to another anecdote with a specimen of
Leigh's wit. It appears that a member of the Club
had recently been knighted, and had returned to
Adelphi Terrace after some months' absence, with
a very swelled head. On being asked where he had
been, he replied, " At my old ancestral home in
Essex."

" What do you call your ancestral home? " asked
Leigh.

" Burnburry *Court*," replied the newly made
knight, with emphasis.

" Oh, we know *that*," said Leigh, " but what's the
number? "

On my making the commonplace remark that it
had been a cold blustry day, Hamilton said, " Yes,
I keep wishing that some shorn lambs might be in
my vicinity," referring to Lawrence Sterne's well-
known *dictum* that " there is One who tempereth

167

the wind to the shorn lamb," a statement which not a few people believe to be in the Bible.

Tales of car drivers were common, one of the best of them being that Jehu when asked what did his fares usually pay him, replied, " Well, yer honour, the *meanest* of them gives me half-a-crown! "

Tyrrell, referring to an intolerable bore of colossal proportions, remarked, " Don't you think that S—— has all the qualities of an elephant except sagacity? "

Someone in speaking of the choir in his native country town, said, " Even the old tenor who was there in my father's time is still a member. Of course, he has quite lost his voice but I was glad to see the old man in his accustomed place," whereupon Hamilton said, referring to a familiar line in Gray's " Elegy "—

" So they kept the noiseless tenor."

My readers will understand that I only give the recollections of years ago, and have, perforce, to give only " the top-most froth of thought." The conversation often took a deeper tone, as when, for instance, Tyrrell maintained that Walter Savage Landor, in the immortal lines on Rose Aylmer, verses beloved of Charles Lamb, should have written in the plural instead of the singular—

" Nights of memories and of sighs."
instead of—
" A night of memories and of sighs
I consecrate to thee."

With profound respect for a great scholar and one

possessing keen discernment in poetic literature, I feel sure that all lovers of Landor will demur at this *dictum.*

An amusing story is told of an American lady who on being informed that at dinner she would meet Judge Madden, author of a delightful book on Shakespeare, entitled, " The Diary of Master William Silence," determined to refer to it when introduced to the author. This she did by telling the judge, " Oh, Judge, I've been reading that charming book of yours on Dutch William."

" Dutch William? " queried the puzzled judge.

" Yes, your book on William the Silent! "

A reference being made to the great Bed of Ware which could hold 40 persons, Colquhoun remarked, " D——d awkard piece of furniture, fancy having to whistle for your wife."

There was a rumour that a Civic Official, a butcher in Dublin, was to be knighted in connection with a Royal visit—Burtchaell at once suggested, on account of his calling, that the new knight should be dubbed, " *Sir Loin* O'Rafferty " (or whatever the name was).

CHAPTER XVIII

SOME LITERARY CORRESPONDENCE

Some Literary Correspondence—Errors of Authors—Sir Leslie Stephen's "Hours in a Library"—Danger of quoting from Memory—Bret Harte's Poems—Shenstone, not Herrick—My Letters to William Morris and Robert Browning—Letters to William Ernest Henley—Matthew Arnold and Arthur Hugh Clough—Swinburne's Solitary "Limerick"—Count Tolstoy—Report of his Death "greatly exaggerated."

IN my youth, with all the arrogance of youth, I was fond of finding fault with my elders, and undoubtedly my "betters." But it was indeed in no spirit of faultfinding that I wrote to some eminent men from time to time, seizing the opportunity to do so, not with a view to autograph collecting, for such was never my hobby, as I gave away many of the replies I received, especially if the letters were merely perfunctory acknowledgments of my own.

One of the first letters I addressed to a public man was written to Mr (afterwards Sir) Leslie Stephen, advocating the publication of a cheaper edition, of his delightful series of studies, entitled, "Hours in a Library"; and at the same time pointing out that the quotations in the essay on " The Ethics of Wordsworth " were incorrect in nearly every instance. Leslie Stephen sent me a very gracious acknowledgment, and said that my suggestion in connection with " Hours in a Library " had been anticipated, and added, " I regret to learn that so many errors are to be found in my Wordsworth essay; it was the first time I attempted to rely on my memory for my quotations, and you may be sure it shall be the last."

When thanking the great writer for his letter, I took the opportunity to send him a transcript I had made of his essay on Wordsworth, thus giving him irrefutable evidence of the great store I set by the essay for I had transcribed it when still a boy, and when, owing to lack of pence, I was not in a position to buy the volumes, which were then sold in sets only, at something like nine shillings per volume. Sir Leslie Stephen was evidently touched by this fact, and expressed his gratification in a later letter which is remarkable chiefly for an expression of his opinion that " to be known is a very doubtful blessing," and thus my correspondence with him ended. The essay on "Wordsworth's Ethics," I may add, still appears with all its imperfections.

With Bret Harte my " correspondence " was a one-sided affair, possibly owing to the fact that he was travelling through the States when I wrote to him, suggesting the correction of the sub-title of one of his poems, which was erroneously stated to be " after Herrick." The verses contain the following lines,

and are to be found in Bret Harte's earlier, racier
work—

> "She wished (I remember it well,
>   And esteemed her the more for that wish)
> For a perfect cystidean shell
>   And a whole holocephalic fish."

This is not an imitation of Robert Herrick, but of
Shenstone, whose poem " I have found out a gift for
my fair " it follows closely—

> " I have found out a gift for my fair—
>   I have found where the wood pigeons breed;
> But let me that plunder beware—
>   She would say 'twas a barbarous deed.

> " For none could be true, she averred,
>   Who would rob a poor bird of its young;
> And I loved her the more when I heard
>   Such tenderness fall from her tongue."

Bret Harte never replied to my letter, but I noticed
that in later editions of his poems, the incorrect
ascription to Herrick was dropped.

In much the same spirit I wrote to William Morris,
asking him why the lines in " King Arthur's Tomb "
had been altered for the worse from—

> The Moon shone like a star she shed
> When she dwelt up in heaven a while ago,
> And ruled all things but God:

to—

> " The Moon shone like a tear she shed ";

and also why the reading—

> " O sickle cutting harvest the day long! " had been
given instead of " cutting hemlock."

Some Literary Correspondence

Morris replied that " it was a long time ago," and added, with something like a sigh for the " tender grace of a day that is dead," " star! " is evidently the correct reading, as also " hemlock," which is obviously right.

Early in 1888, I was handed, one fine morning by my dear friend, William Ponsonby, of Ponsonby and Weldrick of the Dublin University Press, a curious little book of poems, published by another friend of mine, for whom I had a great respect, and one whose memory all Britishers must honour, the late Alfred Nutt. The title was " A Book of Verses." " What do you think of them? " asked Mr Ponsonby. I could scarcely tell at first glance, but paid my half crown, and read—

" Out in the bay a bugle is lilting a gallant song."

A gallant song indeed, was that lilted by William Ernest Henley. I read and re-read his " Rhymes and Rhythms." To my untutored ears the rhythms consisted of " prose cut into lengths," but, nevertheless, ears attuned to Walt Whitman, found music in Henley. I amused myself by writing a column and a half in *The Dublin Evening Mail*, and sent the cutting to Mr Alfred Nutt, whose untimely death, which took place recently in Paris, in endeavouring to save the life of his son who survives him, all interested in Celtic literature deeply deplore.

In acknowledgment I got a long letter from Henley, who wrote from Chiswick. He said I was right in my conjecture that the title " A Book of Verses " was from FitzGerald's "Omar Khayyam." He deprecated my statement that his rhythms were " prose cut into lengths," and added that if I couldn't find any music in his verse, he regretted the fact. He thanked me for my review, and said that Whitman at his best sang, and sang clearly. The letter was signed, as all Henley's were as a rule, with his initials only, " W. E. H.," and closed by saying that he had been in bed some time with " a twisted foot."

Of course, I was aware of the fact that Henley had suffered, and had been operated on quite recently at the Old Edinburgh Infirmary, but I thought it might divert him if I continued the discussion, so I wrote telling him that I had bought about a dozen copies of his book, a fact calculated to cheer him, and that I had read aloud his fine poem " Out of the Night " to some half dozen young men, and that it and others of his poems had been received with applause.

I remembered my audience on the occasion to which I referred included the late William Larminie, whose work is quoted by Professor Saintsbury in his " History of English Prosody "; Frederick J. Gregg, William Butler Yeats, George Russell, better known as " A. E.," and Charles Weekes, all of whom have written poems of very excellent quality. At the same time I added that I could not accept such a line as—

" The poor old beggar explains his poor old ulcers "

as poetry.

Some Literary Correspondence

Henley replied saying that he was indeed glad to hear from me in such memorable terms, and defending himself as a realist in verse. He again stated that if I found no poetry in his rhythms he was sorry for me, and that he would not willingly " exchange ears " with anyone who did not. I replied that I loved and honoured Wordsworth as a poet, but that I did not accept such lines as—

> " A common tub like one of those
> Which women use to wash their clothes."

as poetry of any kind whatsoever, but that I should not trouble him further on the matter, and wound up by thanking him for " Out of the Night," which was, indeed, in Elizabeth Barrett Browning's phrase " medicated music suited to mankind's forlornest uses," and there the matter ended. I have referred to this poem of Henley's more than once, and may be pardoned for quoting it here—

> " Out of the night that covers me,
>   Black as the pit from pole to pole,
>   I thank whatever gods may be
>   For my unconquerable soul.
>
> In the fell clutch of circumstance
>   I have not winced nor cried aloud.
>   Under the bludgeonings of chance
>   My head is bloody, but unbowed.
>
> Beyond this place of wrath and tears
>   Looms but the horror of the shade;
>   And yet the menace of the years
>   Finds, and shall find, me unafraid.

In Castle and Court House

> It matters not how strait the gate,
> How charged with punishments the scroll,
> I am the master of my fate:
> I am the captain of my soul.

At the risk of appearing frivolous I cannot refrain from quoting my friend Dr Robertson Wallace, who with this poem in his mind, said:

" No married man is the Captain of his soul. As a general rule the Captain of his soul is his Mate."

One of the most popular of Robert Browning's shorter poems is " The Lost Leader "—

> Just for a handful of silver he left us,
> Just for a riband to stick in his coat.

For many years the identity of " The Lost Leader " was matter for conjecture, and having heard the point disputed, I resolved to settle the matter by appealing to the poet. At the time I was unaware that Browning had written on the subject to Dr Alexander B. Grossart, the Editor of Herrick and of Giles and Phineas Fletcher, and that Grossart, in his edition of the prose works of William Wordsworth had printed Browning's letter, from which it appears that Browning had replied to the same question from private inquiries scores of times. Luckily the poet was one of the most patient and courteous of mortals, and by return post I got a letter from the author of " The Lost Leader," dated from Warwick Crescent, in which he wrote:

" Dear Sir,—I confess to having taken Wordsworth as a kind of lay figure for my poem, but never meant to breathe a word against the genius of the master."

Some Literary Correspondence

I submitted this note to Mrs Sutherland Orr when she compiled her " Life of Robert Browning," but she did not deem it important enough to include in her book.

Readers of " The Cornhill Magazine," if they possess the volumes edited by Thackeray, will remember an excellent article on the genius of Arthur Hugh Clough, the author of " The Bothie of Tober na Vuolich." It was on Clough that Swinburne, I believe, composed the only " Limerick " of which he was ever guilty—

> There was a bad poet named Clough
> Who wrote some detestable stuff;
> But the public, though dull,
> Had not quite such a skull
> As belongs to believers in Clough.

J. Russell Lowell, on the contrary, held that Clough was the most representative English poet of his time. A judgment with which many will feel inclined to agree. Someone in a small literary society to which I belonged in those days, having stated that the article in " The Cornhill " was by Matthew Arnold, I wrote to Pain's Hill Cottage, Cobham, and had a reply from Arnold, dated " Christmas Eve, 1889," in which Arnold wrote that he did not write the article in question, " though some words on Clough will be found in my lecture on translating Homer."

When Vizitelly published the first translation into English of Tolstoy's " Anna Karenina " and Matthew Arnold declared that in consequence of its excellence we should all soon be learning Russian, I wrote to Count Tolstoy congratulating him on the fact and asking his acceptance of a small volume of selections from Walt Whitman. The little book reached Tolstoy's hands, at Yasnáya Polyána with obliterations made by the Press Censor on nearly every page!

When Count Leo Tolstoy's cousin, also a Count Tolstoy died in 1887, I was asked by the Editor of *The Dublin Evening Mail* to write a leading article on the subject for the morning edition. The Editor appeared to be under the impression that it was the great Russian writer who was dead, and my instructions, accordingly, were to deal with the career of the author of "War and Peace" and "Anna Karenina." I wrote the article with genuine sorrow for the decease of a great literary artist. Judge my surprise on the following day, when, having seen by the morning's papers that Tolstoy the writer was not dead, and that the false report was in connection with the death of a distant relative, I found my article in the *Mail!* There had been no time to substitute another article, mine was simply prefaced by a few words stating the facts of the case, and to these my article had been dovetailed!

When six months had elapsed I sent a copy of that issue to Tolstoy, but whether it reached him or not I never heard.

History repeats itself, and Tolstoy's death has again been prematurely reported, this time, alas! to be confirmed in the end.

CHAPTER XIX

MASONIC MEMORIES

Freemasonry in Ireland and Freemasonry in England—
The Irish Volunteer Lodge—Old Records—The
" Firing Glass "—The Duke of York's Lodge
XXV. — Sir Charles A. Cameron, C.B. — Lord
Roberts—Lord Kitchener—The Earl of Shaftesbury—
Lodge XXV. dines in the Temple—The Munificence
of the late Bro. Henry Arthur Blyth—Sir Thomas
Devereux Pile, Bt.—" Irish Masonry Illustrated "—
Letter from Sir James Creed Meredith, LL.D.—The
Duke of Abercorn—Viscount Templetown—Lord
Castletown—Bro. W. Harding Lawder—The Quatuor
Coronati Lodge—General John Corson Smith of
Chicago—The Duke of Connaught and Lodge XXV.

MASONRY in Ireland differs considerably from
Masonry in England. In Ireland there is no rivalry
between the Mark Mason and his brother the Free
and Accepted member of the Order who is to be
found at labour in Freemason's Hall. In Ireland
the Freemason is readily accepted as a Mark Mason
and as readily as a Knight Templar, and I was
therefore astonished when told by that learned
member of the Order, Bro. Henry Sadler, the
librarian of Freemason's Hall, that the Mark Masons
had a hall of their own.

In Castle and Court House

I have been a Master Mason since 1893. I knew nothing of the Craft prior to that date, but it had long been my ambition to be enrolled among its members. Accordingly, when an opportunity presented itself I was nominated for Lodge 153, by the late Frederick Charles Ramsay, who was my partner in a timber-importing business in which I was engaged: one of the many phases of my strangely diversified life. I was admitted and initiated by Bro. George Bell, a well-known and highly respected ship-broker of Dublin.

But Lodge 153 did not fulfil my requirements in Masonry, and I therefore was affiliated to Lodge 620 being struck by the glamour of the history of this ancient lodge, which bears the proud title of " The Irish Volunteers' Lodge," a Lodge founded prior to the Volunteer Movement of 1852, the year in which this country was supposed to be threatened by invasion from France, just as at the present time she is supposed to be regarded as the prey of Germany. The Lodge was undoubtedly founded in troublous times, and faced them with spirit. The late R. W. Bro. Keating Clay used to delight in telling how Lodge 620 used to be held on the sands at Sandymount when the tide was out, and how it was " tiled by the serried bayonets of the Irish Volunteers."

It was at one time my sincere wish to write the history of the rise and progress of this remarkable lodge. With this view I borrowed, and had for a long time in my possession the minute books and other records of the lodge, lent me for the purpose

Masonic Memories

by Bro. the Rev. T. B. Gibson, M.A., now Canon of Ferns, who was succeeded as Secretary to the Lodge by his brother-in-law, Bro. J. T. Ray, an Inspector of the Bank of Ireland.

These ancient documents, marvellously preserved, were indeed a delight to handle. They proved that the light of Freemasonry burned brightly in Ireland during dark and troublous times. In one of the volumes were recorded the minutes of a meeting held on the eve of the Battle of Waterloo.

It is strange the association of ideas in a single word. The word " Waterloo " recalls to me the fact that a friend of mine being in a desperate hurry to catch a train from the well-known terminus jumped into a taxi-cab in the Strand, shouting the single word " Waterloo." " The station, sir? " queried the driver, " No," yelled my irate friend, " the bloody battle field! " The epithet " bloody," I may remark, is not inappropriate when applied to a battlefield.

But to return to the minutes of Lodge 620. To look over those ancient documents with their dis-coloured pages and faded ink, their solemn style and faded signatures, was indeed to get a glimpse of the doings of a day that is dead. In these pages, with all due ceremony, there was recorded such an important fact that Bro. So and So was fined for non-attendance, and that such and such an amount had to be paid for " glass broke."

Not being quite *au fait* with the history of Masonry, I could not discover why so many glasses were " broke," until my friend Dr Chetwoode

In Castle and Court House

Crawley told me that heavy and almost solid glasses were used in those days and were called "firing glasses," being employed for what is now done by clapping the hands when a "running fire" is called for.

When at refreshment the Brethren of Lodge 620 produced with justifiable pride the ancient flags and banners which had braved the battle and the breeze in the old days of the Irish Volunteers, and especially did they pride themselves on a waxen effigy, life size, of an Irish Volunteer in his uniform as he lived!

In 1895 I was affiliated to Lodge 25, known as The Duke of York's Lodge, the lodge having been named after the Duke of York, whose monument turns its back on Waterloo Place, and is adorned by an aggressive lightning conductor, which rises like an indignant single hair from the head of the statue. It cannot be said that in this case "beauty draws us by a single hair," though it may draw the lightning!

Lodge 25 has for its able secretary Sir Charles Cameron, C.B. (City Analyst of Dublin), a fact to which the lodge owes not a little of its numerical strength and its popularity. It numbers among its members, honorary and otherwise, Lord Roberts and Lord Kitchener; and when I was in Dublin and an active member of it, the W.M. of the Lodge was the Earl of Shaftesbury, a very energetic musical member, who often delighted the Lodge during refreshment, with his songs, the accompaniment to which his Lordship played himself.

Lodge 25 is, I believe, a revival of the old and long extinct Lodge of Munster.

Masonic Memories

The Warrant, No. 25, was first issued on the 13th November, 1733, to a Lodge in Youghal, County of Cork, and after some vicissitudes passed into the possession of another Co. Cork Lodge in 1809, by whom it was retained until 1823. The number was next used by a Lodge connected with the 25th Regt., whose warrant was surrendered in 1839 to Grand Lodge. The present Warrant of Lodge No. 25 is dated 4th November, 1853, and was issued to Bros. E. C. Carleton, Rev. C. E. Tisdall, and T. P. Swan, Members of Lodge 494. The Lodge met for the first time on 5th November, 1853. No regular meeting of the Lodge was held from 14th October, 1859, until 11th January, 1866, when a large number of Brethren were proposed for affiliation, and were elected on the 18th January, 1866. Since that date 218 initiations and 123 affiliations have made the Lodge by far the largest in Dublin. All the important professions are represented in it. The Present Members (of whom 45 are Graduates of Dublin University) include 21 Army Officers, 12 Barristers, 8 Clergymen, 28 Medical Men (civilians), 10 Solicitors, 4 Engineers and Architects, 2 Constabulary Officers, 2 Stockbrokers, 4 Bank Officials, and 6 Professors of Music. Total—97. The number of Present Members (including Honorary Members) is 147. Through the kindness of Bro. Anderson Cooper the Original Warrant, dated 1733, is now in the possession of the Lodge. It was never surrendered to Grand Lodge.

When I founded in 1901 the only Masonic Journal

worthy of the craft, a sixpenny monthly, printed on art paper and entitled " Irish Masonry, Illustrated," I devoted an early number to the history of Lodge 25, and gave a facsimile of the original charter, several portraits, and many interesting facts.

One of the most curious facts in connection with the Lodge was that on one occasion it invited its guests to refreshment in the Temple! The facts are these. When the late Henry Arthur Blyth, brother of Lord Blyth (at that time Sir James Blyth), well known in connection with the great firm of Walter Gilbey, was W.M. it was found that the applications for seats for refreshment were so numerous that no hall in Dublin was available, suitable for so large a gathering of members of an avowedly esoteric body. The matter was desperate, and despair had seized the officers of the Lodge until it was decided, permission being granted, to hold the dinner in the Temple itself! and dine in the Temple, Lodge 25 did! being the first to do so, as it is assuredly the last Lodge that ever will. I was present on the occasion, my guests included my friend the late James Pile, brother of Sir Thomas Devereux Pile, J.P., D.L., ex-Lord Mayor of Dublin. The W.M., Bro. Henry Arthur Blyth, marked the occasion by subscribing two hundred guineas each to the Boys' School, the Girls' School, and the Centenary Fund.

In founding " Irish Masonry Illustrated," in Dublin in 1901, I believe I supplied a very much needed organ for the Order in Ireland. It was a

Masonic Memories

handsome publication, and with a view to give increased interest to the election of candidates for the schools, I introduced a feature which might be copied by *The Freemason* or some of the provincial masonic journals in England with good effect.

This feature consisted of pages devoted to portraits of the candidates, by means of which it was possible for the Governors of the schools (I am myself a Life Governor of both) to gain some idea of the appearance of the boys or girls for whom they give their votes; and it also assisted those who were soliciting votes for the candidates to emphasize their claims by sending copies of the paper which contained the portraits. If a Governor saw a particularly bright and intelligent face, he naturally voted for the little boy or girl whose appearance seemed to contain a promise that he or she would be a credit to the schools.

That this monthly paper gained the approval of Sir James Creed Meredith, LL.D., one of the Secretaries of the Royal University of Ireland, and the Deputy-Grand Master of the Masonic Body in Ireland, the following letter clearly proves.

" CLONEVIN, PEMBROKE ROAD, DUBLIN,
13th May, 1901.

" MY DEAR COLLES,—I must thank you most sincerely for the copy you were good enough to send me of the first number of 'Irish Masonry Illustrated.'

The design of the publication is good, and it has

185

been carried into effect in a manner which leaves nothing to be desired.

" I am sure that you will continue to provide most interesting information in connection with the progress of Masonry at Home and Abroad.

" May I once more renew my good wishes for the success of your very interesting and useful publication? Yours fraternally,—

"J. C. MEREDITH, D.G.M."

I also had letters from the Grand Master, the Duke of Abercorn, Lord Castletown, Viscount Templetown, the Earl of Shaftesbury, and other prominent members of the Order in Ireland, including that great authority on the literature of the Order, Bro. Crossle.

In connection with this publication, I devised another, in order to produce which I had the hearty co-operation of Bro. W. Harding Lawder, the Managing Director of the Irish branch of the well known photographers, Lafayette Ltd. This consisted of photographs of prominent masons in Ireland at the close of the century, and included portraits of all the Provincial Grand Officers throughout Ireland. The photographs were done on India paper, and the Album, when completed, was thoroughly representative of the Masonic Body in Ireland.

During my residence in Ireland I was the local Honorary Secretary of the " Quatuor Coronati " (The Four Crowned Martyrs) Lodge 2076, London, and succeeded in getting many Freemasons interested

186

in the work of this Lodge, which is a literary Lodge, and was founded by the late Sir Walter Besant the novelist and historian of London. It consists of a very limited number of members, and a Circle of Correspondents. The Lodge publishes a Quarterly which is profusely illustrated and the literary matter is as a rule entertaining as well as erudite. Bro. G. Dames Burtchaell, B.L., Athlone Pursuivant is now, I believe, the Local Secretary in Ireland of this Lodge, and a more learned Mason than he is, would be most difficult to find.

One of my pleasantest masonic memories is the visit to Ireland of that fine old Freemason, General John Corson Smith of Chicago, who was entertained by Lodge 25 as was also the Duke of Connaught, the Grand Master of the Order in England.

CHAPTER XX

AN IRISH HUMORIST

Edwin Hamilton—His Prize Poem, "Ariadne "—" Dublin
Doggerels "—" Mongrel Doggerels "—" A Visit to
the Zoo "—" The Chimpanzor and the Chimpanzee "
—Mr F. R. Benson—" General Macbeth "—Practical
Jokes—" The Song of the False Tooth "—J. M.
Lowry — " The Pedigror and the Pedigree " —
" Bully's Acre "—The Bigot's Club—" Faust " up
to Date — Society for Prevention of Cruelty to
Children—Sara de Groot in "School."

I HAVE referred several times to my friend Edwin
Hamilton, whom many called the Sir William
Schwenck Gilbert of Ireland. This may seem an
exaggerated estimate of Hamilton to those
unacquainted with his prose and verse, but I believe
that if my readers have patience enough to glance
through my account of my friend's work, and
the extracts I give from it, that my contention that
he is one of the greatest living humorists will be
allowed.

Edwin Hamilton's merit as a rhymer was recognised in 1872 when he gained the Vice-Chancellor's
prize for poetry in T.C.D. by his metrical drama,
" Ariadne," a skilful parody of Swinburne's metres
in " Atalanta in Calydon," but though it contains

some excellent "fooling," in deftly woven metres, I pass on to his first volume, entitled, "Dublin Doggerels," in which the poet, as Civic Laureate, celebrated the public buildings, squares, and streets of his native city, and devoted verses to such subjects as the Zoo and the river Liffey. Of his method let the following lines from his verses on the Zoo serve as an illustration—

> See anon the lithe libretto
>   Lightly spring from bough to bough;
> Hear the strains of the stiletto—
>   Ah! methinks I hear him now.
> See, by yonder weeping willow,
>   At the margin of the lake,
> How the snowy peccadillo
>   Leaves her nest and comes for cake.

A charming little poem which has been set to music by Herr Löhr is—

> TO MY FIRST LOVE.
>
> I remember
>   Meeting you
> In September
>   Sixty-two
> We were eating,
>   Both of us;
> And the meeting
>   Happened thus:—
> Accidental,
>   On the road;
> (Sentimental
>   Episode.)
> I was gushing,
>   You were shy,

In Castle and Court House

You were blushing,
  So was I.
I was smitten,
  So were you.
(All that's written
  Here is true.)
Any money?
  Not a bit.
Rather funny,
  Wasn't it?
Vows we plighted,
  Happy pair!
How delighted
  People were!
But your father,
  To be sure,
Thought it rather
  Premature.
And your mother,
  Strange to say,
Was another
  In the way.
What a heaven
  Vanished then!
(You were seven,
  I was ten.)
That was many
  Years ago;
Don't let any-
  body know.

This poem, which is worthy of Hood, was charmingly illustrated by Harry Furniss when reprinted in Hamilton's second volume, " The Moderate Man and Other Verses."

Of the poems in this second volume which was published by Ward and Downey, one of the most

An Irish Humorist

characteristic is "The Chimpanzor and the Chimpanzee" which is a capital poem for recitation, as indeed, are many of Hamilton's poems. Perhaps one of the best for this form of entertainment is his "General Macbeth" which has never appeared in any collected edition of his work. The author recited it by request on the occasion of a dinner at which Mr F. R. Benson, himself an able exponent of Macbeth was present.

GENERAL MACBETH.

There were three unmarried sisters, who were elderly
    and weird,
  Inhabiting a blighted heath—an uninviting spot;
Each had fingers long and skinny, and moustaches, and
    a beard,
  And they mixed up toads and snakes and babies' fingers
    in a pot—
          In a pot,
          Boiling hot,
          An unappetising lot
Of promiscuous ingredients were compounded in a pot.

Well, a Caledonian General—Macbeth—was there one
    night;
  They hailed him as a future king. He said, " It's all
    a joke;
Because the king is living and has sons." Said they,
    " You're right;
  But that's not hard to remedy "—and vanished in the
    smoke—
          In the smoke.
          What they spoke
          Might be taken as a joke;
But couldn't kings be taught the knack of vanishing in
    smoke?

In Castle and Court House

Macbeth and the unscrupulous but lovely Lady M.,
    Determined upon regicide, which wasn't strictly fair,
    Considering their monarch was a visitor to them;
    And Macbeth, when on the job, perceived a dagger in
        the air.
                    In the air,
                    He could swear
                    It was actually there;
Though daggers as a class are very seldom in the air.

The inhospitable couple put their project into force,
    And he polished off the servants who beside their
        monarch lay,
Alleging that those varlets were the murderers, of course,
    For the sons of the deceased had found him rather in
        the way.
                    " By the way,
                    Would it pay
                    To assassinate them, eh? "
Thought Lady M., " Those youngsters are extremely in
    the way."

When the sons of the departed were communicated with,
    Being rather unassuming, they determined upon flight.
The suggestion of complicity was obviously a myth;
    But they thought themselves in danger, and absconded
        in the night.
                    In the night,
                    And a fright,
                    For they didn't want to fight;
But they left Macbeth the kingdom by decamping in the
    night.

Well, as King, he gave a party, and a lot of people came,
    And his Majesty expressed regret that Banquo wasn't
        there;
That warrior had died at his dictation all the same;
    And now his ghost came striding in, and settled in a
        chair.

An Irish Humorist

In a chair,
One to spare,
Kept for Banquo, as it were.
Though the company saw nothing but an ordinary chair.

Then his Majesty, to everyone's unqualified surprise,
  Shouted queer things at the phantom, which eventually
      fled;
And the Queen said, " Never mind him; he is generally
      wise,
  Though occasionally more or less affected in the head."
            " In the head,"
            So she said,
            But she wilfully misled,
For she knew that he had never been affected in the head.

" Now gentlemen and ladies," she continued, " if I may
  Give a practical suggestion—though you've not had
      much to eat—
Of course, I don't insinuate it's time to go away,
  But, I may remark, your carriages are waiting in the
      street."
            In the street—
            They retreat.
            The policeman on his beat
Said, " They're early out, and positively sober, in the
      street."

Now, a nobleman, the other Mac, whose father's name
      was Duff,
  Was prejudiced against the King, as anybody might
Whose family had not been treated tenderly enough,
  So he made an affidavit he would meet him in a fight.
            In a fight,
            That was right;
            In a mediæval light,
All contemporary differences ended in a fight.

Then the Queen was taken ill and took to walking in
      her sleep,

In Castle and Court House

And she told a lot of secrets of the murders she had
    planned—
Such secrets as an ordinary personage would keep—
And she trotted round the bedroom with a candle in
    her hand.
             In her hand,
             Understand,
             In a candlestick japanned;
No queen would condescend to take a candle in her hand.

Macbeth was disconcerted, so he sought the witches out—
    And was promised that, till Birnam Wood should come
        to Dunsinane,
Of his personal indemnity he needn't have a doubt;
    Which uncanny reassurance made him happy in the
        main.
             In the main,
             To retain
             His anxiety was vain,
For woods are fairly stationary—taken in the main.

At last his fortress—Dunsinane—was menaced by a
    crowd—
    An enemy who scorned to run, but simply cut their
        sticks,
And carried such, with leaves and all, their forces to
        enshroud;
    So, when the wood appeared to move, he said, " I'm
        in a fix.
             In a fix,
             For it licks
             All creation, and it sticks
In my gizzard. This unfixity has put me in a fix."

In a plain, before his castle, where Macbeth had sallied
    forth,
    He met with the antagonist who'd sworn to have his
        hide.

An Irish Humorist

They fought with much intensity, these champions of the
      north;
  And his Majesty was ultimately punctured in the side.
         In the side;
         So he died,
         For his head was misapplied,
In addition to a formidable puncture in the side.

MORAL.

Should you hope to lead a prosperous, aristocratic life,
  Take a note of what I say in my capacity of friend:
If you slaughter all your relatives to gratify your wife,
  You may find their representatives unpleasant in the
    end.
        In the end
        They may send
        You to—well, you comprehend.
And now, two monosyllables to finish in—
        " The End."

I may here remark that Edwin Hamilton in speech
is quite as amusing as in his verse. He makes the
most laughable joke with a serious face, and rarely
smiles at jokes made by others. He had a habit of
wearing a beard for a few months and then shaving
it off for some months, only to return to growing it
again. A lady once complained to him:

" Mr Hamilton, I never recognise you, for you are
always shaving off your beard. How many have you
grown altogether? "

" I did not grow them altogether," replied Hamilton, " I grew them one by one."

He sometimes called for me on a Sunday, when
we both lived in Leeson Park, to go for a walk with
him. At the risk (literally) of chronicling " small-

beer" I may add that on one such occasion he asked me had I any money. By some curious accident I found on searching my pockets that I had only one penny!

" Never mind," he said, " that will do."

We were walking along a country road near Dundrum and the weather was sultry. I asked Hamilton what he wanted the money for. He replied, " To get a drink!" I laughed, and inquired what drink could he expect for a penny. He answered:

" This is what we'll do. We go into that house," indicating one which we were approaching. " You ask me what I'll have. I reply ' Brandy and Soda, doctor,' whereupon you say, ' No, you must limit yourself to what I allow you, a pennyworth of stout a day.' Then order a glass of Guinness for me. Of course, you as my medical adviser don't drink!" (A glass of Guinness in Ireland can be had for the humble and heavy coin).

This was a blue look out for me, but I did as I was told. We walked in and the dialogue was as given above, but when the glass of stout arrived, Hamilton put down a sovereign and ordered a brandy and soda, and pointing to the stout, to the astonishment of the barmaid he said, turning to me, " You may drink that stuff yourself!" Of course, I was not limited to the Guinness. The barmaid was unable to change the sovereign as the house had only just opened. Hamilton accordingly took it back, and tendered the necessary sum. When we left he began whistling a hymn. I said:

An Irish Humorist

" You're very religious to-day."

" Yes," he said, " that sovereign makes me so."

"That sovereign," said I, "What's that got to do with it? "

" Don't you recognise the air? " he asked. I did, it was that of " Oh, thou *that changest not*, abide with me! "

This hymn, J. M. Lowry, another Dublin humorist, used to call " The Song of the False Tooth," because of the reference to " change and decay in all around I see."

Edwin Hamilton was, I believe, founder and President of the Bigots' Club, and wrote for the Club an amusing poem on " Faust," a theme he treated on very original lines, introducing snatches of popular songs. One of the most striking of his poems is " The Pedigror and the Pedigree " which is also out of print and runs as follows—

THE PEDIGROR AND THE PEDIGREE.

One Hyphen-Brown-Hyphen-Black-Hyphen-De Rose,
Is a person whose pedigree everyone knows.
     The Browns were Crusaders,
     Or Norman invaders,
And the Hyphens, though small, were redoubtable foes
     In the days of " the Charter,"
     As Knights of the Garter—
At least, so the family history shows.

Then the Blacks were distinguished for medical skill,
Long before the invention of licence to kill;
     Their prescriptions were taken
     By Chaucer and Bacon,

In Castle and Court House

And Caractacus sent for them when he was ill;
  And they cured Alexander
  The Great and Leander,
By dividing between them a Holloway's pill.

The De Roses were poets, when poets could claim
To be true men of genius and worthy the name.
  Their songs were the neatest,
  The purest, and sweetest,
And their works are enshrined in the temple of fame—
  At least, so they should be,
  And probably would be
If down to posterity some of them came.

Then the Hyphen-Brown-Hyphens were lions at Court
In the days when the Joust was a recognised sport.
  They dined on six courses,
  Kept several horses,
Drank sack out of goblets, and bumpers of port.
  Then Oliver Cromwell
  Queen Anne, and Beau Brummel
Were the people with whom they were wont to consort.

Then the Brown-Hyphen-Blacks were the scourge of the
  sea,
From the cave of Adullam to Trincomalee;
  No cruisers were braver
  To capture a slaver
Or to land a rich cargo of pepper or tea.
  Against Frenchmen and Dutchmen,
  Italians and such men,
You could always get odds of eleven to three.

Then the Hyphen-Black-Hyphens were men about town,
For they all had substantial estates from the Crown.
  At the Wars of the Roses
  They turned up their noses—
They despised that particular form of renown;
  But they'd follow the ladies
  (Like Orpheus) to—Cadiz;
There were never such mashers from Solomon down.

An Irish Humorist

Then the Hyphen-De Roses claimed longer descent,
For their name's on the Sphinx, done in Roman cement.
As you find Cain and Abel
But half up their table,
They regarded the Flood as a recent event;
And the Hyphen-De Roses,
With Aaron and Moses,
Went about in the Wilderness sharing a tent.

So much for his ancestors now in the grave.
Does their sole representative also behave
As a man of high station,
A good reputation,
An escutcheon unsullied by coward or knave?
Is he famous in story,
And covered with glory?
Is he true to the name his progenitors gave?

He is very much down, and as up as can be
A remarkable (genealogical) tree;
Branch ever so slender
He'll never surrender—
He would rather be drowned in the depths of the sea—
Though, like many possessors
Of proud predecessors,
His pretensions to grandeur are fiddle-de-dee.

But see—to a wealthy relation he goes—
An uncle, whose name the directory shows.
He's a generous lender,
And ultimate vendor
Of the goods of which anyone cares to dispose.
" On the ticket what name, sir? "
" Not know me? For shame, sir!
Why, Hyphen-Brown-Hyphen-Black-Hyphen-De Rose."

Notwithstanding the pedigree lately unrolled,
Our hero was frequently out in the cold.
Though so aristocratic,
He lived in an attic—

In Castle and Court House

Till the bailiff came up like a wolf on the fold.
  The man in possession
  Would brook no repression,
So the table, the chair, and the mangle were sold.

When he went to the workhouse (where everyone goes
When his assets all told are but one suit of clothes)
  His demeanour was stately,
  But modified greatly
By the fact that his boots didn't cover his toes.
  " Who are you? " said the master.
  " Fell scribe of disaster,
I'm Hyphen-Brown-Hyphen-Black-Hyphen-De Rose."

But the name was too long to be quite taken down
(It appeared, in fact, rather an improper noun);
  Though the lack of his titles
  Might prey on his vitals,
He was ruthlessly, recklessly registered " Brown."
  Still, the Browns were Crusaders,
  Or Norman invaders,
And—perhaps—had some kind of estates from the Crown.

MORAL.

Now, this history's truthful—as history goes;
You anticipate, doubtless, the moral it shows,
  If the past were the present,
  It might be unpleasant,
Or it mightn't, for anything anyone knows.
  Don't rely for your merit
  On what you inherit,
Like Hyphen-Brown-Hyphen-Black-Hyphen-De-Rose.

Striking as is this poem, Hamilton's prose as
exhibited in his " Waggish Tales," is equally remarkable. His story of " Bully's Acre," for instance, opens
with—
  " I bet you the pawn-ticket of my amputation
instruments against your new skeleton."

An Irish Humorist

" Done! though I'm giving you about five to three,
for my skeleton, including the second coat of varnish,
cost close on six pounds, your knives are only worth
about five, and it will cost over two to take them
out."

Hamilton wrote the " T.D.C. Tercentenary Prologue " when the undergraduates performed three
plays at the Gaiety Theatre.   He also wrote the
Prologue for the opening of the Theatre Royal by
Messrs Morell and Mouillot, including a line
referring to the managers, which brought a ten-
shilling telegram of expostulation from them—

" To whom Mouillot (you owe) Morell-oquence than
mine."

At a performance of " School," given at the Gaiety
Theatre, Dublin, to raise funds for the Society for
Prevention of Cruelty to Children; when the
heroine's part was taken by the gifted Sara de Groot,
Hamilton read a Prologue he had written for the
occasion, in which he referred to the fact that " Cats'
Homes and Dogs' Homes reared their heads on
high," but though even—

" The vivisected rabbit had a friend "
and—
"Though the doors of Charity were wide—
Children in arms were not allowed inside."

I cannot dismiss Hamilton from my pages, his
name, like Charles the First's head in Mr Dick's
essays, must crop up now and then, but those who
are interested and require further information can
discover much by referring to " Who's Who."

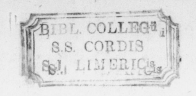
CHAPTER XXI

TWO IRISH HISTORIANS

Sir John T. Gilbert—His History of the Irish Confedera-
tion and the War in Ireland—Dr S. R. Gardiner—
Waits for Appearance of Gilbert's Volumes—History
of the City of Dublin—Dennis Florence MacCarthy's
Sonnet—History of the Viceroys—" Lady Wilde,
from the Author "—Rosa Mulholland—Lord Russell
of Killowen—Villa Nova—A Sunday with Gilbert—Dr
P. W. Joyce—His " Old Celtic Romances "—His
History of Ireland—The Royal Irish Academy—
Ancient Irish Music—The Very Reverend John Henry
Bernard, D.D., Dean of St Patrick's.

" Greatest minds," said Wordsworth, " are often
those of whom the busy world hears least," and this
dictum was often recalled to my memory when I
saw my friend Sir John T. Gilbert enter the doors of
the Royal Irish Academy. Here was a man who had
unobtrusively and patiently toiled for fifty years at
such a great work as the " History of the Irish Con-
federation and the War in Ireland," (1641-1649)
which when completed filled seven volumes, contented with the fact that he was giving a truly noble
gift to his country.

Gilbert, however, was not without his " pepper-
corn of praise," and this was all the more significant

Two Irish Historians

in his eyes in that it was bestowed by his peers.
Dr S. R. Gardiner, the eminent English historian
waited for the appearance of the volumes during the
progress of his own documentary History of
England. "I am getting more interested," he wrote,
"in the appearance of your book on the Irish
Rebellion, as I am approaching the subject more
closely. I am now working at Strafford's trial, so
that I shall be at the Irish Rebellion by next Spring
or Summer. Is there any hope of your book being
out by that time?"

The list of Gilbert's writings is a formidable one,
and includes various works in connection with the
National Manuscripts, Historic and Municipal
Documents of Ireland, "A Contemporary History
of affairs in Ireland, from 1641 to 1652," "A History
of the City of Dublin," in three volumes, and
"History of the Viceroys of Ireland; with Notices
of the Castle of Dublin, and its Chief Occupants in
Former Times."

Of these books the most popular was the "History
of Dublin." This book, of which the first edition
was published in 1854, is a beautiful specimen of
what a Dublin publishing house can do. It was
printed at the University Press, by H. M. Gill, in
whose hands the University Press then was. It has
been out of print for many years, and the copy before
me is marked "very scarce." To anyone to whom
Dublin is dear, Gilbert's History is an invaluable and
deeply interesting record of her past—of "days that
are no more." In its pages will be found recorded

the many and great changes which Dublin has undergone. In the first volume is given a map of Dublin as published by John Speed in 1610, which is, I fear, somewhat lacking in fidelity to fact, but which clearly proves how ancient are many of the present titles of the streets.   Winetavern Street, Castle Street, Whitefriars, St. Andrew's Church, and many others are marked, as well as the position of "The Colledges" (*sic*). The book is brimful of anecdotes and tales of other days. Graphic pictures are presented of various stages in the development of Dublin. Of days when one could order a "chair" to attend Handel's Musical Entertainments at the New Musick Hall in Fishamble Street, or repair to the Smock Alley Theatre to see Sheridan perform.

When Gilbert's "History of Dublin" was first published, Dennis Florence MacCarthy, the Irish poet, author of "Waiting for the May," wrote the following sonnet on the subject.

Long have I loved the beauty of thy streets,
Fair Dublin; long, with unavailing vows,
Sigh'd to all guardian deities who rouse
The spirits of dead nations to new heats
Of life and triumph; vain the fond conceits,
Nestling like eaves-warmed doves 'neath patriot brows!
Vain as the "Hope" that, from thy Custom-House,
Looks o'er the vacant bay in vain for fleets.
Genius alone brings back the days of yore:
Look! look what life is in these quaint old shops;
The loneliest lanes are rattling with the roar
Of coach and chair; fans, feathers, flambeaux, fops
Flutter and flicker through yon open door,
Where Handel's hand moves the great organ-stops.

Two Irish Historians

Gilbert's " History of the Viceroys " came next in popular estimation. It was published in 1865. The copy I possess bears the inscription " Lady Wilde, from the Author." The narrative commences with the Dublin of Romance, and closes with the reign of Henry VIII. To read this book in conjunction with the History of England is to be enlightened on many points, for Gilbert was not satisfied to follow in the footsteps of his predecessors, but gave extracts from hitherto unprinted and little-known archives, and elucidated, for the first time, facts and circumstances, up to that time misunderstood or unnoticed.

Sir John T. Gilbert married one of our most charming story-tellers, Miss Rosa Mulholland, whose sister married the late Lord Chief Justice of England, Lord Russell of Killowen. Lady Gilbert's books, for instance, " The Wild Birds of Killevy," or, indeed, any of the volumes which Messrs Blackie and Son publish annually from her pen, possess a rare fascination for both old and young readers.

The Gilberts lived in a delightful old-fashioned house called " Villa Nova," near Blackrock, in the county of Dublin, not far from the coast. The house had its own enclosure of great old trees, lawn, meadow and stream, and is truly " a haunt of ancient peace." Here Gilbert laboured for fifty years " among the song birds in which he delighted, and in friendship with the squirrels that haunted the ancient walnut trees near his windows." A squirrel cracking a nut was on his book-plate, and I told him once that I thought he was himself a human squirrel cracking some of the hardest of nuts, the falsehoods in Irish History to extract the kernel of truth.

" Sunday was Gilbert's holiday," wrote Lady Gilbert in her admirable Life of the great Historian, " and on the afternoon of that day he delighted to welcome all who would undertake a long walk to enter at the green, jasmine-covered wicket, rest under the great walnut trees, and gather round the afternoon tea-table."

It has often been my privilege and pleasure to walk with Gilbert on the lawn, in which he took a great pleasure, and listen to his wit and wisdom, the former being not unlike the recorded utterances of Charles Lamb. Gilbert loved a jest, and his eyes lit up when he thought he had made a better joke than usual. I seem to see his—

> . . . eyes twinkle yet
> At his own jest. [Those] eyes lit up
> With Summer lightnings of a soul
> So full of Summer warmth, so glad
> So healthy, sound, and clear, and whole,
> His memory scarce can make me sad.

Another Irish Historian whom I have had the honour to know for many years is Dr P. W. Joyce, one of the Commissioners for the Publication of the Ancient Laws of Ireland. Dr Joyce's most popular books are his " The Origin and History of Irish Names of Places," and his " Old Celtic Romances: translated from the Gaelic." He has also written

a fine " History of Ireland from the Earliest Times
to 1608," with much judgment, avoiding exaggera-
tion and bitterness, and showing fair play all round.

Dr Joyce resembles a fine old Roman in appearance, the " unsubduable old Roman," as Carlyle
remarked of Walter Savage Landor. He is a prominent Member of the Royal Irish Academy, and
frequently lightens the debates of that learned body,
by references to the romantic legends of old Ireland.
In this way I have heard him relate the story of
King O'Connor Macnessa who was shot in the head
with a " brain ball," *i.e.*, the brains of a defunct
enemy mixed with clay and baked. O'Connor
carried this strange missile in his head for years and
was told never to get excited or he would die.
When the missionaries related to the king how
Christ had suffered under the Jews, he became
excited—

> The brain-ball leaped forth from his head,
> And bequeathing his soul to that Saviour,
> King O'Connor Macnessa fell dead.

An important contribution to our knowledge of
Ireland is Dr Joyce's great work in two volumes on
the Social History of Ancient Ireland, in which the
author treats of the Government, Military System,
and Law, Religion, Learning, and Art, Trades,
Industries, and Commerce, Manners, Customs, and
Domestic Life of the Ancient Irish People. This
is a beautiful book containing nearly 400 illustrations
and should be read by all who desire to understand
the Irish People. The perusal of it should be made

obligatory on all would-be Members of Parliament who attempt to solve the problem of the Irish question!

Dr Joyce is an authority on Ancient Irish Music, and has collected over a hundred of original Irish airs which are indeed genuine Irish melodies, which until Dr Joyce collected them had never been published. One of these he sent me recently jotted down from memory with the music. It is entitled, "O, come to the Hedgerows," the words by Dr Joyce being charmingly wedded to the old Irish air. The words are—

O come to the hedgerows with gay flowers all bright,
While the green fields are smiling beneath the sun's light;
Through the green lanes we'll wander the long happy day,
While the little birds are singing merrily—
    O come, come away.
O come to the seaside to hear the wild waves,
On the dark rocks we'll stand while the storm wildly raves;
And we'll watch the white seagulls through tempest and
    spray,
While the mighty ocean rages fierce and loud—
    O come, come away.
O come to the blue hills, the wild mountain side,
Where the green fern grows tall and the heath-bell blooms
    wide,
Where the mountain stream dashes o'er mossy rocks grey,
And sings with gentle murmur all day long—
    O come, come away.

This song is a universal favourite among the Irish National Schools.

The Royal Irish Academy, of which I was myself a member, being elected on the recommendation of

Two Irish Historians

Sir John T. Gilbert, Professor Louis Claude Purser, and Edwin Hamilton, has done much good work. The Academy grants out of its funds, money to enable scholars to pursue certain paths. In this way the late Professor Atkinson was assisted while translating The Book of Ballymote and the Yellow Book of Lecan. At one time it was possible for almost any parish priest to be elected, but thanks to the efforts of a wise committee this state of things was altered and even so great a scholar as Professor Mahaffy thought well to place the letters M.R.I.A. on the title page of his " Prolegomena to Ancient History." Matters also improved considerably during the able administration of the Very Rev. the Dean of St. Patrick's Cathedral, who before his succession to the post once held by Swift, was as the Rev. John Henry Bernard, D.D., for a short time Secretary to the Academy. Bernard has done some good work, and with Mahaffy was responsible for a volume on Kant's " Critique of Pure Reason."

CHAPTER XXII

" FAR-OFF THINGS "

Mr F. Moir Bussy's Book—The Last Duel in the Phœnix
Park — Edward Richards Purefoy Colles — Chief
Justice of Sierra Leone—English Ignorance regard-
ing Ireland—A New Theory to solve the Irish
Problem—Priests and People of Ireland—Father
Healy, Parish Priest of Little Bray—Healy and
Fitzpatrick—Secret Service under Pitt—" Throw your
Brogue after Her "—" Don't cut your Old Friends ! "

THE death of Fitzharris the cabman who drove the
Irish Invincibles to the Phœnix Park when on their
fiendish errand to commit a murder, and the publication of Mr Bussy's book incorporating some of Mr
John Mallon's memoirs, have again called attention
to the unhappy differences which existed and in part
still exist between England and Ireland.

I have no intention to plunge into matters political,
" to (fire) the blood I have no ready arts," but Mr
Bussy's recollections and his descriptions of occurrences he has himself witnessed, give additional proof
of how very slow a process is social development.
One would imagine that the custom of duelling was
one of those which belong to a far-away past ; but,
strange as it may seem, one of the last to appear in

the "fifteen acres" in the Phœnix Park, which was the favourite place for duelling appointments, was my father's cousin, Mr Edward Richards Purefoy Colles, at one time Chief Justice of Sierra Leone.

I do not state this on my own authority, but on that of Mr Charles Pelham Mulvany, who in 1880 in "Society in Dublin Thirty Years Ago," wrote:—

"Among the last representatives of the duello, was Mr Colles, a well known and much respected member of the Bar. This gentleman, though of a generous nature, had a sharp tongue, and would often say things which seemed to disprove the theory, often urged in apology for duelling, that it tends to check the disposition to hurt the feelings of those we mix with. Thus in a dispute at the Dublin Society Council with a most respectable clergyman, who happened to be chaplain to the Lock Hospital, Mr Colles said, 'I will not be put down by you who live on the wages of the filthiest vice!' On another occasion Mr Colles actually challenged a Dublin tradesman, a tenant of his, with whom he had a dispute as to rent. Mr Colles, a most punctual and orderly man, was first on the ground. 'Sir,' said he, when his tardy opponent appeared, 'You have neither the honour of a gentleman, nor the punctuality of a tradesman!' For the later years of his life this gentleman led a most peaceable existence. As Librarian of the Royal Dublin Society, he was especially noted for his kindness to the young men who frequented that library as students."

Constitutional progress being, in the British Isles,

largely, if not wholly dependent on social development, it is not strange that the progress towards an *entente cordiale* between England and Ireland has been tardy. Great ignorance with regard to Ireland exists in England to-day. What was that ignorance fifty years ago when the means of inter-communication between the two countries did not include one-tenth of the facilities we enjoy to-day?

What the ignorance of the average Englishman with regard to Ireland was in those days may be gathered from these humorous verses, written evidently by a believer in Home Rule.

Before I came across the sea
  To this delightful place,
I thought the native Irish were
  A funny sort of race.
I thought they bore shillelagh-sprigs,
  And that they always said—
" Ochone, acushla, tare-an-ouns,
  Begorrah! " and " Bedad! "

I thought their noses all turned up,
  Just like a crooked pin;
I thought their mouths six inches wide
  And always on the grin;
I thought their heads were made of stuff
  As hard as any nails;
I half-suspected that they were
  Possessed of little tails.

But when I came unto the land
  Of which I heard so much,
I found that the inhabitants
  Were not entirely such.

"Far-Off Things"

I found their features were not all
    Exactly like baboons';
I found that some wore billycocks,
    And some had pantaloons.

It seems that praties in their skins
    Are not their only food,
And that they have a house or two
    Which is not built of mud.
In fact, they're not all brutes or fools,
    And I suspect that when
They rule themselves they'll be as good,
    Almost, as Englishmen!

A propos of the Irish ruling themselves, one of
the best theories I ever heard propounded to solve
the Irish question, I heard from a Mr Cavanagh.
The country is, as is well known, very largely Roman
Catholic. The Priesthood of Ireland are not noted
for their activity and the people follow suit.
The Irish are not over industrious. Mr
Cavanagh's idea was that the problem should be
attacked through the country's religion. The
authority of Rome should be secured and an
exchange of the priests of Ireland for the priests of
the United States be effected.

The priest from U.S.A. would introduce fresh
ideas to his flock. One of these would be the Gospel
of Work, a gospel which if energetically preached
would in time lead to the regeneration of all Ireland,
especially of the South and West, while the priesthood of Ireland, instead of dry-rotting in Ireland
would learn to move with the times, surrounded as
they would be by the bustling people of America.
Such is Mr Cavanagh's proposal which I recommend
to Mr Birrell.

In Castle and Court House

To learn how extraordinary is the ignorance on matters theological which exist in Ireland, one has only to turn to the pages of Mr McCarthy, whose " Five Years in Ireland," " Priests and People," and other books prove clearly that the belief in fairies and demons and other supernatural agencies exist among the ignorant peasants of the West as strongly to-day as in the dark ages. Mr McCarthy quoted the case of the peasants in the West who put their sister sitting on the fire to drive the devil out of her.

But ignorance of this kind does not exist among the peasantry only. A son of the late Sir Dominick Corrigan, the great surgeon, was a captain in the Army during the first Kaffir War. Lady Corrigan was much distressed on learning that several dusky warriors were killed by her son, and in her zeal for the departed, she wished to pay for masses for the souls of the Kaffirs, who had, the good lady believed, gone to Purgatory. Of course, masses for these heathen were refused, but a ballad immortalised her action in the following terms—

Oh, pray for them poor haythen Kaffirs! How quare!
The nagurs they knew not the Captain was there;
Oh, pray to the Vargin to pardon the guilt
Of the sowls of the Kaffirs young Corrigan kilt!

Like the Cats of Kilkenny, those pretty pusheens,
Sure the Captain he cut them to small smithereens.
Sure his sword it was all dripping red to the hilt
With the blood of the Kaffirs brave Corrigan kilt!

Musha! dear dirty Dublin grew sad at the tale,
And the boys they were silent that shouted "Repale!"

And with people the churches and chapels were filt
That prayed for them Kaffirs brave Corrigan kilt.

The belief in Purgatory was never more humor-
ously commented on than by Father Healy, Parish
Priest of Little Bray. Some young fellows seeing a
priest in the railway carriage, declared loudly their
disbelief in the doctrine. Father Healy said nothing
until his station was reached, when on getting out
of the carriage and having shut the door, he looking
in at the window, remarked, " Well, boys, I'm sorry
for ye, for if ye don't believe in Purgatory, ye may
go to Hell! "

Father Healy's Life was written by the late Mr
Fitzpatrick, author of " Secret Service under Pitt."
Once when I was walking with Sir Charles Cameron,
we met Father Healy. Sir Charles asked the genial
priest to dine with him. " No, Sir Charles, thank
ye," said Father Healy. Cameron pressed him to
come and finally demanded his reason for refusing.
" To tell you the truth, Sir Charles," responded the
witty priest, " I'm afraid that you've asked Fitzpatrick, and he's bound to write my life some day,
and I don't want to meet him, God forgive me."
Healy's surmise was correct; his life *was* written by
Fitzpatrick.

Two stories of Healy which, I believe, have not
been chronicled in Fitzpatrick's Life, are as follows—
At a wedding the bride was given away by Lord
Morris, familiarly known as Peter the Packer.
Morris prided himself on his Irish accent, and at the
wedding breakfast, addressing the bride, said, " And

now, my dear, having given ye away, shure I can do no more for ye." "Oh, yes, you can, my Lord," said Father Healy, "you can throw your *brogue* after her."

The other story is that Healy, when the guest of a wealthy but illiterate Baronet, remarked on the excellence of his library. "Ah, yes," said his pompous and ignorant host, "my old friends, Father Healy, my old friends." " I'm glad to see," said Healy, examining a book of which the pages showed utter ignorance of the paper-knife, " I'm glad to see you don't *cut* your old friends."

CHAPTER XXIII

ANOTHER DUBLIN HUMORIST——J. M. LOWRY

Edwin Hamilton not the only Dublin Humorist—James
Moody Lowry—His " The Keys ' At Home ' "—" A
Lay of Kilcock "—A Parody of Tennyson—" Jack
Spratt "—A Parody of Macaulay—" The Battle at the
Asses' Bridge "—" Spasmodeus in Swinburnia "—A
Bogus Review—A Story of Cremation—Mr Edward
Terry.

EDWIN HAMILTON is not the only Dublin Humorist
as I think my readers will admit when they have read
some of the specimens of the verse which I am
privileged to reproduce in this chapter.

James Moody Lowry is the author of a very
amusing booklet, entitled " The Keys' ' At Home.' "
It is a Christmas fantasy and a very quaint one it
is. The Keys of the household are supposed to be
" At Home " on Christmas night, and the party
consists of an orange, a mouse, a much mutilated
roast duck, a sunflower, and a boiled lobster, as well
as several members of the Key family, including a
watch-key and two cross-keys.

The conversation recorded is full of innocent fun,
with such remarks by members of the Key family

as that the French members were known as Mon Key and the Spanish as Don Key!

The little volume was published at Ye Leaden-hall Press, and quickly ran out of print, but was reprinted in Dublin more than once, and the lyrics for which it was eagerly sought have been issued, with additions, in one volume, entitled, "A Lay of Kilcock with Other Lays and Relays," by Messrs Hodges, Figgis & Co. Here is a parody of the Tennysonian metre having for its subject the famous Jack Spratt of Nursery Rhyme—

> Within the limits of well-ordered law
> They lived, this trusty squire and eke his spouse,
> No discord marked the genial dinner hour,
> Where union rooted in disunion stood,
> And tastes divergent served the end in view,
> What he would not, she would, what she not, he;
> So in all courtesy the meal progressed,
> And soon the viands wholly passed from sight.

One of the most notable parodies by Mr Lowry is his rendering of Macaulay's well-known poem, as may be judged from the following lines, entitled—

THE BATTLE AT THE ASSES' BRIDGE.

> Triangle Equilateral
>   By Algebra he swore
> That his good friend Isosceles
>   Should suffer wrong no more.
> By Algebra he swore it,
>   And named a fighting-day,
> And bade his Angles hurry forth—
> East and West, and South and North—
>   To summon to the fray.

Another Dublin Humorist

East and West and North and South
  The Angles hurry fast,
And Problem old and Theorem
  Have heard the trumpet-blast.
Shame on the Point that hath no parts,
  The circle that would quake,
When Equilateral has sworn
  The Asses' Bridge to take!
    .   .   .   .

And now they are assembled,
  The tale of fighting men;
The Decimals in hundreds are,
  The Units one to ten.
Equations all quadratical,
  Drawn out in long array;
Oh, proud was Equilateral
  Upon the fighting-day.

But on the Bridge of Asses
  Was tumult and affright,
For all the lines below the base
  Were stricken at the sight.
They held a council standing
  Upon the narrow ridge;
Hard lines, I wis, in times like this
  'Twould take to save the Bridge.

Then out spake gallant Alpha,
  On the Apex full in view,
" A Dog," they say, shall have his day,
  A Bridge shall have it, too;
And how can man die better,
  When things come to this pass,
Than fighting as first letter
  In the sacred name of ASS?

" Know then, false Equilateral,
  No Bridge thou'lt take to-day;
I, with two more to help me,
  Will keep ye all at bay.

In Castle and Court House

In these five lines a thousand
  May well be stopped by three;
Now who will stand, on either hand,
  And keep the Bridge with me?"

Then out spake gallant Beta
  (Of Grecian blood was he),
"Lo! I will stand on thy right hand,
  And keep the Bridge with thee."
And spake a stout Centurion,
  A Roman, surnamed C,
"I will abide on thy left side,
  And keep the Bridge with thee."

The three stood calm and silent,
  And watched the foeman's line,
As from its right stepped out to fight
  Theta's well-known Co-sine
And Vector the Quaternion—
  Vector, whose fourfold power
Had puzzled many a weary head,
And kept it aching out of bed
  Long past the midnight hour.

C went at once for Vector,
  And with a deadly blow
Of his good blade he quickly laid
The great Quaternion low:
For in that hour had Vector's power
  Been risen to the tenth.
Little cared C, I ween, for he
  Had smote him to the Nth.

Next Beta marked how Theta
  Advanced against his line,
So with his trusty tangent he
  Bisected the Co-sine.
"Lie there," he cried, "Fell tyrant!

Another Dublin Humorist

No longer shalt thou mark
How Girton's gold-haired graduates sigh,
,With vain endeavours, to descry
The variable length of Pi
    In thine accursed Arc.''

Then X, on his Equation,
    Advanced, and all were mute,
For in his hand he waved his brand—
    A knotty old cube root.
Thrice round his head he waved it,
    And then the weapon sprung
Like bolt from bow—a mighty blow
    On Alpha's crest it rung.

He reeled, and first on Beta
    Leaned for a breathing-space,
Then dashed his Co-efficient
    In the Equation's face,
And loud he cried, '' No more thy pride
    My inmost soul shall vex '';
Then with a stroke, 'twould cleave an oak,
    Eliminated X.

.   .   .   .

They gave him out of Euclid
    Ten cuts so erudite,
Not thrice ten Senior Wranglers
    Could solve 'twixt day and night;
They gave a square (it still is there),
    And every dunce derides,
With twice the double ratio
    Of its homologous sides.

And on the square they raised him,
    A vast triangle high,
His name is on the Apex
    (To witness if I lie)

In Castle and Court House

And underneath is written,
In letters all of brass,
How well brave Alpha held the Bridge
That's sacred to the ASS.

Like Edwin Hamilton in "Ariadne," Lowry has parodied Swinburne, but the parody is by no means as ambitious as was that by Hamilton. The parody is entitled "Spasmodeus in Swinburnia," the argument being as follows—

"Gorgonzola, a beautiful damsel betrothed to Spasmodeus, having rejected the overtures of Mars, is turned by him into a cheese. In this form she is presented to Spasmodeus, who unconsciously devours her. The father of Gorgonzola, Gripeus, and her mother, Kolera, having sought her in vain, consult the Delphic Oracle, who reveals to them her fate, and commands them to punish Spasmodeus. They accordingly inflict on him divers torments. Spasmodeus implores the aid of Æsculapius, who, with the assistance of Mercury, overcomes Gripeus and Kolera. In the struggle the teeth of Spasmodeus become loosened, and in the act of thanking Æsculapius he swallows the whole set, and is choked to death."

Here is Lowry's parody of the famous chorus—

Before the beginning of lays
There came to the making of rhyme,
Dust and delicious days,
Dew on the dawn of time,
Crying, and sighing, and laughter,
Weeping, and loathing, and love,
With little before or after,
And less beneath and above.

222

Another Dublin Humorist

And the poet takes in hand
   Kisses, and foam, and tears,
And sobbings, and slides of sand,
   Under the feet of the years;
He laughs while he writes in derision
   Thoughts that he cannot *think*—
His life is a sort of vision
   Betwixt a drink, and a drink.

Lowry's muse is best known in connection with such original work as his " Lay of Kilcock," and " The Last of the Leprachauns." He has also written some prose including a delightful little book entitled " A Doll's Garden Party," and " The Book of Jousts." His popularity in Dublin was once proved in a curious way. I used at the time to write about four columns of reviews in the Wednesday issue of *The Dublin Evening Mail*. As a practical joke I solemnly reviewed the non-existent " Collected Works of James Lowry, B.L., in two Volumes," mentioning incidentally such purely apochryphal poems as " The Lay of the Last Bantam." The result was marvellous, for the book-sellers of Dublin were deluged with orders for the book! Lowry generously forgave me, though his life must have been made miserable by references to the review, and requests for copies of the unpublished book. He once told me a long and elaborate story about a man who in the early days of cremation took no casquet for the remains of the deceased, and had to use an empty cigar box, which he placed in the hat rack in the railway carriage on his return from Woking. Feeling done up he took advantage of a stoppage and ran into the refreshment room for a drink only to find that a thief, deeming the contents of the box to be cigars, had disappeared with it.

Lowry did not tell me he had used this story for a chapter in a novel he wrote, and in my ignorance I anticipated him! Mr Lowry is, like his friend Mr Edward Terry, an enthusiastic Mason, and holds the same position in the Grand Lodge of Ireland that Mr W. S. Penley, another of his friends, holds in the Grand Lodge of England.

An American Man of Letters, the late
GEORGE PELLEW OF KATONAH, NEW YORK

WALT WHITMAN
(From a photograph sent by him to the Author)

CHAPTER XXIV

SOME AMERICAN MEN OF LETTERS

James Russell Lowell and John Pentland Mahaffy—Canon
Ainger—George Pellew of New York—His Visit to
Ireland—" The Decay of Modern Preaching "—
Pulpit Absurdities — Edgar Fawcett — Thomas
Sergeant Perry—Lillah Cabot Perry—John Fiske—
Poetic Vein *v.* Varicaux Vein! Sarah B. Piatt—
John James Piatt—His Poems praised by Lowell and
Longfellow.

JAMES RUSSELL LOWELL, we are told on the authority
of Canon Ainger, said as he got into his hansom, in
reference to Professor Mahaffy, from whom he had
just parted, " that is one of the wittiest men I have
ever met, and I have met many witty men in my lifetime." Ainger, one of the most genial of hosts, who
had seen his guest as far as he could, came back
and delightedly told Mahaffy of this *dictum* of the
author of " The Biglow Papers."

" Ah, poor fellow," said Mahaffy, " Lowell, I see,
never met an Irishman before! "

I think it is this appreciation of whatever there
is of Irish in me, that has led to the many and warm
friendships I have had the happiness to experience in

meeting Americans. I delight in American methods I revel in their intellectual and physical activity, and I even rejoice in their accent, for have I not a horrible one of my own!

One of the most delightful American men of letters I ever met, I have already mentioned, George Pellew. He visited Ireland in 1887, when I met him as already stated, at Whitehall, Clondalkin, the residence at that time of Katharine Tynan. He was then engaged in compiling notes for his book on Ireland, a book to which I contributed by giving Pellew introductions to my cousin, Mr Richard Colles, J.P., who appeared in its pages as " A Kilkenny Manufacturer," and to Mr E. B. Ivatts, at that time Goods Manager of the Midland Great Western Railway. He also received letters of introduction from W. E. H. Lecky; the Marquis of Sligo; Lady O'Hagan; Mrs Penrose Fitzgerald; Sir Louis Mallet; Sir James Caird, and Sir George Young, to representative Unionists, and to representative Nationalists from the Hon. W. R. Grace of New York, John E. Ellis, M.P., Mrs Alice Stopford Green, widow of J. R. Green the historian, A. P. Graves and Charles E. Mallet of London. Thus he was enabled to hear both sides of the question, and certainly his book betrays no personal bias whatever, but rather the cool, critical conclusions of the true lawyer. He was a member of the Suffolk Bar, Massachusetts. The book ran into three or four editions.

Pellew was a fellow of infinite jest. I had one or

two postcards from him, while in Ireland, one of them commencing—

> " ' An infant crying in the night,
> An infant crying for the light '

of your countenance is at the Imperial Hotel," etc.

At the Imperial I found him one afternoon, and as we discussed " The Love Sonnets of Proteus " and the " Wanderings of Oisin," for both of which he expressed great admiration, I noticed Mahaffy pass by. " There," said I, " goes the Decay of Modern Preaching," referring thereby to Professor Mahaffy's latest book. Pellew could not pronounce the letter " R," and his speech was the most un-American in accent I ever heard, being soft and liquid in tone. He replied: " Pweaching is a quaint thing. I heard a parson in the west pweach. He got into a high pulpit and this is something like what he said: ' Satan, my bwethwen, would be wevvy glad to-mowwow if Michael or Gabwiel were to come to him and say—God will forgive you if you shed one little tear—and Satan, my bwethwen, would weep, and his tears would become a little twickling will, and that will would become a wivver, and that wivver would become an ocean, and the billows of that ocean would flow up to the thwone of God, and God would say—Satan, I forgive you! ' "

These absurdities are quite possible. I remember when I came to London in 1902 hearing a preacher in St. Clements Dane say the following bit of bathos from the pulpit. He was holding forth on the miraculous draught of fishes. First he told how

Christ said " Cast in on the right side of the boat,"
and then he asked his congregation " Why, my
brethren, did our Lord say ' Cast in on the right side
of the boat '? " Of course a discreet silence followed
this important query, which the preaching-man, to
use Browning's phrase (a phrase which students of
Browning will remember is followed by the words,
" intense stupidity "), repeated. Again solemn silence,
followed by a triumphant thump on the pulpit cushion
and the announcement, as if clenching the argument,
" Because, my brethren, it *was* the *right* side of the
boat! "

George Pellew's full name was William Henry
Edward George Pellew. He was the eldest son
of Henry E. Pellew of Katonah, New York, who is
a cousin of Viscount Exmouth, a title bestowed on
Admiral Pellew for his successful attack on the Bey
of Algiers in 1816. Walter Savage Landor in his
" Dry Sticks Fagotted " included a poem in which
are associated the names Blake, Collingwood, and
Pellew. George Pellew's great-grand-uncle was
Henry Addington, Viscount Sidmouth, at one time
Prime Minister of England. On his maternal side
he was no less distinguished, his great grandfather
being John Jay, Chief Justice of the United States,
of whom he wrote the life as a contribution to the
" American Statesmen " series.

Pellew was born in 1859, he graduated at Harvard
in 1880, and three years later took his degree at the
Harvard Law School, and was admitted to
the Suffolk Bar, being admitted five years later to the

Some American Men of Letters

New York Bar. When in College he was Editor of the "Advocate," and wrote the Pudding Poem and his class ode. The Pudding Club Poem contained some memorable lines, notably the following which I have preserved in my memory—

> " Full of infinite suggestions,
>   In the mind that ever questions,
>   For a nobler faith inspires it
>   When the questioning is done."

When, after extensive wanderings through Ireland, he returned to America, Pellew wrote frequently to me. His letters were chiefly about literature and to him I owe any knowledge I possess of Thomas Sergeant Perry, Edgar Saltus, Edgar Fawcett, Richard Hovey, and other American writers. His own contribution to criticism was a monograph on Jane Austen. He also wrote an able pamphlet on "Woman and the Commonwealth, or a Question of Expediency." A volume of his poems with an introduction by W. D. Howells was published after his death, which took place very suddenly in 1892, and was due to an accident. Thus I lost a friend who to this day is constantly in my thoughts, and for whom my regret can never die.

In one of Pellew's letters to me he quoted the following verses by Edgar Fawcett, entitled, " Dei Gratia "—

> The height of his dead father's throne he gained,
>   With servile courtiers cringing at his nod;
> A shallow and beardless boy thenceforth he reigned,
>   By the grace of God.

In Castle and Court House

And oft, when following some rash whim of rule,
   O'er laws and liberties he rode rough-shod,
And proved a reprobate no less than fool,
   By the grace of God.
For years the crown did he thus coarsely keep,
   Wearing its grandeur like a dolt or clod,
Then died one even in a drunken sleep,
   By the grace of God.

Later I got some poems from Fawcett, and bought, when in Germany, at Leipsig Railway Station some of his novels in the Tauchnitz edition. They did not strike me as being very forcible.

Another American, a man of letters with whom I have had the pleasure of a long correspondence, is Mr Thomas Sergeant Perry, author of " From Opitz to Lessing: A Study in Neo-Classicism "; " The Evolution of the Snob "; " English Literature in the Eighteenth Century "; and " A History of Greek Literature." Mr Perry lately sent me his monograph on John Fiske.

A propos of John Fiske, I met at Professor Dowden's in Dublin a namesake, Mr John Fiske, who wrote " The Dog in British Poetry," published by my friend the late Alfred Nutt, whose tragic death in Paris when attempting to save his son from drowning, created a serious gap in the ranks of Celtic scholars.

To return to Mr Perry, we have in him a great grandson of Benjamin Franklin. He is a great believer in realism in literature, and in the application of scientific methods in criticism. He was, until lately, Professor of English literature in Tokio

University. Latterly he has taken to the study of Russian, and delights in reading Gogol, Dostoieffsky, Lermentoff, and Tolstoy, in that difficult language. His wife, Lillah Cabot Perry, is the author of " The Heart of the Weed," which I have already quoted, and of a charming verse translation of the Greek Anthology, published under the title of " From the Garden of Hellas." The late William Sharp, no mean judge of poetry, included the following sonnet by Mrs Perry in his collection of " American Sonnets "—

To One Despondent

Sometimes you doubt my love, and sad tears rise
    To eyes like shady pools, grown dark and clear
    With wistful questioning if I hold you dear,
And thus my answering smile to you replies.
We breathe to live—yet 'neath these summer skies,
    Though we scarce feel our breathing, do not fear
    That life has ceased, or long for winter drear
To show each snowy breath that heavenward flies.

And though I laugh while others sing your praise,
    If the world scorn and hold you in despite,
Then shall you more rejoice than you have grieved,
Seeing love greater far than you believed,
    As first we see the eternal stars' bright rays
    When creeps the dark imponderable night.

Mrs Perry, in addition to being a deft " weaver of the sonnet," and possessed of an exquisite lyrical gift, is also an artist of the impressionist school, and has studied under some of the greatest masters in Europe.

In Castle and Court House

There are poets and poets.   When living in
Dublin I illustrated one of my own jokes by using
a sketch by Du Maurier!   The artist himself had
used it to illustrate the following—

SHE.—" But I am married now."
HE.—" Too late for congratulations? "

The base use to which I put an admirable sketch
was as follows—

AT A LITERARY GATHERING.

Enthusiastic Lady.—" But you must admit that our
President has a poetic vein."

Indifferent Lover of Prose.—" Well, if he has, it's a
varicaux vein "!

There are not many instances of poet wedded to
poetess.   The Brownings are, of course, the great
example, but another instance of note is that of the
Elizabeth Barrett Browning of America, Mrs Sarah
B. Piatt, the writer of some exquisite verse, and
whose husband, Mr John James Piatt is the author
of " A Dream of Church Windows," and other poems
highly praised by J. Russell Lowell, and Longfellow.
I had the pleasure of meeting both Mr and Mrs
Piatt when the former was U.S. Consul in Dublin.
He had previously held the same position in Cork.
Here is a fine sonnet by Mr Piatt, and with it I
close this chapter—

ABRAHAM LINCOLN.

Stern be the pilot in the dreadful hour
  When a great nation, like a ship at sea
  With the wrath breakers whitening at her lee,
Feels her last shudder if her Helmsman cower;

232

Some American Men of Letters

A godlike manhood be his mighty dower!
  Such and so gifted, Lincoln, mayst thou be,
  With thy high wisdom's low simplicity
And awful tenderness of voted power.
For our hot records then thy name shall stand
  On Time's calm ledger out of passionate days—
    With the pure debt of gratitude begun,
  And only paid in never-ending praise—
One of the many of a mighty Land,
    Made by God's providence the Anointed One.

CHAPTER XXV

MORE AMERICAN MEN OF LETTERS

Richard Hovey—His "Launcelot and Guenevere"—
His Lyrics — A Presentation Volume — Arthur
McMorrough Kavanagh — John Burroughs — His
Prose Poems on Nature—Jonathan Heard, Jr.—
Hermann Schaffeur—Lady Cooke—Edgar Fawcett—
Fred Lake—W. B. Yeats and A. C. Swinburne at
fault!—Paul Fleury Mottelay—His Translations.

ONE of the ablest and most promising of young
American poets was the late Richard Hovey who,
alas! died early. In the words of William Watson
relative to the early death of Keats—

" The Gods, alas! gave him their fatal love."

It is to Thomas Sergeant Perry I owe my friendship for Richard Hovey, who many years ago sent
me his beautiful elegy on the death of Thomas W.
Parsons, entitled " Seaward," which is one of the
very finest threnodies in the language. The poem
is, unfortunately, out of print.

Hovey next sent me his " Launcelot and
Guenevere," a poem in dramas, the first portion of
which was published in one volume, entitled " The
Marriage of Guenevere," followed by four other
volumes, of which the subjects are " The Quest of
Merlin: A Masque "; " The Birth of Galahad: A

Romantic Drama"; "Taliesin: A Masque"; and
a posthumous volume "The Holy Graal and Other
Fragments," edited with Introduction and Notes by
Mrs Richard Hovey, and a Preface by Bliss Carman.

The difference between Hovey's conception of
Guenevere and those of his predecessors in song, is
shown by Mrs Hovey; she says: "Our time has
given us three Gueneveres: the Guenevere of
Tennyson, who sinned and came to repentance and
remorse; the Guenevere of Morris, who appeals to
the tenderness of the human heart, who explains and
asks human sympathies; and the Guenevere of
Hovey, who only loves, who never sins, who never
repents. The truly tragic Guenevere is the one
Richard Hovey chose for the Poem in Dramas—a
woman who typifies in her sorrows womanhood at
the point in civilisation where the might of a system
—presses heaviest upon woman; and especially on
the type of woman furthest developed in emotional
and intellectual power. The broadest physical and
intellectual base is the preparation for the highest
spiritual flight into the realms of love, the miracle
love that involves those wonder realms in which it
may be hoped Galahads may be born."

The lyrics which this beautiful poem in dramas
contains can best be judged by the following:

> You remind me, sweeting,
>   Of the glow,
> Warm and pure and fleeting—
> Blush of apple-blossoms—
> On cloud bosoms,
>   When the sun is low.

In Castle and Court House

Like a golden apple
  'Mid the far
Topmost leaves that dapple
Stretch of summer blue—
There are you,
  Sky-set like a star.

Fearful lest I bruise you,
  How should I
Dare to reach you, choose you,
Stain you with my touch?
It is much
  That you star the sky.

Why should I be climbing,
  So to seize
All that sets me rhyming—
In my hand enfold
All the gold
  Of Hesperides?

I would not enfold you
  If I might;
I would just behold you,
Sigh, and turn away,
While the day
  Darkens into night.

Hovey frequently wrote to me, delightful letters, and sent me amongst other books, a copy of " Songs from Vagabondia," written by him in conjunction with another true poet, Bliss Carman. This little book, published by Mr John Lane of The Bodley Head, was inscribed—

" To Ramsay Colles,—from Richard Hovey."
             " London, 2nd November, 1894."

More American Men of Letters

and a quotation from one of his poems—

> Here's a health to thee, Colles,
> And here's a health to me;
> And here's to all the pretty girls
> From Denver to the sea!

Readers of Dr Joyce's " History of Ireland," a
fascinating book, by the way, will remember the
story of the King of Leinster, McMurrough
Kavanagh, from whom the late Arthur Kavanagh
of Carlow, for some time M.P. claimed descent.
Kavanagh was a man of genius. Nature had cruelly
deprived him of both arms and legs, but he
nevertheless, followed the hounds, and wrote a capital
clear hand as more than one of his letters to me
proved. Here are Hovey's lines on the kindly, and
let me add, kingly spirit of McMorrough Kavanagh,
whose life story has been published, and is well worth
reading if only as a proof of how mind can triumph
over matter.

> A stone jug and a pewter mug,
> And a table set for three!
> A jug and a mug at every place,
> And a biscuit or two with Brie!
> Three stone jugs of Cruiskeen Lawn,
> And a cheese like crusted foam!
> The Kavanagh receives to-night!
> McMorrough is at home!
>
> Throw ope the window to the stars
> And let the warm night in!
> Who knows what revelry in Mars
> May rhyme with rouse akin?

In Castle and Court House

Fill up and drain the loving-cup,
  And leave no drop to waste!
The moon looks in to see what's up—
  Begad, she'd like a taste!

What odds if Leinster's kingly roll
  Be now an idle thing?
The world is his who takes his toll,
  A vagrant or a king.
What though the crown be melted down,
  And the heir a gipsy roam?
The Kavanagh receives to-night!
  McMurrough is at home!

We three and the barley-bree!
  And the moonlight on the floor!
Who were a man to do with less?
  What emperor has more?
Three stone jugs of Cruiskeen Lawn,
  And three stout hearts to drain,
A slanter to the truth in the heart of youth,
  And the joy of the love of men.

Many a pleasant letter was interchanged and many
a quip and jest, for I sent Hovey impromptus on
postcards, of which I inflict but one on my indulgent
reader—

    If you were the King of Diamonds
      And I were the Knave of Clubs,
      We'd have many convivial rubs,
      And knocking about in pubs.,
      But I'm hanged if I'd stand any snubs
    If you were the King of Diamonds
      And I were the Knave of Clubs.

Hovey, genial soul, wrote "this clamours to be
finished," and added much more to the same effect,

238

sending me at the same time a walking-stick surrounded by leathern thongs interlaced. I acknowledged the gift, sending him the following—

> If you were the top o' the morning,
>   And I were the dead o' night,
> Together we'd study the weather,
> And always be in high feather—
> We'd sing, " Oh, there's nothing like leather "—
> If you were the top o' the morning,
>   And I were the dead 'o night!

Hovey wrote to me saying he was about to be married, and I was, therefore, not surprised when I did not hear from him for some time. I knew he was wandering about and kept silence for at least twelve months or more. Then I wrote to him, care of Mr John Lane, his publisher. My letter was returned to me unopened, and bore on the envelope the single and significant word " Dead."

Other American men of letters with whom I corresponded were John Burroughs, whose Nature studies are a source of perpetual delight; " Birds and Poets "; " Winter Sunshine "; " Wake Robin "; and a " Study of Walt Whitman," which is one of the best books on the Good Gray Poet ever published; and Jonathan Heard, Jr., who under the title of " The Odd Number," translated thirteen short stories from Guy de Maupassant. Quite recently I met Herman Schaffeur at an " At Home " given by Lady Cooke (Tenessee Clafflin) at the Lyceum Club in Piccadilly. This young poet hails from San Francisco. He drew me on the subject of Tennyson, Browning, Arnold, Rossetti, and others, my contemporaries, and listened with evident interest until I rose to depart, when he exclaimed, as he held my hand, " I've had a splendid afternoon! I seem to have been listening to a voice from the Past!" I bear no ill-will to this young man. His voice, when it becomes one of the past, will, I feel sure, be more potent than mine could possibly be, but as Oliver Wendell Holmes remarked, " How we love the man who is the first in public to refer to us as ' the venerable ' so-and-so! "

Returning for a moment to Edgar Fawcett, we all know Browning's " Flower Fancies "; I used to think, and indeed think now, that Fawcett's " conceit " about the toad among the lilies was quaint and clever. He likens the toad squat among the lilies to—

> Thick-lipped slaves of ebon skin
> Who guard the drowsy ladies in
> The dim seraglios.

A propos of Browning. He declared on one occasion, "I only met one poet in my life." My own experience has been that poets are as plentiful as potatoes.

Few men in their hours of expansion—I don't mean when they are suffering from swelled head—will deny that they have at one time or another indulged in verse making. One such I met who in broad daylight announced to me that he claimed to be a poet! I was at the moment, in the expressive

words of Mr George Graves "pirouetting towards
the pewter," and having on the same authority
"dipped my beak in the foaming fourpenny," I
talked somewhat audibly, I fancy, to my companion
about one Fred Lake a descendant of Sir
Launcelot du Lake, or as I fear I somewhat
flippantly described him, " Guenevere's Mash." Judge
my astonishment when there arose at my elbow a
man such as I deem to be a familiar figure on a race-
course (I never was on one in my life). He turned
to me and said, " I'm a pote, guvernor."

I said, " I'm sorry to hear it."

He said, " This is the sort of stuff I write—

' You should always keep yer hosses on the go,
You should always keep yer hosses on the go;
    The sure and steady pace,
    It's that as wins the race;
You should always keep yer hosses on the go! ' "

My companion maintained that this was much
better and had certainly more sense than some of
Yeats or Swinburne. " Yeats," he said, " wrote—

' She brings in the dishes and she lays them in a row;
With her to an isle in the water I would go.' "

" Now," said he, " why did she lay the dishes in
a row instead of one on top of another? Simply
because the poet must find a rhyme to 'go.' And
where on earth," he added, " should an isle be but
in the water? " I murmured something about Shorts

being on an *island* in the Strand, but he treated the remark with the contempt it deserved. " Then," said he, " take Swinburne's—

> Before the beginning of years
>   There came to the making of man
> Time with a gift of tears,
>   Grief with a glass that ran.
>
> .   .   .   .
>
> And the great gods took in hand
>   Fire and the falling of tears,
> And a measure of sliding sand
>   From under the feet of the years."

" How on earth can anyone ' before the beginning of years '—' take a measure of sliding sand ' or anything else from under their feet? "

This conundrum I was unable to solve!

I will include in this chapter a verse of my own. Every student of English literature knows Landor's divine lines on Lady Godiva, written when he was a very young man—

> In every hour, in every mood,
> O Lady, it is sweet and good
>   To bathe the soul in prayer;
> And, at the close of such a day,
> When we have ceased to bless and pray,
>   To dream of thy long hair.

Hair was a favourite subject with Landor. He would have agreed with Pope that—

> Beauty draws us with a single hair.

More American Men of Letters

But we must first catch our hair! Landor wrote "on seeing a hair of Lucretia Borgia"—

> Borgia, thou once wert almost too august
> And high for adoration; now thou'rt dust.
> All that remains of thee these plaits unfold—
> Calm hair, meandering in pellucid gold.

Like the tortoise, which having no hair of its own has by the irony of Fate its shell utilised to make combs, I take a great interest in human hair and agree with St. Paul on this particular subject if on no other, when therefore I was asked by a lady at a gathering of poets, if I, too, were a poet, I replied, "yes." She then asked "Can you write a poem about me?" "Certainly," I replied, and scribbled on the back of the menu—

> Alas, she had a niggard heart
> Who in your hair those hairpins placed;
> Had I such wealth—nay, do not start—
> I'd let it run to waist!

I must conclude this account of my American friends by referring to my most recent acquisition in this respect, that gifted translator Paul Fleury Mottelay whose friendship I acquired through the good services of R. W. Brother James Ruddock, a gifted musician and one who is not alone a source of music in himself but also in that of others. Mr Mottelay's literary labours include the accepted translation of Gilbert of Colchester's great work, and an authoritative treatise entitled "The Bridge Blue Book."

CHAPTER XXVI

EDGAR SALTUS: PUBLICIST

Wainwright's Essays, edited by W. Carew Hazlitt—
Copies sent to W. D. Howells, Oscar Wilde, and
Edgar Saltus—G. P. Putnams' Sons—Greening &
Co.—Edgar Everston Saltus—Eduard von Hartmann
—Saltus the Chief Exponent of Pessimism in
America—The Greatest Character in Fiction—The
Inventor of Cloakrooms—Alphabet Jones—Saltus's
Novels—His Poems—William Sharp.

ONE of the American authors to whom I sent a copy
of " The Essays of Thomas Griffiths Wainwright,"
edited by W. Carew Hazlitt, was Edgar Saltus. I
have already said that my sending a copy to Oscar
Wilde led to Wilde's essay on " Pen, Palette, and
Poison," but though Mr W. D. Howells was much
impressed by the volume and wrote me a kindly
letter thanking me for it, the essays do not appear to
have made much impression on Mr Saltus.

Why Edgar Saltus as a writer is not more widely
known has been and remains a puzzle to me. Ever
since I read his " A Transaction in Hearts," which
I picked up in 1890, I have been deeply interested
in the man and his writings, and with considerable
difficulty I succeeded, thanks to the untiring efforts

244

of Messrs Putnams' Sons of New York, in procuring all his published writings, including some translations from the French.

With these volumes I have now long been familiar, and I feel sure that all who enjoy true artistic workmanship in a story cannot fail to be interested in them, as they can now, in many instances be procured in the excellent reprints of Messrs Greening & Co.

Edgar Everston Saltus was born in New York on 8th October, 1858. He is a descendant of Admiral Cornelius Everston, who as Commander of the Dutch Fleet, captured on 9th August, 1673, the City of New York. He was educated at Columbia College and Heidelberg University.

Saltus started his literary career as a philosopher, by no means a bad *rôle* for one who aims at being a searcher of human hearts and a penetrative revealer of their deepest secrets. His initial performance was "The Philosophy of Disenchantment," published in 1884, the work, no doubt, the result of his University career at Heidelberg, and the tone of which is, I believe, due in no small measure to personal contact with the late Eduard von Hartmann.

The volume, which consists of some 200 pages, octavo, presents in a simple and attractive style the teachings of Schopenhauer, of whose career an interesting sketch is given. Chapters are devoted to such subjects as " The Sphinx's Riddle "; " The Borderlands of Happiness "; " The Great Quietus "; and to such questions as " Is Life an Infliction? "

In Castle and Court House

To the truths enunciated by Schopenhauer as the High Priest of Pessimism is added a summary of the deductions of von Hartmann, to the personality and philosophy of whom a chapter is devoted.

As it is not to Saltus the philosopher, but to Saltus the story-teller I wish to refer, I shall merely mention the fact that " The Philosophy of Disenchantment " was followed in 1885 by a kindred work entitled " The Anatomy of Negation," in which is given a tableau of anti-theism from Kapila to Leconte de Lisle. This little book—in which there is no attempt made to prove anything—is a notable contribution to the literature of pessimism, and it ran to more than one edition.

Saltus' first work of fiction, " Mr Incoul's Misadventure," was published in 1886, and was referred to by William Sharp as full of brilliant talent. His " The Truth about Tristrem Varick," and " Eden " were also very remarkable novels. The latter contained such gems as—

" There is nothing more talkative than the foot of a pretty woman ";

" A woman who marries a second time does not deserve to have lost her first husband," and this beautiful simile—

" Eden sat very still, *surprised as February at a violet.*"

In " Tristrem Varick " Edgar Saltus wrote his most ambitious novel ; witness the following elaborate description of the heroine, Viola Raritan—

" She was dressed in a gown of canary, draped

with madeira and fluttered with lace. Her arms and neck were bare and unjewelled. Her hair was cimmerian, the black of basalt that knows no shade more dark, and it was arranged in such wise that it fell on either side of her forehead, circling a little space above the ear, and then wound into a coil on the neck. This arrangement was not modish, but it was becoming—the only arrangement, in fact, that would have befitted her features which resembled those of the Cleopatra unearthed by Lieutenant Gorringe. Her eyes were not oval, but round, and they were amber as those of leopards, the yellow of living gold. The corners of her mouth drooped a little, and the mouth itself was rather large than small. When she laughed one could see her tongue; it was like an inner cut of water melon, and sometimes when she was silent the point of it caressed her under lip. Her skin was of that quality which artificial light makes radiant, and yet of which the real delicacy is only apparent by day. She just lacked being tall, and in her face and about her bare arms and neck was the perfume of health. She moved indolently with a grace of her own. She was not twenty, a festival of beauty in the festival of life."

In this and other passages Saltus' mannerisms are markedly apparent, as when, for instance, he tells us that a girl's eyes " were not black, they were of that sultry blue which is observable in the ascension of tobacco smoke through a sunbeam," and again he says of the eyes of a young man that they " were of that green-grey which is caught in an icicle held over grass."

In Castle and Court House

The description of the opera in New York is so good that I quote it as a specimen of our author's method of making an inventory of human puppets:

"At the opera that night the aristocrats of the New World were in full force. Among them were men who could not alone have wedded the Adriatic, but have dowered her as well. Venice in her greatest splendour had never dreamed such wealth as theirs. There was Jabez Robinson, his wife and children, familiarly known as the Swiss Family Robinson, the founder of their dynasty having emigrated from some Helvetian vale. A lightning calculator might have passed a week in the summing up of their possessions. There was old Jerolomon, who, through the manipulation of the monopolies, exhaled an odour of Sing-Sing, the which had been so attractive to the nostrils of an English peer that he had taken his daughter as wife. There was Madden who controlled an entire State. There was Bucholz, who declared himself above the law, and who had erupted in New York three decades before with the seven deadly sins for sole capital. There was Bleecker Bleecker, who each year gave away a Pope's ransom to charity and pursued his debtors to the grave. There was Dunwoodie, whose coat smelled of benzine and whose signature was potent as a king's. There was Forbush, who lunched furtively on an apple and had given a private establishment to each of his twelve children. There was Gwathmeys, who had twice ruined himself for his enemies and made a fortune for his friends. There was Attersoll, who could have bought the White House, and whose sole pleasures were window-gardening and the accord of violins.

"On the grand-tier was Mrs Besalul, on whom society had shut her door because she had omitted to close her own. In an adjoining box was Mrs Smithwick, the bride of a month, fairer than any queen whose face was worth the world to kiss, and who, the previous winter, had written a novel of such impropriety that when it was published her mother forbade her to read it. There was Miss Pickett, a *débutante*, who possessed the disquieting ugliness of a monkey, who had announced that there was nothing so immoral as *ennui*. There was Mrs Bouvery, who claimed connection with everyone whose name began with Van. Mrs Hackensack, one of the few surviving Knickerbockers. The Coenties twins, known as Dry and Extra Mumm. And there were others less interesting. Mrs Pender, for instance, famous for her musicales, which no one could be bribed to attend. . . Mrs Nevers, mailed in diamonds; Mrs Goodloe, mailed in pearls, and a senator's wife in a bonnet."

Edgar Saltus' books are all enlivened by a very pretty wit indeed, as, for instance, when he declared, " Hell is supposed to be hot, but fancy it cold, and there cannot be a pin to choose between it and London in December." It was Saltus, I believe, who, when asked " Who is the greatest character in fiction? " replied, " God." He is fond of asserting that though there is a land where there is much joy over the sinner that repents; in this world we live in, the joy is at his detection!

Alphabet Jones, the novelist who saunters through several volumes, is an amusing if somewhat an adumbrative character. One of his conundrums is "Who invented cloakrooms?" The reply is "Potaphar's wife." It is Jones who makes the remark that "in ancient days women who lapsed from virtue were stoned," and adds, "for that matter they are still, but the stones are from Tiffani's."

"Tristrem Varick" is the most artistic of Edgar Saltus' novels, but "A Transaction in Hearts" is the most powerful study of human nature he has done so far. In this book he depicts the conflicting emotions which run riot in the breast of the Rev. Christopher Gonfallon, who falls in love with his wife's sister. Sympathy with his subject may seem strange in a professor of anatomy, but without genuine love for his profession no man can use the scalpel with supreme success. Saltus may be a vivisector, but he never "murders to dissect." He is the deft anatomist who lays bare the very source of life while he searches for the roots of the disease, the cure of which he would discover; but in all his operations his actions are marked by judgment and skill, and in the beneficial result of his labours the whole world shares and rejoices.

The story of "A Transaction in Hearts" is simple. When Gonfallon married Ruth, the elder daughter of Bucholz the monopolist, her sister Claire was but an undeveloped girl. She returns at the period dealt with, from a European trip extending over four years, and little by little her beauty and waywardness infatuate the susceptible rector, her brother-in-law, whose wife is permanently on the sick-list, a victim to neuralgia.

The mental tortures endured by Gonfallon, the spiritual struggles, the gradual sapping of the foundations of his moral nature, are depicted with marvellous skill, and though pages are devoted to the exposition, there is not a sentence which any save the most vacuous readers would willingly skip.

The picture of the enchantress is drawn in a few strokes.

" She was worse than pretty. In her skin was the hue of that white rose which has a sulphur heart. Her features had the surety of an intaglio ; her head was small, the brow low ; in her hair, which was short and curled, was the glisten of gold-leaf shown to the sun. Her eyes were of porcelain blue, the under lids retreating and shorter than the upper."

That such a physically doll-like creature should act a heroic part appears almost incredible ; but the novelist in relating the tale leaves no doubt in the mind of his reader that Claire acts in a thoroughly natural manner, and convincingly proves once more that in the most unpromising natures lurk great possibilities, a fact which the more superficial student of humanity is apt to overlook. Claire compromises herself in order to save the reputation of her father.

Saltus has written many other books some of which have not been reprinted in England, notably a collection of short stories in which one entitled " A Transient Guest " is worthy of Maupassant, and " Love and Lore," a volume of delightful essays, with interludes in verse of the excellence of which the following may serve as an illustration—

IMEROS.

My heart a haunted manor is, where Time
  Has fumbled noiselessly with mouldering hands:
  At sunset ghosts troop out in sudden bands,
'At noon 'tis vacant as a house of crime;

But when, unseen as sound, the night-winds climb
  The higher keys with their unstilled demands,
  It wakes to memories of other lands,
'And thrills with echoes of enchanted rhyme.

Then, through the dreams and hopes of earlier years,
  A fall of phantom footsteps on the stair
    Approaches near, and ever nearer yet,
  A voice rings through my life's deserted ways;
  I turn to greet thee, Love. The empty air
    Holds but the spectre of my own regret.

In October, 1904, I wrote an article on Saltus in "The Westminster Review," in which I expressed the hope that the popular recognition, which is undoubtedly his due, should soon be accorded a writer of such marked individuality and literary ability, and this essay I sent to Mr Saltus, who wrote me a pleasant letter in acknowledgment signed " Yours attentively." It is pleasant to learn that he is now frequently in London, and is a naturalised Englishman to the extent that he is a member of The Authors' Club.

Edgar Saltus : Publicist

Messrs Greening have issued a little volume entitled " The Wit and Wisdom of Edgar Saltus," by G. F. Monkshood and George Gamble, which is a very representative collection of epigrams by Saltus.

CHAPTER XXVII

A CHAPTER OF ACCIDENTS

Ignorance of Ireland and the Irish—The Irish Jarvey—
Lord Annaly and the Peerage—Tobacco and the
Toad—White Horse Whisky—" Alive with Dead
Dogs "—" Same Bill-Sticker? "—J. Sheridan Le
Fanu—" Well, Molly, did he pop? "—Greenleaf
Withers Brown—Silver Hairs *v.* Gold—A Perfectly
Beautiful Mummy—Plât Deutsch.

I HAVE always maintained that if one knows all the
rest of the world but is ignorant of Ireland and the
Irish, there is then something one does not know,
whereas if one is acquainted with Ireland that fact
helps one to understand the rest of the world!

Ireland has never suffered from " that dull stagna-
tion of the soul-content." Even Walter Savage
Landor, who warmly espoused her cause, winning
thereby the gratitude of both O'Connell and Davis,
is ironical on this subject :—

> Ireland never was contented—
> Say you so? You are demented.
> Ireland was contented when
> All could use the sword and pen,
> And when Tara rose so high
> That her turrets split the sky,
> And about her courts were seen
> Liveried Angels robed in green,
> Wearing, by Saint Patrick's bounty,
> Emeralds big as half a county.

A Chapter of Accidents

Charles Lever and Samuel Lover were largely to blame for the general acceptance of the Irishman as a buffoon. This has led to Irishmen accepting this verdict, and too often the sorry spectacle is witnessed, of a truly intellectual representative of a thoughtful, artistic, and imaginative race, devoting his energies to humouring fools until he is despised by the very fools whom he humours.

Let us hope that in the near future such wilfully mis-drawn figures as Handy Andy and Harry Lorriquer will no longer be accepted as faithful portraits of the average son of Erin.

To this very desirable end the "Bogland Sketches," and other studies by Miss Jane Barlow will help not a little. Miss Barlow is one of the most modest of writers and her work in prose and verse is but too little known. A natural outcome of the Barrie school of fiction, she is, nevertheless, original, and her work is by no means confined to fiction, for she has translated with marvellous force and fidelity the "Battle of the Frogs and Mice," from Homer, in which task she has but one rival— George Chapman.

The Irish jarvey is responsible for many of the erroneous ideas about Ireland, entertained by Englishmen or Americans who have visited the country. Seated on either side of an "outside car," in close proximity to the driver, the tourist very naturally falls into conversation with him, asks questions and seeks information, and as Jehu is loath to be considered ignorant on any subject, he often makes statements which are wide of the truth.

255

In Castle and Court House

But whether the information given be truthful or not, it is always tinged with humour, of which the following may be taken as an example:

A callow youth, having successfully qualified at one of the great military schools in England, is sent to Richmond Barracks, Dublin, to commence his career as a soldier. On arriving at, say, the North Wall, he takes an outside car and directs the driver to the barracks.

"Richmond Barracks, all right, Captain," says the jarvey, as he starts on a trip for which the legal fare is sixpence, but for which a shilling is usually tendered.

"What is the fare?" asks the "Captain."

"Well, Colonel," says the driver again, in a tone of voice which precludes the idea of any attitude save that of profound respect for the exalted person he is driving, "the meanest of thim gives me half-a-crown."

But the Irish are by no means a subservient race. The late Professor J. W. Corbett, a member of the Senate of T.C.D., and father of the Rev. F. St. John Corbett, M.A., rector of St. George-in-the-East, once told me an amusing story, which is as follows:

Dr Corbett called with Lord Annaly to see Sir Patrick Joseph Keenan, Chief Commissioner for National Education in Ireland. The flunkey in a scarlet waistcoat of portly proportions on being asked if Sir Patrick were in or not, said:

"I'll see. What name shall I say?"

A Chapter of Accidents

Dr Corbett replied, " Just say Lord Annaly wishes to see him."

The hall porter disappeared upstairs, and kept the enquirers for Sir Patrick waiting at least twenty minutes. On his return he delivered himself as follows:

" Sir Patrick is not in, but *I* see no ' Lord Annaly ' in the Peerage! "

Travelling on one occasion from Dublin to Kilkenny, I was in a smoking compartment on the Great Southern and Western Railway. The only other person in the carriage was a gentleman who was smoking a pipe with evident satisfaction, but which to my olfactory nerves held tobacco of a particularly disgusting aroma. Not having any tobacco myself with which to overcome this truly appalling smell, I opened the window, but as the weather was very cold, was obliged to shut it very soon. It then struck me that good-humoured remonstrance might prevail and abate the nuisance, so I said in a conciliatory tone:

" Pardon me, sir, but really your tobacco would poison a toad."

Without moving a facial muscle the smoker removed his pipe and replied " Evidently! " He then offered me with a smile one of the best cigars I ever smoked.

On another occasion, when travelling from Dublin to Belfast, during severe and gloomy weather, I said to a fellow-traveller who had been, like myself, listening to the pattering of the rain which, as my

friend William Wilkins, the author of " Songs of
Study" says in his celebrated contribution to
" Kottabos," " fell on the pane like a pile of fetters."

" Sir, although you are a stranger to me, would
you feel insulted if I offered you a glass of Scotch
whisky?" pulling out, as I put my query, a bottle
of White Horse from my handbag.

Lightly tapping with his forefinger the familiar
white horse with its flowing tail, he said, with
emphasis:

" My dear sir, it would take *gallons* of *that*
whisky to insult me!"

The drawer of the long-bow, or the tall-tale man
is not unknown in Ireland. Here is a specimen.

" Yes, sir, my friend when skating was caught by
a truant balloon, and, would you believe it, one of
his skates fell off and killed a retriever, and later the
other also fell off and killed a poodle!"

" Is that so?" I asked.

" Yes, and if my friend had had as many feet as a
centipede and skates on each foot, the whole country-
side would have been *alive* with *dead* dogs!"

Another strange specimen of Irish humour consists of the following:

In the City and County Conservative Club in
Dublin was a member who was occasionally intoxi-
cated with something stronger than the " exuberance
of his own verbosity." He was a well-known man
and some fellow member of the club usually saw him
home on such occasions.

The night following one of these episodes, someone inquired, " Did anyone see A—— home last night ? "

" I did," replied a recently elected member, whereupon an old member asked :

" Did he tell you his father was a bill-sticker?"

" Well, strange to say, he did refer to the fact."

" What of that," said another member of the company, " the late Lord Mayor's father was also a bill-sticker."

" Yes," added a third, " and the father of Bartholomew Buggins, the baritone, was a bill-sticker! "

Silence for a second, when the Hon. Secretary asks, in mild surprise :

" *Same* Bill Sticker? "

This kind of humour was well displayed by Joseph Sheridan Le Fanu, the author of " Uncle Silas." Le Fanu as a boy was always late for family prayers. Coming into the room one morning, late as usual, his father cried, holding out his watch as he spoke, " Joseph, Joseph, can this be right? " " No, sir," replied Joseph, " I'm sure you're fast."

My uncle, the Rev. Thomas Garde of Cloyne, Co Cork, was fond of telling an experience of his in the days when he was a pale young curate. He was paying his addresses to a young lady who resided in a rural district not far from Blarney. As her mother did not think the curate pursued his wooing with celerity, she, in order to bring matters to a crisis, left the young couple alone in the drawing-room, while she proceeded to a floor above.

In Castle and Court House

The curate was shy and diffident, and after some small-talk on nothing in particular, he bade the girl farewell, and went downstairs, unaccompanied, to the entrance hall. Here he was engaged in putting on his gloves, prior to making his exit, when he overheard the following conversation between mother and daughter, the former speaking loudly from the upper floor to her daughter on the lower:

"Well, Molly, did he pop?" To which the girl replied:

"Oh, the divil a pop!"

Whereupon the mother exclaimed, "Oh, the mane baste!"

A propos of clergymen, I used, when living in Dublin, to delight in attending the services at the little church in Lower Leeson Street, whenever the Rev. F. F. Carmichael, D.D. preached the sermon. Canon Carmichael is an eloquent preacher, but his expressions are sometimes unconventional as, for instance, when he, on one occasion declared that the Patriarch Isaac was "a hen-pecked man," and on another when from the pulpit he recommended the congregation to take seats in the gallery of the church, and glancing round, said in convincing tones, "There are several very respectable people rent seats in the gallery," whereupon being seated in the gallery I seized the opportunity to rise and bow towards the pulpit.

One of the many attractions of Dublin used to be the Pantomimes written in couplets by Greenleaf Withers Brown. Some of these couplets in which

A Chapter of Accidents

I used to take special delight, occur in "Cinderella," when the Fairy Godmother, visiting her little charge, says—

You've got a cold, my Jewel—
Drink a warm bath and put your feet in gruel!

In another Pantomime, I think "The Yellow Dwarf," the King exclaims—

My plates are dished, my dishes only plated,
My very gates with bills are variegated,

and adds—

My little *pages* have to take their *leaves!*

There was also a double play on words in—

I am *well on* in days
And badly *off* for knights.

I had a curious experience at Killarney once. There was a large party staying at the hotel there one evening in early spring. I did not know any one of the company, but after dinner there was a concert given in the entrance hall and I found myself discussing music with a young lady with a face like a beautiful rose and with a wealth of pure white hair like snow on a dish of strawberries. For the moment I forgot that she was young and was foolish enough to inquire if she remembered Decca the American cantatrice.

"No," she replied, and added, "do not think I am old because my hair is white."

Recognising the mistake I had made, I at once apologised by saying, "I can assure you that one of your *silver* hairs is worth all the *gold* ones in the world!"

She smiled. ("Her bright smile haunts me still.")

"That is such a pretty speech," she said, "that I wish you would write it down for me."

I had no paper in my pocket so wrote the declaration on the back of my visiting card and was rewarded by her putting it safely into the bosom of her evening dress.

Next morning as I repaired to the drive in front of the hotel to mount a hired steed for a morning ride, I found a second horse which had just been mounted by a somewhat gloomy but handsome man.

We rode side by side in silence for some time, when I ventured to remark:

"Allow me to introduce myself. My name is Colles."

"Ah," he said, pulling up suddenly, "so you're the d——d scoundrel whose card I found on my wife's dressing table when I arrived late last night."

"Calm yourself," I replied. "Surely a simple statement of facts is not wrong?"

"Compliments like that you paid to a married woman are not right," he said, wrathfully. "Don't let me catch you doing it again!"

"There was no compliment meant," I said.

"What!" he exclaimed; "No compliment! What do you mean?"

"Only that I take no interest save in brunettes," I replied.

"Oh, you d——d Irishmen!" he shouted, as he put his horse to a gallop, "you'd wriggle out of anything!"

A Chapter of Accidents

I let him ride ahead and ride his ill-humour off. When he returned he invited me to breakfast, and we have been the best of friends ever since. He is not now averse to his wife being complimented, for he understands how frothy my compliments are.

A few months after his last son was born, we went in a small party to the British Museum, and visited the Egyptian galleries. His wife was looking radiant, and I inquired affectionately about the latest arrival. One of the party came up, and addressing her while he pointed to a mummy case, asked:

" Is not that a perfectly lovely mummy? "

I replied, as I patted her shoulder, " Not in it, my boy, with this ' perfectly lovely *Mummy!* ' "

This time, being an old friend, her husband merely remarked, " I agree with you."

At the risk of chronicling small-beer, I may give the following to conclude this chapter.

My friend Max Deutsch, President of the Francis Joseph Institute for the relief of suffering Austrians and Hungarians, is the proud possessor of two hand-some Blenheim spaniels. These dogs are allowed after supper to sit on chairs on either side of Mrs Deutsch and have plates laid before them which, when filled with their suppers are taken elsewhere and the dogs follow.

On one occasion these intelligent creatures spent their time in alternately gazing at the empty plates in front of them and into their mistress' face, to learn why their supper was delayed.

"One would almost think they could speak," someone remarked.

"What language would they speak, if they did?" I inquired. "Not Dog Latin."

As no one guessed I answered my own question —"*Plât* Deutsch!"

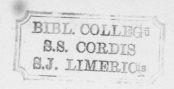
CHAPTER XXVIII

THE FAMILY OF COLLES IN IRELAND

The Colles Family in Worcester — William Colles,
Secretary to Sir Henry Harrington—Sir Roger
Purefoy—Job Colles serves under Gustavus
Adolphus, King of Sweden—Is wounded at the Battle
of Leipzic, 1631—Is presented by the King with a
Silver-handled Sword on the Field of Battle—The
Fate of the Sword—William Colles (1702-1770), the
Inventor of Machinery for Boring and Polishing
Marble—The Marble Works in Kilkenny in 1748—
Pococke's " Tour in Ireland in 1752 "—Barry Colles
(1697-1785)—Susan Colles and The Meredyth Family
—Sir Joshua Colles Meredyth, Bt.—The Cabman
Claimant to the Title—Charles Colles of Maghera-
more—His Funeral Entry—Richard Colles of Gyah,
Bengal, India — His Invention — Major-General
William Ramsay—The Maha-Bodhi Society.

In a book that is frankly egotistical and cannot, of
necessity, be otherwise, some facts in connection
with the family of Colles may be of interest.

The family of Colles, of Co Worcester (13th
Century), and other counties in England appears
to have been connected with Ireland since the year
1600, or the end of the reign of Queen Elizabeth.

William Colles, born in 1585, went to Ireland
with Sir Henry Harrington, Knight, Seneschal of

O'Byrne's country. Sir Henry, who was a brother of John, first Lord Harrington of Exton, had grants of land in Counties Kildare, Wexford, and Westmeath. He returned to England, engaged his uncle, Sir Roger Purefoy, eight Gentlemen, and twenty yeomen, of Coleshill (or Colles-hill) and Caldecote, Co Warwick, and Drayton Co Leicester, to follow him and settle in Ireland.

William's son, Job Colles, went to Sweden with Sir Frederick Hamilton, father of the first Viscount Boyne, and served under Gustavus Adolphus, King of Sweden. He was wounded at the battle of Leipzic, 1631, and was presented by the King on the field of battle with a silver-handled sword. This sword his great-grand-nephew, William, to whom it descended, " having a great value for the said sword as a relic, and wishing to preserve it in some more ostensible shape than as an unfashionable and useless implement, had its hilt worked into a pair of shoe buckles, with a wrought inscription in very indifferent verse on them (for he was a poet and wrote several tragedies), which being in a ruinous state, his son Richard had again in London in 1812 fashioned into a snuff-box."

Of this William Colles, who was born in 1702, and died in 1770, it has been recorded that " he was a man of great mechanical abilities and abounding in a variety of those eccentric schemes which mark original genius, though success only, in the eyes of the world can stamp them with rationality, one of which was an attempt to make dogs weave linen by

WILLIAM COLLES OF KILKENNY
Surgeon (b. 1648, d. 1719)

WILLIAM COLLES OF ABBEYVALE, CO. KILKENNY
(1702-1770)

turning wheels; another, the supplying the Corporation of Dublin with bored marble tubes, as pipes for distributing water through the city, was defeated only by a combination of pump-borers and other mechanics, who rose in a mob and destroyed them on their arrival. Such was the impression his abilities made on the common people, that to this day his feats are proverbial among them, and they speak of him as a necromancer."

William Colles was the inventor of the machinery used for boring and polishing marble. He first tried a model in a small stream, and finding it succeed, he took a perpetual lease of the marble quarry in Kilkenny. "While he amused the populace," says the writer of some " Statistical Observations Relative to the County of Kilkenny, made in the years 1800 and 1801," " by various devices, such as that of a musical instrument which played by itself, as it floated down the stream of the river, and many others, he applied himself to the construction of useful machinery for different purposes; and invented a water-mill, and an engine for dressing flax, simple and efficacious, but now no longer used."

William Colles applied his marble to the construction of a vast variety of articles. There was in Kilkenny a room lined with it by him, in imitation of wainscot; and he used it instead of leaden pipes in one or two houses. In "A Tour in Ireland, by two Englishmen," a book published in 1748, it is stated " near the mill are apartments called warehouses, where you may see such a diversity of chimney-pieces, cisterns, buffets, vases, punch-bowls, mugs of different dimensions, frames for looking-glasses, pictures, etc., that they would employ the eye the longest day, and yet find something to admire," and much to the same effect will be found in " Pococke's Tour in Ireland in 1752," unearthed by the diligence of the late Dr G. T. Stokes. The English traveller observes justly, that the marble " is full as durable, and bears as fine a polish as any brought from Italy," and he continues, " though the stones in the quarry sometimes weigh several ton, yet the method the contriver has to lift them, draw them out, and convey them to the mill, without any other than manual operation, adds still more to the surprise. I am informed that this ingenious gentleman sends yearly shiploads to England, which gives me a particular satisfaction, that they mind a native of Ireland has outdone all they have hitherto seen. . . I cannot hear that anyone has imitated the machinery. It is perpetually at work, by night as well as by day, and requires little attendance."

William Colles was an Alderman of the City of Kilkenny of which his uncle, Barry Colles (born 1697, died 1785), was twice Mayor. St. John's Bridge in Kilkenny, of greaty beauty, was built by him, and some remains of fine architectural pieces prove the universality of his genius.

Susan, the only daughter and heiress of Barry Colles carried the Kilkenny estates to the Meredyth family, when she married Joshua Paul Meredyth, fourth son of Sir Richard Meredyth, 2nd Bart. of

Greenhills, Co Kildare. Her son, Sir Barry Colles Meredyth, 7th Bart., succeeded to the title on the death of his uncle, Sir Moore Meredyth, 6th Bart., and her grandson, Sir Joshua Colles Meredyth's granddaughter was married to the late Sir Bernard Burke, C.B., Ulster King-at-Arms.

The tenth Baronet in the Meredyth family was Sir Edward Meredyth, a Military Knight of Windsor, who died leaving no male heir, and the title was claimed by George Augustus Jervis Meredyth of Hobart, Tasmania, who was known as the cabman claimant, he having in his long life played many parts, including those of shoemaker, stoker, storeman, policeman, and finally acted in the capacity by which his claim to be heir to a creation of 1660, was designated.

But to return to Job Colles; his brother, William, suffered in the Irish Rebellion of 1641, as a loyalist. he escaped to Coventry, but returned in 1658—" to repair his fortunes " to Ireland. Here in 1659 he took a house in Skinner's Row (now Christchurch Place), Dublin, where it appears he became a merchant. His brother Charles Colles served as a soldier in the Cromwellian army, and got large grants of land in the counties of Sligo, Wexford, and Kilkenny. He resided in Magheramore, near Sligo, and Collesford on the Drumcliff river takes its name from him. The Rev. Dr O'Rorke in his " History of Sligo: Town and County " refers to the fact that the local tradition or gossip represents Colles as having a gallows at Collesford " for

hanging the political suspects of the neighbourhood."
This tradition probably arose from the fact that
Colles was Provost Marshall of Connaught for
fourteen years, and High Sheriff of Co Sligo, 1685.

His funeral entry registered in Ulster's office, of
which I have a certified copy, is an interesting
document, and reads as follows:

Charles Colles of Magherymore in the County of
Sligo, Esqr., third sonn of William Colles of Doghill
in the King's county and of......... dar. of.........
Lyons of Phillipstowne in the King's county afore-
said. The said Charles was Justice of the peace
in the said county of Sligo in the Reigne of his late
Majestie King Charles the second of blessed
memory and of King James the second and
Provost Marshall of Connaught for fourteen years
and high Sheriffe of the said county of Sligo at the
time of his decease. He took to his first wife Ann
daughter of Anthony Strattford who was Governour
of Duncannon in Com Wexford by whome he had
issue four sons (vizt.) William eldest sonn md. to
Allice daughter of Deane Dudley Persse by whom
he had issue two sonns Peirce and Charles both died
young and five daughters (vizt.) Sarah, Ann, Dorcas,
Lettice and Mary liveing and two more died young,
Charles second sonn died young. Anthony Colles
third sonn maried to Mary dar. of Walter Johnson
of Magherimenagh in the County of Fermanagh
Esqr. by whome he had issue three sonns (vizt.)
Charles and Francis died young, and Anthony now
liveing Robert Colles fourth sonn maried unto Jane

The Family of Colles in Ireland

daughter of Thomas Jones of Carrigin in Com Sligo Esqr. by whome he hath issue one daughter named Ann. The said Charles had alsoe by his first wife four dars. (vizt.) Dorcas eldest md. to George Crofton Esqr. by whome she hath issue Henry, George, Addam, Thomas and William, Mary, Ann, Elizabeth and Hanah now liveing, Frances, Charles and Sidney died young Sidney second dar. md. to William Johnson by whome she hath issue William, Arnold, George, Charles, Frances, Mary and Ann and James that died young, Lucey 3rd daughter md. to William Parkes by whome she hath issue one sonn named Roger and one daughter named Ellenor; Ismy fourth dr. unmaried and Ann and Mary died young. The first menconed Charles tooke to his second wife Affra dar. of . . . . Stinson of . . . in the County of . . . who died sans issue. The said first menconed Charles departed this mortall life at Phibbestowne in the County of Dublin on Sunday the fifteenth of November, one thousand six hundred eighty and five and was interred the twenty fourth of the same month in the chancell of the Parish church of St. Michael's, Dublin. The truth of the premisses is certified by the subscription of the said William Colles, eldest sonn and heire of this Defunct, who hath returned this certificate to be recorded in the office of Sr. Richd. Carney Kt. Ulster King at Armes this twenty seventh day of November Anno Domini 1685.

My father, Richard Colles, was a descendant of

Charles, "this Defunct." He was a Civil Engineer in India, and invented a machine for cutting and drying indigo. I was born on 5th October, 1862, in the holy city of Buddha Gaya, Bengal, under the shadow of the great Maha-Bodhi Temple. Gaya is so sacred a place that the natives believe that, as in Benares, one can even eat beef there and yet go to heaven. My father died at the age of thirty-nine, on the 10th January, 1868, the anniversary of his wedding day. He was, like his great-great-grand-father, an inventor and mechanician, and I possess a watch of which the hour hand was constructed by him from a lady's hairpin, and in which he supplied the place of a lost jewel with the head of a pin!

My connection with India was brief, but I hope to visit it before I die. I owe such education as I received to my mother's brother, the late William Ramsay, a Major-General in the Madras Tenth Native Infantry. So much interested was I in the fact that I was born in Buddha Gaya, that in 1901 I became representative in Ireland of the Maha-Bodhi Society.

CHAPTER XXIX

THE FAMILY OF COLLES IN ENGLAND

The Colleses of Worcestershire—Members of Parliament,
1298-1341—William Colles, 1310—Gualterus Colles,
scriba principis, 1415 — Constable of Bordeaux —
Michael Colles hanged by Yorkists during Wars of
the Roses—Edmund Colles of Leigh—The Colles
Ghost—Tombs of the Family in Leigh Church—
Sydney Smith on Ancestors.

IN a fine work, published in two portly folios in 1781,
entitled " Collections for the History of Worcestershire," by T. Nash, there is much interesting
information given with regard to the family of Colles,
and a page is devoted to " Monuments in Leigh
Church," some of which appear in the beautiful
engravings which adorn the book and make it much
sought for by collectors; the current price being
about four pounds for the two volumes. In volume
one there is an incidental reference to Richard
Colles who was Member of Parliament in the Reign
of Edward II.

The family of Colles appears to have been settled
at Leigh, in Worcestershire, as early as the middle
of the 13th Century. In 1240 Peter Colles held
land in fee farm, and paid ninepence quarterly to

the Priory of St. Mary at Worcester, on behalf of
the Lord of the Manor. In 1298 (time of Edward
I.) William Colles represented the City of Worcester
in Parliament. Richard Colles in 1302 was one of
the " Bailiffes " of the City of Worcester, and as
such did penance on the 3rd day of February in that
year, for a breach of the Cathedral sanctuary, committed by certain " viri sanguinum et dolore," who
had treacherously allured a fugitive from the churchyard where he had taken refuge, and kept him
prisoner until he agreed to leave the kingdom.

That members of the family served their country
in the senate as well as on the field is proved by
the following table compiled from lists published by
the Camden Society and from references made in the
Registry of Worcester Priory—

A.D.	1298,	26	Edward I.,	William Colles.
,,	1305,	33	do.	Peter Colles.
,,	1313,	6	Edward II.,	Peterus Colles.
,,	1315,	8	do.	Ricardus Colles.
,,	1316,	9	do.	do.
,,	1316,	9	do.	Peter Colles.
,,	1319,	12	do.	Ricardus Colles.
,,	1320,	14	do.	Ricardus Colles, junior.
,,	1320,	14	do.	Ricardus Colles.
,,	1321,	14	do.	William Colles.
,,	1322,	15	do.	Ricardus Colles.
,,	1323,	16	do.	Peter Colles.
,,	1325,	19	do.	do.
,,	1327,	1	Edward III.,	do.
,,	1341,	14	do.	Richard Colles.

I hope no wicked wag will accuse me of having

RICHARD COLLES
of St. Stephen's Green, Dublin, and of Prospect, Co. Dublin
(*b.* 1748; called to the Bar, 1783; *d.* 1816)

MONUMENTS IN LEIGH CHURCH
(From engravings in "Collections for the History of Worcestershire," by T. Nash, 1781.
The tomb on the right is that of William Colles, who died in 1615. The lower tomb in the
centre is that of Edmund Colles, who died in 1606)

anything in common with the De Rougement referred to in the following. He, no doubt, was an ancestor of the wonderful liar whose exploits were chronicled in " The Wide World " magazine.

The passage referred to runs as follows—

In 1310, William Colles of Worcester granted to the Master and Brethren of the Hospital or Commanding of St. Walstan in the Parish of St. Peter's, City of Worcester, " all that land called Chestall, Oldcastle, Edward's Church, with common for six beasts in Lulsley after the hay had been carried off as also a messuage held there by one Peter de Rougemente." The License of the Bishop of Worcester, Lord of the Manor, allowing him to alienate the land is dated London, 8id July, 1310. The Commanding or Hospital of St. Walstan was a community of secular priests and had nothing to do with the Knights of St. John. It still gives, I think, its name to a street in Worcester, viz., Commanding Street.

There is a farm called Colles Place (*vulgo* Coles Place or Cold Place) in Lulsley, which is mentioned in a ledger of the Priory of Malvern, in the reign of Henry III., as belonging to the family of Colles.

In 1415, Gualterus Colles " scriba principis," was a member of the Embassy sent to France by King Henry V. Twenty years later we find Walter Colles Constable of Bordeaux and appointed with six others by Henry VI. in a Commission under his Privy Seal dated Westminster, 9th July, 1435, to investigate the claims of Bertrand de Monteferando to the estate of his uncle Baron de la Bret. Three Commissioners to be a quorum. These facts will be found stated in Redman's " Life of Henry V." The text in Rymer's " Foedera " runs as follows—

" The Kyng at Shene ye XIth day of May ye XIXth year by y' advys of my Lordes his councillers commanded ye keeper of his privy seal to make sufficiaunt warrant unto ye Tresorer of Englande and Chamberlyns to delyvere money for payment of all servys after ye payment of Fraunce unto my lorde Duke of York under his furme. Yat is to say ye sayde money to be put in a secure coffre under two lokkes of which Maistre Walter Collys shall have one Kay and Lewys John Knyght anoyer, which coffre shall be opennyd in ye landyng of ye saide Duk beyond ye sees and after muster taken by ye sayde Walter and Lewys with oyer of ye sayde speres ye saide money be employde in ye payment of John on his appointment as one of the King's Council in Normandy."

The Royal Palace, it will be remembered, was at the time at Shene, near Richmond.

In 1442, on the 9th of October, the King in Council in the Great Chamber at Eltham debated the terms of the truce lately made " betwix the Duc of York and ye Duchess of Bourgoyne," and ordered a Commission to be issued, in which Walter Colles' name appears as " Magister Walter Colles præcentoris Ecclesiæ Cathedralis Exoniæ," which, allowing for the spelling of the period, seems to point to Walter's having been a precentor of Exeter Cathedral.

During the Wars of the Roses the Colleses (as might be expected from Walter Colles' position in the service of Henry VI.), were Lancastrians. After the Battle of Wakefield (29th December, 1461) one of them, Michael Colles, was seized and hanged by some of the fugitive Yorkists.

It was in Henry VIth's reign that the intermarriage between the Purefoys and the ancestor of the Irish family of Colles took place.

The first of the Colles family that settled in Worcestershire, appears to have been Richard Colles of Alfrick, said in the Visitation Book of Warwickshire, 1619, to have been " e familiâ Collesorum de com. Somerset." He was buried at Powick, in 1440. His grandson, William Colles, married Margaret, sister and co-heiress of John Hitch, and died in 1558, aged 63, having had issue Edmund Colles, Michael Colles, of Hampton in Arden, Co Warwick; and Bradwell, Bucks; William Colles of Parkbury, Herts; and John Colles of Hatfield Court, Co Hereford. The eldest, Edmund Colles, purchased the Manor of Leigh, and was in the Commission of the Peace, and Deputy Lieutenant of the County. He was High Sheriff of the County in the time of Queen Elizabeth and was a Justice of the Council of the Marches in Wales.

Referring to this Edward Colles, Nash says—

" This respectable person, whose ancestors were

possessed of lands in Leigh, Bransford, Hallow, Grimley, Sukley, Broadwas, and Cotheridge, married Joane, daughter of Robert Somerville of Somerville's, Ashton com. Glouc., by whom he had one daughter married to Mr Dansey of Brinsop, in the County of Hereford, and a son, William, who married Mary Palmer, daughter and heir of Jerome Palmer, by Eleanor Paget, third daughter of William Baron Paget, Lord Privy Seal and Knight of the Garter. His issue are mentioned in Sukley. Mr Edmund Colles had a second wife of the name and family of Townsend, anciently in Norfolk, but most esteemed in the Marches of Wales. His issue by her were Susan Colles, wife of Sir Edmund Harewell, Knight of the Bath, t. James I., and Edmund Colles of Grimley, whose wife was descended from the knightly families of Cornwall, and Blunt of Kinlet, com. Staff., and was of the blood of Acton, of Acton, a name existing before the Conquest. A brother of that eminent man, Mr Edmund Colles, was Mr John Colles, of Hatfield, com. Heref., whose son's heir, Mr Colles, married the apparent heir of Mr Ingram of Earle's Court, near Worcester."

In the Habingdon MSS., the following passage is quoted from " The White Book of the Bishoprick of Worcester "—" This Manor (Suckley) being the Abbot's of Tewkesbury, together with the Parsonage of Bushley appropriate, falling into the King's hands by the suppression of Monasteries, was afterwards passed away (3 and 4 Philip and Mary) to John Handby, or Hundby; from whom it came to Edmund Colles, of Leigh, Esq.; who gave it to John Colles, the son of his younger son, Mr Richard Colles," and Nash in his remarks on Berrington says

" it is a manor one mile north west of Tenbury, and was annexed to the Priory of St. John the Evangelist in Pembroke. After the dissolution of this priory, it was granted (36 Henry VIII.) to Richard Andrews, who conveyed it to Mr Richard Palmer, from whom it passed to Mr Matthew Palmer, from whom it descended to Mr Jerome Palmer, whose daughter and heir, Mary, brought it to her husband, William Colles."

Nash also says in his account of Leigh, " This ancient lordship of the abbots of Pershore falling by the dissolution of monasteries into the King's hands, remained there until Elizabeth's time. The tenants of the house and demesne, both under the abbot and under the King and Queen, were the Colleses, of which family was Mr Edmund Colles, ' a grave and learned justice of this shire, who purchased the inheritance of this manor,' whose son, William Colles, succeeded him, whose son and heir, Mr Edmund Colles, lived in the time of Mr Habingdon, and being loaded with debts (which like a snowball from Malvern Hill gathered increase), thought fit to sell it to Sir Walter Devereux, Bart."

This sale led to the Colleses of Leigh being

accredited with a family ghost! The legend, as told by a correspondent of *The Athenæum*, 26th September, 1846, is as follows—

"I well remember that in my juvenile days old people used to speak of a spectre that formerly appeared in the parish of Leigh, in Co Worcester, whom they called 'Old Coles'; and said that he frequently used, at dead of night, to ride as swift as the wind down that part of the public road between Bransford and Brocamin, called Leigh Walk, in a coach drawn by four horses, with fire flying out of their nostrils—and that they invariably dashed right over the great barn at Leigh Court, and then on into the river Teme. It was likewise said that this perturbed spirit was at length *laid* in a neighbouring pool by twelve parsons at dead of night, by the light of an inch of candle; and as he was not to rise again until the candle was quite burnt out, it was, therefore, thrown into the pool, and to make all sure the pool was filled up—

"And peaceful after that slept old Colles' shade."

My cousin, the late Surgeon John Armstrong Purefoy Colles of the Bengal Army told me that when he visited Leigh in 1869 that this ghost was by no means laid, but was still supposed to haunt the cellars of Leigh Court "where he sits on the largest beer barrel and squeaks like a rat." A rope hanging from the vault of the cellar is known as "Colles' Bell." This, however, I think is quite too undignified behavour for any Colles to indulge in.

The Family of Colles in England

From ghosts to monuments is an easy transition. The descriptions in " Nash's History," of the tombs which I have had photographed, run as follows—

" On the north side of the church Mr Edmund Colles' arms, who was the first that bore them, a man esteemed the wisest of his age in the government of this country. This first coat of the Colles' is impaled with three birds. The arms of his family about the reign of Henry IV., are a chevron between three birds."

In the Habingdon MS., the description of Edmund Colles' tomb is given—

" On the south side (of Leigh Church) is a raised monument, having the portraiture of a man in civil habit, with a lion at his feet, and some verses over him that are scarce legible, and not worth much trouble. About the tomb is this inscription ' Hic jacet sepultus Edmundus Colles arm. qui. obiit 19 Dec., A.D. 1606, æt. suæ. 76.' " Then follows a description of his arms which I spare my indulgent reader.

Of another of my illustrations of tombs the following description is given by Nash—

" On the north side of the chancel, on a raised tomb and under an arch supported by two pillars is the portraiture of a Knight armed and kneeling ; behind him his wife kneeling ; over them the arms and crest of Colles. On the dexter pillar the arms of Colles, and over it some emblems, and above that the crest of Colles. On the sinister pillar his wife's single coat. This Inscription in great letters: 'Hic jacet sepulta Maria Colles, uxor Gulielmi Colles armigeri, qui Obiit 14 Aprilis, A.D. 1602'; and about the tomb these words, 'Here lieth William Colles, of Leigh, in the County of Worcester, Esq., with Mary, his wife, daughter and heir of Jerome Palmer, Esq., by Esther Paget, his wife, third daughter of William Lord Paget, Baron of Beaudefert, Lord Keeper of the Privy Seal, Knight of the Most Noble Order of the Garter, and a Privy Counsellor to Henry VIII., Edward VI., and Queen Mary. William Colles died 20th Sept., 1615; and Mary his wife, died 15th April, 1602.' Beneath are his seven sons and five daughters kneeling."

In 1892 I had the particulars given above printed in a little pamphlet for private circulation, and as I glance at descriptions of the crest "A sea-pye Sable seizing on a fish proper, wounded and bleeding," I recall the words of Sydney Smith: "My ancestors had no arms, but invariably sealed their letters with their thumbs."

CHAPTER XXX

THE FAMILY OF COLLES IN THE UNITED STATES

Christopher Colles, the First Projector of Inland Naviga-
tion in America—A Pupil of Richard Pococke, the
Famous Oriental Traveller, later Bishop of Ossory—
Death of Pococke in 1765—Colles leaves for Phila-
delphia in 1771—His Public Lectures—His proposals
for Construction of Reservoirs—The Revolutionary
War—Colles teaches Gunnery to American Artillery—
His Pamphlets on Joining the Waters of the Great
Lakes—His Proposals for the Introduction of the
Telegraph—His Death in 1816—John Colles (1751-
1807)—E. G. T. Colles, Inventor of the Colles
Fourfold Heater and Live Steam Purifier—Pioneers
of American Progress.

" To no single individual is the system of American
improvements more indebted than to Christopher
Colles," so wrote John Austin Stephens the Editor
of " The Magazine of American History," in an
article which appeared in that magazine in June,
1878, headed " Christopher Colles, the First Projector of Inland Navigation in America."

Christopher Colles was born in Ireland in the
year 1738.   Left an orphan at an early age, he
passed into the charge of the renowned Richard
Pococke, the famous Oriental traveller, later Bishop

of Ossory. The pursuits of Pococke led the mind of his adopted pupil to physical investigation, and, it would appear, that to considerable attainments in languages, he added a fair acquaintance with mathematics, mineralogy, climate, antiquities, and geographical science.

Upon the death of Pococke in 1765, Colles started upon his wanderings. The first reference to his name, in connection with New York, appears in Watson's annals of that city, in which it is stated he delivered public lectures in Philadelphia in 1772, upon pneumatics, illustrated by experiments in an air pump of his invention.

He is also said to have been the first in the United States to undertake the building of a steam engine, for a distillery in Philadelphia, but failed for want of means, although his plans secured the approval of David Ritterhouse and the Philosophical Society. In 1773 he lectured at the Exchange, in New York, on the advantages in *lock navigation*.

Colles was the first person who suggested canals, and improvements on the Ontario route. In November, 1784, according to the records of the Assembly, he presented a memorial on the subject, and, in April following, a favourable report was had thereon. Colles visited the country, and took an actual survey of the principal obstructions upon the Mohawk river as far as Wood Creek. He published the results of his tour in a pamphlet in 1785. "The amazing extent," he wrote, "of the five great lakes to which the proposed navigation will communicate, will be found to have five times as much coast as all England; and the countries watered by the numerous rivers which fall into these lakes, full seven or eight times as great as that valuable island."

In an article on the " Water Chronology of the City of New York," published in that valuable repository, the Corporation Manual of Valentine for 1854, the services of Colles only are noticed by the writer, Theodore R. de Forest.

Colles, in 1774, proposed the construction of a reservoir and other works, and the laying down of a system of conduit pipes. With the aid of the corporation of the city, a steam pumping engine was erected near the collect pond. This enterprise was completed in March, 1776. The engine carried a pump eleven inches in diameter and six feet stroke, which lifted 417,600 gallons daily. The War of the Revolution arrested the undertaking, yet in 1778 the people petitioned that Colles' plan might be carried out. When later, the Manhattan Company was chartered to supply New York with water, it is claimed that the original proposal to look without its limits for a supply came from Colles.

On the breaking out of the war, Colles turned his remarkable fertility of resource to a military enterprise, giving lectures on gunnery, and teaching the American artillery the principles of projectiles, in which employment, his biographer in Appleton's Encyclopædia says, he was continued until this branch of the service was remodelled on the arrival of Baron Steuben in 1777.

Immediately on the close of the war, he again devoted his attention to his favourite project of internal improvement. All the authorities concur in giving to Colles the credit of having been not only the first to propose, but the first to bring before the public, in a practical form, the feasibility and vast national advantage of a system of water communication, which should unite the great lakes and their boundless tributory territory with the Atlantic ocean.

The priority of Christopher Colles in the conception of the grand design is demonstrated by several passages in his pamphlet of 1785. For instance, where he says that " by this the internal trade will be promoted; by this the country will be settled; by this the frontiers will be secured; by this a variety of articles, as masts, yards, and ship timber, may be brought to New York, which will not bear the expense of land carriage, and which, notwithstanding, will be a very considerable remittance to Europe; by this in time of war provisions and military stores may be moved with facility in sufficient quantity to meet any emergency, and by this in time of peace, all the necessary conveniences, and if we please the luxuries of life, may be distributed to the romotest parts of the GREAT LAKES which so beautifully diversify the face of this extensive continent, and to the smallest branches of the numerous rivers which shoot from these lakes upon any point of the compass."

Although this great project temporarily failed, Colles contrived to interest himself in matters of public interest, and issued proposals for publishing a Survey of the Roads of the United States of America. This was published in 1789. The plates were of copper, neatly engraved, "each page containing a delineation of near twelve miles of road on a scale of about an inch and three-quarters to a mile."

In 1808, encouraged, perhaps, by the improvement of inland navigation in the State of New York, Colles proposed a plan of navigation between New York and Philadelphia, but as before, without practical benefit to himself. His views were made public in a little tract issued at his own expense. The plan proposed was to erect canals not dug into the soil, as in Europe, but built of *timber*, entirely elevated above the ground, with perpendicular sides!

In a series of articles by Henry O'Reilly, which appeared in "The Historical Magazine," entitled "Material for Telegraph History," the writer in the article which appeared in April, 1869, recognises Colles as having been the first to make "formal proposal for telegraphic intercourse along the whole American coast, from Passamaquoddy to New Orleans." This was in the Summer of 1812, by means of public lectures and newspaper articles. Colles only partially succeeded in his endeavours. A Semaphoric Telegraph was established to signalise intelligence between New York and Sandy Hook, which for many years was under his personal direction. In a little pamphlet published in the year following, he described this numerical telegraph to be a machine composed of a frame of timber in the form of a five-pointed star, to be erected on eminences, so as to be distinctly visible with a telescope at a distance of ten miles. A revolving index carried a circular board, on which were marked nine digits and a cypher.

Mr O'Reilly wrote with regard to this matter: "Had the wise suggestions of Mr Colles been promptly sustained by the Government or by the business community—had his proposed telegraph system been extended along the coast to any considerable extent—so as to transmit intelligence rapidly among the American people; many movements of British fleets and armies might have been essentially impeded, if not entirely frustrated, and our national feelings, as well as the public and private interests of our countrymen, might have been saved from various painful ordeals. But in 1812, even the citizens of New York were as slow in appreciating the value of Colles' Semaphoric Telegraph as they were in 1845, when little or nothing could be raised in that city towards extending the Electro-magnetic Telegraph northward of Baltimore—to which place the National Government had built a forty-mile experimental line from Washington during the previous year."

It is pleasant to learn from a sketch contributed by Dr John W. Francis to "The Knickerbocker Gallery," published in New York in 1855; a handsome volume to which Washington Irving, Oliver Wendell Holmes, William Cullen Bryant, Bayard

CHRISTOPHER COLLES (1739-1816)
The First Projector of Inland Navigation in America
(From the portrait by Jarvis in the Gallery of
the New York Historical Society)

ABRAHAM COLLES (1773-1843)
Professor of Surgery and Anatomy, T.C.D., and twice President
of the Royal College of Surgeons, Ireland
(From the painting by Martin Creegan, P.R.H.A.)

The Family of Colles in United States

Taylor, John G. Saxe, James Russell Lowell, N. P. Willis, and Henry Wadsworth Longfellow, and other well-known American writers also contributed; that though many of Colles' projects failed, he bore his losses philosophically. In Dr Francis' article, which fills twenty pages, and is entitled "Reminiscences of Christopher Colles," we read:

"Many paid deference to him amid all his disappointments. De Witt Clinton included him among the prominent promoters of internal improvement. Dr Mitchell often visited him, and lauded his services in the advancement of public works. Jarvis, the painter, pronounced him a genius, and painted his portrait with great fidelity. 'My pencil,' said Jarvis, 'will render you hereafter better known; you have done too much good to be forgotten.' The picture is in the Historical Society. Dr Hosack commemorated him, in his 'Life of Clinton,' as an early pioneer in behalf of the canal policy of New York, and caused an engraving of his portrait to occupy a niche on the column of his canal worthies. Senator Seward has not overlooked him in his elaborate introduction to the 'Natural History of New York.' Trumbull, the historical painter, often cheered him onward, and bid him hope, for on that article he himself had long lived. Nor was that genuine Knickerbocker, G. C. Verplanck, indifferent to his condition, nor backward in suggestions. In the great celebration which took place in New York in November, 1825, when the waters of Erie united with the Atlantic, the effigy of Colles was borne with appropriate dignity among the emblems of that vast procession." And Dr Francis added:

"Had I encountered Colles in any land I would have been willing to have naturalised him to our soil and institutions. He had virtues, the exercise of which must prove profitable to any people. . . . The ardent and untiring man was so connected with divers affairs, even after he had domesticated himself among us, that every movement in which he took a part must have had salutary influences on the masses of those days."

Christopher Colles died on the 4th of October, 1816, in the 79th year of his age, and was buried in St. Paul's Cemetery in New York. Mr Henry O'Reilly thus closes his account of him: "As unostentatious as he was sagacious, he was indeed one of those gifted men whose misfortune consists in being ahead of their times. The New York Historical Society has a portrait painted by Jarvis as a mark of respect from some of the eminent contemporaries of Colles; and that valuable Society may well point to it as a memento of one of the best men that ever trod its halls or honoured its membership. Be his memory ever honoured as one of the worthiest pioneers of American Progress!"

John Colles (1751-1807), at one time a publisher in Dublin, went to America with his Cousin Christopher in 1771. His son, James Colles (1788-1883) was a merchant in New Orleans, and lived to the great age of ninety-five. His son of the same name also lived to a good old age (1828-1898) and

The Family of Colles in United States

Taylor, John G. Saxe, James Russell Lowell, N. P. Willis, and Henry Wadsworth Longfellow, and other well-known American writers also contributed; that though many of Colles' projects failed, he bore his losses philosophically. In Dr Francis' article, which fills twenty pages, and is entitled " Reminiscences of Christopher Colles," we read:

" Many paid deference to him amid all his disappointments. De Witt Clinton included him among the prominent promoters of internal improvement. Dr Mitchell often visited him, and lauded his services in the advancement of public works. Jarvis, the painter, pronounced him a genius, and painted his portrait with great fidelity. ' My pencil,' said Jarvis, ' will render you hereafter better known; you have done too much good to be forgotten.' The picture is in the Historical Society. Dr Hosack commemorated him, in his ' Life of Clinton,' as an early pioneer in behalf of the canal policy of New York, and caused an engraving of his portrait to occupy a niche on the column of his canal worthies. Senator Seward has not overlooked him in his elaborate introduction to the ' Natural History of New York.' Trumbull, the historical painter, often cheered him onward, and bid him hope, for on that article he himself had long lived. Nor was that genuine Knickerbocker, G. C. Verplanck, indifferent to his condition, nor backward in suggestions. In the great celebration which took place in New York in November, 1825, when the waters of Erie united with the Atlantic, the effigy of Colles was borne with appropriate dignity among the emblems of that vast procession." And Dr Francis added:

"Had I encountered Colles in any land I would have been willing to have naturalised him to our soil and institutions. He had virtues, the exercise of which must prove profitable to any people. . . . The ardent and untiring man was so connected with divers affairs, even after he had domesticated himself among us, that every movement in which he took a part must have had salutary influences on the masses of those days."

Christopher Colles died on the 4th of October, 1816, in the 79th year of his age, and was buried in St. Paul's Cemetery in New York. Mr Henry O'Reilly thus closes his account of him: "As unostentatious as he was sagacious, he was indeed one of those gifted men whose misfortune consists in being ahead of their times. The New York Historical Society has a portrait painted by Jarvis as a mark of respect from some of the eminent contemporaries of Colles; and that valuable Society may well point to it as a memento of one of the best men that ever trod its halls or honoured its membership. Be his memory ever honoured as one of the worthiest pioneers of American Progress!"

John Colles (1751-1807), at one time a publisher in Dublin, went to America with his Cousin Christopher in 1771. His son, James Colles (1788-1883) was a merchant in New Orleans, and lived to the great age of ninety-five. His son of the same name also lived to a good old age (1828-1898) and his grandson, Christopher John Colles, practises as a physician in New York, and is the author of some medical works of which some specimens are in the Library of the British Museum.

That the faculty for invention is not dead in the Colles family is proved by the fact that Edward Taylor Gillespie Colles, a son of William Henry George Colles (1803-1880), who settled in Canada in 1859, and nephew of Edward Richards Purefoy Colles (1798-1883) already referred to, is the inventor of much useful machinery, notably The Colles Fourfold Heater and Live Steam Purifier, which can be seen at work to-day in Clinton Street, Chicago, where the inventor has his factory and from which these heaters not alone are despatched throughout the United States and Canada, but leave for shipment to Europe.

CHAPTER XXXI

KINGS AND CORONATIONS

In this year of the coronation of King George V., I recall the fact that in 1902 I was one of the many who were saddened by the intelligence of the sudden illness of King Edward VII. That sage King and genial gentleman may be said, without fear of contradiction, to have been the most deeply loved monarch that ever sat on the throne of England. He was in the realms of Royalty all that Oliver Goldsmith was in the realms of literature. Of him also it might be said that he touched nothing that he did not adorn. And for once Mr Bernard Shaw was right, we might admire in Edward VII. His Majesty the King, but it was the Man we loved, " the genial figure with the race-glass and the cigar ; the pattern for all good stockbrokers from Friday to Monday."

I wonder do many of my readers know the work

of Ella Mary Gordon, whose poems were the favourite reading of Queen Victoria, a fact which won for the poetess the pleasing title of " The Queen's Poetess." It is to Dr Charles Forshaw I owe my acquaintance with Mrs Gordon, who is a daughter of the great Rosarian, Mr Paul, of Waltham Cross, and wife of the genial Town Clerk of Aberdeen. Mrs Gordon's sister, Miss Florence Paul is an artist of exceptional ability, and has illustrated the Poems of the Queen's Poetess in a truly charming style.

The chief characteristics of Mrs Gordon's poems are simplicity and directness. She does not toy with her subject, nor view it in different lights, nor does she, even in the poems most steeped in pathos, indulge in introspection or in tears. There is the strength which springs from serenity in all her work, and this strength is communicated to her readers, thus making her poems a source of consolation to those who are sad of heart. Mrs Gordon seems to have accepted the *dictum* of Lucretius, that " true religion consists in beholding all things with a calm soul." Her poems breathe a spirit of resignation and of steadfastness.

In illustration I may quote the following poem which does not, as the work of many other poets on the same theme, prove the speaker to be a dweller in a region roofed by repentance and paved with despair. The situation is none the less painful, the grief is none the less poignant because the utterance is deliberately calm. Love may exist whole-hearted though the love cannot " starve, feast, despair, and be happy."

> " Although another's name I bear,
>   I still am true;
> And when I too have reached the goal,
>   Shall look for you.
>
> Had we walked daily hand in hand,
>   Care might have pressed;
> Now, looking back on what has been—
>   'Twas for the best.
>
> One sweet ray shines when cloudy mists
>   Fall on my soul—
> Our love has not been worn by time;
>   It still lives whole."

Being by Royal Deeside in July, 1902, staying at the Huntly Arms Hotel, in Aboyne, I ventured to call upon Mrs Gordon who resided during the summer months at a delightful châlet called Auchintoul, a beautiful little structure with a lower story of granite and an upper of pinewood, the whole being surrounded with climbing roses, and from the window could be heard the soothing sound of the river as it rounded the garden to flow under a fine suspension bridge.

I found Mrs Gordon in a charming little sitting-room, which overlooked the garden. I had had some correspondence with her in connection with the cheap edition of her poetical works entitled " Poems for the People," and at once recognised her from a fine portrait which had been reproduced as frontispiece to that book.

Kings and Coronations

At the moment of my entry she was examining some rare wild birds' eggs which her son, Paul Seaton Gordon, a fine, manly young fellow of eighteen, or thereabouts, had recently acquired for his collection. Young Gordon, who is a capital amateur photographer, was showing his mother some photographs he had taken of eggs to illustrate an article on the subject, and Mrs Gordon's private secretary, a lady, was evidently also much interested.

It is now eight years since I was at Aboyne, but I remember well the impression created by this gentle and refined woman as she spoke of Sir John Stainer and others of her friends, and, going to the piano played for me the simple air to which the following verses had just been set—

The One I loved the best
Has entered into rest,
Above the clouds' white crest.

The One I loved of old
Has won her crown of gold,
And knows the joys untold.

No breakers lash the Bar,
No sorrows surge afar,
Where shines my guiding star.

The work of life is done,
The cloudless day begun,
God guards my dearest One.

The sun has sunk to rest
For ever in the West
With her my soul loved best.

In Castle and Court House

A little later the Town Clerk of Aberdeen entered the room, and was good enough to say that in anticipation of my visit he had made arrangements for Mrs Gordon, her Secretary, and myself to visit Balmoral on the morrow. Accordingly, the following morning found me travelling with these two ladies by train from Aboyne to Ballater, from which a coach-and-four runs to Braemar.

As we neared the latter place we saw from our seats on the box that three large motor cars were rapidly coming towards us. The driver of the coach becoming uneasy on account of the restiveness of one of the leaders, pulled up and asked me to hold his head. I was dressed in riding breeches and leathers, and at once complied, but as I reached the ground, Mrs Gordon, who had recently been in a carriage accident, becoming nervous, leaped from the top of the coach. Luckily I was just in time to catch her, and leave her to the care of the other passengers, before running to the horse's head and quieting him as the motors containing a number of coloured people and one or two whites dashed past.

These cars, I learned later, contained King Lewanika, the enlightened ruler of Barotseland, who was accompanied by members of his suite and by Colonel Colin Harding, the British Commandant of Barotseland, who did much in British interests in connection with the Anglo-Portuguese Barotse Boundary question.

After a few moments Mrs Gordon recovered from her fright, and we proceeded to Braemar, where we had a pleasant luncheon party at the Fife Arms. Later we went in a brougham to Balmoral, which we had permission to inspect, thanks to the good offices of Mr Gordon.

On the day following, Mrs Gordon kindly took me for a drive round Aboyne, in the course of which she called upon Mr and Mrs Williams, with whom King Lewanika, Colonel Harding, and the entire party from Barotseland were staying. Here we found the Monarch and his dusky suite being photographed, and I was presented to his Majesty, and had a pleasant chat with Colonel Harding, who is a splendid type of Englishman. I may mention here, that in 1904 I heard, with great regret, that this gallant officer was severely mauled by lions when travelling near Kalomo, his right shoulder being badly smashed and both his legs severely bitten.

A day or two after the visit to Balmoral, Mr and Mrs Gordon took me with them to Balcorry Castle, the seat of Sir David Stewart. Here a large number of guests were entertained on a lovely summer afternoon, one of the chief attractions being a visit from the party of Fijians who had come over in connection with the Coronation. Amongst other things, such as dances, we witnessed the ceremony of making Kava, a drink much esteemed in Fiji. It was not made in orthodox fashion, a not very savoury method on which I shall not expatiate, but was brewed; the root being alternately soused in water and wrung out by the Chief, who plunged his brawny brown arms up to the elbows in the liquid, while his followers, clad in light garments, and with chaplets of roses on their heads, marched round him singing some weird hymn tunes!

When the ceremony of consecration was over, and the liquor was deemed to be ready, half-cocoa-nuts and calabashes were dipped in it and offered to the guests to imbibe. I tasted the fluid, which resembled in flavour a mixture of soap and water with a dash of red pepper. This liquor is said when indulged in too freely to affect the legs but not the head. I am glad to say that I took my departure as sober as a judge.

I saw King Lewanika several times during my short stay in Aboyne, and that shrewd Monarch is, I am glad to see, still on the throne of Barotseland. The latest intelligence received concerning him is that the Duke of Connaught devoted an afternoon to reviewing the Barotse Police and to a reception of Lewanika the Barotse Chief and his fellow tribes-men, who presented the Duke with a Royal Blue Monkey, and a grey Kaross. A sham hippopotamus hunt was got up by Lewanika for the Duke's entertainment, the hunt being partaken in by skilled hunters in dug-out canoes.

While staying in Aboyne, I had the pleasure of meeting some clergy of the district, one of them kindly asking me to visit his kirk on the following Sabbath day. I accepted the invitation and also the suggestion that I should call at the manse before entering the kirk. This accordingly I did, and found my reverend friend in his study with his second in command. I was a little bit curious to discover why I had been asked to call at the minister's house, but I had not long to wait for a solution of the mystery, for turning to me a few minutes after I had entered, he said:

" I thought that perhaps you might be weary, and that a glass of whisky and potass might not be amiss."

I thanked him for his kindly thought which was the outcome of genuine Scottish hospitality, and I have no doubt that in consequence of this glass of whisky and potass I sang " All people that on earth do dwell " with more unction than I would otherwise have done!

I returned to London in time for the Coronation, which took place on 9th August, 1902. The last time I saw King Edward was at the ceremony of opening Kingsway, when I stood little more than the length of a walking stick in front of him, and he looked in magnificent health and strength. Much work and worry were, however, in store for him, and he never shirked a duty. The King is dead. Long live the King! In his Majesty, George V. we have a Monarch who will not alone profit by the great example of his father, but strike out a line of his own, a line which will render his name illustrious, the indications of which are, in my humble judgment, already markedly perceptible.

CHAPTER XXXII

"THE PROVOST AND FELLOWS OF TRINITY"

"Father O'Flynn" and Alfred Perceval Graves—
Provosts Jellett and Salmon—Provost Anthony
Traill, LL.D.—A "Learic" by Father Matthew
Russell—Professor R. Yelverton Tyrrell—His Essays
and Translations—Professor Starkie—"The Story of
Cupid and Psyche," edited by Professor Louis Claude
Purser—George Ferdinand Shaw—His Articles in
The Dublin Evening Mail—The Nemean Odes of
Pindar, edited by Professor Bury—Henry Stewart
Macran, F.T.C.D.—Robert Russell, F.T.C.D.—"The
Book of Trinity College"—A Fine Irish Bull.

EVERYONE knows, or ought to know, "Father
O'Flynn," that capital song by Alfred Perceval
Graves, a song which will last as long as there is a
priest in Ireland. Owing to his being resident in
England I did not see much of Mr Graves, but when
Mr Arthur à Beckett's ill-fated paper *John Bull*,
was about to be started, he called on me with the
view of my becoming a contributor, and since then
I have met him once or twice.

My reason for referring to "Father O'Flynn" is
on account of the verses in that celebrated song,
which praise the Provost and Fellows of Trinity as
being famous alike for Greek and Latinity. I have

300

already referred to Jellett, who was succeeded as
Provost by Salmon, a celebrated mathematician and
divine. When Salmon died, full of years and
honours, he was succeeded by Dr Anthony Traill,
the present Provost. Long may he reign! Traill
is a robust and athletic man, a good sportsman and
a bulwark of the Protestant Church. He is the beau
ideal of " a strong still man in a blatant land."

Dr Anthony Traill has great strength of character.
He cares for no one's opinions save his own, and he
does not hesitate to plump for himself should occasion
arise. He and his sons are men of muscle. I
remember on one occasion when father and sons
were on the cricket field, an English visitor asking:
" Are those buffaloes which have evolved into men,
or men who have degenerated into buffaloes? " The
name of Traill is famous in another direction, for
Dr Anthony Traill's brother ran the first electric
train in the world; that from Portrush to the Giant's
Causeway, and another brother was Major R. G.
Traill, a Resident Magistrate in the West of Ireland,
who was a terror to evil-doers. All honour to
Anthony Traill, he is the right man for such a
position in troublous times for the old University of
Dublin.

I have already referred more than once to
Professor Mahaffy, who is a Doctor of Divinity, a
Doctor of Music, and a Doctor of Civil Law of
Oxford. His " History of Greek Literature " is a
delightful book, and is never likely to be superseded.
Mahaffy's kindliness of heart is unbounded. I

proposed, on one occasion, to lecture on the works of Henrik Ibsen and asked Mahaffy to take the chair. He wrote saying he was going for a holiday, but would, nevertheless, postpone it if I could alter the date of my lecture. I would not, however, hear of the Professor depriving himself of a well-earned holiday. One of the most entertaining of Mahaffy's books has long been out of print, his " Prolegomena to Ancient History."

Another Professor of Trinity College, Dublin, has thus been referred to by a contemporary poet, the Rev. Matthew Russell, S.J., Editor of *The Irish Monthly*, which he founded in 1873. Father Russell terms his verses " Learics," after Edward Lear. He wrote—

> Professor R. Yelverton Tyrrell
> In Latin is brisk as a squirrel;
>   And eke his Greek prose
>   As pleasantly flows
> As the language of Lang or of Birrell.

Of course, Father Russell's reference is to " Obiter Dicta." What " the language of Birrell " was, or could be, when he was kicked in the leg by a suffragette, we can only guess at.

Father Russell is a younger brother of the late Lord Russell of Killowen, Chief Justice of England. After his ecclesiastical education at Maynooth, he joined the Jesuit Order, and has worked in schools and churches in Limerick and Dublin. He is well-known in the world of letters as the compiler of

The Provost and Fellows of Trinity

" Sonnets on the Sonnet," published by Longmans in 1898. This collection contains no less than a hundred and fifty-seven sonnets, the subject of each of which is the Sonnet itself regarded from some point of view. Among the contributors were Swinburne, Austin Dobson, W. E. Henley, Wilfrid Blunt, Archbishop Alexander, and Professor W. W. Skeat.

Father Russell is a poet of no mean powers. His verses, entitled, " Land! Land! " was the last poem which caught Gladstone's attention just before he died—

> My dying hour, how near art thou?
> Or near or far, my head I bow
>   Before God's ordinance supreme;
>   But ah, how priceless then will seem
> Each moment rashly squandered now!
>
> Teach me, for thou can'st teach me, how
> These fleeting instants to endow
> With worth that may the past redeem,
>   My dying hour!
>
> My barque that late with buoyant prow
> The sunny waves did gaily plough,
> Now through the sunset's fading gleam
> Drifts dimly shorewards in a dream.
> I feel the land-breeze on my brow,
>   My dying hour!

Professor Tyrrell's " Lectures on Latin Poetry," and his " Essays on Greek Literature " are fascinating books, and he has edited with Professor L. C. Purser the " Correspondence of Cicero," in seven volumes. Tyrrell's translation of the

Archarnians of Aristophanes into English verse is excellent. To translate the Archarnians has ever since Frere's days had been the ambition of classical scholars, witness the latest translation by Professor Starkie, also a Fellow of Trinity College, Dublin.

A propos of editions of the Classics, one of the finest achievements in this line is "The Story of Cupid and Psyche as related by Apuleius," edited with an admirable introduction and notes by Professor Louis Claude Purser, F.T.C.D. It is only by a stretch of the imagination that Apuleius can be counted a Classic, for his language is strange and unclassical and therefore by no means easy to edit.

One of the most noted figures in T.C.D., was my dear friend George Ferdinand Shaw, LL.D., for some time the Registrar. So long-lived were the Fellows, that Shaw used to complain that for over forty years he was a Junior Fellow. Shaw used to write brilliant leading articles for *Saunder's Newsletter*, and later for *The Dublin Evening Mail*, when the latter was the property of George Tickell. I also was a contributor to the *Mail*, but as I was chief Accountant of the Ulster Bank, I could not visit the offices, accordingly a book used to be carried from Shaw to me, and from me to Shaw, in which we wrote letters and messages to each other. Some of Shaw's messages were like the language of Walt Whitman full of " hells " and " damns." I secured one of these books when filled, and well remember making my friends laugh over Shaw's remarks on misprints in an article written by him on Professor

Bury's edition of the Nemean Odes of Pindar. The page was lurid with sulphurous sentiments and ill-wishes for the printer's fate! My copy of Bury's edition of the Nemean Odes was presented by the editor to the late Professor Atkinson.

A propos of Atkinson, he edited the "Yellow Book of Leccan" for the Royal Irish Academy. In a little volume entitled "Who is Who in Dublin," Atkinson was stated to be *author* of "The Book of Ballymote" and "The Yellow Book of Leccan!" Out of this little "Who is Who" I had the pleasure of reading to Sir Francis Cruise a notice of his own decease! a fact which greatly amused that able medical man and excellent musician.

Professor J. B. Bury to whom I have just referred was for many years the "marvellous boy" of the University. He secured high honours very early in life, and even now is not fifty. His "History of Greece," and his edition of Gibbon's "Decline and Fall" are fine works. Bury is now Regius Professor of Modern History at Cambridge.

Dr T. K. Abbott, the Librarian of T.C.D. is one of the labourers on Kant's Ethics, but his life has been devoted to his Library, which is one of the best equipped in the world, and enjoys the copyright privilege.

Among the Junior Fellows there are now many brilliant young men; but Death has been busy amongst the Seniors, sweeping away, with others, Thomas Kells Ingram, the author of "Who Fears

to Speak of Ninety-eight?" and of volumes on
"Slavery" and "Comteism."

Of the younger men my friend Henry Stewart
Macran is one of the ablest. I have already referred
to his "History of Greek Music."

The field of mathematics is not a flowery one, but
Robert Russell, F.T.C.D. has gained a world-wide
reputation in this particular branch of learning, and
one in which a name is made only amongst one's
peers.

One of the most amusing pranks ever played on
learned Fellows in T.C.D. was when an under-
graduate named Pococke wrote as a Prize Essay
a long rigmarole entitled, "Signs of the Times," with
obscure quotations from Browning, and without one
word of commonsense. This document, strange to
say, won a gold medal, which, however, the author
refused to accept.

In the Tercentenary Year (1892) a handsome
volume was published, entitled, "The Book of
Trinity College." It contained the text of a sermon
in which the following sentence occurred in reference
to King David's experiences:—"With this *retrospect
before* him, the Psalmist," did so and so! So that
"The Book of Trinity College, Dublin," as is fitting,
is not without its fine specimen of an Irish Bull.

CHAPTER XXXIII

ONMIUM GATHERUM

The Irish Crossing Sweeper—A Generous Employer—
John Murray, Governor of Mount Joy Prison—
" Rattle yer Tins! "—My Only Visible Means of
Support—The Joys of Keeping Aquaria—A Golden
Speech — " No Bill for You, Sir! " — William
Allingham the Poet—A Lord Mayor of Dublin and
His Speech to the Ladies—An Eccentric J.P.

A FRIEND to whom I incautiously mentioned that I
was engaged in writing my reminiscences, asked,
" What on earth are you writing a book for ?" I
replied, " for the same reason as that for which a
crossing sweeper in Ireland told me he swept a
crossing."

" And what reason was that? " asked my obtuse
friend.

" I'll tell you," I replied. " He was sweeping a
crossing as clean as a new sixpence and insinuated
that I should give him a coin. I was in a bad
temper, and asked him, just as you have asked me,
' What on earth are you sweeping this clean crossing
for?' He answered, touching his hat most deferen-
tially, ' I'm only trying to earn my living, sir, *if you
have no objection!*' I need scarcely say I searched

for, found, and handed him a heavy and humble coin."

" Are there any good stories in your book? " asked my friend.

" I cannot say," I said, " the tales are all true and the result of my own experiences, judge from this one. I was asked to preside at a Press Luncheon by Messrs Abbott Bros., the big poultry people and as I entered the room in the hotel in which the luncheon was being held, the head waiter, a grey-haired, solemn old man, somewhat like Mr Asquith in appearance, approached me hurriedly and asked me, ' Are you Mr Abbott's father, sir? ' ' My good man,' said I, ' how can I tell you until I have seen Mr Abbott? ' "

My friend did not care for the story and said that Mr T. W. H. Crosland, the author of " The Unspeakable Scott," and " Lovely Woman," told better. I said, " I agree with you, but then Crosland is a genius. There is one story he told me which is unique, that in which he asked a butcher who claimed to be literary because he wrote for *Answers* and *Comic Cuts* what was his opinion —Did Bacon write Shakespeare? ' Well,' answered the butcher, ' if Bacon did *not* write Shakespeare, he missed the biggest opportunity of his life! ' "

When I was living in Dublin, and writing for the press, while at the same time I was accountant in the Ulster Bank, I received a letter from an official in the Civil Service who occupied a very good position, having at least £1,000 a year, with house, and fire and light. He wrote saying that his wife had left for a visit to the country and that as it was approaching Christmas he wished to give " the cook and the washerwoman's little girl a treat, and asking me to get him for them a couple of seats for the Panto-mime at the Gaiety! After the lapse of twenty-four hours, I replied, saying, " My dear So and So, I have applied for seats, but Mr Hyland, the Manager at the Gaiety, tells me he is booked up for weeks ahead. However, he has placed the Royal Box at my disposal, and I have much pleasure in placing it at yours for the kindly object you have in view, but please remember, evening dress is indispensable! "

I need scarcely say that I heard nothing more about the matter.

One of my earliest friends in Ireland was John Murray, the Governor of Mount Joy Prison. I used to dine with him in his private apartments, and on one occasion was startled by hearing a tremendous uproar in the yard below. He explained that some of the cells had small windows looking out on this yard, and one very refractory woman used her tin drinking mug to bang on the window sill, at the same time calling out to her fellow-prisoners in reference to the Governor, " Rattle yer tins, ye Divils ye, and kape ould Nero from sleepin'!" Such a specimen of womanhood lived before her time. She would be a valuable addition to-day to the ranks of the Suffragettes!

Another friend whom I have known for many years is Fred Mouillot, the actor manager. On one occasion I was Mouillot's guest at a Savage Club dinner. Mouillot was staying at the Tavistock Hotel, and having got into a hansom, he asked me to tell the driver his address. I did so with the best English accent I possessed at the moment, which I fear must have been half-Scotch, for the driver having gone a little distance shouted to his fare, " What part of 'Averstock 'ill did you say, sir? "

My friend A. C. Amoore one day astonished me by presenting me with a very handsome walking stick. As I could not understand his reason for so doing, I inquired. He replied, " My only reason is because I noticed that of late you have had no visible means of support."

From a boy I have been addicted to keeping live fish, beetles, water-snails, diving spiders, and other interesting stock of a like nature. I had quite a large number of aquaria, and, indeed, I still indulge in this innocent recreation, having been, quite recently, presented with a huge aquarium by Val Prince, the well-known artist.

One night I was travelling homeward in the train, and put a paper bag full of gentles and another of mealy-worms in the hat rack. Tired out with my day's work and being solus in a first class carriage, I fell asleep and awoke twenty minutes later to find two ladies gazing at me in a horror-stricken way. I was covered with gentles! These innocent but unpleasant-looking preludes to future blue-bottle flies were crawling in dozens over my coat, and being white while the coat was navy-blue, they were very conspicuous indeed!

310

Omnium Gatherum

If people knew how interesting fish can be when kept as pets, the keeping of aquaria would be a more popular pastime. Fish and water-snails live such placid lives, and to me their lives are so strongly contrasted to my own stormy existence, that they attract me very much indeed. Often when contemplating the serenity of a snail, or the peaceful life of a perch, I have been quite oblivious of being in a work-a-day world! At such times the peregrinations of a periwinkle have been to me more deeply interesting than the platitudes of a Prime Minister. The unruffled existence of a Ruffe has made me long for a peace only rivalled by the peace that passeth all understanding.

Silence is not always golden. Once with a Press party travelling in the North of Ireland, we finished our tour with a banquet at the Great Central Hotel, Belfast. My brethren of the Pen asked me to propose a vote of thanks to the combined railways, the Midland of which Mr John Elliott was then a Manager, and the Northern Counties Railway of Ireland, which is now combined with the Midland. I made a short speech to the best of my ability, saying that the *entente cordiale* between England and France would be nothing in comparison to the *entente cordiale* between England and Ireland; and that in purchasing the Northern Counties Railway the Midland had created a bond between England and Ireland which ignorance and fanaticism would be powerless to destroy, and which would bind the sister countries closer day by day!

In Castle and Court House

Six months later I passed through Belfast and put up at the Great Central Hotel. An hour after I had booked, Mr Felstead the Manager met me and said he remembered me on account of my " great speech!" I was so much pleased that I made the Great Central my head-quarters for a week, and had one or two supper parties. When leaving to catch the 10.20 a.m. for Dublin, I asked to see Mr Felstead to say " Good-bye." I was told he was out. " Well," I said, " I must go. Let me have my bill." The reply was, " Mr Felstead left instructions—no bill for *you*, sir." I have been told quite recently that my reputation as a speech-maker is still remembered at the Great Central!

I had another very pleasant experience in Belfast. Calling during a flying visit to see a friend, I found the house shut up. After repeated knocking at the door, two ladies appeared at the entrance to the next house, and explained that my friend had gone away for a few days. These ladies, hearing I had come a long distance, insisted on my having some tea, and were most kind and hospitable. I learned with much pleasure that they were Mrs Faussett and Mrs Allison, sisters of the Irish poet, William Allingham.

A Lord Mayor of Dublin, who shall be nameless, was asked at a drawing-room meeting of ladies to preside and say a few words in favour of female suffrage.

It was in the closing days of November, when the term of office of the Lord Mayor was also coming to a close at the end of the year. Dublin's Chief Magistrate made a short speech in the course of which he said, " I am glad to see so many ladies here this evening, for the days of my *morality* are nearly over."

A very amusing and erratic magistrate in the West of Ireland used to make extraordinary statements from the Bench. His views of men and things were somewhat strange, as, for instance, when a man was charged with drunkenness, he asked:

" Is he drunk *now?* "

"No, your worship," replied the astonished constable.

" Then," said this modern Solomon, " for God's sake let the poor man go! "

And now my pleasant task is ended, and I must bid farewell to those who have followed me thus far. For the last nine years the scene of my labours has been laid in London, that heart of " the weary Titan," to adopt Matthew Arnold's magnificent simile ; with occasional excursions to Germany and elsewhere, all of which have tended to make me believe with Dr Johnson that he who is tired of London is tired of life.

I am by no means tired of life, or of London. " Stony-hearted Oxford Street," as De Quincey called her, has been, to me " all a wonder and a wild delight." *En route* for Southern Nigeria, I got as far as London, and said " This is the place for me! " Existence has not been an unalloyed source of joy,

In Castle and Court House

but although I have had a more strenuous time than
these pages give any hint of, I can say with Landor's
old philosopher—

> Nature I loved, and, next to Nature, Art;
> I warmed both hands before the fire of life—

and, when it sinks, I shall " be ready to depart! "

My life in England? Ah, as Rudyard Kipling says:
That's another story!

Index

315

Index

Index

Index

Index

319

Index

PRINTED AT THE NEWCASTLE-UPON-TYNE PRESS,
WATERLOO HOUSE, THORNTON STREET

MY WATCH *

AN INSTRUCTIVE LITTLE TALE

MY beautiful new watch had run eighteen months without losing or gaining, and without breaking any part of its machinery or stopping. I had come to believe it infallible in its judgments about the time of day, and to consider its constitution and its anatomy imperishable. But at last, one night, I let it run down. I grieved about it as if it were a recognized messenger and forerunner of calamity. But by and by I cheered up, set the watch by guess, and commanded my bodings and superstitions to depart. Next day I stepped into the chief jeweler's to set it by the exact time, and the head of the establishment took it out of my hand and proceeded to set it for me. Then he said, " She is four minutes slow — regulator wants pushing up." I tried to stop him — tried to make him understand that the watch kept perfect time. But no; all this human cabbage could see was that the watch was four minutes slow, and the regulator *must* be pushed up a little; and so, while I danced around him in

---

* Written about 1870

anguish, and implored him to let the watch alone, he calmly and cruelly did the shameful deed. My watch began to gain. It gained faster and faster day by day. Within the week it sickened to a raging fever, and its pulse went up to a hundred and fifty in the shade. At the end of two months it had left all the timepieces of the town far in the rear, and was a fraction over thirteen days ahead of the almanac. It was away into November enjoying the snow, while the October leaves were still turning. It hurried up house rent, bills payable, and such things, in such a ruinous way that I could not abide it. I took it to the watchmaker to be regulated. He asked me if I had ever had it repaired. I said no, it had never needed any repairing. He looked a look of vicious happiness and eagerly pried the watch open, and then put a small dice box into his eye and peered into its machinery. He said it wanted cleaning and oiling, besides regulating — come in a week. After being cleaned and oiled, and regulated, my watch slowed down to that degree that it ticked like a tolling bell. I began to be left by trains, I failed all appointments, I got to missing my dinner; my watch strung out three days' grace to four and let me go to protest; I gradually drifted back into yesterday, then day before, then into last week, and by and by the comprehension came upon me that all solitary and alone I was lingering along in week before last, and the world was out of sight. I seemed to detect in myself a sort of sneaking

fellow-feeling for the mummy in the museum, and a
desire to swap news with him. I went to a watchmaker again. He took the watch all to pieces while
I waited, and then said the barrel was " swelled."
He said he could reduce it in three days. After this
the watch *averaged* well, but nothing more. For
half a day it would go like the very mischief, and
keep up such a barking and wheezing and whooping
and sneezing and snorting, that I could not hear
myself think for the disturbance; and as long as it
held out there was not a watch in the land that stood
any chance against it. But the rest of the day it
would keep on slowing down and fooling along until
all the clocks it had left behind caught up again.
So at last, at the end of twenty-four hours, it would
trot up to the judges' stand all right and just in
time. It would show a fair and square average, and
no man could say it had done more or less than its
duty. But a correct average is only a mild virtue in
a watch, and I took this instrument to another
watchmaker. He said the kingbolt was broken. I
said I was glad it was nothing more serious. To
tell the plain truth, I had no idea what the kingbolt
was, but I did not choose to appear ignorant to a
stranger. He repaired the kingbolt, but what the
watch gained in one way it lost in another. It would
run awhile and then stop awhile, and then run awhile
again, and so on, using its own discretion about the
intervals. And every time it went off it kicked back
like a musket. I padded my breast for a few days,

2S

but finally took the watch to another watchmaker.
He picked it all to pieces, and turned the ruin over
and over under his glass; and then he said there
appeared to be something the matter with the hair-
trigger. He fixed it, and gave it a fresh start. It
did well now, except that always at ten minutes to
ten the hands would shut together like a pair of
scissors, and from that time forth they would travel
together. The oldest man in the world could not
make head or tail of the time of day by such a
watch, and so I went again to have the thing repaired. This person said that the crystal had got
bent, and that the mainspring was not straight. He
also remarked that part of the works needed half-
soling. He made these things all right, and then
my timepiece performed unexceptionably, save that
now and then, after working along quietly for nearly
eight hours, everything inside would let go all of a
sudden and begin to buzz like a bee, and the hands
would straightway begin to spin round and round so
fast that their individuality was lost completely, and
they simply seemed a delicate spider's web over the
face of the watch. She would reel off the next
twenty-four hours in six or seven minutes, and then
stop with a bang. I went with a heavy heart to one
more watchmaker, and looked on while he took her
to pieces. Then I prepared to cross-question him
rigidly, for this thing was getting serious. The watch
had cost two hundred dollars originally, and I
seemed to have paid out two or three thousand for

repairs. While I waited and looked on I presently recognized in this watchmaker an old acquaintance — a steamboat engineer of other days, and not a good engineer, either. He examined all the parts carefully, just as the other watchmakers had done, and then delivered his verdict with the same confidence of manner.

He said:

" She makes too much steam — you want to hang the monkey-wrench on the safety-valve!"

I brained him on the spot, and had him buried at my own expense.

My uncle William (now deceased, alas!) used to say that a good horse was a good horse until it had run away once, and that a good watch was a good watch until the repairers got a chance at it. And he used to wonder what became of all the unsuccessful tinkers, and gunsmiths, and shoemakers, and engineers, and blacksmiths; but nobody could ever tell him.

POLITICAL ECONOMY *

POLITICAL Economy is the basis of all good government. The wisest men of all ages have brought to bear upon this subject the——

[Here I was interrupted and informed that a stranger wished to see me down at the door. I went and confronted him, and asked to know his business, struggling all the time to keep a tight rein on my seething political economy ideas, and not let them break away from me or get tangled in their harness. And privately I wished the stranger was in the bottom of the canal with a cargo of wheat on top of him. I was all in a fever, but he was cool. He said he was sorry to disturb me, but as he was passing he noticed that I needed some lightning-rods. I said, " Yes, yes — go on — what about it?" He said there was nothing about it, in par-ticular — nothing except that he would like to put them up for me. I am new to housekeeping; have been used to hotels and boarding-houses all my life. Like anybody else of similar experience, I try to ap-pear (to strangers) to be an old housekeeper; con-

---

* Written about 1870.

sequently I said in an off-hand way that I had been
intending for some time to have six or eight lightning-rods put up, but — The stranger started, and
looked inquiringly at me, but I was serene. I thought
that if I chanced to make any mistakes, he would not
catch me by my countenance. He said he would
rather have my custom than any man's in town. I
said, "All right," and started off to wrestle with
my great subject again, when he called me back and
said it would be necessary to know exactly how
many "points" I wanted put up, what parts of the
house I wanted them on, and what quality of rod I
preferred. It was close quarters for a man not used
to the exigencies of housekeeping; but I went
through creditably, and he probably never suspected
that I was a novice. I told him to put up eight
"points," and put them all on the roof, and use
the best quality of rod. He said he could furnish
the "plain" article at 20 cents a foot; "cop-
pered," 25 cents; "zinc-plated spiral-twist," at 30
cents, that would stop a streak of lightning any time,
no matter where it was bound, and "render its errand harmless and its further progress apocryphal."
I said apocryphal was no slouch of a word, emanat-
ing from the source it did, but, philology aside, I
liked the spiral-twist and would take that brand.
Then he said he *could* make two hundred and fifty
feet answer; but to do it right, and make the best
job in town of it, and attract the admiration of the
just and the unjust alike, and compel all parties to

2

say they never saw a more symmetrical and hypo-
thetical display of lightning-rods since they were
born, he supposed he really couldn't get along without four hundred, though he was not vindictive, and
trusted he was willing to try. I said, go ahead and
use four hundred, and make any kind of a job he
pleased out of it, but let me get back to my work.
So I got rid of him at last; and now, after half an
hour spent in getting my train of political economy
thoughts coupled together again, I am ready to go
on once more.]

richest treasures of their genius, their experience of life, and their
learning. The great lights of commercial jurisprudence, international
confraternity, and biological deviation, of all ages, all civilizations, and
all nationalities, from Zoroaster down to Horace Greeley, have——

[Here I was interrupted again, and required to go
down and confer further with that lightning-rod
man. I hurried off, boiling and surging with prodigious thoughts wombed in words of such majesty
that each one of them was in itself a straggling procession of syllables that might be fifteen minutes
passing a given point, and once more I confronted
him — he so calm and sweet, I so hot and frenzied.
He was standing in the contemplative attitude of the
Colossus of Rhodes, with one foot on my infant
tuberose, and the other among my pansies, his hands
on his hips, his hat-brim tilted forward, one eye
shut and the other gazing critically and admiringly
in the direction of my principal chimney. He said
now *there* was a state of things to make a man glad

to be alive; and added, " I leave it to *you* if you ever saw anything more deliriously picturesque than eight lightning-rods on one chimney?" I said I had no present recollection of anything that transcended it. He said that in his opinion nothing on earth but Niagara Falls was superior to it in the way of natural scenery. All that was needed now, he verily believed, to make my house a perfect balm to the eye, was to kind of touch up the other chimneys a little, and thus " add to the generous *coup d'œil* a soothing uniformity of achievement which would allay the excitement naturally consequent upon the first *coup d'état.*" I asked him if he learned to talk out of a book, and if I could borrow it anywhere? He smiled pleasantly, and said that his manner of speaking was not taught in books, and that nothing but familiarity with lightning could enable a man to handle his conversational style with impunity. He then figured up an estimate, and said that about eight more rods scattered about my roof would about fix me right, and he guessed five hundred feet of stuff would do it; and added that the first eight had got a little the start of him, so to speak, and used up a mere trifle of material more than he had calculated on — a hundred feet or along there. I said I was in a dreadful hurry, and I wished we could get this business permanently mapped out, so that I could go on with my work. He said, " I *could* have put up those eight rods, and marched off about my business — some men *would* have done it.

B

But no; I said to myself, this man is a stranger to me, and I will die before I'll wrong him; there ain't lightning-rods enough on that house, and for one I'll never stir out of my tracks till I've done as I would be done by, and told him so. Stranger, my duty is accomplished; if the recalcitrant and dephlogistic messenger of heaven strikes your—'' '' There, now, there,'' I said, '' put on the other eight — add five hundred feet of spiral-twist — do anything and everything you want to do; but calm your sufferings, and try to keep your feelings where you can reach them with the dictionary. Meanwhile, if we understand each other now, I will go to work again.''

I think I have been sitting here a full hour this time, trying to get back to where I was when my train of thought was broken up by the last interruption; but I believe I have accomplished it at last, and may venture to proceed again.]

wrestled with this great subject, and the greatest among them have found it a worthy adversary, and one that always comes up fresh and smiling after every throw. The great Confucius said that he would rather be a profound political economist than chief of police. Cicero frequently said that political economy was the grandest consummation that the human mind was capable of consuming; and even our own Greeley has said vaguely but forcibly that '' *Political*——

[Here the lightning-rod man sent up another call for me. I went down in a state of mind bordering on impatience. He said he would rather have died than interrupt me, but when he was employed to do a job, and that job was expected to be done in a clean, workmanlike manner, and when it was finished and fatigue urged him to seek the rest and recreation he stood so much in need of, and he was about to do it, but looked up and saw at a glance that all the calculations had been a little out, and if a thunder storm were to come up, and that house, which he felt a personal interest in, stood there with nothing on earth to protect it but sixteen lightning-rods — "Let us have peace!" I shrieked. "Put up a hundred and fifty! Put some on the kitchen! Put a dozen on the barn! Put a couple on the cow! — Put one on the cook! — scatter them all over the persecuted place till it looks like a zinc-plated, spiral-twisted, silver-mounted cane-brake! Move! Use up all the material you can get your hands on, and when you run out of lightning-rods put up ram-rods, cam-rods, stair-rods, piston-rods — *anything* that will pander to your dismal appetite for artificial scenery, and bring respite to my raging brain and healing to my lacerated soul!" Wholly unmoved — further than to smile sweetly — this iron being simply turned back his wristbands daintily, and said he would now proceed to hump himself. Well, all that was nearly three hours ago. It is question-able whether I am calm enough yet to write on the noble theme of political economy, but I cannot resist the desire to try, for it is the one subject that is nearest to my heart and dearest to my brain of all this world's philosophy.]

"——*economy is heaven's best boon to man.*" When the loose but gifted Byron lay in his Venetian exile he observed that, if it could be granted him to go back and live his misspent life over again, he would give his lucid and unintoxicated intervals to the composition, not of frivolous rhymes, but of essays upon political economy. Washington loved this exquisite science; such names as Baker, Beckwith, Judson, Smith, are imperishably linked with it; and even imperial Homer, in the ninth book of the Iliad, has said:—

> Fiat justitia, ruat cœlum,
> Post mortem unum, ante bellum,
> Hic jacet hoc, ex-parte res,
> Politicum e-conomico est.

The grandeur of these conceptions of the old poet, together with the felicity of the wording which clothes them, and the sublimity of the imagery whereby they are illustrated, have singled out that stanza, and made it more celebrated than any that ever——

[" Now, not a word out of you — not a single word. Just state your bill and relapse into impenetrable silence for ever and ever on these premises. Nine hundred dollars? Is that all? This check for the amount will be honored at any respectable bank in America. What is that multitude of people gathered in the street for? How? — ' looking at the lightning-rods!' Bless my life, did they never see any lightning-rods before? Never saw ' such a stack of them on one establishment,' did I understand you to say? I will step down and critically observe this popular ebullition of ignorance."]

THREE DAYS LATER.— We are all about worn out. For four-and-twenty hours our bristling premises were the talk and wonder of the town. The

theaters languished, for their happiest scenic inven-
tions were tame and commonplace compared with
my lightning-rods. Our street was blocked night
and day with spectators, and among them were
many who came from the country to see. It was a
blessed relief on the second day when a thunder
storm came up and the lightning began to " go for "
my house, as the historian Josephus quaintly phrases
it. It cleared the galleries, so to speak. In five
minutes there was not a spectator within half a mile
of my place; but all the high houses about that distance away were full, windows, roof, and all. And
well they might be, for all the falling stars and Fourth
of July fireworks of a generation, put together and
rained down simultaneously out of heaven in one
brilliant shower upon one helpless roof, would not
have any advantage of the pyrotechnic display that
was making my house so magnificently conspicuous
in the general gloom of the storm. By actual count,
the lightning struck at my establishment seven hundred and sixty-four times in forty minutes, but
tripped on one of those faithful rods every time,
and slid down the spiral-twist and shot into the
earth before it probably had time to be surprised at
the way the thing was done. And through all that
bombardment only one patch of slates was ripped
up, and that was because, for a single instant, the
rods in the vicinity were transporting all the lightning they could possibly accommodate. Well, nothing was ever seen like it since the world began. For

one whole day and night not a member of my family stuck his head out of the window but he got the hair snatched off it as smooth as a billiard-ball; and, if the reader will believe me, not one of us ever dreamt of stirring abroad. But at last the awful siege came to an end — because there was absolutely no more electricity left in the clouds above us within grappling distance of my insatiable rods. Then I sallied forth, and gathered daring workmen together, and not a bite or a nap did we take till the premises were utterly stripped of all their terrific armament except just three rods on the house, one on the kitchen, and one on the barn — and, behold, these remain there even unto this day. And then, and not till then, the people ventured to use our street again. I will remark here, in passing, that during that fearful time I did not continue my essay upon political economy. I am not even yet settled enough in nerve and brain to resume it.

TO WHOM IT MAY CONCERN.— Parties having need of three thousand two hundred and eleven feet of best quality zinc-plated spiral-twist lightning-rod stuff, and sixteen hundred and thirty-one silver-tipped points, all in tolerable repair (and, although much worn by use, still equal to any ordinary emergency), can hear of a bargain by addressing the publisher.

THE JUMPING FROG*

IN ENGLISH. THEN IN FRENCH. THEN CLAWED BACK INTO A CIVILIZED LANGUAGE ONCE MORE BY PATIENT, UN-RENUMERATED TOIL

EVEN a criminal is entitled to fair play; and certainly when a man who has done no harm has been unjustly treated, he is privileged to do his best to right himself. My attention has just been called to an article some three years old in a French Magazine entitled, " Revue des Deux Mondes " (Review of Some Two Worlds), wherein the writer treats of " Les Humoristes Americaines " (These Humorists Americans). I am one of these humorists Americans dissected by him, and hence the complaint I am making.

This gentleman's article is an able one (as articles go, in the French, where they always tangle up everything to that degree that when you start into a sentence you never know whether you are going to come out alive or not). It is a very good article, and the writer says all manner of kind and complimentary things about me — for which I am sure I

* Written about 1865.

thank him with all my heart; but then why should
he go and spoil all his praise by one unlucky experiment? What I refer to is this: he says my Jumping
Frog is a funny story, but still he can't see why it
should ever really convulse any one with laughter —
and straightway proceeds to translate it into French
in order to prove to his nation that there is nothing
so very extravagantly funny about it. Just there is
where my complaint originates. He has not translated it at all; he has simply mixed it all up; it is
no more like the Jumping Frog when he gets through
with it than I am like a meridian of longitude. But
my mere assertion is not proof; wherefore I print
the French version, that all may see that I do not
speak falsely; furthermore, in order that even the
unlettered may know my injury and give me their
compassion, I have been at infinite pains and trouble
to re-translate this French version back into English;
and to tell the truth I have well nigh worn myself
out at it, having scarcely rested from my work
during five days and nights. I cannot speak the
French language, but I can translate very well,
though not fast, I being self-educated. I ask the
reader to run his eye over the original English
version of the Jumping Frog, and then read the
French or my re-translation, and kindly take notice
how the Frenchman has riddled the grammar. I
think it is the worst I ever saw; and yet the French
are called a polished nation. If I had a boy that
put sentences together as they do, I would polish

him to some purpose. Without further introduction, the Jumping Frog, as I originally wrote it, was as follows [after it will be found the French version, and after the latter my re-translation from the French]:

THE NOTORIOUS JUMPING FROG OF CALAVERAS* COUNTY.

In compliance with the request of a friend of mine, who wrote me from the East, I called on good-natured, garrulous old Simon Wheeler, and inquired after my friend's friend, Leonidas W. Smiley, as requested to do, and I hereunto append the result. I have a lurking suspicion that *Leonidas W.* Smiley is a myth; that my friend never knew such a personage; and that he only conjectured that if I asked old Wheeler about him, it would remind him of his infamous *Jim* Smiley, and he would go to work and bore me to death with some exasperating reminiscence of him as long and as tedious as it should be useless to me. If that was the design, it succeeded.

I found Simon Wheeler dozing comfortably by the barroom stove of the dilapidated tavern in the decayed mining camp of Angel's, and I noticed that he was fat and bald-headed, and had an expression of winning gentleness and simplicity upon his tranquil countenance. He roused up, and gave me good-day. I told him a friend of mine had commissioned me to make some inquiries about a cherished companion of his boyhood named *Leonidas W.* Smiley — *Rev. Leonidas W.* Smiley, a young minister of the Gospel, who he had heard was at one time a resident of Angel's Camp. I added that if Mr. Wheeler could tell me anything about this Rev. Leonidas W. Smiley, I would feel under many obligations to him.

Simon Wheeler backed me into a corner and blockaded me there with his chair, and then sat down and reeled off the monotonous narrative which follows this paragraph. He never smiled, he never frowned, he never changed his voice from the gentle-flowing key to which he tuned his initial sentence, he never betrayed the slightest suspicion of enthusiasm; but all through the interminable narrative there ran a vein

---

* Pronounced Cal-e-*va*-ras.

of impressive earnestness and sincerity, which showed me plainly that, so far from his imagining that there was anything ridiculous or funny about his story, he regarded it as a really important matter, and admired its two heroes as men of transcendent genius in *finesse*. I let him go on in his own way, and never interrupted him once.

"Rev. Leonidas W. H'm, Reverend Le — well, there was a feller here once by the name of *Jim* Smiley, in the winter of '49 — or may be it was the spring of '50 — I don't recollect exactly, somehow, though what makes me think it was one or the other is because I remember the big flume warn't finished when he first come to the camp; but any way, he was the curiosest man about always betting on anything that turned up you ever see, if he could get anybody to bet on the other side; and if he couldn't he'd change sides. Any way that suited the other man would suit *him* — any way just so's he got a bet, *he* was satisfied. But still he was lucky, uncommon lucky; he most always come out winner. He was always ready and laying for a chance; there couldn't be no solit'ry thing mentioned but that feller'd offer to bet on it, and take ary side you please, as I was just telling you. If there was a horse-race, you'd find him flush or you'd find him busted at the end of it; if there was a dog-fight, he'd bet on it; if there was a cat-fight, he'd bet on it; if there was a chicken-fight, he'd bet on it; why, if there was two birds setting on a fence, he would bet you which one would fly first; or if there was a camp-meeting, he would be there reg'lar to bet on Parson Walker, which he judged to be the best exhorter about here, and so he was too, and a good man. If he even see a straddle-bug start to go anywheres, he would bet you how long it would take him to get to — to wherever he was going to, and if you took him up, he would foller that straddle-bug to Mexico but what he would find out where he was bound for and how long he was on the road. Lots of the boys here has seen that Smiley, and can tell you about him. Why, it never made no difference to *him* — he'd bet on *any* thing — the dangdest feller. Parson Walker's wife laid very sick once, for a good while, and it seemed as if they warn't going to save her; but one morning he come in, and Smiley up and asked him how she was, and he said she was considable better — thank the Lord for his inf'nite mercy — and coming on so smart that with the blessing of Prov'dence she'd get well yet; and Smiley, before he thought, says, "Well, I'll resk two-and-a-half she don't anyway."

Thish-yer Smiley had a mare — the boys called her the fifteen-minute nag, but that was only in fun, you know, because of course she was faster than that — and he used to win money on that horse, for all she was so slow and always had the asthma, or the distemper, or the consumption, or something of that kind. They used to give her two or three hundred yards start, and then pass her under way; but always at the fag end of the race she'd get excited and desperate like, and come cavorting and straddling up, and scattering her legs around limber, sometimes in the air, and sometimes out to one side among the fences, and kicking up m-o-r-e dust and raising m-o-r-e racket with her coughing and sneezing and blowing her nose — and *always* fetch up at the stand just about a neck ahead, as near as you could cipher it down.

And he had a little small bull-pup, that to look at him you'd think he warn't worth a cent but to set around and look ornery and lay for a chance to steal something. But as soon as money was up on him he was a different dog; his under-jaw'd begin to stick out like the fo'castle of a steamboat, and his teeth would uncover and shine like the furnaces. And a dog might tackle him and bully-rag him, and bite him, and throw him over his shoulder two or three times, and Andrew Jackson — which was the name of the pup — Andrew Jackson would never let on but what *he* was satisfied, and hadn't expected nothing else — and the bets being doubled and doubled on the other side all the time, till the money was all up; and then all of a sudden he would grab that other dog jest by the j'int of his hind leg and freeze to it — not chaw, you understand, but only just grip and hang on till they throwed up the sponge, if it was a year. Smiley always come out winner on that pup, till he harnessed a dog once that didn't have no hind legs, because they'd been sawed off in a circular saw, and when the thing had gone along far enough, and the money was all up, and he come to make a snatch for his pet holt, he see in a minute how he'd been imposed on, and how the other dog had him in the door, so to speak, and he 'peared surprised, and then he looked sorter discouraged-like, and didn't try no more to win the fight, and so he got shucked out bad. He give Smiley a look, as much as to say his heart was broke, and it was *his* fault, for putting up a dog that hadn't no hind legs for him to take holt of, which was his main dependence in a fight, and then he limped off a piece and laid down and died. It was a good pup, was that Andrew Jackson, and would have made a name for hisself if he'd lived, for the stuff was in him and he had genius — I know it, because he hadn't no opportunities to speak of, and it don't stand to reason that a dog could make such a fight as he could under them circumstances if he hadn't no talent. It always makes me feel sorry when I think of that last fight of his'n, and the way it turned out.

Well, thish-yer Smiley had rat-tarriers, and chicken cocks, and tom-cats and all them kind of things, till you couldn't rest, and you couldn't fetch nothing for him to bet on but he'd match you. He ketched a frog one day, and took him home, and said he cal'lated to educate him; and so he never done nothing for three months but set in his back yard and learn that frog to jump. And you bet you he *did* learn him, too. He'd give him a little punch behind, and the next minute you'd see that frog whirling in the air like a doughnut — see him turn one sum-merset, or may be a couple, if he got a good start, and come down flat-footed and all right, like a cat. He got him up so in the matter of ketching flies, and kep' him in practice so constant, that he'd nail a fly every time as fur as he could see him. Smiley said all a frog wanted was education, and he could do 'most anything — and I believe him. Why, I've seen him set Dan'l Webster down here on this floor — Dan'l Webster was the name of the frog — and sing out, "Flies, Dan'l, flies!" and quicker'n you could wink he'd spring straight up and snake a fly off'n the counter there, and flop down on the floor ag'in as solid as a gob of mud, and fall to scratching the side of his head with his hind foot as indifferent as if he hadn't no idea he'd been doin' any more'n any frog might do. You never see a frog so modest and straightfor'ard as he was, for all he was so gifted. And when it come to fair and square jumping on a dead level, he could get over more ground at one straddle than any animal of his breed you ever see. Jumping on a dead level was his strong suit, you understand; and when it come to that, Smiley would ante up money on him as long as he had a red. Smiley was monstrous proud of his frog, and well he might be, for fellers that had traveled and been everywheres all said he laid over any frog that ever *they* see.

Well, Smiley kep' the beast in a little lattice box, and he used to fetch him down town sometimes and lay for a bet. One day a feller — a stranger in the camp, he was — come acrost him with his box, and says:

"What might it be that you've got in the box?"

And Smiley says, sorter indifferent-like, "It might be a parrot, or it might be a canary, maybe, but it ain't — its only just a frog."

And the feller took it, and looked at it careful, and turned it round this way and that, and says, "H'm — so 'tis. Well, what's *he* good for?"

"FLIES, DAN'L, FLIES!"

"Well," Smiley says, easy and careless, "he's good enough for *one* thing, I should judge — he can outjump any frog in Calaveras county."

The feller took the box again, and took another long, particular look, and give it back to Smiley, and says, very deliberate, "Well," he says, "I don't see no p'ints about that frog that's any better'n any other frog."

"Maybe you don't," Smiley says. "Maybe you understand frogs and maybe you don't understand 'em; maybe you've had experience, and maybe you ain't only a amature, as it were. Anyways, I've got *my* opinion, and I'll resk forty dollars that he can outjump any frog in Calaveras county."

And the feller studied a minute, and then says, kinder sad like, "Well, I'm only a stranger here, and I ain't got no frog; but if I had a frog, I'd bet you."

And then Smiley says, "That's all right — that's all right — if you'll hold my box a minute, I'll go and get you a frog." And so the feller took the box, and put up his forty dollars along with Smiley's, and set down to wait.

So he set there a good while thinking and thinking to hisself, and then he got the frog out and prized his mouth open and took a teaspoon and filled him full of quail shot — filled him pretty near up to his chin — and set him on the floor. Smiley he went to the swamp and slopped around in the mud for a long time, and finally he ketched a frog, and fetched him in, and give him to this feller, and says:

"Now, if you're ready, set him alongside of Dan'l, with his forepaws just even with Dan'l's, and I'll give the word." Then he says, "One — two — three — *git!*" and him and the feller touched up the frogs from behind, and the new frog hopped off lively, but Dan'l give a heave, and hysted up his shoulders — so — like a Frenchman, but it warn't no use — he couldn't budge; he was planted as solid as a church, and he couldn't no more stir than if he was anchored out. Smiley was a good deal surprised, and he was disgusted too, but he didn't have no idea what the matter was, of course.

The feller took the money and started away; and when he was going out at the door, he sorter jerked his thumb over his shoulder — so — at Dan'l, and says again, very deliberate, "Well," he says, "*I* don't see no p'ints about that frog that's any better'n any other frog."

Smiley he stood scratching his head and looking down at Dan'l a long time, and at last he says, "I do wonder what in the nation that frog throw'd off for — I wonder if there ain't something the matter with him — he 'pears to look mighty baggy, somehow." And he ketched Dan'l by the nap of the neck, and hefted him, and says, "Why blame my cats if he don't weigh five pound!" and turned him upside down and he belched out a double handful of shot. And then he see how it was, and he was the maddest man — he set the frog down and took out after that feller, but he never ketched him. And——"

[Here Simon Wheeler heard his name called from the front yard, and got up to see what was wanted.] And turning to me as he moved away, he said: "Just set where you are, stranger, and rest easy — I ain't going to be gone a second."

But, by your leave, I did not think that a continuation of the history of the enterprising vagabond *Jim* Smiley would be likely to afford me much information concerning the Rev. *Leonidas W.* Smiley, and so I started away.

At the door I met the sociable Wheeler returning, and he button-holed me and re-commenced:

"Well, thish-yer Smiley had a yaller one-eyed cow that didn't have no tail, only just a short stump like a bannanner, and——"

However, lacking both time and inclination, I did not wait to hear about the afflicted cow, but took my leave.

Now let the learned look upon this picture and say if iconoclasm can further go:

[From the *Revue des Deux Mondes*, of July 15th, 1872.]

LA GRENOUILLE SANTEUSE DU COMTE DE CALAVERAS.

"—Il y avait une fois ici un individu connu sous le nom de Jim Smiley: c'était dans l'hiver de 49, peut-être bien au printemps de 50, je ne me rappelle pas exactement. Ce qui me fait croire que c'était l'un ou l'autre, c'est que je me souviens que le grand bief n'était pas achevé lorsqu'il arriva au camp pour la premiére fois, mais de toutes façons il était l'homme le plus friand de paris qui se pût voir, pariant sur tout ce qui se présentait, quand il pouvait trouver un adversaire, et, quand il n'en trouvait pas il passait du côté opposé. Tout ce qui convenait à l'autre lui convenait; pourvu qu'il eût un pari, Smiley était satisfait. Et il avait une chance! une chance inouie: presque toujours il gagnait.

Il faut dire qu'il était toujours prêt à s'exposer, qu'on ne pouvait mentionner la moindre chose sans que ce gaillard offrît de parier là-dessus n'importe quoi et de prendre le côté que l'on voudrait, comme je vous le disais tout à l'heure. S'il y avait des courses, vous le trouviez riche ou ruiné à la fin; s'il y avait un combat de chiens, il apportait son enjeu; il l'apportait pour un combat de chats, pour un combat de coqs;—parbleu! si vous aviez vu deux oiseaux sur une haie, il vous aurait offert de parier lequel s'envolerait le premier, et, s'il y avait *meeting* au camp, il venait parier régulièrement pour le curé Walker, qu'il jugeait être le meilleur prédicateur des environs, et qui l'était en effet, et un brave homme. Il aurait rencontré une punaise de bois en chemin, qu'il aurait parié sur le temps qu'il lui faudrait pour aller où elle voudrait aller, et, si vous l'aviez pris au mot, il aurait suivi la punaise jusqu'au Mexique, sans se soucier d'aller si loin, ni du temps qu'il y perdrait. Une fois la femme du curé Walker fut très malade pendant longtemps, il semblait qu'on ne la sauverait pas; mais un matin le curé arrive, et Smiley lui demande comment ella va, et il dit qu'elle est bien mieux, grâce à l'infinie miséricorde, tellement mieux qu'avec la bénédiction de la Providence elle s'en tirerait, et voilá que, sans y penser, Smiley répond:—Eh bien! ye gage deux et demi qu'elle mourra tout de même.

"Ce Smiley avait une jument que les gars appelaient le bidet du quart d'heure, mais seulement pour plaisanter, vous comprenez, parce que, bien entendu, elle était plus *vite* que ça! Et il avait coutume de gagner de l'argent avec cette bête, quoiqu'elle fût poussive, cornarde, toujours prise d'asthme, de coliques ou de consomption, ou de quelque chose d'approchant. On lui donnait 2 ou 300 *yards* au départ, puis on la dépassait sans peine; mais jamais à la fin elle ne manquait de s'échauffer, de s'exaspérer, et elle arrivait, s'écartant, se défendant, ses jambes grêles en l'air devant les obstacles, quelquefois les évitant et faisant avec cela plus de poussière qu'aucun cheval, plus de bruit surtout avec ses éternumens et reniflemens,—crac! elle arrivait donc toujours première d'une tête, aussi juste qu'on peut le mesurer. Et il avait un petit bouledogue qui, à le voir, ne valait pas un sou; on aurait cru que parier contre lui c'était voler, tant il était ordinaire; mais aussitôt les enjeux faits, il devenait un autre chien. Sa mâchoire inférieure commençait à ressortir comme un gaillard d'avant, ses dents se découvraient brillantes commes des fournaises, et un chien pouvait le taquiner, l'exciter, le mordre, le jeter deux ou trois fois par-dessus son

épaule, André Jackson, c'était le nom du chien, André Jackson prenait
cela tranquillement, comme s'il ne se fût jamais attendu à autre chose, et
quand les paris étaient doublés et redoublés contre lui, il vous saisissait
l'autre chien juste à l'articulation de la jambe de derrière, et il ne la
lâchait plus, non pas qu'il la mâchât, vous concevez, mais il s'y serait tenu
pendu jusqu'à ce qu'on jetât l'éponge en l'air, fallût-il attendre un an.
Smiley gagnait toujours avec cette bête-là; malheureusement ils ont fini
par dresser un chien qui n'avait pas de pattes de derrière, parce qu'on les
avait sciées, et quand les choses furent au point qu'il voulait, et qu'il en
vint à se jeter sur son morceau favori, le pauvre chien comprit en un instant qu'on s'était moqué de lui, et que l'autre le tenait. Vous n'avez
jamais vu personne avoir l'air plus penaud et plus découragé; il ne fit
aucun effort pour gagner le combat et fut rudement secoué, de sorte que,
regardant Smiley comme pour lui dire:—Mon cœur est brisé, c'est ta
faute; pourquoi m'avoir livré à un chien qui n'a pas de pattes de derrière,
puisque c'est par là que je les bats?—il s'en alla en clopinant, et se
coucha pour mourir. Ah! c'était un bon chien, cet André Jackson, et
il se serait fait un nom, s'il avait vécu, car il y avait de l'etoffe en lui, il
avait du génie, je la sais, bien que de grandes occasions lui aient
manqué; mais il est impossible de supposer qu'un chien capable de se
battre comme lui, certaines circonstances étant données, ait manqué de
talent. Je me sens triste toutes les fois que je pense à son dernier
combat et au dénoûment qu'il a eu. Eh bien! ce Smiley nourrissait des
terriers à rats, et des coqs de combat, et des chats, et toute sorte de
choses, au point qu'il était toujours en mesure de vous tenir tête, et
qu'avec sa rage de paris on n'avait plus de repos. Il attrapa un jour une
grenouille et l'emporta chez lui, disant qu'il prétendait faire son éducation; vous me croirez si vous voulez, mais pendant trois mois il n'a rien
fait que lui apprendre à sauter dans une cour retirée de sa maison. Et je
vous réponds qu'il avait réussi. Il lui donnait un petit coup par
derrière, et l'instant d'après vous voyiez la grenouille tourner en l'air
comme un beignet au-dessus de la poêle, faire une culbute, quelquefois
deux, lorsqu'elle était bien partie, et retomber sur ses pattes comme un
chat. Il l'avait dressée dans l'art de gober des mouches, et l'y exerçait
continuellement, si bien qu'une mouche, du plus loin qu'elle apparaissait,
était une mouche perdue. Smiley avait coutume de dire que tout ce qui
manquait à une grenouille, c'était l'éducation, qu'avec l'éducation elle
pouvait faire presque tout, et je le crois. Tenez, je l'ai vu poser
Daniel Webster là sur se plancher,—Daniel Webster était le nom de la

grenouille,— et lui chanter:— Des mouches! Daniel, des mouches !—
En un clin d'œil, Daniel avait bondi et saisi une mouche ici sur le
comptoir, puis sauté de nouveau par terre, où il restait vraiment à se
gratter la tête avec sa patte de derrière, comme s'il n'avait pas eu la
moindre idée de sa supériorité. Jamais vous n'avez grenouille vu de
aussi modeste, aussi naturelle, douée comme elle l'était ! Et quand il
s'agissait de sauter purement et simplement sur terrain plat, elle faisait
plus de chemin en un saut qu'aucune bête de son espèce que vous
puissiez connaître. Sauter à plat, c'était son fort ! Quand il s'agissait
de cela, Smiley entassait les enjeux sur elle tant qu'il lui, restait un
rouge liard. Il faut le reconnaître, Smiley était monstrueusement fier
de sa grenouille, et il en avait le droit, car des gens qui avaient voyagé,
qui avaient tout vu, disaient qu'on lui ferait injure de la comparer à une
autre; de façon que Smiley gardait Daniel dans une petite boîte à claire-
voie qu'il emporta it parfois à la ville pour quelque pari.

"Un jour, un individu étranger au camp l'arrête avec sa boîte et lui
dit:— Qu'est-ce que vous avez donc serré là dedans?

"Smiley dit d'un air indifférent:— Cela pourrait être un perroquet
ou un serin, mais ce n'est rien de pareil, ce n'est qu'une grenouille.

"L'individu la prend, la regarde avec soin, la tourne d'un côté et
de l'autre puss il dit.— Tiens ! en effet ! A quoi est-elle bonne?

"—Mon Dieu! répond Smiley, toujours d'un air dégagé, elle est
bonne pour une chose à mon avis, elle peut battre en sautant toute
grenouille du comté de Calaveras.

"L'individu reprend la boîte, l'examine de nouveau longuement, et
la rend à Smiley en disant d'un air délibéré:— Eh bien ! je ne vois pas
que cette grenouille ait rien de mieux qu'aucune grenouille.

"—Possible que vous ne le voyiez paz, dit Smiley, possible que vous
vous entendiez en grenouilles, possible que vous ne vous y entendez
point, possible que vous ayez de l'expérience, et possible que vous ne
soyez qu'un amateur. De toute manière, je parie quarante dollars
qu'elle battra en sautant n'importe quelle grenouille du comté de
Calaveras.

"L'individu réfléchit une seconde et dit comme attristé:— Je ne
suis qu'un étranger ici, je n'ai pas de grenouille; mais, si j'en avais une,
je tiendrais le pari.

"—Fort bien! répond Smiley. Rien de plus facile. Si vous
voulez tenir ma boîte une minute, j'irai vous chercher une grenouille.—
Voilà donc l'individu qui garde la boîte, qui met ses quarante dollars sur

ceux de Smiley et qui attend. Il attend assez longtemps, réfléchissant tout seul, et figurez-vous qu'il prend Daniel, lui ouvre la bouche de force et avec une cuiller à thé l'emplit de menu plomb de chasse, mais l'emplit jusqu'au menton, puis il le pose par terre. Smiley pendant ce temps était à barboter dans une mare. Finalement il attrape une grenouille, l'apporte à cet individu et dit:—Maintenant, si vous êtes prêt, mettez-la tout contre Daniel, avec leurs pattes de devant sur la même ligne, et je donnerai le signal;—puis il ajoute:— Un, deux, trois, sautez!

"Lui et l'individu touchent leurs grenouilles par derrière, et la grenouille neuve se met à sautiller, mais Daniel se soulève lourdement, hausse les épaules ainsi, comme un Français; à quoi bon? il ne pouvait bouger, il était planté solide comme une enclume, il n'avançait pas puis que si on l'eût mis á l'ancre. Smiley fut surpris et dégoûté, mais il ne se doutait pas du tour, bien entendu. L'individu empoche l'argent, s'en va, et en s'en allant est-ce qu'il ne donne pas un coup de pouce par-dessus lé'paule, comme ça, au pauvre Daniel, en disant de son air délibéré:—Eh bien! je ne vois pas que cette grenouille ait rien de mieux qu'une autre.

"Smiley se gratta longtemps la tête, les yeux fixés sur Daniel, jusqu'à ce qu'enfin il dit:—Je me demande comment diable il se fait que cette bête ait refusé. . . Est-ce qu'elle aurait quelque chose? . . On croirait qu'elle est enflée.

"Il empoigne Daniel par la peau du cou, le soulève et dit:—Le loup me croque, s'il ne pèse pas cinq livres.

"Il le retourne, et le malheureux crache deux poignées de plomb. Quand Smiley reconnut ce qui en était, il fut comme fou. Vous le voyez d'ici poser sa grenouille par terre et courir après cet individu, mais il ne le rattrapa jamais, et. . .

[Translation of the above back from the French.]

THE FROG JUMPING OF THE COUNTY OF CALAVERAS.

It there was one time here an individual known under the name of Jim Smiley; it was in the winter of '49, possibly well at the spring of '50, I no me

recollect not exactly. This which me makes to believe that it was the one or the other, it is that I
shall remember that the grand flume is not achieved
when he arrives at the camp for the first time, but
of all sides he was the man the most fond of to bet
which one have seen, betting upon all that which is
presented, when he could find an adversary; and
when he not of it could not, he passed to the side
opposed. All that which convenienced to the other,
to him convenienced also; seeing that he had a bet,
Smiley was satisfied. And he had a chance! a
chance even worthless; nearly always he gained.
It must to say that he was always near to himself
expose, but one no could mention the least thing
without that this gaillard offered to bet the bottom,
no matter what, and to take the side that one him
would, as I you it said all at the hour (tout à
l'heure). If it there was of races, you him find
rich or ruined at the end; if it there is a combat of
dogs, he bring his bet; he himself laid always for a
combat of cats, for a combat of cocks; — by-blue!
If you have see two birds upon a fence, he you
should have offered of to bet which of those birds
shall fly the first; and if there is *meeting* at the
camp (*meeting* au camp) he comes to bet regularly
for the curé Walker, which he judged to be the best
predicator of the neighborhood (prédicateur des
environs) and which he was in effect, and a brave
man. He would encounter a bug of wood in the
road, whom he will bet upon the time which he

shall take to go where she would go — and if you
him have take at the word, he will follow the bug as
far as Mexique, without himself caring to go so far;
neither of the time which he there lost.   One time
the woman of the curé Walker is very sick during
long time, it seemed that one not her saved not;
but one morning the curé arrives, and Smiley him
demanded how she goes, and he said that she is well
better, grace to the infinite misery (lui demande
comment elle va, et il dit qu'elle est bien mieux,
grâce à l'infinie misèricorde) so much better that with
the benediction of the Providence she herself of it
would pull out (elle s'en tirerait) ; and behold that
without there thinking Smiley responds : " Well, I
gage two-and-half that she will die all of same."

This Smiley had an animal which the boys called
the nag of the quarter of hour, but solely for pleasantry, you comprehend, because, well understand,
she was more fast as that! [Now why that excla-
mation? — M. T.] And it was custom of to gain
of the silver with this beast, notwithstanding she
was poussive, cornarde, always taken of asthma, of
colics or of consumption, or something of approaching.   One him would give two or three hundred
yards at the departure, then one him passed without
pain ; but never at the last she not fail of herself
èchauffer, of herself exasperate, and she arrives herself écartant, se dèfendant, her legs grêles in the air
before the obstacles, sometimes them elevating and
making with this more of dust than any horse, more

of noise above with his éternumens and reniflemens
— crac! she arrives then always first by one head,
as just as one can it measure. And he had a small
bull dog (boule dogue!) who, to him see, no value,
not a cent; one would believe that to bet against
him it was to steal, so much he was ordinary; but
as soon as the game made, she becomes another
dog. Her jaw inferior commence to project like a
deck of before, his teeth themselves discover brilliant
like some furnaces, and a dog could him tackle (le
taquiner), him excite, him murder (le mordre), him
throw two or three times over his shoulder, André
Jackson — this was the name of the dog — André
Jackson takes that tranquilly, as if he not himself
was never expecting other thing, and when the bets
were doubled and redoubled against him, he you
seize the other dog just at the articulation of the
leg of behind, and he not it leave more, not that he
it masticate, you conceive, but he himself there shall
be holding during until that one throws the sponge
in the air, must he wait a year. Smiley gained
always with this beast-là; unhappily they have
finished by elevating a dog who no had not of feet
of behind, because one them had sawed; and when
things were at the point that he would, and that he
came to himself throw upon his morsel favorite, the
poor dog comprehended in an instant that he himself was deceived in him, and that the other dog him
had. You no have never see person having the air
more penaud and more discouraged; he not made

no effort to gain the combat, and was rudely shucked.

Eh bien! this Smiley nourished some terriers à rats, and some cocks of combat, and some cats, and all sorts of things; and with his rage of betting one no had more of repose. He trapped one day a frog and him imported with him (et l'emporta chez lui) saying that he pretended to make his education. You me believe if you will, but during three months he not has nothing done but to him apprehend to jump (apprendre ă sauter) in a court retired of her mansion (de sa maison). And I you respond that he have succeeded. He him gives a small blow by behind, and the instant after you shall see the frog turn in the air like a grease-biscuit, make one sum-mersault, sometimes two, when she was well started, and re-fall upon his feet like a cat. He him had accomplished in the art of to gobble the flies (gober des mouches), and him there exercised continually — so well that a fly at the most far that she appeared was a fly lost. Smiley had custom to say that all which lacked to a frog it was the education, but with the education she could do nearly all — and I him believe. Tenez, I him have seen pose Daniel Webster there upon this plank — Daniel Webster was the name of the frog — and to him sing, "Some flies, Daniel, some flies!" — in a flash of the eye Daniel had bounded and seized a fly here upon the counter, then jumped anew at the earth, where he rested truly to himself scratch the head with his behind foot, as if he no had not the least idea of his superiority. Never you not have seen frog as modest, as natural, sweet as she was. And when he himself agitated to jump purely and simply upon plain earth, she does more ground in one jump than any beast of his species than you can know. To jump plain — this was his strong. When he himself agitated for that, Smiley multiplied the bets upon her as long as there to him remained a red. It must to know, Smiley was monstrously proud of his frog, and he of it was right, for some men who were traveled, who had all seen, said that they to him would be injurious to him compare to another frog. Smiley guarded Daniel in a little box latticed which he carried bytimes to the village for some bet.

One day an individual stranger at the camp him arrested with his box and him said:

"What is this that you have then shut up there within?"

Smiley said, with an air indifferent:

"That could be a paroquet, or a syringe (ou un serin), but this no is nothing of such, it not is but a frog."

The individual it took, it regarded with care, it turned from one side and from the other, then he said:

"Tiens! in effect! — At what is she good?"

"My God!" respond Smiley, always with an air disengaged, "she is good for one thing, to my notice (à mon avis), she can batter in jumping (elle peut batter en sautant) all frogs of the county of Calaveras."

The individual re-took the box, it examined of new longly, and it rendered to Smiley in saying with an air deliberate:

"Eh bien! I no saw not that that frog had nothing of better than each frog." (Je ne vois pas que cette grenouille ait rien de mieux qu'aucune grenouille.) [If that isn't grammar gone to seed, then I count myself no judge.—M. T.]

"Possible that you not it saw not," said Smiley, "possible that you — you comprehend frogs; possible that you not you there comprehend nothing; possible that you had of the experience, and possible that you not be but an amateur. Of all manner (De toute manière) I bet forty dollars that she batter in jumping no matter which frog of the county of Calaveras."

The individual reflected a second, and said like sad:

"I not am but a stranger here, I no have not a frog; but if I of it had one, I would embrace the bet."

"Strong well!" respond Smiley; "nothing of more facility. If you will hold my box a minute, I go you to search a frog (j' irai vous chercher)."

Behold, then, the individual, who guards the box, who puts his forty dollars upon those of Smiley, and who attends (et qui attend). He attended enough longtimes, reflecting all solely. And figure

you that he takes Daniel, him opens the mouth by
force and with a teaspoon him fills with shot of the
hunt, even him fills just to the chin, then he him
puts by the earth. Smiley during these times was
at slopping in a swamp. Finally he trapped (attrape) a frog, him carried to that individual, and said :

"Now if you be ready, put him all against
Daniel, with their before feet upon the same line,
and I give the signal "— then he added : "One,
two, three — advance !"

Him and the individual touched their frogs by
behind, and the frog new put to jump smartly, but
Daniel himself lifted ponderously, exalted the shoulders thus, like a Frenchman — to what good? he
not could budge, he is planted solid like a church,
he not advance no more than if one him had put at
the anchor.

Smiley was surprised and disgusted, but he not
himself doubted not of the turn being intended
(mais il ne se doutait pas du tour, bien entendu).
The individual empocketed the silver, himself with
it went, and of it himself in going is it that he no
gives not a jerk of thumb over the shoulder — like
that — at the poor Daniel, in saying with his air
deliberate — (L'individu empoche l'argent, s'en va
et en s'en allant est ce qu'il ne donne pas un coup de
pouce par-dessus l'épaule, comme ca, au pauvre
Daniel, endisant de son air délibéré) :

"Eh bien! *I no see not that that frog has nothing
of better than another.*"

Smiley himself scratched longtimes the head, the eyes fixed upon Daniel, until that which at last he said:

"I me demand how the devil it makes itself that this beast has refused. Is it that she had something? One would believe that she is stuffed."

He grasped Daniel by the skin of the neck, him lifted and said:

"The wolf me bite if he no weigh not five pounds."

He him reversed and the unhappy belched two handfuls of shot (et le malhereus, etc.). When Smiley recognized how it was, he was like mad. He deposited his frog by the earth and ran after that individual, but he not him caught never.

Such is the Jumping Frog, to the distorted French eye. I claim that I never put together such an odious mixture of bad grammar and delirium tremens in my life. And what has a poor foreigner like me done, to be abused and misrepresented like this? When I say, "Well, I don't see no p'ints about that frog that's any better'n any other frog," is it kind, is it just, for this Frenchman to try to make it appear that I said, "Eh bien! I no saw not that that frog had nothing of better than each frog?" I have no heart to write more. I never felt so about anything before.

HARTFORD, March, 1875.

JOURNALISM IN TENNESSEE*

The editor of the Memphis *Avalanche* swoops thus mildly down upon a correspondent who posted him as a Radical:—" While he was writing the first word, the middle, dotting his i's, crossing his t's, and punching his period, he knew he was concocting a sentence that was saturated with infamy and reeking with falsehood."—*Exchange*.

I WAS told by the physician that a Southern climate would improve my health, and so I went down to Tennessee, and got a berth on the *Morning Glory and Johnson County War-Whoop* as associate editor. When I went on duty I found the chief editor sitting tilted back in a three-legged chair with his feet on a pine table. There was another pine table in the room and another afflicted chair, and both were half buried under newspapers and scraps and sheets of manuscript. There was a wooden box of sand, sprinkled with cigar stubs and " old soldiers," and a stove with a door hanging by its upper hinge. The chief editor had a long-tailed black cloth frock coat on, and white linen pants. His boots were small and neatly blacked. He wore a ruffled shirt, a large seal ring, a standing collar of

---

* Written about 1871.

obsolete pattern, and a checkered neckerchief with the ends hanging down. Date of costume about 1848. He was smoking a cigar, and trying to think of a word, and in pawing his hair he had rumpled his locks a good deal. He was scowling fearfully, and I judged that he was concocting a particularly knotty editorial. He told me to take the exchanges and skim through them and write up the " Spirit of the Tennessee Press," condensing into the article all of their contents that seemed of interest.

I wrote as follows:

"SPIRIT OF THE TENNESSEE PRESS.

"The editors of the *Semi-Weekly Earthquake* evidently labor under a misapprehension with regard to the Ballyhack railroad. It is not the object of the company to leave Buzzardville off to one side. On the contrary, they consider it one of the most important points along the line, and consequently can have no desire to slight it. The gentlemen of the *Earthquake* will, of course, take pleasure in making the correction.

"John W. Blossom, Esq., the able editor of the Higginsville *Thunderbolt and Battle Cry of Freedom*, arrived in the city yesterday. He is stopping at the Van Buren House.

"We observe that our contemporary of the Mud Springs *Morning Howl* has fallen into the error of supposing that the election of Van Werter is not an established fact, but he will have discovered his mistake before this reminder reaches him, no doubt. He was doubtless misled by incomplete election returns.

"It is pleasant to note that the city of Blathersville is endeavoring to contract with some New York gentlemen to pave its well-nigh impassable streets with the Nicholson pavement. The *Daily Hurrah* urges the measure with ability, and seems confident of ultimate success."

I passed my manuscript over to the chief editor for acceptance, alteration, or destruction. He glanced at it and his face clouded. He ran his

eye down the pages, and his countenance grew portentous. It was easy to see that something was
wrong. Presently he sprang up and said:

"Thunder and lightning! Do you suppose I am
going to speak of those cattle that way? Do you
suppose my subscribers are going to stand such
gruel as that? Give me the pen!"

I never saw a pen scrape and scratch its way so
viciously, or plow through another man's verbs and
adjectives so relentlessly. While he was in the midst
of his work, somebody shot at him through the
open window, and marred the symmetry of my ear.

"Ah," said he, "that is that scoundrel Smith,
of the *Moral Volcano* — he was due yesterday."
And he snatched a navy revolver from his belt and
fired. Smith dropped, shot in the thigh. The shot
spoiled Smith's aim, who was just taking a second
chance, and he crippled a stranger. It was me.
Merely a finger shot off.

Then the chief editor went on with his erasures
and interlineations. Just as he finished them a hand-
grenade came down the stove pipe, and the explosion shivered the stove into a thousand fragments.
However, it did no further damage, except that a
vagrant piece knocked a couple of my teeth out.

"That stove is utterly ruined," said the chief
editor.

I said I believed it was.

"Well, no matter — don't want it this kind of
weather. I know the man that did it. I'll get

him. Now, *here* is the way this stuff ought to be written."

I took the manuscript. It was scarred with erasures and interlineations till its mother wouldn't have known it if had had one. It now read as follows:

"SPIR'T OF THE TENNESSEE PRESS.

"The inveterate liars of the *Semi-Weekly Earthquake* are evidently endeavoring to palm off upon a noble and chivalrous people another of their vile and brutal falsehoods with regard to that most glorious conception of the nineteenth century, the Ballyhack railroad. The idea that Buzzardville was to be left off at one side originated in their own fulsome brains — or rather in the settlings which *they* regard as brains. They had better swallow this lie if they want to save their abandoned reptile carcasses the cowhiding they so richly deserve.

"That ass, Blossom, of the Higginsville *Thunderbolt and Battle Cry of Freedom*, is down here again sponging at the Van Buren.

"We observe that the besotted blackguard of the Mud Spring *Morning Howl* is giving out, with his usual propensity for lying, that Van Werter is not elected. The heaven-born mission of journalism is to disseminate truth; to eradicate error; to educate, refine, and elevate the tone of public morals and manners, and make all men more gentle, more virtuous, more charitable, and in all ways better, and holier, and happier; and yet this black-hearted scoundrel degrades his great office persistently to the dissemination of falsehood, calumny, vituperation, and vulgarity.

"Blathersville wants a Nicholson pavement — it wants a jail and a poorhouse more. The idea of a pavement in a one-horse town composed of two gin mills, a blacksmith shop, and that mustard-plaster of a newspaper, the *Daily Hurrah!* The crawling insect, Buckner, who edits the *Hurrah*, is braying about this business with his customary imbecility, and imagining that he is talking sense."

"Now *that* is the way to write — peppery and to the point. Mush-and-milk journalism gives me the fan-tods."

About this time a brick came through the window with a splintering crash, and gave me a considerable of a jolt in the back. I moved out of range — I began to feel in the way.

The chief said, " That was the Colonel, likely. I've been expecting him for two days. He will be up now right away."

He was correct. The Colonel appeared in the door a moment afterward with a dragoon revolver in his hand.

He said, " Sir, have I the honor of addressing the poltroon who edits this mangy sheet?"

" You have. Be seated, sir. Be careful of the chair, one of its legs is gone. I believe I have the honor of addressing the putrid liar, Colonel Blatherskite Tecumseh?"

" Right, sir. I have a little account to settle with you. If you are at leisure we will begin."

" I have an article on the ' Encouraging Progress of Moral and Intellectual Development in America ' to finish, but there is no hurry. Begin."

Both pistols rang out their fierce clamor at the same instant. The chief lost a lock of his hair, and the Colonel's bullet ended its career in the fleshy part of my thigh. The Colonel's left shoulder was clipped a little. They fired again. Both missed their men this time, but I got my share, a shot in the arm. At the third fire both gentlemen were wounded slightly, and I had a knuckle chipped. I then said, I believed I would go out and take a walk, as this was a private matter, and I had a delicacy about participating in it further. But both gentlemen begged me to keep my seat, and assured me that I was not in the way.

They then talked about the elections and the crops while they reloaded, and I fell to tying up my wounds. But presently they opened fire again with animation, and every shot took effect — but it is proper to remark that five out of the six fell to my share. The sixth one mortally wounded the Colonel, who remarked, with fine humor, that he would have to say good morning now, as he had business up town. He then inquired the way to the undertaker's and left.

The chief turned to me and said, " I am expecting company to dinner, and shall have to get ready. It will be a favor to me if you will read proof and attend to the customers."

I winced a little at the idea of attending to the customers, but I was too bewildered by the fusillade that was still ringing in my ears to think of anything to say.

He continued, " Jones will be here at 3 — cowhide him. Gillespie will call earlier, perhaps — throw him out of the window. Ferguson will be along about 4 — kill him. That is all for to-day, I believe. If you have any odd time, you may write a blistering article on the police — give the chief inspector rats. The cowhides are under the table; weapons in the drawer — ammunition there in the corner — lint and bandages up there in the pigeon-holes. In case of accident, go to Lancet, the surgeon, downstairs. He advertises — we take it out in trade."

He was gone. I shuddered. At the end of the next three hours I had been through perils so awful that all peace of mind and all cheerfulness were gone from me. Gillespie had called and thrown *me* out of the window. Jones arrived promptly, and when I got ready to do the cowhiding he took the job off my hands. In an encounter with a stranger, not in the bill of fare, I had lost my scalp. Another stranger, by the name of Thompson, left me a mere wreck and ruin of chaotic rags. And at last, at bay in the corner, and beset by an infuriated mob of editors, blacklegs, politicians, and desperadoes, who raved and swore and flourished their weapons about my head till the air shimmered with glancing flashes of steel, I was in the act of resigning my berth on the paper when the chief arrived, and with him a rabble of charmed and enthusiastic friends. Then ensued a scene of riot and carnage such as no human pen, or steel one either, could describe. People were shot, probed, dismembered, blown up, thrown out of the window. There was a brief tornado of murky blasphemy, with a confused and frantic war-dance glimmering through it, and then all was over. In five minutes there was silence, and the gory chief and I sat alone and surveyed the sanguinary ruin that strewed the floor around us.

D

He said, " You'll like this place when you get used to it."

I said, " I'll have to get you to excuse me; I think maybe I might write to suit you after a while; as soon as I had had some practice and learned the language I am confident I could. But, to speak the plain truth, that sort of energy of expression has its inconveniences, and a man is liable to interruption. You see that yourself. Vigorous writing is calculated to elevate the public, no doubt, but then I do not like to attract so much attention as it calls forth. I can't write with comfort when I am interrupted so much as I have been to-day. I like this berth well enough, but I don't like to be left here to wait on the customers. The experiences are novel, I grant you, and entertaining, too, after a fashion, but they are not judiciously distributed. A gentleman shoots at you through the window and cripples *me;* a bomb-shell comes down the stove-pipe for your gratification and sends the stove door down *my* throat; a friend drops in to swap compliments with you, and freckles *me* with bullet-holes till my skin won't hold my principles; you go to dinner, and Jones comes with his cowhide, Gillespie throws me out of the window, Thompson tears all my clothes off, and an entire stranger takes my scalp with the easy freedom of an old acquaintance; and in less than five minutes all the blackguards in the country arrive in their war-paint, and proceed to scare the rest of me to death with their tomahawks. Take it

altogether, I never had such a spirited time in all
my life as I have had to-day. No; I like you, and
I like your calm unruffled way of explaining things
to the customers, but you see I am not used to it.
The Southern heart is too impulsive; Southern hospitality is too lavish with the stranger. The paragraphs which I have written to-day, and into whose
cold sentences your masterly hand has infused the
fervent spirit of Tennessean journalism, will wake up
another nest of hornets. All that mob of editors
will come — and they will come hungry, too, and
want somebody for breakfast. I shall have to bid
you adieu. I decline to be present at these festivi-
ties. I came South for my health, I will go back
on the same errand, and suddenly. Tennesseean
journalism is too stirring for me."

After which we parted with mutual regret, and I
took apartments at the hospital.

STORY OF THE BAD LITTLE BOY *

ONCE there was a bad little boy whose name was Jim — though, if you will notice, you will find that bad little boys are nearly always called James in your Sunday-school books. It was strange, but still it was true, that this one was called Jim.

He didn't have any sick mother, either — a sick mother who was pious and had the consumption, and would be glad to lie down in the grave and be at rest but for the strong love she bore her boy, and the anxiety she felt that the world might be harsh and cold towards him when she was gone. Most bad boys in the Sunday books are named James, and have sick mothers, who teach them to say, " Now, I lay me down," etc., and sing them to sleep with sweet, plaintive voices, and then kiss them good night, and kneel down by the bedside and weep. But it was different with this fellow. He was named Jim, and there wasn't anything the matter with his mother — no consumption, nor anything of that kind. She was rather stout than otherwise, and she was not pious; moreover, she was not anxious on Jim's account. She said if he were to

* Written about 1865.

break his neck it wouldn't be much loss. She always spanked Jim to sleep, and she never kissed him good night; on the contrary, she boxed his ears when she was ready to leave him.

Once this little bad boy stole the key of the pantry, and slipped in there and helped himself to some jam, and filled up the vessel with tar, so that his mother would never know the difference; but all at once a terrible feeling didn't come over him, and something didn't seem to whisper to him, " Is it right to disobey my mother? Isn't it sinful to do this? Where do bad little boys go who gobble up their good kind mother's jam?" and then he didn't kneel down all alone and promise never to be wicked any more, and rise up with a light, happy heart, and go and tell his mother all about it, and beg her forgiveness, and be blessed by her with tears of pride and thankfulness in her eyes. No; that is the way with all other bad boys in the books; but it happened otherwise with this Jim, strangely enough. He ate that jam, and said it was bully, in his sinful, vulgar way; and he put in the tar, and said that was bully also, and laughed, and observed " that the old woman would get up and snort " when she found it out; and when she did find it out, he denied knowing anything about it, and she whipped him severely, and he did the crying himself. Everything about this boy was curious — everything turned out differently with him from the way it does to the bad Jameses in the books.

Once he climbed up in Farmer Acorn's apple tree to steal apples, and the limb didn't break, and he didn't fall and break his arm, and get torn by the farmer's great dog, and then languish on a sick bed for weeks, and repent and become good. Oh, no; he stole as many apples as he wanted and came down all right; and he was all ready for the dog, too, and knocked him endways with a brick when he came to tear him. It was very strange — nothing like it ever happened in those mild little books with marbled backs, and with pictures in them of men with swallow-tailed coats and bell-crowned hats, and pantaloons that are short in the legs, and women with the waists of their dresses under their arms, and no hoops on. Nothing like it in any of the Sunday-school books.

Once he stole the teacher's penknife, and, when he was afraid it would be found out and he would get whipped, he slipped it into George Wilson's cap — poor Widow Wilson's son, the moral boy, the good little boy of the village, who always obeyed his mother, and never told an untruth, and was fond of his lessons, and infatuated with Sunday-school. And when the knife dropped from the cap, and poor George hung his head and blushed, as if in conscious guilt, and the grieved teacher charged the theft upon him, and was just in the very act of bringing the switch down upon his trembling shoulders, a white-haired, improbable justice of the peace did not suddenly appear in their midst, and strike an attitude and say, " Spare this noble boy — there stands the cowering culprit! I was passing the school door at recess, and, unseen myself, I saw the theft committed!" And then Jim didn't get whaled, and the venerable justice didn't read the tearful school a homily, and take George by the hand and say such a boy deserved to be exalted, and then tell him to come and make his home with him, and sweep out the office, and make fires, and run errands, and chop wood, and study law, and help his wife do household labors, and have all the balance of the time to play, and get forty cents a month, and be happy. No; it would have happened that way in the books, but it didn't happen that way to Jim. No meddling old clam of a justice dropped in to make trouble, and so the model boy George got thrashed, and Jim was glad of it because, you know, Jim hated moral boys. Jim said he was " down on them milksops." Such was the coarse language of this bad, neglected boy.

But the strangest thing that ever happened to Jim was the time he went boating on Sunday, and didn't get drowned, and that other time that he got caught out in the storm when he was fishing on Sunday, and didn't get struck by lightning. Why, you might look, and look, all through the Sunday-school books from now till next Christmas, and you would never come across anything like this. Oh, no; you would find that all the bad boys who go boating on Sunday nvariably get drowned; and all the bad boys who

get caught out in storms when they are fishing on
Sunday infallibly get struck by lightning. Boats
with bad boys in them always upset on Sunday, and
it always storms when bad boys go fishing on the
Sabbath. How this Jim ever escaped is a mystery
to me.

This Jim bore a charmed life — that must have
been the way of it. Nothing could hurt him. He
even gave the elephant in the menagerie a plug of
tobacco, and the elephant didn't knock the top of
his head off with his trunk. He browsed around the
cupboard after essence of peppermint, and didn't
make a mistake and drink *aqua fortis*. He stole his
father's gun and went hunting on the Sabbath, and
didn't shoot three or four of his fingers off. He
struck his little sister on the temple with his fist
when he was angry, and she didn't linger in pain
through long summer days, and die with sweet words
of forgiveness upon her lips that redoubled the
anguish of his breaking heart. No; she got over
it. He ran off and went to sea at last, and didn't
come back and find himself sad and alone in the
world, his loved ones sleeping in the quiet churchyard, and the vine-embowered home of his boyhood
tumbled down and gone to decay. Ah, no; he
came home as drunk as a piper, and got into the
station-house the first thing.

And he grew up and married, and raised a large
family, and brained them all with an axe one night,
and got wealthy by all manner of cheating and ras-

cality; and now he is the infernalest wickedest scoundrel in his native village, and is universally respected, and belongs to the legislature.

So you see there never was a bad James in the Sunday-school books that had such a streak of luck as this sinful Jim with the charmed life.

THE STORY OF THE GOOD LITTLE BOY *

ONCE there was a good little boy by the name of Jacob Blivens. He always obeyed his parents, no matter how absurd and unreasonable their demands were; and he always learned his book, and never was late at Sabbath-school. He would not play hookey, even when his sober judgment told him it was the most profitable thing he could do. None of the other boys could ever make that boy out, he acted so strangely. He wouldn't lie, no matter how convenient it was. He just said it was wrong to lie, and that was sufficient for him. And he was so honest that he was simply ridiculous. The curious ways that that Jacob had, surpassed everything. He wouldn't play marbles on Sunday, he wouldn't rob birds' nests, he wouldn't give hot pennies to organ-grinders' monkeys; he didn't seem to take any interest in any kind of rational amusement. So the other boys used to try to reason it out and come to an understanding of him, but they couldn't arrive at any satisfactory conclusion. As I said be-

---

* Written about 1865.

fore, they could only figure out a sort of vague idea
that he was "afflicted," and so they took him under
their protection, and never allowed any harm to
come to him.

This good little boy read all the Sunday-school
books; they were his greatest delight. This was the
whole secret of it. He believed in the good little
boys they put in the Sunday-school books; he had
every confidence in them. He longed to come
across one of them alive once; but he never did.
They all died before his time, maybe. Whenever
he read about a particularly good one he turned over
quickly to the end to see what became of him, because he wanted to travel thousands of miles and
gaze on him; but it wasn't any use; that good little
boy always died in the last chapter, and there was a
picture of the funeral, with all his relations and the
Sunday-school children standing around the grave in
pantaloons that were too short, and bonnets that
were too large, and everybody crying into handkerchiefs that had as much as a yard and a half of
stuff in them. He was always headed off in this
way. He never could see one of those good little
boys on account of his always dying in the last
chapter.

Jacob had a noble ambition to be put in a Sunday-
school book. He wanted to be put in, with pictures
representing him gloriously declining to lie to his
mother, and her weeping for joy about it; and pictures representing him standing on the doorstep

5ˢ

giving a penny to a poor beggar-woman with six
children, and telling her to spend it freely, but not
to be extravagant, because extravagance is a sin;
and pictures of him magnanimously refusing to tell
on the bad boy who always lay in wait for him
around the corner as he came from school, and
welted him over the head with a lath, and then
chased him home, saying, "Hi! hi!" as he proceeded. That was the ambition of young Jacob
Blivens. He wished to be put in a Sunday-school
book. It made him feel a little uncomfortable sometimes when he reflected that the good little boys
always died. He loved to live, you know, and this
was the most unpleasant feature about being a
Sunday-school book boy. He knew it was not
healthy to be good. He knew it was more fatal
than consumption to be so supernaturally good as
the boys in the books were; he knew that none of
them had ever been able to stand it long, and it
pained him to think that if they put him in a book
he wouldn't ever see it, or even if they did get the
book out before he died it wouldn't be popular
without any picture of his funeral in the back part
of it. It couldn't be much of a Sunday-school book
that couldn't tell about the advice he gave to the
community when he was dying. So at last, of
course, he had to make up his mind to do the best
he could under the circumstances — to live right,
and hang on as long as he could, and have his dying
speech all ready when his time came.

But somehow nothing ever went right with this good little boy; nothing ever turned out with him the way it turned out with the good little boys in the books. They always had a good time, and the bad boys had the broken legs; but in his case there was a screw loose somewhere, and it all happened just the other way. When he found Jim Blake stealing apples, and went under the tree to read to him about the bad little boy who fell out of a neighbor's apple tree and broke his arm, Jim fell out of the tree, too, but he fell on *him* and broke *his* arm, and Jim wasn't hurt at all. Jacob couldn't understand that. There wasn't anything in the books like it.

And once, when some bad boys pushed a blind man over in the mud, and Jacob ran to help him up and receive his blessing, the blind man did not give him any blessing at all, but whacked him over the head with his stick and said he would like to catch him shoving *him* again, and then pretending to help him up. This was not in accordance with any of the books. Jacob looked them all over to see.

One thing that Jacob wanted to do was to find a lame dog that hadn't any place to stay, and was hungry and persecuted, and bring him home and pet him and have that dog's imperishable gratitude. And at last he found one and was happy; and he brought him home and fed him, but when he was going to pet him the dog flew at him and tore all the clothes off him except those that were in front, and made a spectacle of him that was astonishing. He examined authorities, but he could not understand the matter. It was of the same breed of dogs that was in the books, but it acted very differently. Whatever this boy did he got into trouble. The very things the boys in the books got rewarded for turned out to be about the most unprofitable things he could invest in.

Once, when he was on his way to Sunday-school, he saw some bad boys starting off pleasuring in a sailboat. He was filled with consternation, because he knew from his reading that boys who went sailing on Sunday invariably got drowned. So he ran out on a raft to warn them, but a log turned with him and slid him into the river. A man got him out pretty soon, and the doctor pumped the water out of him, and gave him a fresh start with his bellows, but he caught cold and lay sick abed nine weeks. But the most unaccountable thing about it was that the bad boys in the boat had a good time all day, and then reached home alive and well in the most surprising manner. Jacob Blivens said there was nothing like these things in the books. He was perfectly dumbfounded.

When he got well he was a little discouraged, but he resolved to keep on trying anyhow. He knew that so far his experiences wouldn't do to go in a book, but he hadn't yet reached the allotted term of life for good little boys, and he hoped to be able to make a record yet if he could hold on till his time

was fully up. If everything else failed he had his
dying speech to fall back on.

He examined his authorities, and found that it
was now time for him to go to sea as a cabin-boy.
He called on a ship captain and made his application,
and when the captain asked for his recommenda-
tions he proudly drew out a tract and pointed to the
words, " To Jacob Blivens, from his affectionate
teacher." But the captain was a coarse, vulgar man,
and he said, " Oh, that be blowed! *that* wasn't any
proof that he knew how to wash dishes or handle a
slush-bucket, and he guessed he didn't want him."
This was altogether the most extraordinary thing
that ever happened to Jacob in all his life. A
compliment from a teacher, on a tract, had never
failed to move the tenderest emotions of ship
captains, and open the way to all offices of honor
and profit in their gift — it never had in any book
that ever *he* had read. He could hardly believe his
senses.

This boy always had a hard time of it. Nothing
ever came out according to the authorities with him.
At last, one day, when he was around hunting up
bad little boys to admonish, he found a lot of them
in the old iron foundry fixing up a little joke on
fourteen or fifteen dogs, which they had tied together in long procession, and were going to orna-
ment with empty nitro-glycerine cans made fast to
their tails. Jacob's heart was touched. He sat
down on one of those cans (for he never minded

grease when duty was before him), and he took hold of the foremost dog by the collar, and turned his reproving eye upon wicked Tom Jones. But just at that moment Alderman McWelter, full of wrath, stepped in. All the bad boys ran away, but Jacob Blivens rose in conscious innocence and began one of those stately little Sunday-school book speeches which always commence with " Oh, sir!" in dead opposition to the fact that no boy, good or bad, ever starts a remark with " Oh, sir." But the alderman never waited to hear the rest. He took Jacob Blivens by the ear and turned him around, and hit him a whack in the rear with the flat of his hand; and in an instant that good little boy shot out through the roof and soared away toward the sun, with the fragments of those fifteen dogs stringing after him like the tail of a kite. And there wasn't a sign of that alderman or that old iron foundry left on the face of the earth; and, as for young Jacob Blivens, he never got a chance to make his last dying speech after all his trouble fixing it up, unless he made it to the birds; because, although the bulk of him came down all right in a tree-top in an adjoining county, the rest of him was apportioned around among four townships, and so they had to hold five inquests on him to find out whether he was dead or not, and how it occurred. You never saw a boy scattered so.*

* This glycerine catastrophe is borrowed from a floating newspaper item, whose author's name I would give if I knew it.—[M. T.]

Thus perished the good little boy who did the best he could, but didn't come out according to the books. Every boy who ever did as he did prospered except him. His case is truly remarkable. It will probably never be accounted for.

A COUPLE OF POEMS BY TWAIN AND MOORE *

THOSE EVENING BELLS.

BY THOMAS MOORE.

Those evening bells! those evening bells!
How many a tale their music tells
Of youth, and home, and that sweet time
When last I heard their soothing chime.

Those joyous hours are passed away;
And many a heart that then was gay,
Within the tomb now darkly dwells,
And hears no more those evening bells.

And so 'twill be when I am gone—
That tuneful peal will still ring on;
While other bards shall walk these dells,
And sing your praise, sweet evening bells.

THOSE ANNUAL BILLS.

BY MARK TWAIN.

These annual bills! these annual bills!
How many a song their discord trills
Of "truck" consumed, enjoyed, forgot,
Since I was skinned by last year's lot!

* Written about 1865.

Those joyous beans are passed away;
Those onions blithe, O where are they?
Once loved, lost, mourned — *now* vexing ILLS
Your shades troop back in annual bills!

And so 'twill be when I'm aground —
These yearly duns will still go round,
While other bards, with frantic quills.
Shall damn and *damn* these annual bills!

NIAGARA *

NIAGARA FALLS is a most enjoyable place of resort. The hotels are excellent, and the prices not at all exorbitant. The opportunities for fishing are not surpassed in the country; in fact, they are not even equaled elsewhere. Because, in other localities, certain places in the streams are much better than others; but at Niagara one place is just as good as another, for the reason that the fish do not bite anywhere, and so there is no use in your walking five miles to fish, when you can depend on being just as unsuccessful nearer home. The advantages of this state of things have never heretofore been properly placed before the public.

The weather is cool in summer, and the walks and drives are all pleasant and none of them fatiguing. When you start out to " do " the Falls you first drive down about a mile, and pay a small sum for the privilege of looking down from a precipice into the narrowest part of the Niagara river. A railway " cut " through a hill would be as comely if it had the angry river tumbling and foaming through

---

* Written about 1871.

its bottom. You can descend a staircase here a hundred and fifty feet down, and stand at the edge of the water. After you have done it, you will wonder why you did it; but you will then be too late.

The guide will explain to you, in his blood-curdling way, how he saw the little steamer, *Maid of the Mist*, descend the fearful rapids — how first one paddle-box was out of sight behind the raging billows and then the other, and at what point it was that her smokestack toppled overboard, and where her planking began to break and part asunder — and how she did finally live through the trip, after accomplishing the incredible feat of traveling seventeen miles in six minutes, or six miles in seventeen minutes, I have really forgotten which. But it was very extraordinary, anyhow. It is worth the price of admission to hear the guide tell the story nine times in succession to different parties, and never miss a word or alter a sentence or a gesture.

Then you drive over to Suspension Bridge, and divide your misery between the chances of smashing down two hundred feet into the river below, and the chances of having the railway train overhead smashing down on to you. Either possibility is discomforting taken by itself, but, mixed together, they amount in the aggregate to positive unhappiness.

On the Canada side you drive along the chasm between long ranks of photographers standing guard behind their cameras, ready to make an ostentatious frontispiece of you and your decaying ambulance, and your solemn crate with a hide on it, which you are expected to regard in the light of a horse, and a diminished and unimportant background of sublime Niagara; and a great many people *have* the incredible effrontery or the native depravity to aid and abet this sort of crime.

Any day, in the hands of these photographers, you may see stately pictures of papa and mamma, Johnny and Bub and Sis, or a couple of country cousins, all smiling vacantly, and all disposed in studied and uncomfortable attitudes in their carriage, and all looming up in their awe-inspiring imbecility before the snubbed and diminished presentment of that majestic presence whose ministering spirits are the rainbows, whose voice is the thunder, whose awful front is veiled in clouds, who was monarch here dead and forgotten ages before this hackful of small reptiles was deemed temporarily necessary to fill a crack in the world's unnoted myriads, and will still be monarch here ages and decades of ages after they shall have gathered themselves to their blood relations, the other worms, and been mingled with the unremembering dust.

There is no actual harm in making Niagara a background whereon to display one's marvelous insignificance in a good strong light, but it requires a sort of superhuman self-complacency to enable one to do it.

When you have examined the stupendous Horseshoe Fall till you are satisfied you cannot improve on it, you return to America by the new Suspension Bridge, and follow up the bank to where they exhibit the Cave of the Winds.

Here I followed instructions, and divested myself of all my clothing, and put on a waterproof jacket and overalls. This costume is picturesque, but not beautiful. A guide, similarly dressed, led the way down a flight of winding stairs, which wound and wound, and still kept on winding long after the thing ceased to be a novelty, and then terminated long before it had begun to be a pleasure. We were then well down under the precipice, but still considerably above the level of the river.

We now began to creep along flimsy bridges of a single plank, our persons shielded from destruction by a crazy wooden railing, to which I clung with both hands — not because I was afraid, but because I wanted to. Presently the descent became steeper, and the bridge flimsier, and sprays from the American Fall began to rain down on us in fast increasing sheets that soon became blinding, and after that our progress was mostly in the nature of groping. Now a furious wind began to rush out from behind the waterfall, which seemed determined to sweep us from the bridge, and scatter us on the rocks and among the torrents below. I remarked that I wanted to go home; but it was too late. We were almost under the monstrous wall of water thundering down from above, and speech was in vain in the midst of such a pitiless crash of sound.

In another moment the guide disappeared behind the deluge, and, bewildered by the thunder,
driven helplessly by the wind, and smitten by the
arrowy tempest of rain, I followed. All was darkness. Such a mad storming, roaring, and bellowing
of warring wind and water never crazed my ears before. I bent my head, and seemed to receive the
Atlantic on my back. The world seemed going to destruction. I could not see anything, the flood poured
down so savagely. I raised my head, with open
mouth, and the most of the American cataract went
down my throat. If I had sprung a leak now I had
been lost. And at this moment I discovered that
the bridge had ceased, and we must trust for a foothold to the slippery and precipitous rocks. I never
was so scared before and survived it. But we got
through at last, and emerged into the open day,
where we could stand in front of the laced and
frothy and seething world of descending water, and
look at it. When I saw how much of it there was,
and how fearfully in earnest it was, I was sorry I
had gone behind it.

The noble Red Man has always been a friend and
darling of mine. I love to read about him in tales
and legends and romances. I love to read of his
inspired sagacity, and his love of the wild free life
of mountain and forest, and his general nobility of
character, and his stately metaphorical manner of
speech, and his chivalrous love for the dusky
maiden, and the picturesque pomp of his dress and

accoutrements. Especially the picturesque pomp of
his dress and accoutrements. When I found the
shops at Niagara Falls full of dainty Indian bead-
work, and stunning moccasins, and equally stunning
toy figures representing human beings who carried
their weapons in holes bored through their arms and
bodies, and had feet shaped like a pie, I was filled
with emotion. I knew that now, at last, I was going
to come face to face with the noble Red Man.

A lady clerk in a shop told me, indeed, that all
her grand array of curiosities were made by the
Indians, and that they were plenty about the Falls,
and that they were friendly, and it would not be
dangerous to speak to them. And sure enough, as
I approached the bridge leading over to Luna Island,
I came upon a noble Son of the Forest sitting under
a tree, diligently at work on a bead reticule. He
wore a slouch hat and brogans, and had a short
black pipe in his mouth. Thus does the baneful
contact with our effeminate civilization dilute the
picturesque pomp which is so natural to the Indian
when far removed from us in his native haunts. I
addressed the relic as follows:

" Is the Wawhoo-Wang-Wang of the Whack-a-
Whack happy? Does the great Speckled Thunder
sigh for the warpath, or is his heart contented with
dreaming of the dusky maiden, the Pride of the
Forest? Does the mighty Sachem yearn to drink
the blood of his enemies, or is he satisfied to make
bead reticules for the pappooses of the paleface?

Speak, sublime relic of bygone grandeur — venerable ruin, speaĸ!"

The relic said:

" An' is it mesiif, Dennis Hooligan, that ye'd be takin' for a dirty injin, ye drawlin', lantern-jawed, spider-legged divil! By the piper that played before Moses, I'll ate ye!"

I went away from there.

By and by, in the neighborhood of the Terrapin Tower, I came upon a gentle daughter of the aborigines in fringed and beaded buckskin moccasins and leggins, seated on a bench with her pretty wares about her. She had just carved out a wooden chief that had a strong family resemblance to a clothespin, and was now boring a hole through his abdomen to put his bow through. I hesitated a moment, and then addressed her:

" Is the heart of the forest maiden heavy? Is the Laughing Tadpole lonely? Does she mourn over the extinguished council-fires of her race, and the vanished glory of her ancestors? Or does her sad spirit wander afar toward the hunting-grounds whither her brave Gobbler-of-the-Lightnings is gone? Why is my daughter silent? Has she aught against the paleface stranger?"

The maiden said:

" Faix, an' is it Biddy Malone ye dare to be callin' names? Lave this, or I'll shy your lean carcass over the cataract, ye sniveling blaggard!"

I adjourned from there also.

" Confound these Indians!" I said. " They told me they were tame; but, if appearances go for anything, I should say they were all on the war-path."

I made one more attempt to fraternize with them, and only one. I came upon a camp of them gathered in the shade of a great tree, making wampum and moccasins, and addressed them in the language of friendship:

" Noble Red Men, Braves, Grand Sachems, War Chiefs, Squaws, and High Muck-a-Mucks, the pale-face from the land of the setting sun greets you! You, Beneficent Polecat — you, Devourer of Mountains — you, Roaring Thundergust — you, Bully Boy with a Glass eye — the paleface from beyond the great waters greets you all! War and pestilence have thinned your ranks and destroyed your once proud nation. Poker and seven-up, and a vain modern expense for soap, unknown to your glorious ancestors, have depleted your purses. Appropriating, in your simplicity, the property of others has gotten you into trouble. Misrepresenting facts, in your simple innocence, has damaged your reputation with the soulless usurper. Trading for forty-rod whisky, to enable you to get drunk and happy and tomahawk your families, has played the ever-lasting mischief with the picturesque pomp of your dress, and here you are, in the broad light of the nineteenth century, gotten up like the ragtag and bobtail of the purlieus of New York. For shame!

Remember your ancestors! Recall their mighty
deeds! Remember Uncas! — and Red Jacket! —
and Hole in the Day! — and Whoopdedoodledo!
Emulate their achievements! Unfurl yourselves
under my banner, noble savages, illustrious gutter-
snipes —"

"Down wid him!" "Scoop the blaggard!"
"Burn him!" "Hang him!" "Dhround him!"

It was the quickest operation that ever was. I
simply saw a sudden flash in the air of clubs, brick-
bats, fists, bead-baskets, and moccasins — a single
flash, and they all appeared to hit me at once, and
no two of them in the same place. In the next
instant the entire tribe was upon me. They tore half
the clothes off me; they broke my arms and legs;
they gave me a thump that dented the top of my
head till it would hold coffee like a saucer; and, to
crown their disgraceful proceedings and add insult
to injury, they threw me over the Niagara Falls, and
I got wet.

About ninety or a hundred feet from the top, the
remains of my vest caught on a projecting rock, and
I was almost drowned before I could get loose. I
finally fell, and brought up in a world of white foam
at the foot of the Fall, whose celled and bubbly
masses towered up several inches above my head.
Of course I got into the eddy. I sailed round and
round in it forty-four times — chasing a chip and
gaining on it — each round trip a half mile — reaching for the same bush on the bank forty-four times,

and just exactly missing it by a hair's-breadth every time.

At last a man walked down and sat down close to that bush, and put a pipe in his mouth, and lit a match, and followed me with one eye and kept the other on the match, while he sheltered it in his hands from the wind. Presently a puff of wind blew it out. The next time I swept around he said:

" Got a match?"

" Yes; in my other vest. Help me out, please."

" Not for Joe."

When I came round again, I said:

" Excuse the seemingly impertinent curiosity of a drowning man, but will you explain this singular conduct of yours?"

" With pleasure. I am the coroner. Don't hurry on my account. I can wait for you. But I wish I had a match."

I said: " Take my place, and I'll go and get you one."

He declined. This lack of confidence on his part created a coldness between us, and from that time forward I avoided him. It was my idea, in case anything happened to me, to so time the occurrence as to throw my custom into the hands of the opposition coroner over on the American side.

At last a policeman came along, and arrested me for disturbing the peace by yelling at people on shore for help. The judge fined me, but I had the advantage of him. My money was with

my pantaloons. and my pantaloons were with the
Indians.

Thus I escaped.   I am now lying in a very critical
condition.   At least I am lying anyway — critical
or not critical.   I am hurt all over, but I cannot tell
the full extent yet, because the doctor is not done
taking inventory.   He will make out my manifest
this evening.   However, thus far he thinks only
sixteen of my wounds are fatal.   I don't mind the
others.

Upon regaining my right mind, I said:

" It is an awful savage tribe of Indians that do
the bead work and moccasins for Niagara Falls,
doctor.   Where are they from?"

" Limerick, my son."

ANSWERS TO CORRESPONDENTS*

"MORAL STATISTICIAN."— I don't want any of your statistics; I took your whole batch and lit my pipe with it. I hate your kind of people. You are always ciphering out how much a man's health is injured, and how much his intellect is impaired, and how many pitiful dollars and cents he wastes in the course of ninety-two years' indulgence in the fatal practice of smoking; and in the equally fatal practice of drinking coffee; and in playing billiards occasionally; and in taking a glass of wine at dinner, etc., etc., etc. And you are always figuring out how many women have been burned to death because of the dangerous fashion of wearing expansive hoops, etc., etc., etc. You never see more than one side of the question. You are blind to the fact that most old men in America smoke and drink coffee, although, according to your theory, they ought to have died young; and that hearty old Englishmen drink wine and survive it, and portly old Dutchmen both drink and smoke freely, and yet grow older and fatter all the time.

---

* Written about 1865.

6   (81)

And you never try to find out how much solid comfort, relaxation, and enjoyment a man derives from
smoking in the course of a lifetime (which is worth
ten times the money he would save by letting it
alone), nor the appalling aggregate of happiness lost
in a lifetime by your kind of people from *not*
smoking. Of course you can save money by deny-
ing yourself all those little vicious enjoyments for
fifty years; but then what can you do with it?
What use can you put it to? Money can't save
your infinitesimal soul. All the use that money can
be put to is to purchase comfort and enjoyment in
this life; therefore, as you are an enemy to comfort
and enjoyment, where is the use of accumulating
cash? It won't do for you to say that you can use
it to better purpose in furnishing a good table, and
in charities, and in supporting tract societies, because you know yourself that you people who have
no petty vices are never known to give away a cent,
and that you stint yourselves so in the matter of
food that you are always feeble and hungry. And
you never dare to laugh in the daytime for fear some
poor wretch, seeing you in a good humor, will try
to borrow a dollar of you; and in church you are
always down on your knees, with your eyes buried
in the cushion, when the contribution box comes
around; and you never give the revenue officers a
full statement of your income. Now you know all
these things yourself, don't you? Very well, then,
what is the use of your stringing out your miserable

lives to a lean and withered old age? What is the use of your saving money that is so utterly worthless to you? In a word, why don't you go off somewhere and die, and not be always trying to seduce people into becoming as " ornery " and unloveable as you are yourselves, by your villainous " moral statistics "? Now I don't approve of dissipation, and I don't indulge in it, either; but I haven't a particle of confidence in a man who has no redeeming petty vices, and so I don't want to hear from you any more. I think you are the very same man who read me a long lecture last week about the degrading vice of smoking cigars, and then came back, in my absence, with your reprehensible fire-proof gloves on, and carried off my beautiful parlor stove.

" YOUNG AUTHOR."— Yes, Agassiz *does* recommend authors to eat fish, because the phosphorus in it makes brain. So far you are correct. But I cannot help you to a decision about the amount you need to eat — at least, not with certainty. If the specimen composition you send is about your fair usual average, I should judge that perhaps a couple of whales would be all you would want for the present. Not the largest kind, but simply good middling-sized whales.

" SIMON WHEELER," *Sonora.*— The following simple and touching remarks and accompanying

F

poem have just come to hand from the rich gold-mining region of Sonora:

To Mr. Mark Twain: The within parson, which I have set to poetry under the name and style of " He Done His Level Best," was one among the whitest men I ever see, and it ain't every man that knowed him that can find it in his heart to say he's glad the poor cuss is busted and gone home to the States.   He was here in an early day, and he was the handyest man about takin' holt of anything that come along you most ever see, I judge.   He was a cheerful, stirrin' cretur, always doin' somethin', and no man can say he ever see him do anything by halvers.   Preachin' was his nateral gait, but he warn't a man to lay back and twidle his thumbs because there didn't happen to be nothin' doin' in his own especial line — no, sir, he was a man who would meander forth and stir up something for hisself.   His last acts was to go his pile on " Kings-*and* " (calklatin' to fill, but which he didn't fill), when there was a " flush " out agin him, and naterally, you see, he went under.   And so he was cleaned out, as you may say, and he struck the home-trail, cheerful but flat broke.   I knowed this talonted man in Arkansaw, and if you would print this humbly tribute to his gorgis abilities, you would greatly obleege his onhappy friend.

HE DONE HIS LEVEL BEST

Was he a mining on the flat —
    He done it with a zest;
Was he a leading of the choir —
    He done his level best.

If he'd a reg'lar task to do,
    He never took no rest;
Or if 'twas off-and-on — the same —
    He done his level best.

If he was preachin' on his beat,
    He'd tramp from east to west,
And north to south — in cold and heat
    He done his level best.

He'd yank a sinner outen (Hades),*
  And land him with the blest;
Then snatch a prayer'n waltz in again,
  And do his level best.

He'd cuss and sing and howl and pray,
  And dance and drink and jest,
And lie and steal — all one to him —
  He done his level best.

Whate'er this man was sot to do,
  He done it with a zest;
No matter *what* his contract was,
  HE'D DO HIS LEVEL BEST.

Verily, this man *was* gifted with ' gorgis abilities,'' and it is a happiness to me to embalm the memory of their luster in these columns. If it were not that the poet crop is unusually large and rank in California this year, I would encourage you to continue writing, Simon Wheeler; but, as it is, perhaps it might be too risky in you to enter against so much opposition.

" PROFESSIONAL BEGGAR."— No; you are not obliged to take greenbacks at par.

" MELTON MOWBRAY,"† *Dutch Flat.*— This cor-

---

* Here I have taken a slight liberty with the original MS. "Hades" does not make such good meter as the other word of one syllable, but it sounds better.

†This piece of pleasantry, published in a San Francisco paper, was mistaken by the country journals for seriousness, and many and loud were the denunciations of the ignorance of author and editor, in not knowing that the lines in question were " written by Byron."

respondent sends a lot of doggerel, and says it has been regarded as very good in Dutch Flat. I give a specimen verse:

> "The Assyrian came down like a wolf on the fold,
> And his cohorts were gleaming with purple and gold;
> And the sheen of his spears was like stars on the sea,
> When the blue wave rolls nightly on deep Galilee."

There, that will do. That may be very good Dutch Flat poetry, but it won't do in the metropolis. It is too smooth and blubbery; it reads like butter-milk gurgling from a jug. What the people ought to have is something spirited — something like "Johnny Comes Marching Home." However, keep on practicing, and you may succeed yet. There is genius in you, but too much blubber.

"St. Clair Higgins." *Los Angeles.*—"My life is a failure; I have adored, wildly, madly, and she whom I love has turned coldly from me and shed her affections upon another. What would you advise me to do?"

You should set your affections on another also — or on several, if there are enough to go round. Also, do everything you can to make your former dame unhappy. There is an absurd idea dissemi-nated in novels, that the happier a girl is with another man, the happier it makes the old lover she has blighted. Don't allow yourself to believe any such nonsense as that. The more cause that girl finds to regret that she did not marry you, the more comfortable you will feel over it. It isn't poetical, but it is mighty sound doctrine.

"ARITHMETICUS." *Virginia, Nevada.*—"If it would take a cannon ball $3\frac{1}{3}$ seconds to travel four miles, and $3\frac{3}{8}$ seconds to travel the next four, and $3\frac{5}{8}$ to travel the next four, and if its rate of progress continued to diminish in the same ratio, how long would it take it to go fifteen hundred million miles?"

I don't know.

"AMBITIOUS LEARNER," *Oakland.*— Yes; you are right — America was not discovered by Alexander Selkirk.

"DISCARDED LOVER."— I loved, and still love, the beautiful Edwitha Howard, and intended to marry her. Yet, during my temporary absence at Benicia, last week, alas! she married Jones. Is my happiness to be thus blasted for life? Have I no redress?"

Of course you have. All the law, written and unwritten, is on your side. The *intention* and not the *act* constitutes crime — in other words, constitutes the *deed*. If you call your bosom friend a fool, and *intend* it for an insult, it *is* an insult; but if you do it playfully, and meaning no insult, it is *not* an insult. If you discharge a pistol *accidentally*, and kill a man, you can go free, for you have done no murder; but if you try to kill a man, and manifestly *intend* to kill him, but fail utterly to do it, the law still holds that the *intention* constituted the crime, and you are guilty of murder. Ergo, if you had married Edwitha *accidentally*, and without really *intending* to do it, you would not actually be married to her at all, because the *act* of marriage could not be complete without the *intention*. And ergo, in the strict spirit of the law, since you deliberately *intended* to marry Edwitha, and didn't do it, you are married to her all the same — because, as I said before, the *intention* constitutes the crime. It is as clear as day that Edwitha is your wife, and your redress lies in taking a club and mutilating Jones with it as much as you can. Any man has a right to protect his own wife from the advances of other men. But you have another alternative — you were married to Edwitha *first*, because of your deliberate intention, and now you can prosecute her for bigamy, in subsequently marrying Jones. But there is another phase in this complicated case: You *intended* to marry Edwitha, and consequently, according to law, she is your wife — there is no getting around that; but she didn't marry you, and if she *never intended* to marry you, *you are not her husband*, of course. Ergo, in marrying Jones, she was guilty of bigamy, because she was the wife of another man at the time; which is all very well as far as it goes — but then, don't you see, she had no other *husband* when she married Jones, and consequently she was *not* guilty of bigamy. Now, according to this view of the case, Jones married a *spinster*, who was a *widow* at the same time and another man's *wife* at the same time, and yet who had no *husband* and *never had one*, and never had any *intention* of getting married, and therefore, of course, *never had* been married; and by the same reasoning you are a *bachelor*, because you have never been any one's *husband;* and a *married man,*

because you have a wife living; and to all intents
and purposes a *widower*, because you have been
deprived of that wife; and a consummate *ass* for
going off to Benicia in the first place, while things
were so mixed. And by this time I have got myself
so tangled up in the intricacies of this extraordinary
case that I shall have to give up any further attempt
to advise you — I might get confused and fail to
make myself understood. I think I could take up
the argument where I left off, and by following it
closely a while, perhaps I could prove to your satisfaction, either that you never existed at all, or that
you are dead now, and consequently don't need the
faithless Edwitha — I think I could do that, if it
would afford you any comfort.

"ARTHUR AUGUSTUS."— No; you are wrong;
that is the proper way to throw a brickbat or a
tomahawk; but it doesn't answer so well for a bouquet; you will hurt somebody if you keep it up.
Turn your nosegay upside down, take it by the
stems, and toss it with an upward sweep. Did you
ever pitch quoits? that is the idea. The practice of
recklessly heaving immense solid bouquets, of the
general size and weight of prize cabbages, from the
dizzy altitude of the galleries, is dangerous and very
reprehensible. Now, night before last, at the Academy of Music, just after Signorina ———— had finished that exquisite melody, "The Last Rose of
Summer," one of these floral pile-drivers came

cleaving down through the atmosphere of applause, and if she hadn't deployed suddenly to the right, it would have driven her into the floor like a shingle-nail. Of course that bouquet was well meant; but how would you like to have been the target? A sincere compliment is always grateful to a lady, so long as you don't try to knock her down with it.

" YOUNG MOTHER."— And so you think a baby is a thing of beauty and a joy forever? Well, the idea is pleasing, but not original; every cow thinks the same of its own calf. Perhaps the cow may not think it so elegantly, but still she thinks it neverthe-less. I honor the cow for it. We all honor this touching maternal instinct wherever we find it, be it in the home of luxury or in the humble cow-shed. But really, madam, when I come to examine the matter in all its bearings, I find that the correctness of your assertion does not assert itself in all cases. A soiled baby, with a neglected nose, cannot be conscientiously regarded as a thing of beauty; and inasmuch as babyhood spans but three short years, no baby is competent to be a joy " forever." It pains me thus to demolish two-thirds of your pretty sentiment in a single sentence; but the position I hold in this chair requires that I shall not permit you to deceive and mislead the public with your plausible figures of speech. I know a female baby, aged eighteen months, in this city, which cannot hold out as a " joy " twenty-four hours on a stretch,

let alone " forever." And it possesses some of the
most remarkable eccentricities of character and ap
petite that have ever fallen under my notice. I will
set down here a statement of this infant's operations
(conceived, planned, and carried out by itself, and
without suggestion or assistance from its mother or
any one else), during a single day; and what I shall
say can be substantiated by the sworn testimony of
witnesses.

It commenced by eating one dozen large blue-mass
pills, box and all; then it fell down a flight of stairs,
and arose with a blue and purple knot on its forehead, after which it proceeded in quest of further
refreshment and amusement. It found a glass
trinket ornamented with brass-work — smashed up
and ate the glass, and then swallowed the brass.
Then it drank about twenty drops of laudanum, and
more than a dozen tablespoonfuls of strong spirits
of camphor. The reason why it took no more
laudanum was because there was no more to take.
After this it lay down on its back, and shoved five
or six inches of a silver-headed whalebone cane
down its throat; got it fast there, and it was all its
mother could do to pull the cane out again, without
pulling out some of the child with it. Then, being
hungry for glass again, it broke up several wine-
glasses, and fell to eating and swallowing the fragments, not minding a cut or two. Then it ate a
quantity of butter, pepper, salt, and California
matches, actually taking a spoonful of butter, a

spoonful of salt, a spoonful of pepper, and three or four lucifer matches at each mouthful. (I will remark here that this thing of beauty likes painted German lucifers, and eats all she can get of them; but she prefers California matches, which I regard as a compliment to our home manufactures of more than ordinary value, coming, as it does, from one who is too young to flatter.) Then she washed her head with soap and water, and afterward ate what soap was left, and drank as much of the suds as she had room for; after which she sallied forth and took the cow familiarly by the tail, and got kicked heels over head. At odd times during the day, when this joy for ever happened to have nothing particular on hand, she put in the time by climbing up on places, and falling down off them, uniformly damaging herself in the operation. As young as she is, she speaks many words tolerably distinctly; and being plain-spoken in other respects, blunt and to the point, she opens conversation with all strangers, male or female, with the same formula, " How do, Jim?" Not being familiar with the ways of children, it is possible that I have been magnifying into matter of surprise things which may not strike any one who is familiar with infancy as being at all astonishing. However, I cannot believe that such is the case, and so I repeat that my report of this baby's performances is strictly true; and if any one doubts it, I can produce the child. I will further engage that she will devour anything that is given her (reserving to myself only the right to exclude anvils), and fall down from any place to which she may be elevated (merely stipulating that her preference for alighting on her head shall be respected, and, therefore, that the elevation chosen shall be high enough to enable her to accomplish this to her satisfaction). But I find I have wandered from my subject; so, without further argument, I will reiterate my conviction that not *all* babies are things of beauty and joys forever.

"ARITHMETICUS." *Virginia, Nevada.*—" I am an enthusiastic student of mathematics, and it is so vexatious to me to find my progress constantly impeded by these mysterious arithmetical technicalities. Now do tell me what the difference is between geometry and conchology? "

Here *you* come again with your arithmetical conundrums, when I am suffering death with a cold in the head. If you could have seen the expression of scorn that darkened my countenance a moment ago, and was instantly split from the center in every direction like a fractured looking-glass by my last sneeze, you never would have written that disgraceful question. Conchology is a science which has nothing to do with mathematics; it relates only to shells. At the same time, however, a man who opens oysters for a hotel, or shells a fortified town, or sucks eggs, is not, strictly speaking, a conchologist — a fine stroke of sarcasm that, but it will be lost on such an unintellectual clam as you. Now compare conchology and geometry together, and you will see what the difference is, and your ques-

7S

tion will be answered. But don't torture me with any more arithmetical horrors until you know I am rid of my cold. I feel the bitterest animosity toward you at this moment — bothering me in this way, when I can do nothing but sneeze and rage and snort pocket handkerchiefs to atoms. If I had you in range of my nose now I would blow your brains **out.**

TO RAISE POULTRY *

SERIOUSLY, from early youth I have taken an especial interest in the subject of poultry-raising, and so this membership touches a ready sympathy in my breast. Even as a schoolboy, poultry-raising was a study with me, and I may say without egotism that as early as the age of seventeen I was acquainted with all the best and speediest methods of raising chickens, from raising them off a roost by burning lucifer matches under their noses, down to lifting them off a fence on a frosty night by insinuating the end of a warm board under their heels. By the time I was twenty years old, I really suppose I had raised more poultry than any one individual in all the section round about there. The very chickens came to know my talent by and by. The youth of both sexes ceased to paw the earth for worms, and old roosters that came to crow, " remained to pray," when I passed by.

I have had so much experience in the raising of fowls that I cannot but think that a few hints from

---

* Being a letter written to a Poultry Society that had conferred a complimentary membership upon the author. Written about 1870.

me might be useful to the society. The two methods I have already touched upon are very simple, and are only used in the raising of the commonest class of fowls; one is for summer, the other for winter. In the one case you start out with a friend along about eleven o'clock on a summer's night (not later, because in some States — especially in California and Oregon — chickens always rouse up just at midnight and crow from ten to thirty minutes, according to the ease or difficulty they experience in getting the public waked up), and your friend carries with him a sack. Arrived at the henroost (your neighbor's, not your own), you light a match and hold it under first one and then another pullet's nose until they are willing to go into that bag without making any trouble about it. You then return home, either taking the bag with you or leaving it behind, according as circumstances shall dictate. *N. B.*— I *have* seen the time when it was eligible and appropriate to leave the sack behind and walk off with considerable velocity, without ever leaving any word where to send it.

In the case of the other method mentioned for raising poultry, your friend takes along a covered vessel with a charcoal fire in it, and you carry a long slender plank. This is a frosty night, understand. Arrived at the tree, or fence, or other henroost (your own if you are an idiot), you warm the end of your plank in your friend's fire vessel, and then raise it aloft and ease it up gently against a slumbering chicken's foot. If the subject of your attentions is a true bird, he will infallibly return thanks with a sleepy cluck or two, and step out and take up quarters on the plank, thus becoming so conspicuously accessory before the fact to his own murder as to make it a grave question in our minds, as it once was in the mind of Blackstone, whether he is not really and deliberately committing suicide in the second degree. [But you enter into a contemplation of these legal refinements subsequently — not then.]

When you wish to raise a fine, large, donkey-voiced Shanghai rooster, you do it with a lasso, just as you would a bull. It is because he must be choked, and choked effectually, too. It is the only good, certain way, for whenever he mentions a matter which he is cordially interested in, the chances are ninety-nine in a hundred that he secures somebody else's immediate attention to it too, whether it be day or night.

The Black Spanish is an exceedingly fine bird and a costly one. Thirty-five dollars is the usual figure, and fifty a not uncommon price for a specimen. Even its eggs are worth from a dollar to a dollar and a half apiece, and yet are so unwholesome that the city physician seldom or never orders them for the workhouse. Still I have once or twice procured as high as a dozen at a time for nothing, in the dark of the moon. The best way to raise the Black Spanish fowl is to go late in the evening and raise

7

coop and all. The reason I recommend this method is that, the birds being so valuable, the owners do not permit them to roost around promiscuously, but put them in a coop as strong as a fireproof safe, and keep it in the kitchen at night. The method I speak of is not always a bright and satisfying success, and yet there are so many little articles of *vertu* about a kitchen, that if you fail on the coop you can generally bring away something else. I brought away a nice steel trap one night, worth ninety cents.

But what is the use in my pouring out my whole intellect on this subject? I have shown the Western New York Poultry Society that they have taken to their bosom a party who is not a spring chicken by any means, but a man who knows all about poultry, and is just as high up in the most efficient methods of raising it as the president of the institution himself. I thank these gentlemen for the honorary membership they have conferred upon me, and shall stand at all times ready and willing to testify my good feeling and my official zeal by deeds as well as by this hastily penned advice and information. Whenever they are ready to go to raising poultry, let them call for me any evening after eleven o'clock, and I shall be on hand promptly.

EXPERIENCE OF THE McWILLIAMSES WITH MEMBRANOUS CROUP*

[As related to the author of this book by Mr. McWilliams, a pleasant New York gentleman whom the said author met by chance on a journey.]

WELL, to go back to where I was before I digressed to explain to you how that frightful and incurable disease, membranous croup, was ravaging the town and driving all mothers mad with terror, I called Mrs. McWilliams's attention to little Penelope and said:

" Darling, I wouldn't let that child be chewing that pine stick if I were you."

" Precious, where is the harm in it?" said she, but at the same time preparing to take away the stick — for women cannot receive even the most palpably judicious suggestion without arguing it; that is, married women.

I replied:

" Love, it is notorious that pine is the least nutritious wood that a child can eat."

My wife's hand paused, in the act of taking the

—————
* Written about 1878.

stick, and returned itself to her lap. She bridled perceptibly, and said:

" Hubby, you know better than that. You know you do. Doctors *all* say that the turpentine in pine wood is good for weak back and the kidneys."

" Ah — I was under a misapprehension. I did not know that the child's kidneys and spine were affected, and that the family physician had recommended —"

" Who said the child's spine and kidneys were affected?"

" My love, you intimated it."

" The idea! I never intimated anything of the kind."

" Why, my dear, it hasn't been two minutes since you said —"

" Bother what I said! I don't care what I did say. There isn't any harm in the child's chewing a bit of pine stick if she wants to, and you know it perfectly well. And she *shall* chew it, too. So there, now!"

" Say no more, my dear. I now see the force of your reasoning, and I will go and order two or three cords of the best pine wood to-day. No child of mine shall want while I —"

" Oh, *please* go along to your office and let me have some peace. A body can never make the simplest remark but you must take it up and go to arguing and arguing and arguing till you don't know what you are talking about, and you *never* do."

" Very well, it shall be as you say. But there is a want of logic in your last remark which —"

However, she was gone with a flourish before I could finish, and had taken the child with her. That night at dinner she confronted me with a face as white as a sheet:

" Oh, Mortimer, there's another! Little Georgie Gordon is taken."

" Membranous croup?"

" Membranous croup."

" Is there any hope for him?"

" None in the wide world. Oh, what is to become of us!"

By and by a nurse brought in our Penelope to say good night and offer the customary prayer at the mother's knee. In the midst of " Now I lay me down to sleep," she gave a slight cough! My wife fell back like one stricken with death. But the next moment she was up and brimming with the activities which terror inspires.

She commanded that the child's crib be removed from the nursery to our bedroom; and she went along to see the order executed. She took me with her, of course. We got matters arranged with speed. A cot bed was put up in my wife's dressing room for the nurse. But now Mrs. McWilliams said we were too far away from the other baby, and what if *he* were to have the symptoms in the night — and she blanched again, poor thing.

We then restored the crib and the nurse to the

nursery and put up a bed for ourselves in a room adjoining.

Presently, however, Mrs. McWilliams said suppose the baby should catch it from Penelope? This thought struck a new panic to her heart, and the tribe of us could not get the crib out of the nursery again fast enough to satisfy my wife, though she assisted in her own person and well nigh pulled the crib to pieces in her frantic hurry.

We moved downstairs; but there was no place there to stow the nurse, and Mrs. McWilliams said the nurse's experience would be an inestimable help. So we returned, bag and baggage, to our own bedroom once more, and felt a great gladness, like storm-buffeted birds that have found their nest again.

Mrs. McWilliams sped to the nursery to see how things were going on there. She was back in a moment with a new dread. She said:

" What *can* make Baby sleep so?"

I said:

" Why, my darling, Baby *always* sleeps like a graven image."

" I know. I know; but there's something peculiar about his sleep now. He seems to — to — he seems to breathe so *regularly*. Oh, this is dreadful."

" But, my dear, he always breathes regularly."

" Oh, I know it, but there's something frightful about it now. His nurse is too young and inexperienced.   Maria shall stay there with her, and be on hand if anything happens.''

" That is a good idea, but who will help *you* ?"

" You can help me all I want.   I wouldn't allow anybody to do anything but myself, anyhow, at such a time as this.''

I said I would feel mean to lie abed and sleep, and leave her to watch and toil over our little patient all the weary night.   But she reconciled me to it. So old Maria departed and took up her ancient quarters in the nursery.

Penelope coughed twice in her sleep.

" Oh, why *don't* that doctor come !   Mortimer, this room is too warm.   This room is certainly too warm.   Turn off the register — quick !''

I shut it off, glancing at the thermometer at the same time, and wondering to myself if 70 *was* too warm for a sick child.

The coachman arrived from down town now with the news that our physician was ill and confined to his bed.   Mrs. McWilliams turned a dead eye upon me, and said in a dead voice:

" There is a Providence in it.   It is foreordained. He never was sick before.   Never.   We have not been living as we ought to live, Mortimer.   Time and time again I have told you so.   Now you see the result.   Our child will never get well.   Be thankful if you can forgive yourself; I never can forgive *my*self.''

I said, without intent to hurt, but with heedless

choice of words, that I could not see that we had been living such an abandoned life.

" *Mortimer !* Do you want to bring the judgment upon Baby, too !"

Then she began to cry, but suddenly exclaimed:

" The doctor must have sent medicines !"

I said:

" Certainly. They are here. I was only waiting for you to give me a chance."

" Well do give them to me! Don't you know that every moment is precious now? But what was the use in sending medicines, when he *knows* that the disease is incurable?"

I said that while there was life there was hope.

" Hope ! Mortimer, you know no more what you are talking about than the child unborn. If you would — As I live, the directions say give one teaspoonful once an hour! Once an hour ! — as if we had a whole year before us to save the child in ! Mortimer, please hurry. Give the poor perishing thing a tablespoonful, and *try* to be quick !"

" Why, my dear, a tablespoonful might —"

" *Don't* drive me frantic !......There, there, there, my precious, my own; it's nasty bitter stuff, but it's good for Nelly — good for mother's precious darling; and it will make her well. There, there, there, put the little head on mamma's breast and go to sleep, and pretty soon — oh, I know she can't live till morning ! Mortimer, a tablespoonful every half hour will — Oh, the child needs belladonna,

too ; I know she does — and aconite. Get them,
Mortimer. Now do let me have my way. You
know nothing about these things."

We now went to bed, placing the crib close to my
wife's pillow. All this turmoil had worn upon me,
and within two minutes I was something more than
half asleep. Mrs. McWilliams roused me :

" Darling, is that register turned on ? "

" No."

" I thought as much. Please turn it on at once.
This room is cold."

I turned it on, and presently fell asleep again. I
was aroused once more :

" Dearie, would you mind moving the crib to
your side of the bed? It is nearer the register."

I moved it, but had a collision with the rug and
woke up the child. I dozed off once more, while
my wife quieted the sufferer. But in a little while
these words came murmuring remotely through the
fog of my drowsiness :

" Mortimer, if we only had some goose grease —
will you ring? "

I climbed dreamily out, and stepped on a cat,
which responded with a protest and would have got
a convincing kick for it if a chair had not got it
instead.

" Now, Mortimer, why do you want to turn up
the gas and wake up the child again? "

" Because I want to see how much I am hurt,
Caroline."

'Well, look at the chair, too — I have no doubt it is ruined. Poor cat, suppose you had —''

"Now I am not going to suppose anything about the cat. It never would have occurred if Maria had been allowed to remain here and attend to these duties, which are in her line and are not in mine."

"Now, Mortimer, I should think you would be ashamed to make a remark like that. It is a pity if you cannot do the few little things I ask of you at such an awful time as this when our child —"

"There, there, I will do anything you want. But I can't raise anybody with this bell. They're all gone to bed. Where is the goose grease?"

"On the mantel-piece in the nursery. If you'll step there and speak to Maria —"

I fetched the goose grease and went to sleep again. Once more I was called:

"Mortimer, I so hate to disturb you, but the room is still too cold for me to try to apply this stuff. Would you mind lighting the fire? It is all ready to touch a match to."

I dragged myself out and lit the fire, and then sat down disconsolate.

"Mortimer, don't sit there and catch your death of cold. Come to bed."

As I was stepping in she said:

"But wait a moment. Please give the child some more of the medicine."

Which I did. It was a medicine which made a

child more or less lively; so my wife made use of
its waking interval to strip it and grease it all over
with the goose oil. I was soon asleep once more,
but once more I had to get up.

"Mortimer, I feel a draft. I feel it distinctly.
There is nothing so bad for this disease as a draft.
Please move the crib in front of the fire."

I did it; and collided with the rug again, which I
threw in the fire. Mrs. McWilliams sprang out of
bed and rescued it and we had some words. I had
another trifling interval of sleep, and then got up,
by request, and constructed a flax-seed poultice.
This was placed upon the child's breast and left
there to do its healing work.

A wood fire is not a permanent thing. I got up
every twenty minutes and renewed ours, and this
gave Mrs. McWilliams the opportunity to shorten
the times of giving the medicines by ten minutes,
which was a great satisfaction to her. Now and
then, between times, I reorganized the flax-seed
poultices, and applied sinapisms and other sorts of
blisters where unoccupied places could be found
upon the child. Well, toward morning the wood
gave out and my wife wanted me to go down cellar
and get some more. I said:

"My dear, it is a laborious job, and the child
must be nearly warm enough, with her extra
clothing. Now mightn't we put on another layer
of poultices and —"

I did not finish, because I was interrupted. I

lugged wood up from below for some little time, and then turned in and fell to snoring as only a man can whose strength is all gone and whose soul is worn out. Just at broad daylight I felt a grip on my shoulder that brought me to my senses suddenly. My wife was glaring down upon me and gasping. As soon as she could command her tongue she said:

" It is all over! All over! The child's perspiring! What *shall* we do?"

" Mercy, how you terrify me! *I* don't know what we ought to do. Maybe if we scraped her and put her in the draft again —"

" Oh, idiot! There is not a moment to lose! Go for the doctor. Go yourself. Tell him he *must* come, dead or alive."

I dragged that poor sick man from his bed and brought him. He looked at the child and said she was not dying. This was joy unspeakable to me, but it made my wife as mad as if he had offered her a personal affront. Then he said the child's cough was only caused by some trifling irritation or other in the throat. At this I thought my wife had a mind to show him the door. Now the doctor said he would make the child cough harder and dislodge the trouble. So he gave her something that sent her into a spasm of coughing, and presently up came a little wood splinter or so.

" This child has no membranous croup," said he. " She has been chewing a bit of pine shingle or something of the kind, and got some little slivers in her throat. They won't do her any hurt."

"No," said I, "I can well believe that. Indeed, the turpentine that is in them is very good for certain sorts of diseases that are peculiar to children. My wife will tell you so."

But she did not. She turned away in disdain and left the room; and since that time there is one episode in our life which we never refer to. Hence the tide of our days flows by in deep and untroubled serenity.

[Very few married men have such an experience as McWilliams', and so the author of this book thought that maybe the novelty of it would give it a passing interest to the reader.]

8s

MY FIRST LITERARY VENTURE

I WAS a very smart child at the age of thirteen — an unusually smart child, I thought at the time. It was then that I did my first newspaper scribbling, and most unexpectedly to me it stirred up a fine sensation in the community. It did, indeed, and I was very proud of it, too. I was a printer's "devil," and a progressive and aspiring one. My uncle had me on his paper (the *Weekly Hannibal Journal*, two dollars a year in advance — five hundred subscribers, and they paid in cordwood, cabbages, and unmarketable turnips), and on a lucky summer's day he left town to be gone a week, and asked me if I thought I could edit one issue of the paper judiciously. Ah! didn't I want to try! Higgins was the editor on the rival paper. He had lately been jilted, and one night a friend found an open note on the poor fellow's bed, in which he stated that he could no longer endure life and had drowned himself in Bear Creek. The friend ran down there and discovered Higgins wading back to shore. He had concluded he wouldn't. The village was full of it for several days, but Higgins did not suspect it. I thought this was a fine opportunity. I wrote an elaborately wretched account of the whole matter, and then illustrated it with villainous cuts engraved on the bottoms of wooden type with a jackknife — one of them a picture of Higgins wading out into the creek in his shirt, with a lantern, sounding the depth of the water with a walking stick. I thought it was desperately funny, and was densely unconscious that there was any moral obliquity about such a publication. Being satisfied with this effort I looked around for other worlds to conquer, and it struck me that it would make good, interesting matter to charge the editor of a neighboring country paper with a piece of gratuitous rascality and " see him squirm."

I did it, putting the article into the form of a parody on the "Burial of Sir John Moore" — and a pretty crude parody it was, too.

Then I lampooned two prominent citizens outrageously — not because they had done anything to deserve it, but merely because I thought it was my duty to make the paper lively.

Next I gently touched up the newest stranger — the lion of the day, the gorgeous journeyman tailor from Quincy. He was a simpering coxcomb of the first water, and the " loudest " dressed man in the State. He was an inveterate woman-killer. Every week he wrote lushy " poetry " for the " Journal," about his newest conquest. His rhymes for my week were headed, " TO MARY IN H——L," mean-

ing to Mary in Hannibal, of course. But while setting up the piece I was suddenly riven from head to
heel by what I regarded as a perfect thunderbolt of
humor, and I compressed it into a snappy footnote
at the bottom — thus: " We will let this thing pass,
just this once; but we wish Mr. J. Gordon Runnels
to understand distinctly that we have a character to
sustain, and from this time forth when he wants to
commune with his friends in h—l, he must select
some other medium than the columns of this
journal!"

The paper came out, and I never knew any little
thing attract so much attention as those playful
trifles of mine.

For once the *Hannibal Journal* was in demand —
a novelty it had not experienced before. The whole
town was stirred. Higgins dropped in with a double-
barreled shotgun early in the forenoon. When he
found that it was an infant (as he called me) that
had done him the damage, he simply pulled my ears
and went away; but he threw up his situation that
night and left town for good. The tailor came with
his goose and a pair of shears; but he despised me,
too, and departed for the South that night. The
two lampooned citizens came with threats of libel,
and went away incensed at my insignificance. The
country editor pranced in with a warwhoop next
day, suffering for blood to drink; but he ended by
forgiving me cordially and inviting me down to the
drug store to wash away all animosity in a friendly

bumper of " Fahnestock's Vermifuge." It was his
little joke. My uncle was very angry when he got
back — unreasonably so, I thought, considering what
an impetus I had given the paper, and considering
also that gratitude for his preservation ought to have
been uppermost in his mind, inasmuch as by his
delay he had so wonderfully escaped dissection,
tomahawking, libel, and getting his head shot off.
But he softened when he looked at the accounts and
saw that I had actually booked the unparalleled
number of thirty-three new subscribers, and had the
vegetables to show for it, cordwood, cabbage, beans,
and unsalable turnips enough to run the family for
two years!

HOW THE AUTHOR WAS SOLD IN NEWARK*

IT is seldom pleasant to tell on one's self, but
sometimes it is a sort of relief to a man to make
a confession. I wish to unburden my mind now,
and yet I almost believe that I am moved to do it
more because I long to bring censure upon another
man than because I desire to pour balm upon my
wounded heart. (I don't know what balm is, but I
believe it is the correct expression to use in this
connection — never having seen any balm.) You
may remember that I lectured in Newark lately for
the young gentlemen of the ——— Society? I did
at any rate. During the afternoon of that day I
was talking with one of the young gentlemen just
referred to, and he said he had an uncle who, from
some cause or other, seemed to have grown permanently bereft of all emotion. And with tears in
his eyes, this young man said, " Oh, if I could only
see him laugh once more! Oh, if I could only see
him weep!" I was touched. I could never withstand distress.

* Written about 1869.

I said: " Bring him to my lecture. I'll start him for you."

" Oh, if you could but do it! If you could but do it, all our family would bless you for evermore — for he is so very dear to us. Oh, my benefactor, can you make him laugh? can you bring soothing tears to those parched orbs?"

I was profoundly moved. I said: " My son, bring the old party round. I have got some jokes in that lecture that will make him laugh if there is any laugh in him; and if they miss fire, I have got some others that will make him cry or kill him, one or the other." Then the young man blessed me, and wept on my neck, and went after his uncle. He placed him in full view, in the second row of benches that night, and I began on him. I tried him with mild jokes, then with severe ones; I dosed him with bad jokes and riddled him with good ones; I fired old stale jokes into him, and peppered him fore and aft with red-hot new ones; I warmed up to my work, and assaulted him on the right and left, in front and behind; I fumed and sweated and charged and ranted till I was hoarse and sick and frantic and furious; but I never moved him once — I never started a smile or a tear! Never a ghost of a smile, and never a suspicion of moisture! I was astounded. I closed the lecture at last with one despairing shriek — with one wild burst of humor, and hurled a joke of supernatural atrocity full at him!

Then I sat down bewildered and exhausted.

The president of the society came up and bathed my head with cold water, and said: " What made you carry on so toward the last?"

I said: " I was trying to make that confounded old fool laugh, in the second row."

And he said: " Well, you were wasting your time, because he is deaf and dumb, and as blind as a badger!"

Now, was that any way for that old man's nephew to impose on a stranger and orphan like me? I ask you as a man and brother, if that was any way for him to do?

THE OFFICE BORE*

HE arrives just as regularly as the clock strikes nine in the morning. And so he even beats the editor sometimes, and the porter must leave his work and climb two or three pair of stairs to unlock the " Sanctum " door and let him in. He lights one of the office pipes — not reflecting, perhaps, that the editor may be one of those " stuck-up " people who would as soon have a stranger defile his toothbrush as his pipestem. Then he begins to loll — for a person who can consent to loaf his useless life away in ignominious indolence has not the energy to sit up straight. He stretches full length on the sofa a while; then draws up to half length; then gets into a chair, hangs his head back and his arms abroad, and stretches his legs till the rims of his boot-heels rest upon the floor; by and by sits up and leans forward, with one leg or both over the arm of the chair. But it is still observable that with all his changes of position, he never assumes the upright or a fraudful affectation of dignity. From time to time he yawns, and stretches, and scratches

* Written about 1869.

himself with a tranquil, mangy enjoyment, and now
and then he grunts a kind of stuffy, overfed grunt,
which is full of animal contentment. At rare and
long intervals, however, he sighs a sigh that is the
eloquent expression of a secret confession, to wit:
" I am useless and a nuisance, a cumberer of the
earth." The bore and his comrades — for there
are usually from two to four on hand, day and
night — mix into the conversation when men come
in to see the editors for a moment on business;
they hold noisy talks among themselves about politics in particular, and all other subjects in general —
even warming up, after a fashion, sometimes, and
seeming to take almost a real interest in what they
are discussing. They ruthlessly call an editor from
his work with such a remark as: " Did you see this,
Smith, in the *Gazette ?*" and proceed to read the
paragraph while the sufferer reins in his impatient
pen and listens; they often loll and sprawl round
the office hour after hour, swapping anecdotes and
relating personal experiences to each other — hair-
breadth escapes, social encounters with distinguished
men, election reminiscences, sketches of odd characters, etc. And through all those hours they never
seem to comprehend that they are robbing the
editors of their time, and the public of journalistic
excellence in next day's paper. At other times
they drowse, or dreamily pore over exchanges, or
droop limp and pensive over the chair-arms for an
hour. Even this solemn silence is small respite to

the editor, for the next uncomfortable thing to
having people look over his shoulders, perhaps, is
to have them sit by in silence and listen to the
scratching of his pen. If a body desires to talk
private business with one of the editors, he must
call him outside, for no hint milder than blasting
powder or nitro-glycerine would be likely to move
the bores out of listening distance. To have to sit
and endure the presence of a bore day after day; to
feel your cheerful spirits begin to sink as his footstep sounds on the stair, and utterly vanish away
as his tiresome form enters the door; to suffer
through his anecdotes and die slowly to his reminiscences; to feel always the fetters of his clogging
presence; to long hopelessly for one single day's
privacy; to note with a shudder, by and by, that to
contemplate his funeral in fancy has ceased to
soothe, to imagine him undergoing in strict and
fearful detail the tortures of the ancient Inquisition
has lost its power to satisfy the heart, and that even
to wish him millions and millions and millions of
miles in Tophet is able to bring only a fitful gleam
of joy; to have to endure all this, day after day,
and week after week, and month after month, is an
affliction that transcends any other that men suffer.
Physical pain is pastime to it, and hanging a pleasure
excursion.

JOHNNY GREER

"THE church was densely crowded that lovely summer Sabbath," said the Sunday-school superintendent, " and all, as their eyes rested upon the small coffin, seemed impressed by the poor black boy's fate. Above the stillness the pastor's voice rose, and chained the interest of every ear as he told, with many an envied compliment, how that the brave, noble, daring little Johnny Greer, when he saw the drowned body sweeping down toward the deep part of the river whence the agonized parents never could have recovered it in this world, gallantly sprang into the stream, and, at the risk of his life, towed the corpse to shore, and held it fast till help came and secured it. Johnny Greer was sitting just in front of me. A ragged street boy, with eager eye, turned upon him instantly, and said in a hoarse whisper:

" ' No; but did you, though?'

" ' Yes.'

" ' Towed the carkiss ashore and saved it yo' self?'

" ' Yes.'

" ' Cracky! What did they give you?'

" ' Nothing.'

" ' W-h-a-t [with intense disgust]! D'you know what I'd a done? I'd a anchored him out in the stream, and said, *Five dollars, gents, or you carn't have yo' nigger.* ' "

THE FACTS IN THE CASE OF THE GREAT BEEF CONTRACT*

IN as few words as possible I wish to lay before the nation what share, howsoever small, I have had in this matter — this matter which has so exercised the public mind, engendered so much ill-feeling, and so filled the newspapers of both continents with distorted statements and extravagant comments.

The origin of this distressful thing was this — and I assert here that every fact in the following *résumé* can be amply proved by the official records of the General Government:

John Wilson Mackenzie, of Rotterdam, Chemung county, New Jersey, deceased, contracted with the General Government, on or about the 10th day of October, 1861, to furnish to General Sherman the sum total of thirty barrels of beef.

Very well.

He started after Sherman with the beef, but when he got to Washington Sherman had gone to Manassas; so he took the beef and followed him there,

* Written about 1867.

but arrived too late; he followed him to Nashville,
and from Nashville to Chattanooga, and from Chattanooga to Atlanta — but he never could overtake
him.   At Atlanta he took a fresh start and followed
him clear through his march to the sea.   He arrived
too late again by a few days; but hearing that Sherman was going out in the *Quaker City* excursion to
the Holy Land, he took shipping for Beirut, calculating to head off the other vessel.   When he arrived
in Jerusalem with his beef, he learned that Sherman
had not sailed in the *Quaker City*, but had gone to
the Plains to fight the Indians.   He returned to
America and started for the Rocky Mountains.
After sixty-eight days of arduous travel on the
Plains, and when he had got within four miles of
Sherman's headquarters, he was tomahawked and
scalped, and the Indians got the beef.   They got
all of it but one barrel.   Sherman's army captured
that, and so, even in death, the bold navigator partly
fulfilled his contract.   In his will, which he had kept
like a journal, he bequeathed the contract to his son
Bartholomew W.   Bartholomew W. made out the
following bill, and then died:

THE UNITED STATES
　　In account with JOHN WILSON MACKENZIE, of New
　　　　Jersey, deceased, ...   Dr.
To thirty barrels of beef for General Sherman, at $100, $3,000
To traveling expenses and transportation, ... 14,000
　　　　　　　　　　　　　　　　　　　　　　　───────
　　　　　　　　　　　　　Total, . . . $17,000
　　　　　　　　　　Rec'd Pay't.

He died then; but he left the contract to Wm. J. Martin, who tried to collect it, but died before he got through. *He* left it to Barker J. Allen, and he tried to collect it also. He did not survive. Barker J. Allen left it to Anson G. Rogers, who attempted to collect it, and got along as far as the Ninth Auditor's Office, when Death, the great Leveler, came all unsummoned, and foreclosed on *him* also. He left the bill to a relative of his in Connecticut, Vengeance Hopkins by name, who lasted four weeks and two days, and made the best time on record, coming within one of reaching the Twelfth Auditor. In his will he gave the contract bill to his uncle, by the name of O-be-joyful Johnson. It was too undermining for Joyful. His last words were: " Weep not for me — *I* am willing to go." And so he was, poor soul. Seven people inherited the contract after that; but they all died. So it came into my hands at last. It fell to me through a relative by the name of Hubbard — Bethlehem Hubbard, of Indiana. He had had a grudge against me for a long time; but in his last moments he sent for me, and forgave me everything, and weeping gave me the beef contract.

This ends the history of it up to the time that I succeeded to the property. I will now endeavor to set myself straight before the nation in everything that concerns my share in the matter. I took this beef contract, and the bill for mileage and transportation, to the President of the United States.

He said, " Well, sir, what can I do for you?"

I said, " Sire, on or about the 10th day of October, 1861, John Wilson Mackenzie, of Rotterdam, Chemung county, New Jersey, deceased, contracted with the General Government to furnish to General Sherman the sum total of thirty barrels of beef —"

He stopped me there, and dismissed me from his presence — kindly, but firmly. The next day I called on the Secretary of State.

He said, " Well, sir?"

I said, " Your Royal Highness: on or about the 10th day of October, 1861, John Wilson Mackenzie, of Rotterdam, Chemung county, New Jersey, deceased, contracted with the General Government to furnish to General Sherman the sum total of thirty barrels of beef —"

" That will do, sir — that will do; this office has nothing to do with contracts for beef."

I was bowed out. I thought the matter all over, and finally, the following day, I visited the Secretary of the Navy, who said, " Speak quickly, sir; do not keep me waiting."

I said, " Your Royal Highness, on or about the 10th day of October, 1861, John Wilson Mackenzie, of Rotterdam, Chemung county, New Jersey, deceased, contracted with the General Government to furnish to General Sherman the sum total of thirty barrels of beef —"

Well, it was as far as I could get. *He* had nothing to do with beef contracts for General Sherman, either. I began to think it was a curious kind of a government. It looked somewhat as if they wanted to get out of paying for that beef. The following day I went to the Secretary of the Interior.

I said, " Your Imperial Highness, on or about the 10th day of October —"

" That is sufficient, sir. I have heard of you before. Go, take your infamous beef contract out of this establishment. The Interior Department has nothing whatever to do with subsistence for the army."

I went away. But I was exasperated now. I said I would haunt them; I would infest every department of this iniquitous Government till that contract business was settled. I would collect that bill, or fall, as fell my predecessors, trying. I assailed the Postmaster-General; I besieged the Agricultural Department; I waylaid the Speaker of the House of Representatives. *They* had nothing to do with army contracts for beef. I moved upon the Commissioner of the Patent Office.

I said, " Your August Excellency, on or about —"

" Perdition! have you got *here* with your incendiary beef contract, at last? We have *nothing* to do with beef contracts for the army, my dear sir."

" Oh, that is all very well — but *somebody* has got to pay for that beef. It has got to be paid *now*, too, or I'll confiscate this old Patent Office and everything in it."

" But, my dear sir —"

9s

" It don't make any difference, sir. The Patent Office is liable for that beef, I reckon; and, liable or not liable, the Patent Office has got to pay for it."

Never mind the details. It ended in a fight. The Patent Office won. But I found out something to my advantage. I was told that the Treasury Department was the proper place for me to go to. I went there. I waited two hours and a half, and then I was admitted to the First Lord of the Treasury.

I said, " Most noble, grave, and reverend Signor, on or about the 10th day of October, 1861, John Wilson Macken —"

" That is sufficient, sir. I have heard of you. Go to the First Auditor of the Treasury."

I did so. He sent me to the Second Auditor. The Second Auditor sent me to the Third, and the Third sent me to the First Comptroller of the Corn-Beef Division. This began to look like business. He examined his books and all his loose papers, but found no minute of the beef contract. I went to the Second Comptroller of the Corn-Beef Division. He examined his books and his loose papers, but with no success. I was encouraged. During that week I got as far as the Sixth Comptroller in that division; the next week I got through the Claims Department; the third week I began and completed the Mislaid Contracts Department, and got a foothold in the Dead Reckoning Department. I finished that in three days. There was only one piace left for it now. I laid siege to the Commissioner of

Odds and Ends. To his clerk, rather — he was not there himself. There were sixteen beautiful young ladies in the room, writing in books, and there were seven well-favored young clerks showing them how. The young women smiled up over their shoulders, and the clerks smiled back at them, and all went merry as a marriage bell. Two or three clerks that were reading the newspapers looked at me rather hard, but went on reading, and nobody said anything. However, I had been used to this kind of alacrity from Fourth Assistant Junior Clerks all through my eventful career, from the very day I entered the first office of the Corn-Beef Bureau clear till I passed out of the last one in the Dead Reckoning Division. I had got so accomplished by this time that I could stand on one foot from the moment I entered an office till a clerk spoke to me, without changing more than two, or maybe three, times.

So I stood there till I had changed four different times. Then I said to one of the clerks who was reading:

" Illustrious Vagrant, where is the Grand Turk?"

" What do you mean, sir? whom do you mean? If you mean the Chief of the Bureau, he is out."

" Will he visit the harem to-day?"

The young man glared upon me a while, and then went on reading his paper. But I knew the ways of those clerks. I knew I was safe if he got through before another New York mail arrived. He only had two more papers left. After a while he finished

them, and then he yawned and asked me what I
wanted.

" Renowned and honored Imbecile: on or
about —"

" You are the beef contract man. Give me your
papers."

He took them, and for a long time he ransacked
his odds and ends. Finally he found the North-
west Passage, as *I* regarded it — he found the long
lost record of that beef contract — he found the
rock upon which so many of my ancestors had split
before they ever got to it. I was deeply moved.
And yet I rejoiced — for I had survived. I said
with emotion, " Give it me. The Government will
settle now." He waved me back, and said there
was something yet to be done first.

" Where is this John Wilson Mackenzie?" said
he.

" Dead."

" When did he die?"

" He didn't die at all — he was killed."

" How?"

" Tomahawked."

" Who tomahawked him?"

" Why, an Indian, of course. You didn't suppose it was the superintendent of a Sunday-school,
did you?"

" No. An Indian, was it?"

" The same."

" Name of the Indian?"

"His name? *I* don't know his name."

"*Must* have his name. Who saw the tomahawking done?"

"I don't know."

"You were not present yourself, then?"

"Which you can see by my hair. I was absent."

"Then how do you know that Mackenzie is dead?"

"Because he certainly died at that time, and I have every reason to believe that he has been dead ever since. I *know* he has, in fact."

"We must have proofs. Have you got the Indian?"

"Of course not."

"Well, you must get him. Have you got the tomahawk?"

"I never thought of such a thing."

"You must get the tomahawk. You must produce the Indian and the tomahawk. If Mackenzie's death can be proven by these, you can then go before the commission appointed to audit claims with some show of getting your bill under such headway that your children may possibly live to receive the money and enjoy it. But that man's death *must* be proven. However, I may as well tell you that the Government will never pay that transportation and those traveling expenses of the lamented Mackenzie. It *may* possibly pay for the barrel of beef that Sherman's soldiers captured, if you can get a relief bill through Congress making an appropriation for that purpose;

but it will not pay for the twenty-nine barrels the Indians ate.''

" Then there is only a hundred dollars due me, and *that* isn't certain! After all Mackenzie's travels in Europe, Asia, and America with that beef; after all his trials and tribulations and transportation; after the slaughter of all those innocents that tried to collect that bill! Young man, why didn't the First Comptroller of the Corn-Beef Division tell me this?''

" He didn't know anything about the genuineness of your claim.''

" Why didn't the Second tell me? why didn't the Third? why didn't all those divisions and departments tell me?''

" None of them knew. We do things by routine here. You have followed the routine and found out what you wanted to know. It is the best way. It is the only way. It is very regular, and very slow, but it is very certain.''

" Yes, certain death. It has been, to the most of our tribe. I begin to feel that I, too, am called. Young man, you love the bright creature yonder with the gentle blue eyes and the steel pens behind her ears — I see it in your soft glances; you wish to marry her — but you are poor. Here, hold out your hand — here is the beef contract; go, take her and be happy! Heaven bless you, my children!''

This is all I know about the great beef contract that has created so much talk in the community.

The clerk to whom I bequeathed it died. I know nothing further about the contract, or any one connected with it. I only know that if a man lives long enough he can trace a thing through the Circumlocution Office of Washington and find out, after much labor and trouble and delay, that which he could have found out on the first day if the business of the Circumlocution Office were as ingeniously systematized as it would be if it were a great private mercantile institution.

THE CASE OF GEORGE FISHER*

THIS is history. It is not a wild extravaganza, like " John Williamson Mackenzie's Great Beef Contract," but is a plain statement of facts and circumstances with which the Congress of the United States has interested itself from time to time during the long period of half a century.

I will not call this matter of George Fisher's a great deathless and unrelenting swindle upon the Government and people of the United States — for it has never been so decided, and I hold that it is a grave and solemn wrong for a writer to cast slurs or call names when such is the case — but will simply present the evidence and let the reader deduce his own verdict. Then we shall do nobody injustice, and our consciences shall be clear.

---

* Some years ago, about 1867, when this was first published, few people believed it, but considered it a mere extravaganza. In these latter days it seems hard to realize that there was ever a time when the robbing of our government was a novelty. The very man who showed me where to find the documents for this case was at that very time spending hundreds of thousands of dollars in Washington for a mail steamship concern, in the effort to procure a subsidy for the company—a fact which was a long time in coming to the surface, but leaked out at last and underwent Congressional investigation.

On or about the 1st day of September, 1813, the Creek war being then in progress in Florida, the crops, herds, and houses of Mr. George Fisher, a citizen, were destroyed, either by the Indians or by the United States troops in pursuit of them. By the terms of the law, if the *Indians* destroyed the property, there was no relief for Fisher; but if the *troops* destroyed it, the Government of the United States was debtor to Fisher for the amount involved.

George Fisher must have considered that the *Indians* destroyed the property, because, although he lived several years afterward, he does not appear to have ever made any claim upon the Government.

In the course of time Fisher died, and his widow married again. And by and by, nearly twenty years after that dimly-remembered raid upon Fisher's cornfields, *the widow Fisher's new husband* petitioned Congress for pay for the property, and backed up the petition with many depositions and affidavits which purported to prove that the troops, and not the Indians, destroyed the property; that the troops, for some inscrutable reason, deliberately burned down " houses " (or cabins) valued at $600, the same belonging to a peaceable private citizen, and also destroyed various other property belonging to the same citizen. But Congress declined to believe that the troops were such idiots (after overtaking and scattering a band of Indians proved to have been found destroying Fisher's property) as to calmly continue the work of destruction themselves, and make a complete job of what the Indians had only commenced. So Congress denied the petition of the heirs of George Fisher in 1832, and did not pay them a cent.

We hear no more from them officially until 1848, sixteen years after their first attempt on the Treasury, and a full generation after the death of the man whose fields were destroyed. The new generation of Fisher heirs then came forward and put in a bill for damages. The Second Auditor awarded them $8,873, being half the damage sustained by Fisher. The Auditor said the testimony showed that at least half the destruction was done by the Indians " *before the troops started in pursuit*," and of course the Government was not responsible for that half.

2. That was in April, 1848. In December, 1848, the heirs of George Fisher, deceased, came forward and pleaded for a " revision " of their bill of damages. The revision was made, but nothing new could be found in their favor except an error of $100 in the former calculation. However, in order to keep up the spirits of the Fisher family, the Auditor concluded to go back and allow *interest* from the date of the first petition (1832) to the date when the bill of damages was awarded. This sen. the Fishers home happy with sixteen years' interest on $8,873 — the same amounting to $8,997.94. Total, $17,870.94.

3. For an entire year the suffering Fisher family

remained quiet—even satisfied, after a fashion.   Then they swooped down upon Government with their wrongs once more.   That old patriot, Attorney-General Toucey, burrowed through the musty papers of the Fishers and discovered one more chance for the desolate orphans — interest on that original award of $8,873 from date of destruction of the property (1813) up to 1832!   Result, $10,004.89 for the indigent Fishers.   So now we have: First, $8,873 damages; second, interest on it from 1832 to 1848, $8,997.94: third, interest on it dated back to 1813, $10,004.89.   Total, $27,875.83!   What better investment for a great-grandchild than to get the Indians to burn a cornfield for him sixty or seventy years before his birth, and plausibly lay it on lunatic United States troops?

4. Strange as it may seem, the Fishers let Congress alone for five years — or, what is perhaps more likely, failed to make themselves heard by Congress for that length of time.   But at last, in 1854, they got a hearing.   They persuaded Congress to pass an act requiring the Auditor to re-examine their case.   But this time they stumbled upon the misfortune of an honest Secretary of the Treasury (Mr. James Guthrie), and he spoiled everything. He said in very plain language that the Fishers were not only not entitled to another cent, but that those children of many sorrows and acquainted with grief *had been paid too much already.*

5. Therefore another interval of rest and silence

ensued — an interval which lasted four years — viz.,
till 1858. The " right man in the right place " was
then Secretary of War — John B. Floyd, of peculiar
renown! Here was a master intellect; here was the
very man to succor the suffering heirs of dead and
forgotten Fisher. They came up from Florida with
a rush — a great tidal wave of Fishers freighted with
the same old musty documents about the same immortal cornfields of their ancestor. They straightway got an act passed transferring the Fisher matter
from the dull Auditor to the ingenious Floyd.
What did Floyd do? He said, " IT WAS PROVED
*that the Indians destroyed everything they could before
the troops entered in pursuit*." He considered, therefore, that what they destroyed must have consisted
of " *the houses with all their contents, and the
liquor* " (the most trifling part of the destruction,
and set down at only $3,200 all told), and that the
Government troops then drove them off and calmly
proceeded to destroy —

*Two hundred and twenty acres of corn in the field,
thirty-five acres of wheat, and nine hundred and
eighty-six head of live stock !* [What a singularly
intelligent army we had in those days, according to
Mr. Floyd — though not according to the Congress
of 1832.]

So Mr. Floyd decided that the Government was
not responsible for that $3,200 worth of rubbish
which the Indians destroyed, but was responsible for
the property destroyed by the troops — which prop-

erty consisted of (I quote from the printed United States Senate document):

	DOLLARS.
Corn at Bassett's Creek, ...	3,000
Cattle, ...	5,000
Stock hogs, ...	1,050
Drove hogs, ...	1,204
Wheat, ...	350
Hides, ...	4,000
Corn on the Alabama River, ...	3,500
Total, ...	18,104

That sum, in his report, Mr. Floyd calls the "*full value* of the property destroyed by the troops." He allows that sum to the starving Fishers, TOGETHER WITH INTEREST FROM 1813. From this new sum total the amounts already paid to the Fishers were deducted, and then the cheerful remainder (a fraction under *forty thousand dollars,*) was handed to them, and again they retired to Florida in a condition of temporary tranquillity. Their ancestor's farm had now yielded them altogether nearly *sixty-seven thousand dollars* in cash.

6. Does the reader suppose that that was the end of it? Does he suppose those diffident Fishers were satisfied? Let the evidence show. The Fishers were quiet just two years. Then they came swarming up out of the fertile swamps of Florida with their same old documents, and besieged Congress once more. Congress capitulated on the 1st of June, 1860, and instructed Mr. Floyd to overhaul

those papers again and pay that bill. A Treasury
clerk was ordered to go through those papers and
report to Mr. Floyd what amount was still due the
emaciated Fishers. This clerk (I can produce him
whenever he is wanted) discovered what was apparently a glaring and recent forgery in the papers,
whereby a witness's testimony as to the price of
corn in Florida in 1813 was made to name double
the amount which that witness had originally speci-
fied as the price! The clerk not only called his
superior's attention to this thing, but in making up
his brief of the case called particular attention to it
in writing. That part of the brief *never got before
Congress*, nor has Congress ever yet had a hint of a
forgery existing among the Fisher papers. Nevertheless, on the basis of the double prices (and
totally ignoring the clerk's assertion that the figures
were manifestly and unquestionably a recent forgery), Mr. Floyd remarks in his new report that
" the testimony, *particularly in regard to the corn
crops*, DEMANDS A MUCH HIGHER ALLOWANCE than
any *heretofore* made by the Auditor or myself." So
he estimates the crop at *sixty bushels* to the acre
(double what Florida acres produce), and then vir-
tuously allows pay for only half the crop, *but* allows
two dollars and a half a bushel for that half, when
there are rusty old books and documents in the
Congressional library to show just what the Fisher
testimony showed before the forgery — viz., that in
the fall of 1813 corn was only worth from $1.25 to

$1.50 a bushel. Having accomplished this, what does Mr. Floyd do next? Mr. Floyd (" with an earnest desire to execute truly the legislative will," as he piously remarks) goes to work and makes out an entirely new bill of Fisher damages, and in this new bill he placidly *ignores the Indians* altogether — puts no particle of the destruction of the Fisher property upon them, but, even repenting him of charging them with burning the cabins and drinking the whisky and breaking the crockery, lays the *entire* damage at the door of the imbecile United States troops, down to the very last item! And not only that, but uses the forgery to double the loss of corn at " Bassett's Creek," and uses it again to absolutely *treble* the loss of corn on the " Alabama River." This new and ably conceived and executed bill of Mr. Floyd's figures up as follows (I copy again from the printed United States Senate document) :

The United States in account with the legal representatives of George Fisher, deceased.

	DOL. C.
1813.—To 550 head of cattle, at 10 dollars, . . .	5,500.00
To 86 head of drove hogs, ...	1,204.00
To 350 head of stock hogs, ...	1,750.00
TO 100 ACRES OF CORN ON BASSETT'S CREEK,	6,000.00
To 8 barrels of whisky, ...	350.00
To 2 barrels of brandy, ...	280.00
To 1 barrel of rum, ...	70.00
To dry goods and merchandise in store, .	1,100.00
To 35 acres of wheat, ...	350.00
To 2,000 hides, ...	4,000.00

To furs and hats in store, ...	600.00
To crockery ware in store, ...	100.00
To smiths' and carpenters' tools, . . .	250.00
To houses burned and destroyed, . . .	600.00
To 4 dozen bottles of wine, ...	48.00
1814.—To 120 acres of corn on Alabama River, .	9,500.00
To crops of peas, fodder, etc., ...	3,250.00
Total, ...	34,952.00
To interest on $22,202, from July 1813 to November 1860, 47 years and 4 months,	63,053.68
To interest on $12,750, from September 1814 to November 1860, 46 years and 2 months, ...	35,317.50
Total, ...	133,323.18

He puts everything in this time. He does not even allow that the Indians destroyed the crockery or drank the four dozen bottles of (currant) wine. When it came to supernatural comprehensiveness in "gobbling," John B. Floyd was without his equal, in his own or any other generation. Subtracting from the above total the $67,000 already paid to George Fisher's implacable heirs, Mr. Floyd announced that the government was still indebted to them in the sum of *sixty-six thousand five hundred and nineteen dollars and eighty-five cents,* "which," Mr. Floyd complacently remarks, "will be paid, accordingly, to the administrator of the estate of George Fisher, deceased, or to his attorney in fact."

But, sadly enough for the destitute orphans, a new President came in just at this time, Buchanan and Floyd went out, and they never got their money. The first thing Congress did in 1861 was

to rescind the resolution of June 1, 1860, under
which Mr. Floyd had been ciphering. Then Floyd
(and doubtless the heirs of George Fisher likewise)
had to give up financial business for a while, and go
into the Confederate army and serve their country.

Were the heirs of George Fisher killed? No.
They are back now at this very time (July, 1870),
beseeching Congress through that blushing and diffident creature, Garrett Davis, to commence making
payments again on their interminable and insatiable
bill of damages for corn and whisky destroyed by a
gang of irresponsible Indians, so long ago that even
government red-tape has failed to keep consistent
and intelligent track of it.

Now the above are facts. They are history. Any
one who doubts it can send to the Senate Document
Department of the Capitol for H. R. Ex. Doc. No.
21, 36th Congress, 2d Session, and for S. Ex. Doc.
No. 106, 41st Congress, 2d Session, and satisfy himself. The whole case is set forth in the first volume
of the Court of Claims Reports.

It is my belief that as long as the continent of
America holds together, the heirs of George Fisher,
deceased, will still make pilgrimages to Washington
from the swamps of Florida, to plead for just a little
more cash on their bill of damages (even when they
received the last of that sixty-seven thousand dollars, they said it was only *one-fourth* what the Government owed them on that fruitful cornfield), and as
long as they choose to come they will find Garrett

Davises to drag their vampire schemes before Congress. This is not the only hereditary fraud (if fraud it is — which I have before repeatedly remarked is not proven) that is being quietly handed down from generation to generation of fathers and sons, through the persecuted Treasury of the United States.

DISGRACEFUL PERSECUTION OF A BOY

IN San Francisco, the other day, " A well-dressed boy, on his way to Sunday-school, was arrested and thrown into the city prison for stoning Chinamen."

What a commentary is this upon human justice! What sad prominence it gives to our human disposition to tyrannize over the weak! San Francisco has little right to take credit to herself for her treatment of this poor boy. What had the child's education been? How should he suppose it was wrong to stone a Chinaman? Before we side against him, along with outraged San Francisco, let us give him a chance — let us hear the testimony for the defense.

He was a "well-dressed" boy, and a Sunday-school scholar, and therefore the chances are that his parents were intelligent, well-to-do people, with just enough natural villainy in their composition to make them yearn after the daily papers, and enjoy them; and so this boy had opportunities to learn all through the week how to do right, as well as on Sunday.

It was in this way that he found out that the great commonwealth of California imposes an unlawful mining-tax upon John the foreigner, and allows Patrick the foreigner to dig gold for nothing — probably because the degraded Mongol is at no expense for whisky, and the refined Celt cannot exist without it.

It was in this way that he found out that a respectable number of the taxgatherers — it would be unkind to say all of them — collect the tax twice, instead of once; and that, inasmuch as they do it solely to discourage Chinese immigration into the mines, it is a thing that is much applauded, and likewise regarded as being singularly facetious.

It was in this way that he found out that when a white man robs a sluice-box (by the term white man is meant Spaniards, Mexicans, Portuguese, Irish, Hondurans, Peruvians, Chileans, etc., etc.), they make him leave the camp; and when a Chinaman does that thing, they hang him.

It was in this way that he found out that in many districts of the vast Pacific coast, so strong is the wild, free love of justice in the hearts of the people, that whenever any secret and mysterious crime is committed, they say, " Let justice be done, though the heavens fall," and go straightway and swing a Chinaman.

It was in this way that he found out that by studying one half of each day's " local items," it would appear that the police of San Francisco were

either asleep or dead, and by studying the other
half it would seem that the reporters were gone
mad with admiration of the energy, the virtue, the
high effectiveness, and the dare-devil intrepidity of
that very police — making exultant mention of how
"the Argus-eyed officer So-and-so," captured a
wretched knave of a Chinaman who was stealing
chickens, and brought him gloriously to the city
prison; and how "the gallant officer Such-and-such-
a-one," quietly kept an eye on the movements of
an " unsuspecting, almond-eyed son of Confucius "
(your reporter is nothing if not facetious), following
him around with that far-off look of vacancy and
unconsciousness always so finely affected by that inscrutable being, the forty-dollar policeman, during
a waking interval, and captured him at last in the
very act of placing his hands in a suspicious manner
upon a paper of tacks, left by the owner in an exposed situation; and how one officer performed this
prodigious thing, and another officer that, and another the other — and pretty much every one of
these performances having for a dazzling central
incident a Chinaman guilty of a shilling's worth of
crime, an unfortunate, whose misdemeanor must be
hurrahed into something enormous in order to keep
the public from noticing how many really important
rascals went uncaptured in the meantime, and how
overrated those glorified policemen actually are.

It was in this way that the boy found out that the
legislature, being aware that the Constitution has
10

made America an asylum for the poor and the oppressed of all nations, and that, therefore, the poor and oppressed who fly to our shelter must not be charged a disabling admission fee, made a law that every Chinaman, upon landing, must be *vaccinated* upon the wharf, and pay to the State's appointed officer *ten dollars* for the service, when there are plenty of doctors in San Francisco who would be glad enough to do it for him for fifty cents.

It was in this way that the boy found out that a Chinaman had no rights that any man was bound to respect; that he had no sorrows that any man was bound to pity; that neither his life nor his liberty was worth the purchase of a penny when a white man needed a scapegoat; that nobody loved Chinamen, nobody befriended them, nobody spared them suffering when it was convenient to inflict it; everybody, individuals, communities, the majesty of the State itself, joined in hating, abusing, and persecuting these humble strangers.

And, therefore, what *could* have been more natural than for this sunny-hearted boy, tripping along to Sunday-school, with his mind teeming with freshly-learned incentives to high and virtuous action, to say to himself:

" Ah, there goes a Chinaman! God will not love me if I do not stone him."

And for this he was arrested and put in the city jail.

Everything conspired to teach him that it was a

high and holy thing to stone a Chinaman, and yet he no sooner attempts to do his duty that he is punished for it—he, poor chap, who has been aware all his life that one of the principal recreations of the police, out toward the Gold Refinery, is to look on with tranquil enjoyment while the butchers of Brannan street set their dogs on unoffending Chinamen, and make them flee for their lives.*

Keeping in mind the tuition in the humanities which the entire " Pacific coast " gives its youth, there is a very sublimity of incongruity in the virtuous flourish with which the good city fathers of San Francisco proclaim (as they have lately done) that " The police are positively ordered to arrest all boys, of every description and wherever found, who engage in assaulting Chinamen."

Still, let us be truly glad they have made the order, notwithstanding its inconsistency; and let us rest perfectly confident the police are glad, too. Because there is no personal peril in arresting boys, provided they be of the small kind, and the reporters

---

* I have many such memories in my mind, but am thinking just at present of one particular one, where the Brannan Street butchers set their dogs on a Chinaman who was quietly passing with a basket of clothes on his head ; and while the dogs mutilated his flesh, a butcher increased the hilarity of the occasion by knocking some of the Chinaman's teeth down his throat with half a brick. This incident sticks in my memory with a more malevolent tenacity, perhaps, on account of the fact that I was in the employ of a San Francisco journal at the time, and was not allowed to publish it because it might offend some of the peculiar element that subscribed for the paper.

will have to laud their performances just as loyally as ever, or go without items.

The new form for local items in San Francisco will now be: " The ever vigilant and efficient officer So-and-so succeeded, yesterday afternoon, in arresting Master Tommy Jones, after a determined resistance," etc., etc., followed by the customary statistics and final hurrah, with its unconscious sarcasm: " We are happy in being able to state that this is the forty-seventh boy arrested by this gallant officer since the new ordinance went into effect. The most extraordinary activity prevails in the police department. Nothing like it has been seen since we can remember."

THE JUDGE'S "SPIRITED WOMAN"

"I WAS sitting here," said the judge, "in this old pulpit, holding court, and we were trying a big, wicked-looking Spanish desperado for killing the husband of a bright, pretty Mexican woman. It was a lazy summer day, and an awfully long one, and the witnesses were tedious. None of us took any interest in the trial except that nervous, uneasy devil of a Mexican woman — because you know how they love and how they hate, and this one had loved her husband with all her might, and now she had boiled it all down into hate, and stood here spitting it at that Spaniard with her eyes; and I tell you she would stir *me* up, too, with a little of her summer lightning, occasionally. Well, I had my coat off and my heels up, lolling and sweating, and smoking one of those cabbage cigars the San Francisco people used to think were good enough for us in those times; and the lawyers they all had their coats off, and were smoking and whittling, and the witnesses the same, and so was the prisoner. Well, the fact is, there warn't any interest in a murder trial then, because the fellow was always brought in ' not guilty,' the jury expecting him to do as much for them some time; and, although the evidence was straight and square against this Spaniard, we knew we could not convict him without seeming to be rather high-handed and sort of reflecting on every gentleman in the community; for there warn't any carriages and liveries then, and so the only ' style ' there was, was to keep your private graveyard. But that woman seemed to have her heart set on hanging that Spaniard; and you'd ought to have seen how she would glare on him a minute, and then look up at me in her pleading way, and then turn and for the next five minutes search the jury's faces, and by and by drop her face in her hands for just a little while as if she was most ready to give up; but out she'd come again directly, and be as live and anxious as ever. But when the jury announced the verdict — Not Guilty, and I told the prisoner he was acquitted and free to go, that woman rose up till she appeared to be as tall and grand as a seventy-four-gun-ship, and says she:

" ' Judge, do I understand you to say that this man is not guilty that murdered my husband without any cause before my own eyes and my little children's, and that all has been done to him that ever justice and the law can do?'

" ' The same,' says I.

" And then what do you reckon she did? Why, she turned on that smirking Spanish fool like a wild cat, and out with a ' navy ' and shot him dead in open court!''

"That *was* spirited, I am willing to admit."

"Wasn't it, though?" said the judge admiringly. "I wouldn't have missed it for anything. I adjourned court right on the spot, and we put on our coats and went out and took up a collection for her and her cubs, and sent them over the mountains to their friends. Ah, she was a spirited wench!"

INFORMATION WANTED

"Washington, *December* 10, 1867.

"COULD you give me any information respecting such islands, if any, as the Government is going to purchase?"

It is an uncle of mine that wants to know. He is an industrious man and well-disposed, and wants to make a living in an honest, humble way, but more especially he wants to be quiet. He wishes to settle down, and be quiet and unostentatious. He has been to the new island St. Thomas, but he says he thinks things are unsettled there. He went there early with an *attaché* of the State department, who was sent down with money to pay for the island. My uncle had his money in the same box, and so when they went ashore, getting a receipt, the sailors broke open the box and took all the money, not making any distinction between Government money, which was legitimate money to be stolen, and my uncle's, which was his own private property, and should have been respected. But he came home and got some more and went back. And then he took the fever. There are seven kinds of fever

down there, you know; and, as his blood was out
of order by reason of loss of sleep and general wear
and tear of mind, he failed to cure the first fever,
and then somehow he got the other six. He is not
a kind of man that enjoys fevers, though he is well
meaning and always does what he thinks is right,
and so he was a good deal annoyed when it appeared he was going to die.

But he worried through, and got well and started
a farm. He fenced it in, and the next day that
great storm came on and washed the most of it over
to Gibraltar, or around there somewhere. He only
said, in his patient way, that it was gone, and he
wouldn't bother about trying to find out where it
went to, though it was his opinion it went to
Gibraltar.

Then he invested in a mountain, and started a
farm up there, so as to be out of the way when the
sea came ashore again. It was a good mountain,
and a good farm, but it wasn't any use; an earthquake came the next night and shook it all down.
It was all fragments, you know, and so mixed up
with another man's property that he could not tell
which were his fragments without going to law; and
he would not do that, because his main object in
going to St. Thomas was to be quiet. All that he
wanted was to settle down and be quiet.

He thought it all over, and finally he concluded
to try the low ground again, especially as he wanted
to start a brickyard this time. He bought a flat,

and put out a hundred thousand bricks to dry
preparatory to baking them. But luck appeared
to be against him. A volcano shoved itself through
there that night, and elevated his brickyard about
two thousand feet in the air. It irritated him a
good deal. He has been up there, and he says the
bricks are all baked right enough, but he can't get
them down. At first, he thought maybe the Government would get the bricks down for him, because
since Government bought the island, it ought to
protect the property where a man has invested in
good faith; but all he wants is quiet, and so he is
not going to apply for the subsidy he was thinking
about.

He went back there last week in a couple of ships
of war, to prospect around the coast for a safe place
for a farm where he could be quiet; but a great
" tidal wave " came, and hoisted both of the ships
out into one of the interior counties, and he came
near losing his life. So he has given up prospecting
in a ship, and is discouraged.

Well, now he don't know what to do. He has
tried Alaska; but the bears kept after him so much,
and kept him so much on the jump, as it were, that
he had to leave the country. He could not be quiet
there with those bears prancing after him all the
time. That is how he came to go to the new island
we have bought — St. Thomas. But he is getting
to think St. Thomas is not quiet enough for a man
of his turn of mind, and that is why he wishes me to

find out if Government is likely to buy some more
islands shortly. He has heard that Government is
thinking about buying Porto Rico. If that is true,
he wishes to try Porto Rico, if it is a quiet place.
How is Porto Rico for his style of man? Do you
think the Government will buy it?

SOME LEARNED FABLES, FOR GOOD OLD BOYS AND GIRLS

IN THREE PARTS

PART FIRST

HOW THE ANIMALS OF THE WOOD SENT OUT A SCIENTIFIC EXPEDITION.

ONCE the creatures of the forest held a great convention and appointed a commission consisting of the most illustrious scientists among them to go forth, clear beyond the forest and out into the unknown and unexplored world, to verify the truth of the matters already taught in their schools and colleges and also to make discoveries. It was the most imposing enterprise of the kind the nation had ever embarked in. True, the government had once sent Dr. Bull Frog, with a picked crew, to hunt for a northwesterly passage through the swamp to the right-hand corner of the wood, and had since sent out many expeditions to hunt for Dr. Bull Frog; but they never could find him, and so government finally gave him up and ennobled his mother to

show its gratitude for the services her son had
rendered to science. And once government sent
Sir Grass Hopper to hunt for the sources of the rill
that emptied into the swamp; and afterwards sent
out many expeditions to hunt for Sir Grass, and at
last they were successful — they found his body, but
if he had discovered the sources meantime, he did
not let on. So government acted handsomely by
deceased, and many envied his funeral.

But these expeditions were trifles compared with
the present one; for this one comprised among its
servants the very greatest among the learned; and
besides it was to go to the utterly unvisited regions
believed to lie beyond the mighty forest — as we
have remarked before. How the members were
banqueted, and glorified, and talked about! Everywhere that one of them showed himself, straightway
there was a crowd to gape and stare at him.

Finally they set off, and it was a sight to see the
long procession of dry-land Tortoises heavily laden
with savans, scientific instruments, Glow-Worms and
Fire-Flies for signal service, provisions, Ants, and
Tumble-Bugs to fetch and carry and delve, Spiders
to carry the surveying chain and do other engineer-
ing duty, and so forth and so on; and after the
Tortoises came another long train of ironclads —
stately and spacious Mud Turtles for marine transportation service; and from every Tortoise and
every Turtle flaunted a flaming gladiolus or other
splendid banner; at the head of the column a great

band of Bumble-Bees, Mosquitoes, Katy-Dids, and Crickets discoursed martial music; and the entire train was under the escort and protection of twelve picked regiments of the Army Worm.

At the end of three weeks the expedition emerged from the forest and looked upon the great Unknown World.   Their eyes were greeted with an impressive spectacle.   A vast level plain stretched before them, watered by a sinuous stream; and beyond there towered up against the sky a long and lofty barrier of some kind, they did not know what.   The Tumble-Bug said he believed it was simply land tilted up on its edge, because he knew he could see trees on it.   But Professor Snail and the others said:

"You are hired to dig, sir — that is all.   We need your muscle, not your brains.   When we want your opinion on scientific matters, we will hasten to let you know.   Your coolness is intolerable, too — loafing about here meddling with august matters of learning, when the other laborers are pitching camp. Go along and help handle the baggage."

The Tumble-Bug turned on his heel uncrushed, unabashed, observing to himself, "If it isn't land tilted up, let me die the death of the unrighteous."

Professor Bull Frog (nephew of the late explorer) said he believed the ridge was the wall that enclosed the earth.   He continued:

"Our fathers have left us much learning, but they had not traveled far, and so we may count this a noble new discovery. We are safe for renown now, even though our labors began and ended with this single achievement. I wonder what this wall is built of? Can it be fungus? Fungus is an honorable good thing to build a wall of."

Professor Snail adjusted his field-glass and examined the rampart critically. Finally he said:

"The fact that it is not diaphanous convinces me that it is a dense vapor formed by the calorification of ascending moisture dephlogisticated by refraction. A few endiometrical experiments would confirm this, but it is not necessary. The thing is obvious."

So he shut up his glass and went into his shell to make a note of the discovery of the world's end, and the nature of it.

"Profound mind!" said Professor Angle-Worm to Professor Field-Mouse; "profound mind! nothing can long remain a mystery to that august brain."

Night drew on apace, the sentinel crickets were posted, the Glow Worm and Fire-Fly lamps were lighted, and the camp sank to silence and sleep. After breakfast in the morning, the expedition moved on. About noon a great avenue was reached, which had in it two endless parallel bars of some kind of hard black substance, raised the height of the tallest Bull Frog above the general level. The scientists climbed up on these and examined and tested them in various ways. They walked along

them for a great distance, but found no end and no
break in them. They could arrive at no decision.
There was nothing in the records of science that
mentioned anything of this kind. But at last the
bald and venerable geographer, Professor Mud
Turtle, a person who, born poor, and of a drudg-
ing low family, had, by his own native force raised
himself to the headship of the geographers of his
generation, said:

" My friends, we have indeed made a discovery
here. We have found in a palpable, compact, and
imperishable state what the wisest of our fathers
always regarded as a mere thing of the imagination.
Humble yourselves, my friends, for we stand in a
majestic presence. These are parallels of latitude!"

Every heart and every head was bowed, so awful,
so sublime was the magnitude of the discovery.
Many shed tears.

The camp was pitched and the rest of the day
given up to writing voluminous accounts of the
marvel, and correcting astronomical tables to fit it.
Toward midnight a demoniacal shriek was heard,
then a clattering and rumbling noise, and the next
instant a vast terrific eye shot by, with a long tail
attached, and disappeared in the gloom, still uttering
triumphant shrieks.

The poor camp laborers were stricken to the heart
with fright, and stampeded for the high grass in a
body. But not the scientists. They had no superstitions. They calmly proceeded to exchange theo-

ries. The ancient geographer's opinion was asked.
He went into his shell and deliberated long and
profoundly. When he came out at last, they all
knew by his worshiping countenance that he brought
light. Said he:

" Give thanks for this stupendous thing which we
have been permitted to witness. It is the Vernal
Equinox!"

There were shoutings and great rejoicings.

" But," said the Angle-Worm, uncoiling after
reflection, " this is dead summer time."

" Very well," said the Turtle, " we are far from
our region; the season differs with the difference of
time between the two points."

" Ah, true. True enough. But it is night. How
should the sun pass in the night?"

" In these distant regions he doubtless passes
always in the night at this hour."

" Yes, doubtless that is true. But it being night,
how is it that we could see him?"

" It is a great mystery. I grant that. But I am
persuaded that the humidity of the atmosphere in
these remote regions is such that particles of daylight adhere to the disk and it was by aid of these
that we were enabled to see the sun in the dark."

This was deemed satisfactory, and due entry was
made of the decision.

But about this moment those dreadful shriekings
were heard again; again the rumbling and thundering came speeding up out of the night; and once

11

more a flaming great eye flashed by and lost itself in gloom and distance.

The camp laborers gave themselves up for lost. The savants were sorely perplexed. Here was a marvel hard to account for. They thought and they talked, they talked and they thought. Finally the learned and aged Lord Grand-Daddy-Longlegs, who had been sitting in deep study, with his slender limbs crossed and his stemmy arms folded, said:

" Deliver your opinions, brethren, and then I will tell my thought — for I think I have solved this problem."

" So be it, good your lordship," piped the weak treble of the wrinkled and withered Professor Woodlouse, " for we shall hear from your lordship's lips naught but wisdom." [Here the speaker threw in a mess of trite, threadbare, exasperating quotations from the ancient poets and philosophers, delivering them with unction in the sounding grandeurs of the original tongues, they being from the Mastodon, the Dodo, and other dead languages.] " Perhaps I ought not to presume to meddle with matters pertaining to astronomy at all, in such a presence as this, I who have made it the business of my life to delve only among the riches of the extinct languages and unearth the opulence of their ancient lore; but still, as unacquainted as I am with the noble science of astronomy, I beg with deference and humility to suggest that inasmuch as the last of these wonderful apparitions proceeded in exactly the opposite direction from that pursued by the first, which you decide to be the Vernal Equinox, and greatly resembled it in all particulars, is it not possible, nay certain, that this last is the *Autumnal* Equi —"

" O-o-o!" " O-o-o! go to bed! go to bed!" with annoyed derision from everybody. So the poor old Woodlouse retreated out of sight, consumed with shame.

Further discussion followed, and then the united voice of the commission begged Lord Longlegs to speak. He said:

" Fellow-scientists, it is my belief that we have witnessed a thing which has occurred in perfection but once before in the knowledge of created beings. It is a phenomenon of inconceivable importance and interest, view it as one may, but its interest to us is vastly heightened by an added knowledge of its nature which no scholar has heretofore possessed or even suspected. This great marvel which we have just witnessed, fellow-savants (it almost takes my breath away), is nothing less than the transit of Venus!"

Every scholar sprang to his feet pale with astonishment. Then ensued tears, handshakings, frenzied embraces, and the most extravagant jubilations of every sort. But by and by, as emotion began to retire within bounds, and reflection to return to the front, the accomplished Chief Inspector Lizard observed:

" But how is this? Venus should traverse the sun's surface, not the earth's."

K

The arrow went home. It carried sorrow to the breast of every apostle of learning there, for none could deny that this was a formidable criticism. But tranquilly the venerable Duke crossed his limbs behind his ears and said:

"My friend has touched the marrow of our mighty discovery. Yes — all that have lived before us thought a transit of Venus consisted of a flight across the sun's face; they thought it, they maintained it, they honestly believed it, simple hearts, and were justified in it by the limitations of their knowledge; but to us has been granted the inestimable boon of proving that the transit occurs across the earth's face, *for we have* SEEN *it!*"

The assembled wisdom sat in speechless adoration of this imperial intellect. All doubts had instantly departed, like night before the lightning.

The Tumble-Bug had just intruded, unnoticed. He now came reeling forward among the scholars, familiarly slapping first one and then another on the shoulder, saying "Nice ('ic!) nice old boy!" and smiling a smile of elaborate content. Arrived at a good position for speaking, he put his left arm akimbo with his knuckles planted in his hip just under the edge of his cut-away coat, bent his right leg, placing his toe on the ground and resting his heel with easy grace against his left shin, puffed out his aldermanic stomach, opened his lips, leaned his right elbow on Inspector Lizard's shoulder, and —

But the shoulder was indignantly withdrawn and

the hard-handed son of toil went to earth. He
floundered a bit but came up smiling, arranged his
attitude with the same careful detail as before, only
choosing Professor Dogtick's shoulder for a support,
opened his lips and —

Went to earth again. He presently scrambled up
once more, still smiling, made a loose effort to brush
the dust off his coat and legs, but a smart pass of
his hand missed entirely, and the force of the un-
checked impulse slewed him suddenly around,
twisted his legs together, and projected him, limber
and sprawling, into the lap of the Lord Longlegs.
Two or three scholars sprang forward, flung the low
creature head over heels into a corner and reinstated
the patrician, smoothing his ruffled dignity with
many soothing and regretful speeches. Professor
Bull Frog roared out:

"No more of this, sirrah Tumble-Bug! Say your
say and then get you about your business with
speed! Quick — what is your errand? Come —
move off a trifle; you smell like a stable; what have
you been at?"

"Please ('ic!) please your worship I chanced to
light upon a find. But no m (*e-uck !*) matter 'bout
that. There's b ('ic!) been another find which —
— beg pardon, your honors, what was that th ('ic!)
thing that ripped by here first?"

"It was the Vernal Equinox."

"Inf ('ic!) fernal equinox. 'At's all right. D
('ic!) Dunno *him*. What's other one?"

" The transit of Venus."

" G ('ic!) Got me again. No matter. Las' one dropped something."

" Ah, indeed! Good luck! Good news! Quick — what is it?"

" M ('ic!) Mosey out 'n' see. It'll pay."

No more votes were taken for four and twenty hours. Then the following entry was made:

" The commission went in a body to view the find. It was found to consist of a hard, smooth, huge object with a rounded summit surmounted by a short upright projection resembling a section of a cabbage stalk divided transversely. This projection was not solid, but was a hollow cylinder plugged with a soft woody substance unknown to our region — that is, it had been so plugged, but unfortunately this obstruction had been heedlessly removed by Norway Rat, Chief of the Sappers and Miners, before our arrival. The vast object before us, so mysteriously conveyed from the glittering domains of space, was found to be hollow and nearly filled with a pungent liquid of a brownish hue, like rainwater that has stood for some time. And such a spectacle as met our view! Norway Rat was perched upon the summit engaged in thrusting his tail into the cylindrical projection, drawing it out dripping, permitting the struggling multitude of laborers to suck the end of it, then straightway reinserting it and delivering the fluid to the mob as before. Evidently this liquor had strangely potent qualities; for all that partook of it were immediately exalted with great and pleasurable emotions, and went staggering about singing ribald songs, embracing, fighting, dancing, discharging irruptions of profanity, and defying all authority. Around us struggled a massed and uncontrolled mob — uncontrolled and likewise uncontrollable, for the whole army, down to the very sentinels, were mad like the rest, by reason of the drink. We were seized upon by these reckless creatures, and 'within the hour we, even we, were undistinguishable from the rest — the demoralization was complete and universal. In time the camp wore itself out with its orgies and sank into a stolid and pitiable stupor, in whose mysterious bonds rank was forgotten and strange bedfellows made, our eyes, at the resurrection, being blasted and our souls petrified with the incredible spectacle of that intolerable stinking scavenger, the Tumble-Bug, and the illustrious patrician my Lord Grand Daddy, Duke of Longlegs, lying soundly steeped in sleep, and clasped lovingly in each other's arms, the like whereof hath not been seen in all the ages that tradition compasseth, and doubtless none shall ever in this world find faith to master the belief of it save only we that have beheld the damnable and unholy vision. Thus inscrutable be the ways of God, whose will be done!

" This day, by order, did the engineer-in-chief, Herr Spider, rig the necessary tackle for the overturning of the vast reservoir, and so its calamitous contents were discharged in a torrent upon the thirsty earth, which drank it up, and now there is no more danger, we reserving but a few drops for experiment and scrutiny, and to exhibit to the king and subsequently preserve among the wonders of the museum. What this liquid is has been determined. It is without question that fierce and most destructive fluid called lightning. It was wrested, in its container, from its storehouse in the clouds, by the resistless might of the flying planet, and hurled at our feet as she sped by. An interesting discovery here results. Which is, that lightning, kept to itself, is quiescent; it is the assaulting contact of the thunderbolt that releases it from captivity, ignites its awful fires and so produces an instantaneous combustion and explosion which spread disaster and desolation far and wide in the earth.''

After another day devoted to rest and recovery, the expedition proceeded upon its way. Some days later it went into camp in a pleasant part of the plain, and the savants sallied forth to see what they might find. Their reward was at hand. Professor Bull Frog discovered a strange tree, and called his comrades. They inspected it with profound interest. It was very tall and straight, and wholly devoid of bark, limbs, or foliage. By triangulation Lord Longlegs determined its altitude; Herr Spider measured its circumference at the base and computed the circumference at its top by a mathematical demonstration based upon the warrant furnished by the uniform degree of its taper upward.   It was considered a very extraordinary find; and since it was a tree of a hitherto unknown species, Professor Woodlouse gave it a name of a learned sound, being none other than that of Professor Bull Frog translated into the ancient Mastodon language, for it had always been the custom with discoverers to perpetuate their names and honor themselves by this sort of connection with their discoveries.

Now Professor Field-Mouse having placed his sensitive ear to the tree, detected a rich, harmonious sound issuing from it.   This surprising thing was tested and enjoyed by each scholar in turn and great was the gladness and astonishment of all. Professor Woodlouse was requested to add to and extend the tree's name so as to make it suggest the musical quality it possessed — which he did, furnishing the addition *Anthem Singer*, done into the Mastodon tongue.

By this time Professor Snail was making some telescopic inspections.   He discovered a great number of these trees, extending in a single rank, with wide intervals between, as far as his instrument would carry, both southward and northward. He also presently discovered that all these trees were bound together, near their tops, by fourteen great ropes, one above another, which ropes were continuous, from tree to tree, as far as his vision could reach.   This was surprising.   Chief Engineer Spider ran aloft and soon reported that these ropes were simply a web hung there by some colossal member of his own species, for he could see its prey dangling here and there from the strands, in the shape of mighty shreds and rags that had a woven look about their texture and were no doubt the discarded skins of prodigious insects which had been caught and eaten. And then he ran along one of the ropes to make a closer inspection, but felt a smart sudden burn on the soles of his feet, accompanied by a paralyzing shock, wherefore he let go and swung himself to the earth by a thread of his own spinning, and advised all to hurry at once to camp, lest the monster should appear and get as much interested in the savants as they were in him and his works. So they departed with speed, making notes about the gigantic web as they went. And that evening the naturalist of the expedition built a beautiful model of the colossal spider, having no need to see it in order to do this, because he had picked up a fragment of its vertebræ by the tree, and so knew exactly what the creature looked like and what its habits and its preferences were by this simple evidence alone. He built it with a tail, teeth, fourteen legs and a snout, and said it ate grass, cattle, pebbles, and dirt with equal enthusiasm. This animal was regarded as a very precious addition to science. It was hoped a dead one might be found to stuff. Professor Woodlouse thought that he and his brother scholars, by lying hid and being quiet, might maybe catch a live one. He was advised to try it. Which was all the attention that was paid to his suggestion. The conference ended with the naming the monster after the naturalist, since he, after God, had created it.

"And improved it, mayhap," muttered the Tumble-Bug, who was intruding again, according to his idle custom and his unappeasable curiosity.

END OF PART FIRST.

SOME FABLES FOR GOOD OLD BOYS AND GIRLS

PART SECOND

HOW THE ANIMALS OF THE WOOD COMPLETED THEIR SCIENTIFIC LABORS

A WEEK later the expedition camped in the midst of a collection of wonderful curiosities. These were a sort of vast caverns of stone that rose singly and in bunches out of the plain by the side of the river which they had first seen when they emerged from the forest. These caverns stood in long straight rows on opposite sides of broad aisles that were bordered with single ranks of trees. The summit of each cavern sloped sharply both ways. Several horizontal rows of great square holes, obstructed by a thin, shiny, transparent substance, pierced the frontage of each cavern. Inside were caverns within caverns; and one might ascend and visit these minor compartments by means of curious winding ways consisting of continuous regular terraces raised one above another. There were many huge shapeless objects in each compartment which were considered to have been living creatures at one time, though now the thin brown skin was shrunken and loose, and rattled when disturbed. Spiders were here in great number, and their cobwebs, stretched in all directions and wreathing the great skinny dead together, were a pleasant spectacle, since they inspired with life and wholesome cheer a scene which would otherwise have brought to the mind only a sense of forsakenness and desolation. Information was sought of these spiders, but in vain. They were of a different nationality from those with the expedition, and their language seemed but a musical, meaningless jargon. They were a timid, gentle race, but ignorant, and heathenish worshipers of unknown gods. The expedition detailed a great detachment of missionaries to teach them the true religion, and in a week's time a precious work had been wrought among those darkened creatures, not three families being by that time at peace with each other or having a settled belief in any system of religion whatever. This encouraged the expedition to establish a colony of missionaries there permanently, that the work of grace might go on.

But let us not outrun our narrative. After close examination of the fronts of the caverns, and much thinking and exchanging of theories, the scientists determined the nature of these singular formations. They said that each belonged mainly to the Old Red Sandstone period; that the cavern fronts rose in

innumerable and wonderfully regular strata high in
the air, each stratum about five frog-spans thick,
and that in the present discovery lay an overpower-
ing refutation of all received geology; for between
every two layers of Old Red Sandstone reposed a
thin layer of decomposed limestone; so instead of
there having been but one Old Red Sandstone
period there had certainly been not less than a
hundred and seventy-five! And by the same token
it was plain that there had also been a hundred and
seventy-five floodings of the earth and depositings
of limestone strata! The unavoidable deduction
from which pair of facts was the overwhelming truth
that the world, instead of being only two hundred
thousand years old, was older by millions upon
millions of years! And there was another curious
thing: every stratum of Old Red Sandstone was
pierced and divided at mathematically regular intervals by vertical strata of limestone. Up-shootings
of igneous rock through fractures in water formations were common; but here was the first instance
where water-formed rock had been so projected. It
was a great and noble discovery and its value to
science was considered to be inestimable.

A critical examination of some of the lower strata
demonstrated the presence of fossil ants and tumble-
bugs (the latter accompanied by their peculiar
goods), and with high gratification the fact was
enrolled upon the scientific record; for this was
proof that these vulgar laborers belonged to the

first and lowest orders of created beings, though at the same time there was something repulsive in the reflection that the perfect and exquisite creature of the modern uppermost order owed its origin to such ignominious beings through the mysterious law of Development of Species.

The Tumble-Bug, overhearing this discussion, said he was willing that the parvenus of these new times should find what comfort they might in their wise-drawn theories, since as far as he was concerned he was content to be of the old first families and proud to point back to his place among the old original aristocracy of the land.

" Enjoy your mushroom dignity, stinking of the varnish of yesterday's veneering, since you like it," said he; " suffice it for the Tumble-Bugs that they come of a race that rolled their fragrant spheres down the solemn aisles of antiquity, and left their imperishable works embalmed in the Old Red Sandstone to proclaim it to the wasting centuries as they file along the highway of Time!"

" Oh, take a walk!" said the chief of the expedition, with derision.

The summer passed, and winter approached. In and about many of the caverns were what seemed to be inscriptions. Most of the scientists said they were inscriptions, a few said they were not. The chief philologist, Professor Woodlouse, maintained that they were writings, done in a character utterly unknown to scholars, and in a language equally unknown. He had early ordered his artists and draughtsmen to make facsimiles of all that were discovered; and had set himself about finding the key to the hidden tongue. In this work he had followed the method which had always been used by decipherers previously. That is to say, he placed a number of copies of inscriptions before him and studied them both collectively and in detail. To begin with, he placed the following copies together:

THE AMERICAN HOTEL.	MEALS AT ALL HOURS.
THE SHADES.	NO SMOKING.
BOATS FOR HIRE CHEAP.	UNION PRAYER MEETING, 4 P.M.
BILLIARDS.	THE WATERSIDE JOURNAL.
THE A1 BARBER SHOP.	TELEGRAPH OFFICE.
KEEP OFF THE GRASS.	TRY BRANDRETH'S PILLS.

COTTAGES FOR RENT DURING THE WATERING SEASON.

FOR SALE CHEAP.	FOR SALE CHEAP.
FOR SALE CHEAP.	FOR SALE CHEAP.

At first it seemed to the professor that this was a sign-language, and that each word was represented by a distinct sign; further examination convinced him that it was a written language, and that every letter of its alphabet was represented by a character of its own; and finally he decided that it was a language which conveyed itself partly by letters, and partly by signs or hieroglyphics. This conclusion was forced upon him by the discovery of several specimens of the following nature:

He observed that cer-
tain inscriptions were
met with in greater
frequency than others.
Such as " FOR SALE
CHEAP;" "BILLIARDS;"
" S. T. — 1860 — X;"
" KENO;" " ALE ON
DRAUGHT." Naturally,
then, these must be re-
ligious maxims. But this
idea was cast aside by
and by, as the mystery
of the strange alphabet
began to clear itself.
In time, the professor
was enabled to translate
several of the inscrip-
tions with considerable
plausibility, though not to
the perfect satisfaction of
all the scholars. Still, he
made constant and en-
couraging progress.

Finally a cavern was
discovered with these inscriptions upon it:

WATERSIDE MUSEUM.

Open at all Hours.   *Admission 50 cents.*

WONDERFUL COLLECTION OF WAX-WORKS, ANCIENT FOSSILS, ETC.

Professor Woodlouse affirmed that the word " Museum " was equivalent to the phrase " *lumgath molo*," or " Burial Place." Upon entering, the scientists were well astonished. But what they saw may be best conveyed in the language of their own official report:

" Erect, in a row, were a sort of rigid great figures which struck us instantly as belonging to the long extinct species of reptile called MAN, described in our ancient records. This was a peculiarly gratifying discovery, because of late times it has become fashionable to regard this creature as a myth and a superstition, a work of the inventive imaginations of our remote ancestors. But here, indeed, was Man, perfectly preserved, in a fossil state. And this was his burial place, as already ascertained by the inscription. And now it began to be suspected that the caverns we had been inspecting had been his ancient haunts in that old time that he roamed the earth — for upon the breast of each of these tall fossils was an inscription in the character heretofore noticed. One read, ' CAPTAIN KIDD THE PIRATE;' another, ' QUEEN VICTORIA;' another, ' ABE LINCOLN;' another, ' GEORGE WASHINGTON,' etc.

" With feverish interest we called for our ancient scientific records to discover if perchance the description of Man there set down would tally with the fossils before us. Professor Woodlouse read it aloud in its quaint and musty phraseology, to wit:

" ' In yͤ time of our fathers Man still walked yͤ

earth, as by tradition we know. It was a creature of exceeding great size, being compassed about with a loose skin, sometimes of one color, sometimes of many, the which it was able to cast at will; which being done, the hind legs were discovered to be armed with short claws like to a mole's but broader, and ye forelegs with fingers of a curious slimness and a length much more prodigious than a frog's, armed also with broad talons for scratching in ye earth for its food. It had a sort of feathers upon its head such as hath a rat, but longer, and a beak suitable for seeking its food by ye smell thereof. When it was stirred with happiness, it leaked water from its eyes; and when it suffered or was sad, it manifested it with a horrible hellish cackling clamor that was exceeding dreadful to hear and made one long that it might rend itself and perish, and so end its troubles. Two Mans being together, they uttered noises at each other like this: '' Haw-haw-haw — dam good, dam good,'' together with other sounds of more or less likeness to these, wherefore ye poets conceived that they talked, but poets be always ready to catch at any frantic folly, God he knows. Sometimes this creature goeth about with a long stick ye which it putteth to its face and bloweth fire and smoke through ye same with a sudden and most damnable bruit and noise that doth fright its prey to death, and so seizeth it in its talons and walketh away to its habitat, consumed with a most fierce and devilish joy.'

L

" Now was the description set forth by our ancestors wonderfully endorsed and confirmed by the
fossils before us, as shall be seen. The specimen
marked ' Captain Kidd ' was examined in detail.
Upon its head and part of its face was a sort of fur
like that upon the tail of a horse. With great labor
its loose skin was removed, whereupon its body was
discovered to be of a polished white texture, thoroughly petrified. The straw it had eaten, so many
ages gone by, was still in its body, undigested —
and even in its legs.

" Surrounding these fossils were objects that
would mean nothing to the ignorant, but to the eye
of science they were a revelation. They laid bare
the secrets of dead ages. These musty Memorials
told us when Man lived, and what were his habits.
For here, side by side with Man, were the evidences
that he had lived in the earliest ages of creation, the
companion of the other low orders of life that belonged to that forgotten time. Here was the fossil
nautilus that sailed the primeval seas; here was the
skeleton of the mastodon, the ichthyosaurus, the
cave bear, the prodigious elk. Here, also, were the
charred bones of some of these extinct animals and
of the young of Man's own species, split length-
wise, showing that to his taste the marrow was a
toothsome luxury. It was plain that Man had
robbed those bones of their contents, since no tooth-
mark of any beast was upon them — albeit the
Tumble-Bug intruded the remark that ' no beast

could mark a bone with its teeth, anyway.' Here were proofs that Man had vague, groveling notions of art; for this fact was conveyed by certain things marked with the untranslatable words, 'FLINT HATCHETS, KNIVES, ARROW-HEADS, AND BONE-ORNAMENTS OF PRIMEVAL MAN.' Some of these seemed to be rude weapons chipped out of flint, and in a secret place was found some more in process of construction, with this untranslatable legend, on a thin, flimsy material, lying by:

"*Jones, if you aon t want to be aischarged from the Musseum, make the next primeaveal weppons more careful—you couldn't even fool one of these sleepy old syentiffic grannys from the Coledge with the last ones. And mind you the animles you carved on some of the Bone Ornaments is a blame sight too good for any primeaveal man that was ever fooled.—Varnum, Manager.*"

"Back of the burial place was a mass of ashes, showing that Man always had a feast at a funeral — else why the ashes in such a place; and showing, also, that he believed in God and the immortality of the soul — else why these solemn ceremonies?

"To sum up. We believe that Man had a written language. We *know* that he indeed existed at one time, and is not a myth; also, that he was the companion of the cave bear, the mastodon, and other extinct species; that he cooked and ate them and likewise the young of his own kind; also, that he bore rude weapons, and knew something of art;

that he imagined he had a soul, and pleased himself with the fancy that it was immortal. But let us not laugh; there may be creatures in existence to whom we and our vanities and profundities may seem as ludicrous."

END OF PART SECOND.

SOME FABLES FOR GOOD OLD BOYS AND GIRLS

PART THIRD

NEAR the margin of the great river the scientists presently found a huge, shapely stone, with this inscription:

"*In 1847, in the spring, the river overflowed its banks and covered the whole township. The depth was from two to six feet. More than 900 head of cattle were lost, and many homes destroyed. The Mayor ordered this memorial to be erected to perpetuate the event. God spare us the repetition of it!*"

With infinite trouble, Professor Woodlouse succeeded in making a translation of this inscription, which was sent home, and straightway an enormous excitement was created about it. It confirmed, in a remarkable way, certain treasured traditions of the ancients. The translation was slightly marred by one or two untranslatable words, but these did not impair the general clearness of the meaning. It is here presented:

"*One thousand eight hundred and forty-seven years*

ago, the (fires ?) descended and consumed the whole city. Only some nine hundred souls were saved, all others destroyed. The (king?) commanded this stone to be set up to . . . . . (untranslatable) . . . . . prevent the repetition of it."

This was the first successful and satisfactory translation that had been made of the mysterious character left behind him by extinct man, and it gave Professor Woodlouse such reputation that at once every seat of learning in his native land conferred a degree of the most illustrious grade upon him, and it was believed that if he had been a soldier and had turned his splendid talents to the extermination of a remote tribe of reptiles, the king would have ennobled him and made him rich. And this, too, was the origin of that school of scientists called Manologists, whose specialty is the deciphering of the ancient records of the extinct bird termed Man. [For it is now decided that Man was a bird and not a reptile.] But Professor Woodlouse began and remained chief of these, for it was granted that no translations were ever so free from error as his. Others made mistakes — he seemed incapable of it. Many a memorial of the lost race was afterward found, but none ever attained to the renown and veneration achieved by the " Mayoritish Stone "— it being so called from the word " Mayor " in it, which, being translated " King," " Mayoritish Stone " was but another way of saying " King Stone."

Another time the expedition made a great " find."
It was a vast round flattish mass, ten frog-spans in
diameter and five or six high.   Professor Snail put
on his spectacles and examined it all around, and
then climbed up and inspected the top.   He said:

" The result of my perlustration and perscontation
of this isoperimetrical protuberance is a belief that it
is one of those rare and wonderful creations left by
the Mound Builders.   The fact that this one is
lamellibranchiate in its formation, simply adds to its
interest as being possibly of a different kind from
any we read of in the records of science, but yet in
no manner marring its authenticity.   Let the megalo-
phonous grasshopper sound a blast and summon
hither the perfunctory and circumforaneous Tumble-
Bug, to the end that excavations may be made and
learning gather new treasures."

Not a Tumble-Bug could be found on duty, so
the Mound was excavated by a working party of
Ants.   Nothing was discovered.   This would have
been a great disappointment, had not the venerable
Longlegs explained the matter.   He said:

" It is now plain to me that the mysterious and
forgotten race of Mound Builders did not always
erect these edifices as mausoleums, else in this case,
as in all previous cases, their skeletons would be
found here, along with the rude implements which
the creatures used in life.   Is not this manifest?"

" True! true!" from everybody.

" Then we have made a discovery of peculiar

value here; a discovery which greatly extends our knowledge of this creature in place of diminishing it; a discovery which will add luster to the achievements of this expedition and win for us the commendations of scholars everywhere. For the absence of the customary relics here means nothing less than this: The Mound Builder, instead of being the ignorant, savage reptile we have been taught to consider him, was a creature of cultivation and high intelligence, capable of not only appreciating worthy achievements of the great and noble of his species, but of commemorating them! Fellow-scholars, this stately Mound is not a sepulchre, it is a monument!"

A profound impression was produced by this.

But it was interrupted by rude and derisive laughter — and the Tumble-Bug appeared.

" A monument!" quoth he. " A monument set up by a Mound Builder! Aye, so it is! So it is, indeed, to the shrewd keen eye of science; but to an ignorant poor devil who has never seen a college, it is not a Monument, strictly speaking, but is yet a most rich and noble property; and with your worships' good permission I will proceed to manufacture it into spheres of exceeding grace and —"

The Tumble-Bug was driven away with stripes, and the draughtsmen of the expedition were set to making views of the Monument from different standpoints, while Professor Woodlouse, in a frenzy of scientific zeal, traveled all over it and all around it hoping to find an inscription. But if there had ever

been one it had decayed or been removed by some
vandal as a relic.

The views having been completed, it was now
considered safe to load the precious Monument itself
upon the backs of four of the largest Tortoises and
send it home to the king's museum, which was
done; and when it arrived it was received with
enormous *éclat* and escorted to its future abiding
place by thousands of enthusiastic citizens, King
Bullfrog XVI. himself attending and condescending
to sit enthroned upon it throughout the progress.

The growing rigor of the weather was now ad-
monishing the scientists to close their labors for the
present, so they made preparations to journey homeward. But even their last day among the Caverns
bore fruit; for one of the scholars found in an
out-of-the-way corner of the Museum or " Burial
Place " a most strange and extraordinary thing. It
was nothing less than a double Man-Bird lashed
together breast to breast by a natural ligament, and
labeled with the untranslatable words, " *Siamese
Twins.*" The official report concerning this thing
closed thus:

" Wherefore it appears that there were in old
times two distinct species of this majestic fowl, the
one being single and the other double. Nature has
a reason for all things. It is plain to the eye of
science that the Double-Man originally inhabited a
region where dangers abounded; hence he was
paired together to the end that while one part slept

the other might watch; and likewise that, danger being discovered, there might always be a double instead of a single power to oppose it. All honor to the mystery-dispelling eye of godlike Science!"

And near the Double Man-Bird was found what was plainly an ancient record of his, marked upon numberless sheets of a thin white substance and bound together. Almost the first glance that Professor Woodlouse threw into it revealed this following sentence, which he instantly translated and laid before the scientists, in a tremble, and it uplifted every soul there with exultation and astonishment:

"*In truth it is believed by many that the lower animals reason and talk together.*"

When the great official report of the expedition appeared, the above sentence bore this comment:

"Then there are lower animals than Man! This remarkable passage can mean nothing else. Man himself is extinct, but *they* may still exist. What can they be? Where do they inhabit? One's enthusiasm bursts all bounds in the contemplation of the brilliant field of discovery and investigation here thrown open to science. We close our labors with the humble prayer that your Majesty will immediately appoint a commission and command it to rest not nor spare expense until the search for this hitherto unsuspected race of the creatures of God shall be crowned with success."

The expedition then journeyed homeward after its long absence and its faithful endeavors, and was re-

ceived with a mighty ovation by the whole grateful
country. There were vulgar, ignorant carpers, of
course, as there always are and always will be; and
naturally one of these was the obscene Tumble-Bug.
He said that all he had learned by his travels was
that science only needed a spoonful of supposition
to build a mountain of demonstrated fact out of;
and that for the future he meant to be content with
the knowledge that nature had made free to all
creatures and not go prying into the august secrets
of the Deity.

13S

MY LATE SENATORIAL SECRETARY-SHIP*

I AM not a private secretary to a senator any more now. I held the berth two months in security and in great cheerfulness of spirit, but my bread began to return from over the waters then — that is to say, my works came back and revealed themselves. I judged it best to resign. The way of it was this. My employer sent for me one morning tolerably early, and, as soon as I had finished inserting some conundrums clandestinely into his last great speech upon finance, I entered the presence. There was something portentous in his appearance. His cravat was untied, his hair was in a state of disorder, and his countenance bore about it the signs of a suppressed storm. He held a package of letters in his tense grasp, and I knew that the dreaded Pacific mail was in. He said:

" I thought you were worthy of confidence."

I said, " Yes, sir."

He said, " I gave you a letter from certain of my constituents in the State of Nevada, asking the

---

* Written about 1867.

establishment of a post-office at Baldwin's Ranch, and told you to answer it, as ingeniously as you could, with arguments which should persuade them that there was no real necessity for an office at that place."

I felt easier. ' Oh, if that is all, sir, I *did* do that."

" Yes, you *did*. I will read your answer for your own humiliation:

" 'WASHINGTON, Nov. 24.

" ' *Messrs. Smith, Jones, and others.*

" ' GENTLEMEN: What the mischief do you suppose you want with a post-office at Baldwin's Ranche? It would not do you any good. If any letters came there, you couldn't read them, you know; and, besides, such letters as ought to pass through, with money in them, for other localities, would not be likely to *get* through, you must perceive at once; and that would make trouble for us all. No, don't bother about a post-office in your camp. I have your best interests at heart, and feel that it would only be an ornamental folly. What you want is a nice jail, you know—a nice, substantial jail and a free school. These will be a lasting benefit to you. These will make you really contented and happy. I will move in the matter at once.

" ' Very truly, etc.,

" ' MARK TWAIN,

" ' For James W. N**, U . S. Senator.'

" That is the way you answered that letter. Those people say they will hang me, if I ever enter that district again; and I am perfectly satisfied they *will*, too."

" Well, sir, I did not know I was doing any harm. I only wanted to convince them."

" Ah. Well, you *did* convince them, I make no manner of doubt. Now, here is another specimen.

I gave you a petition from certain gentlemen of
Nevada, praying that I would get a bill through
Congress incorporating the Methodist Episcopal
Church of the State of Nevada. I told you to say,
in reply, that the creation of such a law came more
properly within the province of the State legislature; and to endeavor to show them that, in the
present feebleness of the religious element in that
new commonwealth, the expediency of incorporating the church was questionable. What did you
write?

"'WASHINGTON, Nov. 24.
"'*Rev. John Halifax and others.*

"'GENTLEMEN: You will have to go to the State Legislature
about that speculation of yours—Congress don't know anything about
religion. But don't you hurry to go there, either; because this thing
you propose to do out in that new country isn't expedient—in fact, it is
ridiculous. Your religious people there are too feeble, in intellect, in
morality, in piety—in everything, pretty much. You had better drop
this—you can't make it work. You can't issue stock on an incorpora-
tion like that—or if you could, it would only keep you in trouble all
the time. The other denominations would abuse it, and "bear" it,
and "sell it short," and break it down. They would do with it just as
they would with one of your silver mines out there—they would try to
make all the world believe it was "wildcat." You ought not to do
anything that is calculated to bring a sacred thing into disrepute. You
ought to be ashamed of yourselves — that is what *I* think about it. You
close your petition with the words: "And we will ever pray." I think
you had better—you need to do it.

"'Very truly, etc.,
"'MARK TWAIN,
"'For James W. N**, U. S. Senator.'

"*That* luminous epistle finishes me with the
religious element among my constituents. But that
my political murder might be made sure, some evil

instinct prompted me to hand you this memorial from the grave company of elders composing the board of aldermen of the city of San Francisco, to try your hand upon — a memorial praying that the city's right to the water lots upon the city front might be established by law of Congress. I told you this was a dangerous matter to move in. I told you to write a non-committal letter to the aldermen — an ambiguous letter — a letter that should avoid, as far as possible, all real consideration and discussion of the water lot question. If there is any feeling left in you — any shame — surely this letter you wrote, in obedience to that order, ought to evoke it, when its words fall upon your ears:

" ' WASHINGTON, Nov. 27.

" ' *The Honorable Board of Aldermen, etc.*

" ' GENTLEMEN: George Washington, the revered Father of his Country is dead. His long and brilliant career is closed, alas! forever. He was greatly respected in this section of the country, and his untimely decease cast a gloom over the whole community. He died on the 14th day of December, 1799. He passed peacefully away from the scene of his honors and his great achievements, the most lamented hero and the best beloved that ever earth hath yielded unto Death. At such a time as this, *you* speak of water-lots!—what a lot was his!

" ' What is fame! Fame is an accident. Sir Isaac Newton discovered an apple falling to the ground—a trivial discovery, truly, and one which a million men had made before him—but his parents were influential, and so they tortured that small circumstance into something wonderful, and, lo! the simple world took up the shout and, in almost the twinkling of an eye, that man was famous. Treasure these thoughts.

" ' Poesy, sweet poesy, who shall estimate what the world owes to thee!

" Mary had a little lamb, its fleece was white as snow—
And everywhere that Mary went, the lamb was sure to go."

18

> " Jack and Gill went up the hill
> To draw a pail of water;
> Jack fell down and broke his crown,
> And Gill came tumbling after."

" ' For simplicity, elegance of diction, and freedom from immoral tendencies, I regard those two poems in the light of gems. They are suited to all grades of intelligence, to every sphere of life—to the field, to the nursery, to the guild. Especially should no Board of Aldermen be without them.

" ' Venerable fossils! write again. Nothing improves one so much as friendly correspondence. Write again—and if there is anything in this memorial of yours that refers to anything in particular, do not be backward about explaining it. We shall always be happy to hear you chirp.

" ' Very truly, etc.,
" ' MARK TWAIN,
" ' For James W. N**, U. S. Senator.'

" That is an atrocious, a ruinous epistle! Distraction !"

" Well, sir, I am really sorry if there is anything wrong about it — but — but it appears to me to dodge the water-lot question."

" Dodge the mischief ! Oh! — but never mind. As long as destruction must come now, let it be complete. Let it be complete — let this last of your performances, which I am about to read, make a finality of it. I am a ruined man. I *had* my misgivings when I gave you the letter from Humboldt, asking that the post route from Indian Gulch to Shakespeare Gap and intermediate points, be changed partly to the old Mormon trail. But I told you it was a delicate question, and warned you to deal with it deftly — to answer it dubiously, and leave them a little in the dark. And your fatal imbecility impelled you to make *this* disastrous reply. I should think you would stop your ears, if you are not dead to all shame:

" ' WASHINGTON, Nov. 30.

" ' *Messrs. Perkins, Wagner, et al.*

" ' GENTLEMEN: It is a delicate question about this Indian trail, but, handled with proper deftness and dubiousness, I doubt not we shall succeed in some measure or otherwise, because the place where the route leaves the Lassen Meadows, over beyond where those two Shawnee chiefs, Dilapidated-Vengeance and Biter-of-the-Clouds, were scalped last winter, this being the favorite direction to some, but others preferring something else in consequence of things, the Mormon trail leaving Mosby's at three in the morning, and passing through Jawbone Flat to Blucher, and then down by Jug-Handle, the road passing to the right of it, and naturally leaving it on the right, too, and Dawson's on the left of the trail where it passes to the left of said Dawson's and onward thence to Tomahawk, thus making the route cheaper, easier of access to all who can get at it, and compassing all the desirable objects so considered by others, and, therefore, conferring the most good upon the greatest number, and, consequently, I am encouraged to hope we shall. However, I shall be ready, and happy, to afford you still further information upon the subject, from time to time, as you may desire it and the Post-office Department be enabled to furnish it to me.

" ' Very truly, etc.,

" ' MARK TWAIN,

" ' For James W. N**, U. S. Senator.'

" There — now *what* do you think of that?"

" Well, I don't know, sir. It — well, it appears to me — to be dubious enough."

" Du — leave the house! I am a ruined man. Those Humboldt savages never will forgive me for tangling their brains up with this inhuman letter. I

M

have lost the respect of the Methodist Church, the board of aldermen —"

" Well, I haven't anything to say about that, because I may have missed it a little in their cases, but I *was* too many for the Baldwin's Ranch people, General !"

" Leave the house! Leave it for ever and for ever, too."

I regarded that as a sort of covert intimation that my service could be dispensed with, and so I resigned. I never will be a private secretary to a senator again. You can't please that kind of people. They don't know anything. They can't appreciate a party's efforts.

A FASHION ITEM*

AT General G——'s reception the other night, the most fashionably dressed lady was Mrs. G. C. She wore a pink satin dress, plain in front but with a good deal of rake to it — to the train, I mean; it was said to be two or three yards long. One could see it creeping along the floor some little time after the woman was gone. Mrs. C. wore also a white bodice, cut bias, with Pompadour sleeves, flounced with ruches; low neck, with the inside handkerchief not visible, with white kid gloves. She had on a pearl necklace, which glinted lonely, high up the midst of that barren waste of neck and shoulders. Her hair was frizzled into a tangled chaparral, forward of her ears, aft it was drawn together, and compactly bound and plaited into a stump like a pony's tail, and furthermore was canted upward at a sharp angle, and ingeniously supported by a red velvet crupper, whose forward extremity was made fast with a half-hitch around a hairpin on the top of her head. Her whole top hamper was neat and becoming. She had a beautiful complexion when

---
* Written about 1867

(197)

she first came, but it faded out by degrees in an unaccountable way. However, it is not lost for good. I found the most of it on my shoulder afterwards. (I stood near the door when she squeezed out with the throng.) There were other ladies present, but I only took notes of one as a specimen. I would gladly enlarge upon the subject were I able to do it justice.

RILEY — NEWSPAPER CORRESPONDENT

ONE of the best men in Washington — or elsewhere — is RILEY, correspondent of one of
the great San Francisco dailies.

Riley is full of humor, and has an unfailing vein
of irony, which makes his conversation to the last
degree entertaining (as long as the remarks are
about somebody else). But notwithstanding the
possession of these qualities, which should enable a
man to write a happy and an appetizing letter,
Riley's newspaper letters often display a more than
earthly solemnity, and likewise an unimaginative
devotion to petrified facts, which surprise and distress all men who know him in his unofficial character. He explains this curious thing by saying
that his employers sent him to Washington to write
facts, not fancy, and that several times he has come
near losing his situation by inserting humorous remarks which, not being looked for at headquarters,
and consequently not understood, were thought to
be dark and bloody speeches intended to convey
signals and warnings to murderous secret societies,
or something of that kind, and so were scratched

out with a shiver and a prayer and cast into the
stove. Riley says that sometimes he is so afflicted
with a yearning to write a sparkling and absorbingly
readable letter that he simply cannot resist it, and
so he goes to his den and revels in the delight of
untrammeled scribbling; and then, with suffering such
as only a mother can know, he destroys the pretty
children of his fancy and reduces his letter to the
required dismal accuracy. Having seen Riley do
this very thing more than once, I know whereof I
speak. Often I have laughed with him over a happy
passage, and grieved to see him plow his pen
through it. He would say, " I had to write that or
die; and I've got to scratch it out or starve. *They*
wouldn't stand it, you know."

I think Riley is about the most entertaining company I ever saw. We lodged together in many
places in Washington during the winter of '67–8,
moving comfortably from place to place, and attracting attention by paying our board — a course which
cannot fail to make a person conspicuous in Washington. Riley would tell all about his trip to California in the early days, by way of the Isthmus and
the San Juan river; and about his baking bread in
San Francisco to gain a living, and setting up ten-
pins, and practicing law, and opening oysters, and
delivering lectures, and teaching French, and tend-
ing bar, and reporting for the newspapers, and keeping dancing schools, and interpreting Chinese in the
courts — which latter was lucrative, and Riley was

doing handsomely and laying up a little money
when people began to find fault because his translations were too " free," a thing for which Riley considered he ought not to be held responsible, since
he did not know a word of the Chinese tongue, and
only adopted interpreting as a means of gaining an
honest livelihood. Through the machinations of
enemies he was removed from the position of official
interpreter, and a man put in his place who was
familiar with the Chinese language, but did not
know any English. And Riley used to tell about
publishing a newspaper up in what is Alaska now,
but was only an iceberg then, with a population
composed of bears, walruses, Indians, and other
animals; and how the iceberg got adrift at last, and
left all his paying subscribers behind, and as soon
as the commonwealth floated out of the jurisdiction
of Russia the people rose and threw off their allegiance and ran up the English flag, calculating to
hook on and become an English colony as they
drifted along down the British Possessions; but a
land breeze and a crooked current carried them by,
and they ran up the Stars and Stripes and steered
for California, missed the connection again and
swore allegiance to Mexico, but it wasn't any use;
the anchors came home every time, and away they
went with the northeast trades drifting off sideways
toward the Sandwich Islands, whereupon they ran
up the Cannibal flag and had a grand human bar-
becue in honor of it, in which it was noticed that

the better a man liked a friend the better he enjoyed
him; and as soon as they got fairly within the
tropics the weather got so fearfully hot that the
iceberg began to melt, and it got so sloppy under
foot that it was almost impossible for ladies to get
about at all; and at last, just as they came in sight
of the islands, the melancholy remnant of the once
majestic iceberg canted first to one side and then to
the other, and then plunged under forever, carrying
the national archives along with it — and not only
the archives and the populace, but some eligible
town lots which had increased in value as fast as
they diminished in size in the tropics, and which
Riley could have sold at thirty cents a pound and
made himself rich if he could have kept the province
afloat ten hours longer and got her into port.

Riley is very methodical, untiringly accommodating, never forgets anything that is to be attended
to, is a good son, a staunch friend, and a permanent
reliable enemy. He will put himself to any amount
of trouble to oblige a body, and therefore always
has his hands full of things to be done for the helpless and the shiftless. And he knows how to do
nearly everything, too. He is a man whose native
benevolence is a wellspring that never goes dry.
He stands always ready to help whoever needs help,
as far as he is able — and not simply with his
money, for that is a cheap and common charity,
but with hand and brain, and fatigue of iimb and
sacrifice of time. This sort of men is rare.

Riley has a ready wit, a quickness and aptness at selecting and applying quotations, and a countenance that is as solemn and as blank as the back side of a tombstone when he is delivering a particularly exasperating joke. One night a negro woman was burned to death in a house next door to us, and Riley said that our landlady would be oppressively emotional at breakfast, because she generally made use of such opportunities as offered, being of a morbidly sentimental turn, and so we should find it best to let her talk along and say nothing back — it was the only way to keep her tears out of the gravy. Riley said there never was a funeral in the neighborhood but that the gravy was watery for a week.

And, sure enough, at breakfast the landlady was down in the very sloughs of woe — entirely brokenhearted. Everything she looked at reminded her of that poor old negro woman, and so the buckwheat cakes made her sob, the coffee forced a groan, and when the beefsteak came on she fetched a wail that made our hair rise. Then she got to talking about deceased, and kept up a steady drizzle till both of us were soaked through and through. Presently she took a fresh breath and said, with a world of sobs:

" Ah, to think of it, only to think of it ! — the poor old faithful creature. For she was *so* faithful. Would you believe it, she had been a servant in that self-same house and that self-same family for twenty-seven years come Christmas, and never a cross word

and never a lick! And, oh, to think she should
meet such a death at last! — a-sitting over the red-
hot stove at three o'clock in the morning and went
to sleep and fell on it and was actually *roasted!*
Not just frizzled up a bit, but literally roasted to a
crisp! Poor faithful creature, how she *was* cooked!
I am but a poor woman, but even if I have to
scrimp to do it, I will put up a tombstone over that
lone sufferer's grave — and Mr. Riley if you would
have the goodness to think up a little epitaph to put
on it which would sort of describe the awful way in
which she met her —"

" Put it, ' *Well done*, good and faithful servant,' "
said Riley, and never smiled.

A FINE OLD MAN

JOHN WAGNER, the oldest man in Buffalo — one hundred and four years old — recently walked a mile and a half in two weeks.

He is as cheerful and bright as any of these other old men that charge around so persistently and tiresomely in the newspapers, and in every way as remarkable.

Last November he walked five blocks in a rainstorm, without any shelter but an umbrella, and cast his vote for Grant, remarking that he had voted for forty-seven presidents — which was a lie.

His " second crop " of rich brown hair arrived from New York yesterday, and he has a new set of teeth coming — from Philadelphia.

He is to be married next week to a girl one hundred and two years old, who still takes in washing.

They have been engaged eighty years, but their parents persistently refused their consent until three days ago.

John Wagner is two years older than the Rhode Island veteran, and yet has never tasted a drop of liquor in his life — unless — unless you count whisky.

SCIENCE VS. LUCK *

A T that time, in Kentucky (said the Hon. Mr.
K——), the law was very strict against what is
termed "games of chance." About a dozen of the
boys were detected playing "seven up" or "old
sledge" for money, and the grand jury found a
true bill against them. Jim Sturgis was retained to
defend them when the case came up, of course.
The more he studied over the matter, and looked
into the evidence, the plainer it was that he must
lose a case at last — there was no getting around
that painful fact. Those boys had certainly been
betting money on a game of chance. Even public
sympathy was roused in behalf of Sturgis. People
said it was a pity to see him mar his successful
career with a big prominent case like this, which
must go against him.

But after several restless nights an inspired idea
flashed upon Sturgis, and he sprang out of bed delighted. He thought he saw his way through. The
next day he whispered around a little among his
clients and a few friends, and then when the case

* Written about 1867.

came up in court he acknowledged the seven-up and
the betting, and, as his sole defense, had the
astounding effrontery to put in the plea that old
sledge was not a game of chance! There was the
broadest sort of a smile all over the faces of that
sophisticated audience. The judge smiled with the
rest. But Sturgis maintained a countenance whose
earnestness was even severe. The opposite counsel
tried to ridicule him out of his position, and did not
succeed. The judge jested in a ponderous judicial
way about the thing, but did not move him. The
matter was becoming grave. The judge lost a little
of his patience, and said the joke had gone far
enough. Jim Sturgis said he knew of no joke in
the matter — his clients could not be punished for
indulging in what some people chose to consider a
game of chance until it was *proven* that it was a
game of chance. Judge and counsel said that would
be an easy matter, and forthwith called Deacons
Job, Peters, Burke, and Johnson, and Dominies
Wirt and Miggles, to testify; and they unanimously
and with strong feeling put down the legal quibble
of Sturgis by pronouncing that old sledge *was* a
game of chance.

" What do you call it *now ?*" said the judge.

" I call it a game of science!" retorted Sturgis;
" and I'll prove it, too!"

They saw his little game.

He brought in a cloud of witnesses, and produced
an overwhelming mass of testimony, to show that

old sledge was not a game of chance but a game of science.

Instead of being the simplest case in the world, it had somehow turned out to be an excessively knotty one. The judge scratched his head over it a while, and said there was no way of coming to a determination, because just as many men could be brought into court who would testify on one side as could be found to testify on the other. But he said he was willing to do the fair thing by all parties, and would act upon any suggestion Mr. Sturgis would make for the solution of the difficulty.

Mr. Sturgis was on his feet in a second.

" Impanel a jury of six of each, Luck *versus* Science. Give them candles and a couple of decks of cards. Send them into the jury room, and just abide by the result!"

There was no disputing the fairness of the proposition. The four deacons and the two dominies were sworn in as the " chance " jurymen, and six inveterate old seven-up professors were chosen to represent the " science " side of the issue. They retired to the jury room.

In about two hours Deacon Peters sent into court to borrow three dollars from a friend. [Sensation.] In about two hours more Dominie Miggles sent into court to borrow a " stake " from a friend. [Sensation.] During the next three or four hours the other dominie and the other deacons sent into court for small loans. And still the packed audience waited, for it was a prodigious occasion in Bull's Corners, and one in which every father of a family was necessarily interested.

The rest of the story can be told briefly. About daylight the jury came in, and Deacon Job, the foreman, read the following

VERDICT.

We, the jury in the case of the Commonwealth of Kentucky vs. John Wheeler *et al.*, have carefully considered the points of the case, and tested the merits of the several theories advanced, and do hereby unanimously decide that the game commonly known as old sledge or seven-up is eminently a game of science and not of chance. In demonstration whereof it is hereby and herein stated, iterated, reiterated, set forth, and made manifest that, during the entire night, the " chance " men never won a game or turned a jack, although both feats were common and frequent to the opposition; and furthermore, in support of this our verdict, we call attention to the significant fact that the " chance " men are all busted, and the " science " men have got the money. It is the deliberate opinion of this jury, that the " chance " theory concerning seven-up is a pernicious doctrine, and calculated to inflict untold suffering and pecuniary loss upon any community that takes stock in it.

" That is the way that seven-up came to be set

apart and particularized in the statute books of Kentucky as being a game not of chance but of science, and therefore not punishable under the law," said Mr. K——. "That verdict is of record, and holds good to this day."

THE LATE BENJAMIN FRANKLIN*

[" Never put off till to-morrow what you can do day after to-morrow just as well." — B. F.]

THIS party was one of those persons whom they call Philosophers. He was twins, being born simultaneously in two different houses in the city of Boston. These houses remain unto this day, and have signs upon them worded in accordance with the facts. The signs are considered well enough to have, though not necessary, because the inhabitants point out the two birthplaces to the stranger any-how, and sometimes as often as several times in the same day. The subject of this memoir was of a vicious disposition, and early prostituted his talents to the invention of maxims and aphorisms calculated to inflict suffering upon the rising generation of all subsequent ages. His simplest acts, also, were contrived with a view to their being held up for the emulation of boys forever — boys who might other-wise have been happy. It was in this spirit that he became the son of a soap-boiler, and probably for no other reason than that the efforts of all future

* Written about 1870.

boys who tried to be anything might be looked upon
with suspicion unless they were the sons of soap-
boilers. With a malevolence which is without parallel in history, he would work all day, and then sit
up nights, and let on to be studying algebra by the
light of a smouldering fire, so that all other boys
might have to do that also, or else have Benjamin
Franklin thrown up to them. Not satisfied with
these proceedings, he had a fashion of living wholly
on bread and water, and studying astronomy at meal-
time — a thing which has brought affliction to
millions of boys since, whose fathers had read
Franklin's pernicious biography.

His maxims were full of animosity toward boys.
Nowadays a boy cannot follow out a single natural
instinct without tumbling over some of those ever-
lasting aphorisms and hearing from Franklin on the
spot. If he buys two cents' worth of peanuts, his
father says, " Remember what Franklin has said,
my son —' A groat a day's a penny a year;' " and
the comfort is all gone out of those peanuts. If he
wants to spin his top when he has done work, his
father quotes, " Procrastination is the thief of time."
If he does a virtuous action, he never gets anything
for it, because " Virtue is its own reward." And
that boy is hounded to death and robbed of his
natural rest, because Franklin said once, in one of
his inspired flights of malignity:

> " Early to bed and early to rise
> Makes a man healthy and wealthy and wise."

As if it were any object to a boy to be healthy and wealthy and wise on such terms. The sorrow that that maxim has cost me through my parents' experimenting on me with it, tongue cannot tell. The legitimate result is my present state of general debility, indigence, and mental aberration. My parents used to have me up before nine o'clock in the morning sometimes when I was a boy. If they had let me take my natural rest where would I have been now? Keeping store, no doubt, and respected by all.

And what an adroit old adventurer the subject of this memoir was! In order to get a chance to fly his kite on Sunday he used to hang a key on the string and let on to be fishing for lightning. And a guileless public would go home chirping about the " wisdom " and the " genius " of the hoary Sabbath-breaker. If anybody caught him playing " mumble-peg " by himself, after the age of sixty, he would immediately appear to be ciphering out how the grass grew — as if it was any of his business. My grandfather knew him well, and he says Franklin was always fixed — always ready. If a body, during his old age, happened on him unexpectedly when he was catching flies, or making mud pies, or sliding on a cellar door, he would immediately look wise, and rip out a maxim, and walk off with his nose in the air and his cap turned wrong side before, trying to appear absent-minded and eccentric. He was a hard lot.

He invented a stove that would smoke your head off in four hours by the clock. One can see the almost devilish satisfaction he took in it by his giving it his name.

He was always proud of telling how he entered Philadelphia for the first time, with nothing in the world but two shillings in his pocket and four rolls of bread under his arm. But really, when you come to examine it critically, it was nothing. Anybody could have done it.

To the subject of this memoir belongs the honor of recommending the army to go back to bows and arrows in place of bayonets and muskets. He observed, with his customary force, that the bayonet was very well under some circumstances, but that he doubted whether it could be used with accuracy at a long range.

Benjamin Franklin did a great many notable things for his country, and made her young name to be honored in many lands as the mother of such a son. It is not the idea of this memoir to ignore that or cover it up. No; the simple idea of it is to snub those pretentious maxims of his, which he worked up with a great show of originality out of truisms that had become wearisome platitudes as early as the dispersion from Babel; and also to snub his stove, and his military inspirations, his unseemly endeavor to make himself conspicuous when he entered Philadelphia, and his flying his kite and fooling away his time in all sorts of such ways when he ought to have been foraging for soap-fat, or constructing candles. I merely desired to do away with somewhat of the prevalent calamitous idea among heads of families that Franklin *acquired* his great genius by working for nothing, studying by moonlight, and getting up in the night instead of waiting till morning like a Christian; and that this programme, rigidly inflicted, will make a Franklin of every father's fool. It is time these gentlemen were finding out that these execrable eccentricities of instinct and conduct are only the *evidences* of genius, not the *creators* of it. I wish I had been the father of my parents long enough to make them comprehend this truth, and thus prepare them to let their son have an easier time of it. When I was a child I had to boil soap, notwithstanding my father was wealthy, and I had to get up early and study geometry at breakfast, and peddle my own poetry, and do everything just as Franklin did, in the solemn hope that I would be a Franklin some day. And here I am.

MR. BLOKE'S ITEM*

OUR esteemed friend, Mr. John William Bloke, of Virginia City, walked into the office where we are sub-editor at a late hour last night, with an expression of profound and heartfelt suffering upon his countenance, and, sighing heavily, laid the following item reverently upon the desk, and walked slowly out again. He paused a moment at the door, and seemed struggling to command his feelings sufficiently to enable him to speak, and then, nodding his head towards his manuscript, ejaculated in a broken voice, " Friend of mine — oh! how sad!" and burst into tears. We were so moved at his distress that we did not think to call him back and endeavor to comfort him until he was gone, and it was too late. The paper had already gone to press, but knowing that our friend would consider the publication of this item important, and cherishing the hope that to print it would afford a melancholy satisfaction to his sorrowing heart, we stopped the press at once and inserted it in our columns:

DISTRESSING ACCIDENT.— Last evening, about six o'clock, as Mr. William Schuyler, an old and respectable citizen of South Park, was

* Written about 1865.

æaving his residence to go down town, as has been his usual custom for many years with the exception only of a short interval in the spring of 1850, during which he was confined to his bed by injuries received in attempting to stop a runaway horse by thoughtlessly placing himself directly in its wake and throwing up his hands and shouting, which if he had done so even a single moment sooner, must inevitably have frightened the animal still more instead of checking its speed, although disastrous enough to himself as it was, and rendered more melancholy and distressing by reason of the presence of his wife's mother, who was there and saw the sad occurrence, notwithstanding it is at least likely, though not necessarily so, that she should be reconnoitering in another direction when incidents occur, not being vivacious and on the lookout, as a general thing, but even the reverse, as her own mother is said to have stated, who is no more, but died in the full hope of a glorious resurrection, upwards of three years ago, aged eighty-six, being a Christian woman and without guile, as it were, or property, in consequence of the fire of 1849, which destroyed every single thing she had in the world. But such is life. Let us all take warning by this solemn occurrence, and let us endeavor so to conduct ourselves that when we come to die we can do it. Let us place our hands upon our heart, and say with earnestness and sincerity that from this day forth we will beware of the intoxicating bowl.—*First Edition of the Californian.*

The head editor has been in here raising the mischief, and tearing his hair and kicking the furniture about, and abusing me like a pickpocket. He says that every time he leaves me in charge of the paper for half an hour, I get imposed upon by the first infant or the first idiot that comes along. And he says that that distressing item of Mr. Bloke's is nothing but a lot of distressing bosh, and has no point to it, and no sense in it, and no information in it, and that there was no sort of necessity for stopping the press to publish it.

Now all this comes of being good-hearted. If I

had been as unaccommodating and unsympathetic as some people, I would have told Mr. Bloke that I wouldn't receive his communication at such a late hour; but no, his snuffling distress touched my heart, and I jumped at the chance of doing something to modify his misery. I never read his item to see whether there was anything wrong about it, but hastily wrote the few lines which preceded it, and sent it to the printers. And what has my kindness done for me? It has done nothing but bring down upon me a storm of abuse and ornamental blasphemy.

Now I will read that item myself, and see if there is any foundation for all this fuss. And if there is, the author of it shall hear from me.

.   .   .   .   .   .

I have read it, and I am bound to admit that it seems a little mixed at a first glance. However, I will peruse it once more.

.   .   .   .   .   .

I have read it again, and it does really seem a good deal more mixed than ever.

.   .   .   .   .   .

I have read it over five times, but if I can get at the meaning of it, I wish I may get my just deserts. It won't bear analysis. There are things about it which I cannot understand at all. It don't say whatever became of William Schuyler. It just says enough about him to get one interested in his career, and then drops him. Who is William Schuyler,

anyhow, and what part of South Park did he live in,
and if he started down town at six o'clock, did he
ever get there, and if he did, did anything happen
to him? Is *he* the individual that met with the
" distressing accident"? Considering the elaborate
circumstantiality of detail observable in the item, it
seems to me that it ought to contain more information than it does. On the contrary, it is obscure —
and not only obscure, but utterly incomprehensible.
Was the breaking of Mr. Schuyler's leg, fifteen
years ago, the " distressing accident " that plunged
Mr. Bloke into unspeakable grief, and caused him
to come up here at dead of night and stop our press
to acquaint the world with the circumstance? Or
did the " distressing accident " consist in the destruction of Schuyler's mother-in-law's property in
early times? Or did it consist in the death of that
person herself three years ago (albeit it does not
appear that she died by accident)? In a word, what
did that " distressing accident " consist in? What
did that driveling ass of a Schuyler stand *in the
wake* of a runaway horse for, with his shouting and
gesticulating, if he wanted to stop him? And how
the mischief could he get run over by a horse that
had already passed beyond him? And what are we
to take " warning " by? And how is this extraordinary chapter of incomprehensibilities going to be a
" lesson " to us? And, above all, what has the
intoxicating "bowl" got to do with it, anyhow? It is
not stated that Schuyler drank, or that his wife

drank, or that his mother-in-law drank, or that the horse drank — wherefore, then, the reference to the intoxicating bowl? It does seem to me that if Mr. Bloke had let the intoxicating bowl alone himself, he never would have got into so much trouble about this exasperating imaginary accident. I have read this absurd item over and over again, with all its insinuating plausibility, until my head swims; but I can make neither head nor tail of it. There certainly seems to have been an accident of some kind or other, but it is impossible to determine what the nature of it was, or who was the sufferer by it. I do not like to do it, but I feel compelled to request that the next time anything happens to one of Mr. Bloke's friends, he will append such explanatory notes to his account of it as will enable me to find out what sort of an accident it was and whom it happened to. I had rather all his friends should die than that I should be driven to the verge of lunacy again in trying to cipher out the meaning of another such production as the above.

A MEDIÆVAL ROMANCE *

CHAPTER I.

THE SECRET REVEALED

IT was night. Stillness reigned in the grand old feudal castle of Klugenstein. The year 1222 was drawing to a close. Far away up in the tallest of the castle's towers a single light glimmered. A secret council was being held there. The stern old lord of Klugenstein sat in a chair of state meditating. Presently he said, with a tender accent: "My daughter!"

A young man of noble presence, clad from head to heel in knightly mail, answered: "Speak, father!"

"My daughter, the time is come for the revealing of the mystery that hath puzzled all your young life. Know, then, that it had its birth in the matters which I shall now unfold. My brother Ulrich is the great Duke of Brandenburgh. Our father, on his deathbed, decreed that if no son were born to Ulrich the succession should pass to my house, provided a *son* were born to me. And further, in case no son

---

* Written about 1868.
15s

were born to either, but only daughters, then the
succession should pass to Ulrich's daughter if she
proved stainless; if she did not, my daughter should
succeed if she retained a blameless name. And so I
and my old wife here prayed fervently for the good
boon of a son, but the prayer was vain. You were
born to us. I was in despair. I saw the mighty
prize slipping from my grasp — the splendid dream
vanishing away! And I had been so hopeful! Five
years had Ulrich lived in wedlock, and yet his wife
had borne no heir of either sex.

" ' But hold,' I said, ' all is not lost.' A saving
scheme had shot athwart my brain. You were born
at midnight. Only the leech, the nurse, and six
waiting-women knew your sex. I hanged them
every one before an hour sped. Next morning all
the barony went mad with rejoicing over the proclamation that a *son* was born to Klugenstein —- an heir
to mighty Brandenburgh! And well the secret has
been kept. You mother's own sister nursed your
infancy, and from that time forward we feared
nothing.

" When you were ten years old a daughter was
born to Ulrich. We grieved, but hoped for good
results from measles, or physicians, or other natural
enemies of infancy, but were always disappointed.
She lived, she throve — Heaven's malison upon her!
But it is nothing. We are safe. For, ha! ha! have
we not a son? And is not our son the future duke?
Our well-beloved Conrad, is it not so? — for woman

of eight-and-twenty years as you are, my child, none other name than that hath ever fallen to *you !*

" Now it hath come to pass that age hath laid its hand upon my brother, and he waxes feeble. The cares of state do tax him sore, therefore he wills that you shall come to him and be already duke in act, though not yet in name. Your servitors are ready — you journey forth to-night.

" Now listen well. Remember every word I say. There is a law as old as Germany, that if any woman sit for a single instant in the great ducal chair before she hath been absolutely crowned in presence of the people — SHE SHALL DIE! So heed my words. Pretend humility. Pronounce your judgments from the Premier's chair, which stands at the *foot* of the throne. Do this until you are crowned and safe. It is not likely that your sex will ever be discovered, but still it is the part of wisdom to make all things as safe as may be in this treacherous earthly life.

" Oh, my father! is it for this my life hath been a lie? Was it that I might cheat my unoffending cousin of her rights? Spare me, father, spare your child!"

" What, hussy! Is this my reward for the august fortune my brain has wrought for thee? By the bones of my father, this puling sentiment of thine but ill accords with my humor. Betake thee to the duke instantly, and beware how thou meddlest with my purpose!"

Let this suffice of the conversation. It is enough

for us to know that the prayers, the entreaties, and the tears of the gentle-natured girl availed nothing. Neither they nor anything could move the stout old lord of Klugenstein. And so, at last, with a heavy heart, the daughter saw the castle gates close behind her, and found herself riding away in the darkness surrounded by a knightly array of armed vassals and a brave following of servants.

The old baron sat silent for many minutes after his daughter's departure, and then he turned to his sad wife, and said:

"Dame, our matters seem speeding fairly. It is full three months since I sent the shrewd and handsome Count Detzin on his devilish mission to my brother's daughter Constance. If he fail we are not wholly safe, but if he do succeed no power can bar our girl from being duchess, e'en though ill fortune should decree she never should be duke!"

"My heart is full of bodings; yet all may still be well."

"Tush, woman! Leave the owls to croak. To bed with ye, and dream of Brandenburgh and grandeur!"

CHAPTER II.

FESTIVITY AND TEARS

SIX days after the occurrences related in the above chapter, the brilliant capital of the Duchy of

Brandenburgh was resplendent with military pageantry, and noisy with the rejoicings of loyal multitudes, for Conrad, the young heir to the crown, was come. The old duke's heart was full of happiness, for Conrad's handsome person and graceful bearing had won his love at once. The great halls of the palace were thronged with nobles, who welcomed Conrad bravely; and so bright and happy did all things seem, that he felt his fears and sorrows passing away, and giving place to a comforting contentment.

But in a remote apartment of the palace a scene of a different nature was transpiring. By a window stood the duke's only child, the Lady Constance. Her eyes were red and swollen, and full of tears. She was alone. Presently she fell to weeping anew, and said aloud:

" The villain Detzin is gone — has fled the dukedom! I could not believe it at first, but, alas! it is too true. And I loved him so. I dared to love him though I knew the duke, my father, would never let me wed him. I loved him — but now I hate him! With all my soul I hate him! Oh, what is to become of me? I am lost, lost, lost! I shall go mad!"

CHAPTER III.

THE PLOT THICKENS

A FEW months drifted by. All men published the praises of the young Conrad's government,

15

and extolled the wisdom of his judgments, the merci-
fulness of his sentences, and the modesty with which
he bore himself in his great office. The old duke
soon gave everything into his hands, and sat apart
and listened with proud satisfaction while his heir
delivered the decrees of the crown from the seat of
the Premier. It seemed plain that one so loved and
praised and honored of all men as Conrad was could
not be otherwise than happy. But, strangely enough,
he was not. For he saw with dismay that the
Princess Constance had begun to love him! The
love of the rest of the world was happy fortune for
him, but this was freighted with danger! And he
saw, moreover, that the delighted duke had discovered his daughter's passion likewise, and was already
dreaming of a marriage. Every day somewhat of
the deep sadness that had been in the princess's
face faded away; every day hope and animation
beamed brighter from her eye; and by and by even
vagrant smiles visited the face that had been so
troubled.

Conrad was appalled. He bitterly cursed himself
for having yielded to the instinct that had made him
seek the companionship of one of his own sex when
he was new and a stranger in the palace — when he
was sorrowful and yearned for a sympathy such as
only women can give or feel. He now began to
avoid his cousin. But this only made matters worse,
for, naturally enough, the more he avoided her the
more she cast herself in his way. He marveled at

this at first, and next it startled him. The girl haunted him; she hunted him; she happened upon him at all times and in all places, in the night as well as in the day. She seemed singularly anxious. There was surely a mystery somewhere.

This could not go on forever. All the world was talking about it. The duke was beginning to look perplexed. Poor Conrad was becoming a very ghost through dread and dire distress. One day as he was emerging from a private anteroom attached to the picture gallery Constance confronted him, and seizing both his hands in hers, exclaimed:

" Oh, why do you avoid me? What have I done — what have I said, to lose your kind opinion of me — for surely I had it once? Conrad, do not despise me, but pity a tortured heart? I cannot, cannot hold the words unspoken longer, lest they kill me — I LOVE YOU, CONRAD! There, despise me if you must, but they *would* be uttered!"

Conrad was speechless. Constance hesitated a moment, and then, misinterpreting his silence, a wild gladness flamed in her eyes, and she flung her arms about his neck and said:

" You relent! you relent! You *can* love me — you *will* love me! Oh, say you will, my own, my worshiped Conrad!"

Conrad groaned aloud. A sickly pallor overspread his countenance, and he trembled like an aspen. Presently, in desperation, he thrust the poor girl from him, and cried:

" You know not what you ask! It is forever and ever impossible!" And then he fled like a criminal, and left the princess stupefied with amazement. A minute afterward she was crying and sobbing there, and Conrad was crying and sobbing in his chamber. Both were in despair. Both saw ruin staring them in the face.

By and by Constance rose slowly to her feet and moved away, saying:

" To think that he was despising my love at the very moment that I thought it was melting his cruel heart! I hate him! He spurned me — did this man — he spurned me from him like a dog!"

CHAPTER IV.

THE AWFUL REVELATION

TIME passed on. A settled sadness rested once more upon the countenance of the good duke's daughter. She and Conrad were seen together no more now. The duke grieved at this. But as the weeks wore away Conrad's color came back to his cheeks, and his old-time vivacity to his eye, and he administered the government with a clear and steadily ripening wisdom.

Presently a strange whisper began to be heard about the palace. It grew louder; it spread farther. The gossips of the city got hold of it. It swept the dukedom. And this is what the whisper said:

" The Lady Constance hath given birth to a child!"

When the lord of Klugenstein heard it he swung his plumed helmet thrice around his head and shouted:

" Long live Duke Conrad! — for lo, his crown is sure from this day forward! Detzin has done his errand well, and the good scoundrel shall be rewarded!"

And he spread the tidings far and wide, and for eight-and-forty hours no soul in all the barony but did dance and sing, carouse and illuminate, to celebrate the great event, and all proud and happy at old Klugenstein's expense.

CHAPTER V.

THE FRIGHTFUL CATASTROPHE

THE trial was at hand. All the great lords and barons of Brandenburgh were assembled in the Hall of Justice in the ducal palace. No space was left unoccupied where there was room for a spectator to stand or sit. Conrad, clad in purple and ermine, sat in the Premier's chair, and on either side sat the great judges of the realm. The old duke had sternly commanded that the trial of his daughter should proceed without favor, and then had taken to his bed broken-hearted. His days were numbered. Poor Conrad had begged, as for his very life, that he might be spared the misery of sitting in judgment upon his cousin's crime, but it did not avail.

The saddest heart in all that great assemblage was in Conrad's breast.

The gladdest was in his father's, for, unknown to his daughter "Conrad," the old Baron Klugenstein was come, and was among the crowd of nobles triumphant in the swelling fortunes of his house.

After the heralds had made due proclamation and the other preliminaries had followed, the venerable Lord Chief Justice said: "Prisoner, stand forth!"

The unhappy princess rose, and stood unveiled before the vast multitude. The Lord Chief Justice continued:

"Most noble lady, before the great judges of this realm it hath been charged and proven that out of holy wedlock your Grace hath given birth unto a child, and by our ancient law the penalty is death excepting in one sole contingency, whereof his Grace the acting duke, our good Lord Conrad, will advertise you in his solemn sentence now; wherefore give heed."

Conrad stretched forth his reluctant scepter, and in the self-same moment the womanly heart beneath his robe yearned pityingly toward the doomed prisoner, and the tears came into his eyes. He opened his lips to speak, but the Lord Chief Justice said quickly:

"Not there, your Grace, not there! It is not

lawful to pronounce judgment upon any of the ducal
line SAVE FROM THE DUCAL THRONE!"

A shudder went to the heart of poor Conrad, and
a tremor shook the iron frame of his old father likewise. CONRAD HAD NOT BEEN CROWNED — dared
he profane the throne? He hesitated and turned
pale with fear. But it must be done. Wondering
eyes were already upon him. They would be suspicious eyes if he hesitated longer. He ascended
the throne. Presently he stretched forth the scepter
again, and said:

" Prisoner, in the name of our sovereign Lord
Ulrich, Duke of Brandenburgh, I proceed to the
solemn duty that hath devolved upon me. Give
heed to my words. By the ancient law of the land,
except you produce the partner of your guilt and
deliver him up to the executioner you must surely
die. Embrace this opportunity — save yourself while
yet you may. Name the father of your child!"

A solemn hush fell upon the great court — a silence
so profound that men could hear their own hearts
beat. Then the princess slowly turned, with eyes
gleaming with hate, and pointing her finger straight
at Conrad, said:

" Thou art the man!"

An appalling conviction of his helpless, hopeless
peril struck a chill to Conrad's heart like the chill of
death itself. What power on earth could save him!
To disprove the charge he must reveal that he was a
woman, and for an uncrowned woman to sit in the

ducal chair was death! At one and the same moment he and his grim old father swooned and fell to
the ground.

.   .   .   .   .

The remainder of this thrilling and eventful story
will NOT be found in this or any other publication,
either now or at any future time.

The truth is, I have got my hero (or heroine)
into such a particularly close place that I do not see
how I am ever going to get him (or her) out of it
again, and therefore I will wash my hands of the
whole business, and leave that person to get out the
best way that offers — or else stay there. I thought
it was going to be easy enough to straighten out
that little difficulty, but it looks different now.

PETITION CONCERNING COPYRIGHT

TO THE HONORABLE THE SENATE AND HOUSE OF
REPRESENTATIVES IN CONGRESS ASSEMBLED:

Whereas, The Constitution guarantees equal rights
to all, backed by the Declaration of Independence;
and

Whereas, Under our laws, the right of property
in real estate is perpetual; and

Whereas, Under our laws, the right of property

in the literary result of a citizen's intellectual labor is restricted to forty-two years; and

Whereas, Forty-two years seems an exceedingly just and righteous term, and a sufficiently long one for the retention of property;

Therefore, Your petitioner, having the good of his country solely at heart, humbly prays that "equal rights" and fair and equal treatment may be meted out to all citizens, by the restriction of rights in *all* property, real estate included, to the beneficent term of forty-two years. Then shall all men bless your honorable body and be happy. And for this will your petitioner ever pray.

MARK TWAIN.

A PARAGRAPH NOT ADDED TO THE PETITION.

The charming absurdity of restricting property-rights in books to forty-two years sticks prominently out in the fact that hardly any man's books ever *live* forty-two years, or even the half of it; and so, for the sake of getting a shabby advantage of the heirs of about one Scott or Burns or Milton in a hundred years, the lawmakers of the "Great" Republic are content to leave that poor little pilfering edict upon the statute books. It is like an emperor lying in wait to rob a phenix's nest, and waiting the necessary century to get the chance.

AFTER-DINNER SPEECH

[AT A FOURTH OF JULY GATHERING, IN LONDON, OF
AMERICANS]

MR. CHAIRMAN AND LADIES AND GEN-
TLEMEN: I thank you for the compliment
which has just been tendered me, and to show my
appreciation of it I will not afflict you with many
words. It is pleasant to celebrate in this peaceful
way, upon this old mother soil, the anniversary of
an experiment which was born of war with this same
land so long ago, and wrought out to a successful
issue by the devotion of our ancestors. It has
taken nearly a hundred years to bring the English
and Americans into kindly and mutually appreciative
relations, but I believe it has been accomplished at
last. It was a great step when the two last mis-
understandings were settled by arbitration instead of
cannon. It is another great step when England
adopts our sewing-machines without claiming the
invention — as usual. It was another when they
imported one of our sleeping cars the other day.
And it warmed my heart more than I can tell,
yesterday, when I witnessed the spectacle of an

Englishman ordering an American sherry cobbler of his own free will and accord — and not only that but with a great brain and a level head reminding the barkeeper not to forget the strawberries. With a common origin, a common language, a common literature, a common religion and — common drinks, what is longer needful to the cementing of the two nations together in a permanent bond of brotherhood?

This is an age of progress, and ours is a progressive land. A great and glorious land, too — a land which has developed a Washington, a Franklin, a Wm. M. Tweed, a Longfellow, a Motley, a Jay Gould, a Samuel C. Pomeroy, a recent Congress which has never had its equal (in some respects), and a United States Army which conquered sixty Indians in eight months by tiring them out — which is much better than uncivilized slaughter, God knows. We have a criminal jury system which is superior to any in the world; and its efficiency is only marred by the difficulty of finding twelve men every day who don't know anything and can't read. And I may observe that we have an insanity plea that would have saved Cain. I think I can say, and say with pride, that we have some legislatures that bring higher prices than any in the world.

I refer with effusion to our railway system, which consents to let us live, though it might do the opposite, being our owners. It only destroyed three thousand and seventy lives last year by collisions,

and twenty-seven thousand two hundred and sixty
by running over heedless and unnecessary people at
crossings. The companies seriously regretted the
killing of these thirty thousand people, and went so
far as to pay for some of them — voluntarily, of
course, for the meanest of us would not claim that
we possess a court treacherous enough to enforce a
law against a railway company. But, thank Heaven,
the railway companies are generally disposed to do
the right and kindly thing without compulsion. I
know of an instance which greatly touched me at
the time. After an accident the company sent
home the remains of a dear distant old relative of
mine in a basket, with the remark, " Please state
what figure you hold him at — and return the
basket." Now there couldn't be anything friendlier
than that.

But I must not stand here and brag all night.
However, you won't mind a body bragging a little
about his country on the fourth of July. It is a fair
and legitimate time to fly the eagle. I will say only
one more word of brag — and a hopeful one. It is
this. We have a form of government which gives
each man a fair chance and no favor. With us no
individual is born with a right to look down upon
his neighbor and hold him in contempt. Let such
of us as are not dukes find our consolation in
that. And we may find hope for the future in
the fact that as unhappy as is the condition of our
political morality to-day, England has risen up out

of a far fouler since the days when Charles I.
ennobled courtesans and all political place was a
matter of bargain and sale. There is hope for us
yet.*

---

* At least the above is the speech which I was *going* to make, but
our minister, Gen. Schenck, presided, and after the blessing, got up and
made a great long inconceivably dull harangue, and wound up by saying
that inasmuch as speech-making did not seem to exhilarate the guests
much, all further oratory would be dispensed with during the evening,
and we could just sit and talk privately to our elbow-neighbors and have
a good sociable time. It is known that in consequence of that remark
forty-four perfected speeches died in the womb. The depression, the
gloom, the solemnity that reigned over the banquet from that time forth
will be a lasting memory with many that were there. By that one
thoughtless remark Gen. Schenck lost forty-four of the best friends he
had in England. More than one said that night, "And this is the sort
of person that is sent to represent us in a great sister empire!"

16s

LIONIZING MURDERERS

I HAD heard so much about the celebrated fortune-teller Madame ———, that I went to see her yesterday. She has a dark complexion naturally, and this effect is heightened by artificial aids which cost her nothing. She wears curls — very black ones, and I had an impression that she gave their native attractiveness a lift with rancid butter. She wears a reddish check handkerchief, cast loosely around her neck, and it was plain that her other one is slow getting back from the wash. I presume she takes snuff. At any rate, something resembling it had lodged among the hairs sprouting from her upper lip. I know she likes garlic — I knew that as soon as she sighed. She looked at me searchingly for nearly a minute, with her black eyes, and then said :

" It is enough. Come !"

She started down a very dark and dismal corridor — I stepping close after her. Presently she stopped, and said that, as the way was so crooked and dark, perhaps she had better get a light. But it seemed ungallant to allow a woman to put herself to so much trouble for me, and so I said :

" It is not worth while, madam. If you will heave another sigh, I think I can follow it."

So we got along all right. Arrived at her official and mysterious den, she asked me to tell her the date of my birth, the exact hour of that occurrence, and the color of my grandmother's hair. I answered as accurately as I could. Then she said:

" Young man, summon your fortitude — do not tremble. I am about to reveal the past."

" Information concerning the *future* would be in a general way, more —"

" Silence! You have had much trouble, some joy, some good fortune, some bad. Your great grandfather was hanged."

" That is a l—"

" Silence! Hanged sir. But it was not his fault. He could not help it."

" I am glad you do him justice."

" Ah — grieve, rather, that the jury did. He was hanged. His star crosses yours in the fourth division, fifth sphere. Consequently you will be hanged also."

" In view of this cheerful —"

" I *must* have silence. Yours was not, in the beginning, a criminal nature, but circumstances changed it. At the age of nine you stole sugar. At the age of fifteen you stole money. At twenty you stole horses. At twenty-five you committed arson. At thirty, hardened in crime, you became an editor. You are now a public lecturer. Worse

things are in store for you. You will be sent to
Congress. Next, to the penitentiary. Finally, happiness will come again — all will be well — you will
be hanged.''

I was now in tears. It seemed hard enough to
go to Congress; but to be hanged — this was too
sad, too dreadful. The woman seemed surprised at
my grief. I told her the thoughts that were in my
mind. Then she comforted me.

"Why, man,"* she said, "hold up your head —

* In this paragraph the fortune-teller details the exact history of the
Pike-Brown assassination case in New Hampshire, from the succoring
and saving of the stranger Pike by the Browns, to the subsequent hanging and coffining of that treacherous miscreant. She adds nothing,
invents nothing, exaggerates nothing (see any New England paper for
November, 1869). This Pike-Brown case is selected merely as a type,
to illustrate a custom that prevails, not in New Hampshire alone, but in
every State in the Union — I mean the sentimental custom of visiting,
petting, glorifying, and snuffling over murderers like this Pike, from the
day they enter the jail under sentence of death until they swing from the
gallows. The following extract from the *Temple Bar* (1866) reveals
the fact that this custom is not confined to the United States: — "On
December 31, 1841, a man named John Johnes, a shoemaker, murdered his sweetheart, Mary Hallam, the daughter of a respectable
laborer, at Mansfield, in the county of Nottingham. He was executed
on March 23, 1842. He was a man of unsteady habits, and gave way
to violent fits of passion. The girl declined his addresses, and he said
if he did not have her no one else should. After he had inflicted the
first wound, which was not immediately fatal, she begged for her life,
but seeing him resolved, asked for time to pray. He said that he would
pray for both, and completed the crime. The wounds were inflicted by
a shoemaker's knife, and her throat was cut barbarously. After this he
dropped on his knees some time, and prayed God to have mercy on two
unfortunate lovers. He made no attempt to escape, and confessed the
crime. After his imprisonment he behaved in a most decorous manner;

you have nothing to grieve about. **Listen.** You will live in New Hampshire. In your sharp need and distress the Brown family will succor you — such of them as Pike the assassin left alive. They will be benefactors to you. When you shall have grown fat upon their bounty, and are grateful and happy, you will desire to make some modest return for these things, and so you will go to the house some night and brain the whole family with an axe. You will rob the dead bodies of your benefactors, and disburse your gains in riotous living among the rowdies and courtesans of Boston. Then you will be arrested, tried, condemned to be hanged, thrown into prison. Now is your happy day. You will be converted — you will be converted just as soon as every effort to compass pardon, commutation, or reprieve has failed — and then! Why, then, every morning and every afternoon, the best and purest young ladies of the village will assemble in your cell and sing hymns. This will show that assassination is respectable. Then you will write a touching letter, in which you will forgive all those recent Browns. This will excite the public admiration. No public can withstand magnanimity. Next, they will

---

he won upon the good opinion of the jail chaplain, and he was visited by the Bishop of Lincoln. It does not appear that he expressed any contrition for the crime, but seemed to pass away with triumphant certainty that he was going to rejoin his victim in heaven. *He was visited by some pious and benevolent ladies of Nottingham, some of whom declared he was a child of God, if ever there was one. One of the ladies sent him a white camelia to wear at his execution."*

16

take you to the scaffold, with great *éclat*, at the
head of an imposing procession composed of clergymen, officials, citizens generally, and young ladies
walking pensively two and two, and bearing bouquets
and immortelles. You will mount the scaffold, and
while the great concourse stand uncovered in your
presence, you will read your sappy little speech
which the minister has written for you. And then,
in the midst of a grand and impressive silence, they
will swing you into per—— Paradise, my son.
There will not be a dry eye on the ground. You
will be a hero! Not a rough there but will envy
you. Not a rough there but will resolve to emulate
you. And next, a great procession will follow you
to the tomb — will weep over your remains — the
young ladies will sing again the hymns made dear
by sweet associations connected with the jail, and,
as a last tribute of affection, respect, and appreciation of your many sterling qualities, they will walk
two and two around your bier, and strew wreaths of
flowers on it. And lo! you are canonized. Think
of it, son — ingrate, assassin, robber of the dead,
drunken brawler among thieves and harlots in the
slums of Boston one month, and the pet of the
pure and innocent daughters of the land the next!
A bloody and hateful devil — a bewept, bewailed,
and sainted martyr — all in a month! Fool! — so
noble a fortune, and yet you sit here grieving!"

"No, madame," I said, "you do me wrong,
you do, indeed. I am perfectly satisfied. I did

not know before that my great-grandfather was
hanged, but it is of no consequence. He has probably ceased to bother about it by this time — and I
have not commenced yet. I confess, madame, that
I do something in the way of editing and lecturing,
but the other crimes you mention have escaped my
memory. Yet I must have committed them — you
would not deceive a stranger. But let the past be
as it was, and let the future be as it may — these
are nothing. I have only cared for one thing. I
have always felt that I should be hanged some day,
and somehow the thought has annoyed me considerably; but if you can only assure me that I shall be
hanged in New Hampshire —"

"Not a shadow of a doubt!"

"Bless you, my benefactress! — excuse this embrace — you have removed a great load from my
breast. To be hanged in New Hampshire is happiness — it leaves an honored name behind a man,
and introduces him at once into the best New
Hampshire society in the other world."

I then took leave of the fortune-teller. But,
seriously, is it well to glorify a murderous villain
on the scaffold, as Pike was glorified in New Hampshire? Is it well to turn the penalty for a bloody
crime into a reward? Is it just to do it? Is it safe?

A NEW CRIME

LEGISLATION NEEDED

THIS country, during the last thirty or forty years, has produced some of the most remarkable cases of insanity of which there is any mention in history. For instance, there was the Baldwin case, in Ohio, twenty-two years ago. Baldwin, from his boyhood up, had been of a vindictive, malignant, quarrelsome nature. He put a boy's eye out once, and never was heard upon any occasion to utter a regret for it. He did many such things. But at last he did something that was serious. He called at a house just after dark one evening, knocked, and when the occupant came to the door, shot him dead, and then tried to escape, but was captured. Two days before, he had wantonly insulted a helpless cripple, and the man he afterward took swift vengeance upon with an assassin bullet had knocked him down. Such was the Baldwin case. The trial was long and exciting; the community was fearfully wrought up. Men said this spiteful, bad-hearted villain had caused grief enough in his time, and now he should satisfy the law. But they were mistaken;

Baldwin was *insane* when he did the deed — they had not thought of that. By the argument of counsel it was shown that at half-past ten in the morning on the day of the murder, Baldwin became insane, and remained so for eleven hours and a half exactly. This just covered the case comfortably, and he was acquitted. Thus, if an unthinking and excited community had been listened to instead of the arguments of counsel, a poor crazy creature would have been held to a fearful responsibility for a mere freak of madness. Baldwin went clear, and although his relatives and friends were naturally incensed against the community for their injurious suspicions and remarks, they said let it go for this time, and did not prosecute. The Baldwins were very wealthy. This same Baldwin had momentary fits of insanity twice afterward, and on both occasions killed people he had grudges against. And on both these occasions the circumstances of the killing were so aggravated, and the murders so seemingly heartless and treacherous, that if Baldwin had not been insane he would have been hanged without the shadow of a doubt. As it was, it required all his political and family influence to get him clear in one of the cases, and cost him not less than ten thousand dollars to get clear in the other. One of these men he had notoriously been threatening to kill for twelve years. The poor creature happened, by the merest piece of ill fortune, to come along a dark alley at the very moment that Baldwin's insanity came upon him, and so he was shot in the back with a gun loaded with slugs.

Take the case of Lynch Hackett, of Pennsylvania. Twice, in public, he attacked a German butcher by the name of Bemis Feldner, with a cane, and both times Feldner whipped him with his fists. Hackett was a vain, wealthy, violent gentleman, who held his blood and family in high esteem, and believed that a reverent respect was due to his great riches. He brooded over the shame of his chastisement for two weeks, and then, in a momentary fit of insanity, armed himself to the teeth, rode into town, waited a couple of hours until he saw Feldner coming down the street with his wife on his arm, and then, as the couple passed the doorway in which he had partially concealed himself, he drove a knife into Feldner's neck, killing him instantly. The widow caught the limp form and eased it to the earth. Both were drenched with blood. Hackett jocosely remarked to her that as a professional butcher's recent wife she could appreciate the artistic neatness of the job that left her in condition to marry again, in case she wanted to. This remark, and another which he made to a friend, that his position in society made the killing of an obscure citizen simply an " eccentricity " instead of a crime, were shown to be evidences of insanity, and so Hackett escaped punishment. The jury were hardly inclined to accept these as proofs at first, inasmuch as the prisoner had never been insane before the murder, and under the tranquilizing effect of the butchering had immediately regained his right mind; but when the defense came to show that a third cousin of Hackett's wife's stepfather was insane, and not only insane, but had a nose the very counterpart of Hackett's, it was plain that insanity was hereditary in the family, and Hackett had come by it by legitimate inheritance. Of course the jury then acquitted him. But it was a merciful providence that Mrs. H.'s people had been afflicted as shown, else Hackett would certainly have been hanged.

However, it is not possible to recount all the marvelous cases of insanity that have come under the public notice in the last thirty or forty years. There was the Durgin case in New Jersey three years ago. The servant girl, Bridget Durgin, at dead of night, invaded her mistress' bedroom and carved the lady literally to pieces with a knife. Then she dragged the body to the middle of the floor, and beat and banged it with chairs and such things. Next she opene¹ the feather beds, and strewed the contents around, saturated everything with kerosene, and set fire to the general wreck. She now took up the young child of the murdered woman in her blood-smeared hands and walked off, through the snow, with no shoes on, to a neighbor's house a quarter of a mile off, and told a string of wild, incoherent stories about some men coming and setting fire to the house; and then she cried piteously, and without seeming to think there was anything suggestive about the blood upon her hands, her clothing, and the baby, volunteered the remark that she was afraid those men had murdered her mistress! Afterward, by her own confession and other testimony, it was proved that the mistress had always been kind to the girl, consequently there was no revenge in the murder; and it was also shown that the girl took nothing away from the burning house, not even her own shoes, and consequently robbery was not the motive. Now, the reader says, " Here comes that same old plea of insanity again." But the reader has deceived himself this time. No such plea was offered in her defense. The judge sentenced her, nobody persecuted the governor with petitions for her pardon, and she was promptly hanged.

There was that youth in Pennsylvania, whose curious confession was published some years ago. It was simply a conglomeration of incoherent drivel from beginning to end, and so was his lengthy speech on the scaffold afterward. For a whole year he was haunted with a desire to disfigure a certain young woman, so that no one would marry her. He did not love her himself, and did not want to marry her, but he did not want anybody else to do it. He would not go anywhere with her, and yet was opposed to anybody else's escorting her. Upon one occasion he declined to go to a wedding with her, and when she got other company, lay in wait for the couple by the road, intending to make them go back or kill the escort. After spending sleepless nights over his ruling desire for a full year, he at last attempted its execution — that is, attempted to disfigure the young woman. It was a success. It was permanent. In trying to shoot her cheek (as she sat at the supper table with her parents and brothers and sisters) in such a manner as to mar its comeliness, one of his bullets wandered a little out of the course, and she dropped dead. To the very last moment of his life he bewailed the ill luck that made her move her face just at the critical moment. And so he died, apparently about half persuaded that somehow it was chiefly her own fault that she got killed. This idiot was hanged. The plea of insanity was not offered.

Insanity certainly is on the increase in the world, and crime is dying out. There are no longer any murders — none worth mentioning, at any rate. Formerly, if you killed a man, it was possible that you were insane — but now, if you, having friends and money, kill a man, it is *evidence* that you are a lunatic. In these days, too, if a person of good family and high social standing steals anything, they call it *kleptomania*, and send him to the lunatic asylum. If a person of high standing squanders his fortune in dissipation, and closes his career with strychnine or a bullet, " Temporary Aberration " is what was the trouble with *him*.

Is not this insanity plea becoming rather common? Is it not so common that the reader confidently expects to see it offered in every criminal case that comes before the courts? And is it not so cheap, and so common, and often so trivial, that the reader smiles in derision when the newspaper mentions it? And is it not curious to note how very often it wins acquittal for the prisoner? Of late years it does not seem possible for a man to so conduct himself, before killing another man, as not to be manifestly insane. If he talks about the stars, he is insane. If he appears nervous and uneasy an hour before the killing, he is insane. If he weeps over a great grief, his friends shake their heads, and fear that he is " not right." If, an hour after the murder, he seems ill at ease, preoccupied and excited, he is unquestionably insane.

Really, what we want now, is not laws against crime, but a law against *insanity*. There is where the true evil lies.

A CURIOUS DREAM*

CONTAINING A MORAL

NIGHT before last I had a singular dream. I seemed to be sitting on a doorstep (in no particular city perhaps) ruminating, and the time of night appeared to be about twelve or one o'clock. The weather was balmy and delicious. There was no human sound in the air, not even a footstep. There was no sound of any kind to emphasize the dead stillness, except the occasional hollow barking of a dog in the distance and the fainter answer of a further dog. Presently up the street I heard a bony clack-clacking, and guessed it was the castanets of a serenading party. In a minute more a tall skeleton, hooded, and half-clad in a tattered and mouldy shroud, whose shreds were flapping about the ribby lattice-work of its person swung by me with a stately stride, and disappeared in the gray gloom of the starlight. It had a broken and worm-eaten coffin on its shoulder and a bundle of something in its hand. I knew what the clack-clacking was then; it was this party's joints working together, and his elbows

---

* Written about 1870.

knocking against his sides as he walked. I may say
I was surprised. Before I could collect my thoughts
and enter upon any speculations as to what this ap-
parition might portend, I heard another one coming
— for I recognized his clack-clack. He had two-
thirds of a coffin on his shoulder, and some foot
and head-boards under his arm. I mightily wanted
to peer under his hood and speak to him, but when
he turned and smiled upon me with his cavernous
sockets and his projecting grin as he went by, I
thought I would not detain him. He was hardly
gone when I heard the clacking again, and another
one issued from the shadowy half-light. This one
was bending under a heavy gravestone, and dragging
a shabby coffin after him by a string. When he got
to me he gave me a steady look for a moment or
two, and then rounded to and backed up to me,
saying:

" Ease this down for a fellow, will you?"

I eased the gravestone down till it rested on the
ground, and in doing so noticed that it bore the
name of " John Baxter Copmanhurst," with " May,
1839," as the date of his death. Deceased sat
wearily down by me, and wiped his os frontis with
his major maxillary — chiefly from former habit I
judged, for I could not see that he brought away
any perspiration.

" It is too bad, too bad," said he, drawing the
remnant of the shroud about him and leaning his
jaw pensively on his hand. Then he put his left

foot up on his knee and fell to scratching his ankle bone absently with a rusty nail which he got out of his coffin.

" What is too bad, friend?"

" Oh, everything, everything. I almost wish I never had died."

" You surprise me. Why do you say this? Has anything gone wrong? What is the matter?"

" Matter! Look at this shroud — rags. Look at this gravestone, all battered up. Look at that disgraceful old coffin. All a man's property going to ruin and destruction before his eyes, and ask him if anything is wrong? Fire and brimstone!"

" Calm yourself, calm yourself," I said. " It *is* too bad — it is certainly too bad, but then I had not supposed that you would much mind such matters, situated as you are."

" Well, my dear sir, I *do* mind them. My pride is hurt, and my comfort is impaired — destroyed, I might say. I will state my case — I will put it to you in such a way that you can comprehend it, if you will let me," said the poor skeleton, tilting the hood of his shroud back, as if he were clearing for action, and thus unconsciously giving himself a jaunty and festive air very much at variance with the grave character of his position in life — so to speak — and in prominent contrast with his distressful mood.

" Proceed," said I.

" I reside in the shameful old graveyard a block

17S

or two above you here, in this street — there, now,
I just expected that cartilage would let go! — third
rib from the bottom, friend, hitch the end of it to
my spine with a string, if you have got such a thing
about you, though a bit of silver wire is a deal
pleasanter, and more durable and becoming, if one
keeps it polished — to think of shredding out and
going to pieces in this way, just on account of the
indifference and neglect of one's posterity!"— and
the poor ghost grated his teeth in a way that gave
me a wrench and a shiver — for the effect is mightily
increased by the absence of muffling flesh and
cuticle. "I reside in that old graveyard, and have
for these thirty years; and I tell you things are
changed since I first laid this old tired frame there,
and turned over, and stretched out for a long sleep,
with a delicious sense upon me of being *done* with
bother, and grief, and anxiety, and doubt, and fear,
forever and ever, and listening with comfortable and
increasing satisfaction to the sexton's work, from
the startling clatter of his first spadeful on my coffin
till it dulled away to the faint patting that shaped
the roof of my new home — delicious! My! I wish
you could try it to-night!" and out of my reverie
deceased fetched me with a rattling slap with a bony
hand.

"Yes, sir, thirty years ago I laid me down there,
and was happy. For it was out in the country then
— out in the breezy, flowery, grand old woods, and
the lazy winds gossiped with the leaves, and the

squirrels capered over us and around us, and the creeping things visited us, and the birds filled the tranquil solitude with music. Ah, it was worth ten years of a man's life to be dead then! Everything was pleasant. I was in a good neighborhood, for all the dead people that lived near me belonged to the best families in the city. Our posterity appeared to think the world of us. They kept our graves in the very best condition; the fences were always in faultless repair, head-boards were kept painted or whitewashed, and were replaced with new ones as soon as they began to look rusty or decayed; monu- ments were kept upright, railings intact and bright, the rosebushes and shrubbery trimmed, trained, and free from blemish, the walks clean and smooth and graveled. But that day is gone by. Our descend- ants have forgotten us. My grandson lives in a stately house built with money made by these old hands of mine, and I sleep in a neglected grave with invading vermin that gnaw my shroud to build them nests withal! I and friends that lie with me founded and secured the prosperity of this fine city, and the stately bantling of our loves leaves us to rot in a dilapidated cemetery which neighbors curse and strangers scoff at. See the difference between the old time and this — for instance: Our graves are all caved in now; our head-boards have rotted away and tumbled down; our railings reel this way and that, with one foot in the air, after a fashion of un- seemly levity; our monuments lean wearily, and our

gravestones bow their heads discouraged; there be
no adornments any more — no roses, nor shrubs,
nor graveled walks, nor anything that is a comfort
to the eye; and even the paintless old board fence
that did make a show of holding us sacred from companionship with beasts and the defilement of heedless feet, has tottered till it overhangs the street, and
only advertises the presence of our dismal resting-
place and invites yet more derision to it.   And now
we cannot hide our poverty and tatters in the
friendly woods, for the city has stretched its withering arms abroad and taken us in, and all that remains of the cheer of our old home is the cluster of
lugubrious forest trees that stand, bored and weary
of a city life, with their feet in our coffins, looking
into the hazy distance and wishing they were there.
I tell you it is disgraceful!

"You begin to comprehend — you begin to see
how it is.   While our descendants are living sumptuously on our money, right around us in the city, we
have to fight hard to keep skull and bones together.
Bless you, there isn't a grave in our cemetery that
doesn't leak — not one.   Every time it rains in the
night we have to climb out and roost in the trees —
and sometimes we are wakened suddenly by the
chilly water trickling down the back of our necks.
Then I tell you there is a general heaving up of old
graves and kicking over of old monuments, and
scampering of old skeletons for the trees!   Bless
me, if you had gone along there some such nights

after twelve you might have seen as many as fifteen of us roosting on one limb, with our joints rattling drearily and the wind wheezing through our ribs! Many a time we have perched there for three or four dreary hours, and then come down, stiff and chilled through and drowsy, and borrowed each other's skulls to bale out our graves with — if you will glance up in my mouth now as I tilt my head back, you can see that my head-piece is half full of old dry sediment — how top-heavy and stupid it makes me sometimes! Yes, sir, many a time if you had happened to come along just before the dawn you'd have caught us baling out the graves and hanging our shrouds on the fence to dry. Why, I had an elegant shroud stolen from there one morning — think a party by the name of Smith took it, that resides in a plebeian graveyard over yonder — I think so because the first time I ever saw him he hadn't anything on but a check-shirt, and the last time I saw him, which was at a social gathering in the new cemetery, he was the best dressed corpse in the company — and it is a significant fact that he left when he saw me; and presently an old woman from here missed her coffin — she generally took it with her when she went anywhere, because she was liable to take cold and bring on the spasmodic rheumatism that originally killed her if she exposed herself to the night air much. She was named Hotchkiss — Anna Matilda Hotchkiss — you might know her? She has two upper front teeth, is tall, but a

17

good deal inclined to stoop, one rib on the left side
gone, has one shred of rusty hair hanging from the
left side of her head, and one little tuft just above
and a little forward of her right ear, has her under
jaw wired on one side where it had worked loose,
small bone of left forearm gone — lost in a fight —
has a kind of swagger in her gait and a ' gallus ' way
of going with her arms akimbo and her nostrils in
the air — has been pretty free and easy, and is all
damaged and battered up till she looks like a queens-
ware crate in ruins — maybe you have met her?''

" God forbid!'' I involuntarily ejaculated, for
somehow I was not looking for that form of question, and it caught me a little off my guard. But I
hastened to make amends for my rudeness, and say,
' I simply meant I had not had the honor — for I
would not deliberately speak discourteously of a
friend of yours. You were saying that you were
robbed — and it was a shame, too — but it appears
by what is left of the shroud you have on that it was
a costly one in its day. How did —.''

A most ghastly expression began to develop
among the decayed features and shriveled integu-
ments of my guest's face, and I was beginning to
grow uneasy and distressed, when he told me he was
only working up a deep, sly smile, with a wink in it,
to suggest that about the time he acquired his
present garment a ghost in a neighboring cemetery
missed one. This reassured me, but I begged him
to confine himself to speech thenceforth, because

his facial expression was uncertain. Even with the most elaborate care it was liable to miss fire. Smiling should especially be avoided. What *he* might honestly consider a shining success was likely to strike me in a very different light. I said I liked to see a skeleton cheerful, even decorously playful, but I did not think smiling was a skeleton's best hold.

"Yes, friend," said the poor skeleton, "the facts are just as I have given them to you. Two of these old graveyards — the one that I resided in and one further along — have been deliberately neglected by our descendants of to-day until there is no occupying them any longer. Aside from the osteological discomfort of it — and that is no light matter this rainy weather — the present state of things is ruinous to property. We have got to move or be content to see our effects wasted away and utterly destroyed. Now, you will hardly believe it, but it is true, nevertheless, that there isn't a single coffin in good repair among all my acquaintance — now that is an absolute fact. I do not refer to low people who come in a pine box mounted on an express wagon, but I am talking about your high-toned, silver mounted burial-case, your monumental sort, that travel under black plumes at the head of a procession and have choice of cemetery lots — I mean folks like the Jarvises, and the Bledsoes and Burlings, and such. They are all about ruined. The most substantial people in our set, they were. And now look at them —

9

utterly used up and poverty-stricken. One of the Bledsoes actually traded his monument to a late barkeeper for some fresh shavings to put under his head. I tell you it speaks volumes, for there is nothing a corpse takes so much pride in as his monument. He loves to read the inscription. He comes after awhile to believe what it says himself, and then you may see him sitting on the fence night after night enjoying it. Epitaphs are cheap, and they do a poor chap a world of good after he is dead, especially if he had hard luck while he was alive. I wish they were used more. Now I don't complain, but confidentially I *do* think it was a little shabby in my descendants to give me nothing but this old slab of a gravestone — and all the more that there isn't a compliment on it. It used to have

GONE TO HIS JUST REWARD '

on it, and I was proud when I first saw it, but by and by I noticed that whenever an old friend of mine came along he would hook his chin on the railing and pull a long face and read along down till he came to that, and then he would chuckle to himself and walk off, looking satisfied and comfortable. So I scratched it off to get rid of those fools. But a dead man always takes a deal of pride in his monument. Yonder goes half-a-dozen of the Jarvises now, with the family monument along. And Smithers and some hired specters went by with his a while ago. Hello, Higgins, good-bye, old friend! That's

Meredith Higgins — died in '44 — belongs to our set in the cemetery — fine old family — great-grandmother was an Injun — I am on the most familiar terms with him — he didn't hear me was the reason he didn't answer me. And I am sorry, too, because I would have liked to introduce you. You would admire him. He is the most disjointed, swaybacked, and generally distorted old skeleton you ever saw, but he is full of fun. When he laughs it sounds like rasping two stones together, and he always starts it off with a cheery screech like raking a nail across a window-pane. Hey, Jones! That is old Columbus Jones — shroud cost four hundred dollars — entire trousseau, including monument, twenty-seven hundred. This was in the spring of '26. It was enormous style for those days. Dead people came all the way from the Alleghanies to see his things — the party that occupied the grave next to mine remembers it well. Now do you see that individual going along with a piece of a head-board under his arm, one leg-bone below his knee gone, and not a thing in the world on? That is Barstow Dalhousie, and next to Columbus Jones he was the most sumptuously outfitted person that ever entered our cemetery. We are all leaving. We cannot tolerate the treatment we are receiving at the hands of our descendants. They open new cemeteries, but they leave us to our ignominy. They mend the streets, but they never mend anything that is about us or belongs to us. Look at that coffin of mine —

yet I tell you in its day it was a piece of furniture that would have attracted attention in any drawing-room in this city. You may have it if you want it — I can't afford to repair it. Put a new bottom in her, and part of a new top, and a bit of fresh lining along the left side, and you'll find her about as comfortable as any receptacle of her species you ever tried. No thanks — no, don't mention it — you have been civil to me, and I would give you all the property I have got before I would seem ungrateful. Now this winding-sheet is a kind of a sweet thing in its way, if you would like to ——. No? Well, just as you say, but I wished to be fair and liberal — there's nothing mean about *me*. Good-bye, friend, I must be going. I may have a good way to go to-night — don't know. I only know one thing for certain, and that is, that I am on the emigrant trail now, and I'll never sleep in that crazy old cemetery again. I will travel till I find respectable quarters, if I have to hoof it to New Jersey. All the boys are going. It was decided in public conclave, last night, to emigrate, and by the time the sun rises there won't be a bone left in our old habitations. Such cemeteries may suit my surviving friends, but they do not suit the remains that have the honor to make these remarks. My opinion is the general opinion. If you doubt it, go and see how the departing ghosts upset things before they started. They were almost riotous in their demonstrations of distaste. Hello, here are some of the

Bledsoes, and if you will give me a lift with this tombstone I guess I will join company and jog along with them — mighty respectable old family, the Bledsoes, and used to always come out in six-horse hearses, and all that sort of thing fifty years ago when I walked these streets in daylight. Good-bye, friend.''

And with his gravestone on his shoulder he joined the grisly procession, dragging his damaged coffin after him, for notwithstanding he pressed it upon me so earnestly, I utterly refused his hospitality. I suppose that for as much as two hours these sad outcasts went clacking by, laden with their dismal effects, and all that time I sat pitying them. One or two of the youngest and least dilapidated among them inquired about midnight trains on the railways, but the rest seemed unacquainted with that mode of travel, and merely asked about common public roads to various towns and cities, some of which are not on the map now, and vanished from it and from the earth as much as thirty years ago, and some few of them never *had* existed anywhere but on maps, and private ones in real estate agencies at that. And they asked about the condition of the cemeteries in these towns and cities, and about the reputation the citizens bore as to reverence for the dead.

This whole matter interested me deeply, and likewise compelled my sympathy for these homeless ones. And it all seeming real, and I not knowing it was a dream, I mentioned to one shrouded wanderer an idea that had entered my head to publish an account of this curious and very sorrowful exodus, but said also that I could not describe it truthfully, and just as it occurred, without seeming to trifle with a grave subject and exhibit an irreverence for the dead that would shock and distress their surviving friends. But this bland and stately remnant of a former citizen leaned him far over my gate and whispered in my ear, and said.

" Do not let that disturb you. The community that can stand such graveyards as those we are emigrating from can stand anything a body can say about the neglected and forsaken dead that lie in them."

At that very moment a cock crowed, and the weird procession vanished and left not a shred or a bone behind. I awoke, and found myself lying with my head out of the bed and " sagging " downwards considerably — a position favorable to dreaming dreams with morals in them, maybe, but not poetry.

NOTE.—The reader is assured that if the cemeteries in his town are kept in good order, this Dream is not leveled at his town at all, but is leveled particularly and venomously at the *next* town.

A TRUE STORY*

IT was summer time, and twilight. We were sitting on the porch of the farmhouse, on the summit of the hill, and " Aunt Rachel " was sitting respectfully below our level, on the steps — for she was our servant, and colored. She was of mighty frame and stature; she was sixty years old, but her eye was undimmed and her strength unabated. She was a cheerful, hearty soul, and it was no more trouble for her to laugh than it is for a bird to sing. She was under fire now, as usual when the day was done. That is to say, she was being chaffed without mercy, and was enjoying it. She would let off peal after peal of laughter, and then sit with her face in her hands and shake with throes of enjoyment which she could no longer get breath enough to express. At such a moment as this a thought occurred to me, and I said:

" Aunt Rachel, how is it that you've lived sixty years and never had any trouble?"

She stopped quaking. She paused, and there was

---

* Written about 1876.

a moment of silence.   She turned her face over her
shoulder toward me, and said, without even a smile
in her voice :

" Misto C——, is you in 'arnest?"

It surprised me a good deal; and it sobered my
manner and my speech, too.   I said :

" Why, I thought — that is, I meant — why, you
can't have had any trouble.   I've never heard you
sigh, and never seen your eye when there wasn't a
laugh in it."

She faced fairly around now, and was full of
earnestness.

" Has I had any trouble?   Misto C——, I's
gwyne to tell you, den I leave it to you.   I was bawn
down 'mongst de slaves; I knows all 'bout slavery,
'case I ben one of 'em my own se'f.   Well, sah,
my ole man — dat's my husban'— he was lovin'
an' kind to me, jist as kind as you is to yo' own
wife.   An' we had chil'en — seven chil'en — an'
we loved dem chil'en jist de same as you loves yo'
chil'en.   Dey was black, but de Lord can't make no
chil'en so black but what dey mother loves 'em an'
wouldn't give 'em up, no, not for anything dat's in
dis whole world.

" Well, sah, I was raised in ole Fo'ginny, but my
mother she was raised in Maryland; an' my *souls !*
she was turrible when she'd git started!   My *lan' !*
but she'd make de fur fly!   When she'd git into
dem tantrums, she always had one word dat she
said.   She'd straighten herse'f up an' put her fists

in her hips an' say, ' I want you to understan' dat I
wa'nt bawn in the mash to be fool' by trash! I's
one o' de ole Blue Hen's Chickens, *I* is!' 'Ca'se,
you see, dat's what folks dat's bawn in Maryland
calls deyselves, an' dey's proud of it. Well, dat
was her word. I don't ever forgit it, beca'se she
said it so much, an' beca'se she said it one day
when my little Henry tore his wris' awful, and most
busted his head, right up at de top of his forehead,
an' de niggers didn't fly aroun' fas' enough to 'tend
to him. An' when dey talk' back at her, she up
an' she says, ' Look-a-heah!' she says, ' I want you
niggers to understan' dat I wa'nt bawn in de mash
to be fool' by trash! I's one o' de ole Blue Hen's
Chickens, *I* is!' an' den she clar' dat kitchen an'
bandage' up de chile herse'f. So I says dat word,
too, when I's riled.

"Well, bymeby my ole mistis say she's broke,
an' she got to sell all de niggers on de place.
An' when I heah dat dey gwyne to sell us all off at
oction in Richmon', oh, de good gracious! I know
what dat mean!"

Aunt Rachel had gradually risen, while she
warmed to her subject, and now she towered above
us, black against the stars.

"Dey put chains on us an' put us on a stan' as
high as dis po'ch — twenty foot high — an' all de
people stood aroun', crowds an' crowds. An' dey'd
come up dah an' look at us all roun', an' squeeze
our arm, an' make us git up an' walk, an' den say

' Dis one too ole,' or ' Dis one lame,' or ' Dis one don't 'mount to much.' An' dey sole my ole man, an' took him away, an' dey begin to sell my chil'en an' take *dem* away, an' I begin to cry; an' de man say, ' Shet up yo' dam blubberin',' an' hit me on de mouf wid his han'. An' when de las' one was gone but my little Henry, I grab' *him* clost up to my breas' so, an' I ris up an' says, ' You shan't take him away,' I says; ' I'll kill de man dat tetches him!' I says. But my little Henry whisper an' say, ' I gwyne to run away, an' den I work an' buy yo' freedom.' Oh, bless de chile, he always so good! But dey got him — dey got him, de men did; but I took and tear de clo'es mos' off of 'em an' beat 'em over de head wid my chain; an' *dey* give it to *me*, too, but I didn't mine dat.

" Well, dah was my ole man gone, an' all my chil'en, all my seven chil'en — an' six of 'em I hain't set eyes on ag'in to dis day, an' dat's twenty-two year ago las' Easter. De man dat bought me b'long' in Newbern, an' he took me dah. Well, bymeby de years roll on an' de waw come. My marster he was a Confedrit colonel, an' I was his family's cook. So when de Unions took dat town, dey all run away an' lef' me all by myse'f wid de other niggers in dat mons'us big house. So de big Union officers move in dah, an' dey ask me would I cook for *dem*. ' Lord bless you,' says I, ' dat's what I's *for*.'

" Dey wa'nt no small-fry officers, mine you, dey

was de biggest dey *is ;* an' de way dey made dem
sojers mosey roun'! De Gen'l he tole me to boss
dat kitchen; an' he say, ' If anybody come meddlin'
wid you, you jist make 'em walk chalk; don't you
be afeared,' he say; ' you's 'mong frens now.'

"Well, I thinks to myse'f, if my little Henry
ever got a chance to run away, he'd make to de
Norf, o' course. So one day I comes in dah whar
de big officers was, in de parlor, an' I drops a
kurtchy, so, an' I up an' tole 'em 'bout my Henry,
dey a-listenin' to my troubles jist de same as if I
was white folks; an' I says, ' What I come for is
beca'se if he got away and got up Norf whar you
gemmen comes from, you might 'a' seen him,
maybe, an' could tell me so as I could fine him
ag'in; he was very little, an' he had a sk-yar on his
lef' wris' an' at de top of his forehead.' Den dey
look mournful, an' de Gen'l says, ' How long sence
you los' him?' an' I say, ' Thirteen year.' Den de
Gen'l say, ' He wouldn't be little no mo' now — he's
a man!'

" I never thought o' dat befo'! He was only
dat little feller to *me* yit. I never thought 'bout
him growin' up an' bein' big. But I see it den.
None o' de gemmen had run acrost him, so dey
couldn't do nothin' for me. But all dat time, do' *I*
didn't know it, my Henry *was* run off to de Norf,
years an' years, an' he was a barber, too, an'
worked for hisse'f. An' bymeby, when de waw
come he ups an' he says: ' I's done barberin',' he

says, 'I's gwyne to fine my ole mammy, less'n she's
dead.' So he sole out an' went to whar dey was
recruitin', an' hired hisse'f out to de colonel for his
servant; an' den he went all froo de battles every-
whah, huntin' for his ole mammy; yes, indeedy,
he'd hire to fust one officer an' den another, tell
he'd ransacked de whole Souf; but you see *I* didn't
know nuffin 'bout *dis*. How was *I* gwyne to know
it?

"Well, one night we had a big sojer ball; de
sojers dah at Newbern was always havin' balls an'
carryin' on. Dey had 'em in my kitchen, heaps o'
times, 'ca'se it was so big. Mine you, I was *down*
on sich doin's; beca'se my place was wid de officers,
an' it rasp me to have dem common sojers cavortin'
roun' my kitchen like dat. But I alway' stood
aroun' an' kep' things straight, I did; an' sometimes dey'd git my dander up, an' den I'd make
'em clar dat kitchen, mine I *tell* you!

"Well, one night—it was a Friday night—dey
comes a whole plattoon f'm a *nigger* ridgment dat
was on guard at de house—de house was head-
quarters, you know—an' den I was jist a-*bilin'*!
Mad? I was jist a-*boomin'*! I swelled aroun', an'
swelled aroun'; I jist was a-itchin' for 'em to do
somefin for to start me. An' dey was a-waltzin' an'
a-dancin'! *my!* but dey was havin' a time! an' I
jist a-swellin' an' a-swellin' up! Pooty soon, 'long
comes *sich* a spruce young nigger a-sailin' down de
room wid a yaller wench roun' de wais'; an' roun'

an' roun' an roun' dey went, enough to make a body
drunk to look at 'em; an' when dey got abreas' o'
me, dey went to kin' o' balacin' aroun' fust on one
leg an' den on t'other, an' smilin' at my big red
turban, an' makin' fun, an' I ups an' says ' *Git*
along wid you! — rubbage!' De young man's face
kin' o' changed, all of a sudden, for 'bout a second,
but den he went to smilin' ag'in, same as he was
befo'. Well, 'bout dis time, in comes some niggers
dat played music and b'long' to de ban', an' dey
never could git along widout puttin' on airs. An'
de very fust air dey put on dat night, I lit into 'em!
Dey laughed, an' dat made me wuss. De res' o'
de niggers got to laughin', an' den my soul *alive*
but I was hot! My eye was jist a-blazin'! I jist
straightened myself up so — jist as I is now, plum
to de ceilin', mos' — an' I digs my fists into my
hips, an' I says, ' Look-a-heah!' I says, ' I want
you niggers to understan' dat I wa'nt bawn in de
mash to be fool' by trash! I's one o' de ole Blue
Hen's Chickens, *I* is!' an' den I see dat young
man stan' a-starin' an' stiff, lookin' kin' o' up at de
ceilin' like he fo'got somefin, an' couldn't 'member
it no mo'. Well, I jist march' on dem niggers —
so, lookin' like a gen'l — an' dey jist cave' away
befo' me an' out at de do'. An' as dis young man
was a-goin' out, I heah him say to another nigger,
' Jim,' he says, ' you go 'long an' tell de cap'n I be
on han' 'bout eight o'clock in de mawnin'; dey's
somefin on my mine,' he says; ' I don't sleep no

mo' dis night. You go 'long,' he says, ' an' leave me by my own se'f.'

" Dis was 'bout one o'clock in de mawnin'. Well, 'bout seven, I was up an' on han', gittin' de officers' breakfast. I was a-stoopin' down by de stove — jist so, same as if yo' foot was de stove — an' I'd opened de stove do' wid my right han'— so, pushin' it back, jist as I pushes yo' foot — an' I'd jist got de pan o' hot biscuits in my han' an' was 'bout to raise up, when I see a black face come aroun' under mine, an' de eyes a-lookin' up into mine, jist as I's a-lookin' up clost under yo' face now; an' I jist stopped *right dah*, an' never budged ! jist gazed an' gazed so; an' de pan begin to tremble, an' all of a sudden I *knowed !* De pan drop' on de flo' an' I grab his lef' han' an' shove back his sleeve — jist so, as I's doin' to you — an' den I goes for his forehead an' push de hair back so, an' ' Boy !' I says, ' if you an't my Henry, what is you doin' wid dis welt on yo' wris' an' dat sk-yar on yo' forehead? De Lord God ob heaven be praise', I got my own ag'in !'

" Oh, no Misto C——, *I* hain't had no trouble. An' no *joy !*"

THE SIAMESE TWINS*

I DO not wish to write of the personal *habits* of these strange creatures solely, but also of certain curious details of various kinds concerning them, which, belonging only to their private life, have never crept into print. Knowing the Twins intimately, I feel that I am peculiarly well qualified for the task I have taken upon myself.

The Siamese Twins are naturally tender and affectionate in disposition, and have clung to each other with singular fidelity throughout a long and eventful life. Even as children they were inseparable companions; and it was noticed that they always seemed to prefer each other's society to that of any other persons. They nearly always played together; and, so accustomed was their mother to this peculiarity, that, whenever both of them chanced to be lost, she usually only hunted for one of them — satisfied that when she found that one she would find his brother somewhere in the immediate neighborhood. And yet these creatures were ignorant and unlettered — barbarians themselves and the offspring of barba-

* Written about 1868.

rians, who knew not the light of philosophy and science. What a withering rebuke is this to our boasted civilization, with its quarrelings, its wranglings, and its separations of brothers!

As men, the Twins have not always lived in perfect accord; but still there has always been a bond between them which made them unwilling to go away from each other and dwell apart. They have even occupied the same house, as a general thing, and it is believed that they have never failed to even sleep together on any night since they were born. How surely do the habits of a lifetime become second nature to us! The Twins always go to bed at the same time; but Chang usually gets up about an hour before his brother. By an understanding between themselves, Chang does all the indoor work and Eng runs all the errands. This is because Eng likes to go out; Chang's habits are sedentary. However, Chang always goes along. Eng is a Baptist, but Chang is a Roman Catholic; still, to please his brother, Chang consented to be baptized at the same time that Eng was, on condition that it should not " count." During the war they were strong partizans, and both fought gallantly all through the great struggle — Eng on the Union side and Chang on the Confederate. They took each other prisoners at Seven Oaks, but the proofs of capture were so evenly balanced in favor of each, that a general army court had to be assembled to determine which one was properly the captor, and which the captive. The jury was unable to agree for a long time; but the vexed question was finally decided by agreeing to consider them both prisoners, and then exchanging them. At one time Chang was convicted of disobedience of orders, and sentenced to ten days in the guardhouse, but Eng, in spite of all arguments, felt obliged to share his imprisonment, notwithstanding he himself was entirely innocent; and so, to save the blameless brother from suffering, they had to discharge both from custody — the just reward of faithfulness.

Upon one occasion the brothers fell out about something, and Chang knocked Eng down, and then tripped and fell on him, whereupon both clinched and began to beat and gouge each other without mercy. The bystanders interfered, and tried to separate them, but they could not do it, and so allowed them to fight it out. In the end both were disabled, and were carried to the hospital on one and the same shutter.

Their ancient habit of going always together had its drawbacks when they reached man's estate, and entered upon the luxury of courting. Both fell in love with the same girl. Each tried to steal clandestine interviews with her, but at the critical moment the other would always turn up. By and by Eng saw, with distraction, that Chang had won the girl's affections; and, from that day forth, he had to bear with the agony of being a witness to all their dainty billing and cooing. But with a magnanimity that

B

did him infinite credit, he succumbed to his fate, and gave countenance and encouragement to a state of things that bade fair to sunder his generous heart-strings. He sat from seven every evening until two in the morning, listening to the fond foolishness of the two lovers, and to the concussion of hundreds of squandered kisses — for the privilege of sharing only one of which he would have given his right hand. But he sat patiently, and waited, and gaped, and yawned, and stretched, and longed for two o'clock to come. And he took long walks with the lovers on moonlight evenings — sometimes traversing ten miles, notwithstanding he was usually suffering from rheumatism. He is an inveterate smoker; but he could not smoke on these occasions, because the young lady was painfully sensitive to the smell of tobacco. Eng cordially wanted them married, and done with it; but although Chang often asked the momentous question, the young lady could not gather sufficient courage to answer it while Eng was by. However, on one occasion, after having walked some sixteen miles, and sat up till nearly daylight, Eng dropped asleep, from sheer exhaustion, and then the question was asked and answered. The lovers were married. All acquainted with the circumstance applauded the noble brother-in-law. His unwavering faithfulness was the theme of every tongue. He had stayed by them all through their long and arduous courtship; and when at last they were married, he lifted his hands above their

heads, and said with impressive unction, " Bless ye,
my children, I will never desert ye !" and he kept
his word. Fidelity like this is all too rare in this
cold world.

By and by Eng fell in love with his sister-in-law's
sister, and married her, and since that day they have
all lived together, night and day, in an exceeding
sociability which is touching and beautiful to behold,
and is a scathing rebuke to our boasted civilization.

The sympathy existing between these two brothers
is so close and so refined that the feelings, the impulses, the emotions of the one are instantly experienced by the other. When one is sick, the other is
sick; when one feels pain, the other feels it; when
one is angered, the other's temper takes fire. We
have already seen with what happy facility they
both fell in love with the same girl. Now Chang is
bitterly opposed to all forms of intemperance, on
principle; but Eng is the reverse — for, while these
men's feelings and emotions are so closely wedded,
their reasoning faculties are unfettered; their *thoughts*
are free. Chang belongs to the Good Templars, and
is a hard working, enthusiastic supporter of all
temperance reforms. But, to his bitter distress,
every now and then Eng gets drunk, and, of course,
that makes Chang drunk too. This unfortunate
thing has been a great sorrow to Chang, for it
almost destroys his usefulness in his favorite field of
effort. As sure as he is to head a great temperance

procession Eng ranges up alongside of him, prompt
to the minute, and drunk as a lord; but yet no more
dismally and hopelessly drunk than his brother, who
has not tasted a drop. And so the two begin to
hoot and yell, and throw mud and bricks at the
Good Templars; and, of course, they break up the
procession. It would be manifestly wrong to punish
Chang for what Eng does, and, therefore, the Good
Templars accept the untoward situation, and suffer
in silence and sorrow. They have officially and
deliberately examined into the matter, and find
Chang blameless. They have taken the two brothers
and filled Chang full of warm water and sugar and
Eng full of whisky, and in twenty-five minutes it was
not possible to tell which was the drunkest. Both
were as drunk as loons — and on hot whisky
punches, by the smell of their breath. Yet all the
while Chang's moral principles were unsullied, his
conscience clear; and so all just men were forced to
confess that he was not morally, but only physically,
drunk. By every right and by every moral evidence
the man was strictly sober; and, therefore, it caused
his friends all the more anguish to see him shake
hands with the pump, and try to wind his watch
with his night-key.

There is a moral in these solemn warnings — or,
at least, a warning in these solemn morals; one or
the other. No matter, it is somehow. Let us heed
it; let us profit by it.

I could say more of an instructive nature about

these interesting beings, but let what I have written suffice.

Having forgotton to mention it sooner, I will remark in conclusion, that the ages of the Siamese Twins are respectively fifty-one and fifty-three years.

SPEECH AT THE SCOTTISH BANQUET IN LONDON*

AT the anniversary festival of the Scottish Corporation of London on Monday evening, in response to the toast of "The Ladies," MARK TWAIN replied. The following is his speech as reported in the London *Observer*:

"I am proud, indeed, of the distinction of being chosen to respond to this especial toast, to 'The Ladies,' or to women if you please, for that is the preferable term, perhaps; it is certainly the older, and therefore the more entitled to reverence. [Laughter.] I have noticed that the Bible, with that plain, blunt honesty which is such a conspicuous characteristic of the Scriptures, is always particular to never refer to even the illustrious mother of all mankind herself as a 'lady,' but speaks of her as a woman. [Laughter.] It is odd, but you will find it is so. I am peculiarly proud of this honor, because I think that the toast to women is one which, by right and by every rule of gallantry, should take precedence of all others — of the army, of the navy, of even royalty itself — perhaps, though the latter is not necessary in this day and in this land, for the reason that, tacitly, you do drink a broad general health to all good women when you drink the health of the Queen of England and the Princess of Wales. [Loud cheers.] I have in mind a poem just now which is familiar to you all, familiar to everybody. And what an inspiration that was (and how instantly the present toast recalls the verses to all our minds) when the most noble, the most gracious, the purest, and sweetest of all poets says:—

---

* Written about 1872.

> " ' Woman! O woman! —— er ——
>   Wom——'

[Laughter.] However, you remember the lines; and you remember how feelingly, how daintily, how almost imperceptibly the verses raise up before you, feature by feature, the ideal of a true and perfect woman; and how, as you contemplate the finished marvel, your homage grows into worship of the intellect that could create so fair a thing out of mere breath, mere words. And you call to mind now, as I speak, how the poet, with stern fidelity to the history of all humanity, delivers this beautiful child of his heart and his brain over to the trials and sorrows that must come to all, sooner or later, that abide in the earth, and how the pathetic story culminates in that apostrophe — so wild, so regretful, so full of mournful retrospection. The lines run thus: —

> " ' Alas! — alas! — a — alas!
>   — — Alas! — — — — alas!'

— and so on. [Laughter.] I do not remember the rest; but, taken together, it seems to me that poem is the noblest tribute to woman that human genius has ever brought forth — [laughter] — and I feel that if I were to talk hours I could not do my great theme completer or more graceful justice than I have now done in simply quoting that poet's matchless words. [Renewed laughter.] The phases of the womanly nature are infinite in their variety. Take any type of woman, and you shall find in it something to respect, something to admire, something to love. And you shall find the whole joining you heart and hand. Who was more patriotic than Joan of Arc? Who was braver? Who has given us a grander instance of self-sacrificing devotion? Ah! you remember, you remember well, what a throb of pain, what a great tidal wave of grief swept over us all when Joan of Arc fell at Waterloo. [Much laughter.] Who does not sorrow for the loss of Sappho, the sweet singer of Israel? [Laughter.] Who among us does not miss the gentle ministrations, the softening influences, the humble piety of Lucretia Borgia? [Laughter.] Who can join in the heartless libel that says woman is extravagant in dress when he can look back and call to mind our simple and lowly mother Eve arrayed in her modification of the Highland costume. [Roars of laughter.] Sir, women have been soldiers, women have been painters, women have been poets. As long as language lives the name of Cleopatra will live. And, not because she conquered George III—[laughter]—but because she wrote those divine lines:—

> " ' Let dogs delight to bark and bite,
>   For God hath made them so.'

[More laughter.] The story of the world is adorned with the names of illustrious ones of our own sex—some of them sons of St. Andrew, too—Scott, Bruce, Burns, the warrior Wallace, Ben Nevis—[laughter]—the gifted Ben Lomond, and the great new Scotchman, Ben Disraeli.* [Great laughter.] Out of the great plains of history tower whole mountain ranges of sublime women—the Queen of Sheba, Josephine, Semiramis, Sairey Gamp; the list is endless—[laughter]—but I will not call the mighty roll, the names rise up in your own memories at the mere suggestion, luminous with the glory of deeds that cannot die, hallowed by the loving worship of the good and the true of all epochs and all climes. [Cheers.] Suffice it for our pride and our honor that we in our day have added to it such names as those of Grace Darling and Florence Nightingale. [Cheers.] Woman is all that she should be—gentle, patient, long suffering, trustful, unselfish, full of generous impulses. It is her blessed mission to comfort the sorrowing, plead for the erring, encourage the faint of purpose, succor the distressed, uplift the fallen, befriend the friendless—in a word, afford the healing of her sympathies and a home in her heart for all the bruised and persecuted children of misfortune that knock at its hospitable door. [Cheers.] And when I say, God bless her, there is none among us who has known the ennobling affection of a wife, or the steadfast devotion of a mother but in his heart will say, Amen! [Loud and prolonged cheering.]

----

* Mr. Benjamin Disraeli, at that time Prime Minister of England, had just been elected Lord Rector of Glasgow University, and had made a speech which gave rise to a world of discussion.

A GHOST STORY

I TOOK a large room, far up Broadway, in a huge old building whose upper stories had been wholly unoccupied for years, until I came. The place had long been given up to dust and cobwebs, to solitude and silence. I seemed groping among the tombs and invading the privacy of the dead, that first night I climbed up to my quarters. For the first time in my life a superstitious dread came over me; and as I turned a dark angle of the stairway and an invisible cobweb swung its slazy woof in my face and clung there, I shuddered as one who had encountered a phantom.

I was glad enough when I reached my room and locked out the mould and the darkness. A cheery fire was burning in the grate, and I sat down before it with a comforting sense of relief. For two hours I sat there, thinking of bygone times; recalling old scenes, and summoning half-forgotten faces out of the mists of the past; listening, in fancy, to voices that long ago grew silent for all time, and to once familiar songs that nobody sings now. And as my reverie softened down to a sadder and sadder pathos, the shrieking of the winds outside softened to a wail, the angry beating of the rain against the panes diminished to a tranquil patter, and one by one the noises in the street subsided, until the hurrying footsteps of the last belated straggler died away in the distance and left no sound behind.

The fire had burned low. A sense of loneliness crept over me. I arose and undressed, moving on tiptoe about the room, doing stealthily what I had to do, as if I were environed by sleeping enemies whose slumbers it would be fatal to break. I covered up in bed, and lay listening to the rain and wind and the faint creaking of distant shutters, till they lulled me to sleep.

I slept profoundly, but how long I do not know. All at once I found myself awake, and filled with a shuddering expectancy. All was still. All but my own heart — I could hear it beat. Presently the bedclothes began to slip away slowly toward the foot of the bed, as if some one were pulling them! I could not stir; I could not speak. Still the blankets slipped deliberately away, till my breast was uncovered. Then with a great effort I seized them and drew them over my head. I waited, listened, waited. Once more that steady pull began, and once more I lay torpid a century of dragging seconds till my breast was naked again. At last I roused my energies and snatched the covers back to their place and held them with a strong grip. I waited. By and by I felt a faint tug, and took a fresh grip. The tug strengthened to a steady strain — it grew stronger and stronger. My hold parted, and for the third time the blankets slid away. I groaned. An answering groan came from the foot of the bed! Beaded drops of sweat stood upon my forehead. I was more dead than alive. Presently I heard a heavy footstep in my room — the step of an elephant, it seemed to me — it was not like anything human. But it was moving *from* me — there was relief in that. I heard it approach the door — pass out without moving bolt or lock — and wander away among the dismal corridors, straining the floors and joists till they creaked again as it passed — and then silence reigned once more.

When my excitement had calmed, I said to myself, " This is a dream — simply a hideous dream.'' And so I lay thinking it over until I convinced myself that it *was* a dream, and then a comforting laugh relaxed my lips and I was happy again. I got up and struck a light; and when I found that the locks and bolts were just as I had left them, another soothing laugh welled in my heart and rippled from my lips. I took my pipe and lit it, and was just sitting down before the fire, when — down went the pipe out of my nerveless fingers, the blood forsook my cheeks, and my placid breathing was cut short with a gasp! In the ashes on the hearth, side by side with my own bare footprint, was another, so vast that in comparison mine was but an infant's! Then I had *had* a visitor, and the elephant tread was explained.

I put out the light and returned to bed, palsied with fear. I lay a long time, peering into the darkness, and listening. Then I heard a grating noise overhead, like the dragging of a heavy body across the floor; then the throwing down of the body, and the shaking of my windows in response to the concussion. In distant parts of the building I heard the muffled slamming of doors. I heard, at intervals, stealthy footsteps creeping in and out among the corridors, and up and down the stairs. Sometimes these noises approached my door, hesitated, and went away again. I heard the clanking of chains faintly, in remote passages, and listened while the clanking grew nearer — while it wearily climbed the stairways, marking each move by the loose surplus of chain that fell with an accented rattle upon each succeeding step as the goblin that bore it advanced. I heard muttered sentences; half-uttered screams that seemed smothered violently; and the swish of invisible garments, the rush of invisible wings. Then I became conscious that my chamber was invaded — that I was not alone. I heard sighs and breathings about my bed, and mysterious whisperings. Three little spheres of soft phosphorescent light appeared on the ceiling directly over my head, clung and glowed there a moment, and then dropped — two of them upon my face and one upon the pillow. They spattered, liquidly, and felt warm. Intuition told me they had turned to gouts of blood as they fell — I needed no light to satisfy myself of that. Then I saw pallid faces, dimly luminous, and white uplifted hands, floating bodiless in the air — floating a moment and then disappearing. The whispering ceased, and the voices and the sounds, and a solemn stillness followed. I waited and listened. I felt that I must have light or die. I was weak with fear. I slowly raised myself toward a sitting posture, and my face came in contact with a clammy hand! All strength went from me apparently, and I fell back like a stricken invalid. Then I heard the rustle of a garment — it seemed to pass to the door and go out.

When everything was still once more, I crept out of bed, sick and feeble, and lit the gas with a hand that trembled as if it were aged with a hundred years. The light brought some little cheer to my spirits. I sat down and fell into a dreamy contemplation of that great footprint in the ashes. By and by its outlines began to waver and grow dim. I glanced up and the broad gas flame was slowly wilting away. In the same moment I heard that elephantine tread again. I noted its approach, nearer and nearer, along the musty halls, and dimmer and dimmer the light waned. The tread reached my very door and paused — the light had dwindled to a sickly blue, and all things about me lay in a spectral twilight. The door did not open, and yet I felt a faint gust of air fan my cheek, and presently was conscious of a huge, cloudy presence before me. I watched it with fascinated eyes. A pale glow stole over the Thing; gradually its cloudy folds took shape — an arm appeared, then legs, then a body, and last a great sad face looked out of the vapor. Stripped of its filmy housings, naked, muscular and comely, the majestic Cardiff Giant loomed above me!

All my misery vanished — for a child might know that no harm could come with that benignant countenance. My cheerful spirits returned at once, and in sympathy with them the gas flamed up brightly again. Never a lonely outcast was so glad to welcome company as I was to greet the friendly giant. I said:

"Why, is it nobody but you? Do you know, I have been scared to death for the last two or three hours? I am most honestly glad to see you. I wish I had a chair — Here, here, don't try to sit down in that thing!

But it was too late. He was in it before I could stop him, and down he went—I never saw a chair shivered so in my life.

"Stop, stop, you'll ruin ev —"

Too late again. There was another crash, and another chair was resolved into its original elements.

"Confound it, haven't you got any judgment at all? Do you want to ruin all the furniture on the place? Here, here, you petrified fool —"

But it was no use. Before I could arrest him he had sat down on the bed, and it was a melancholy ruin.

"Now what sort of a way is that to do? First

you come lumbering about the place bringing a legion of vagabond goblins along with you to worry me to death, and then when I overlook an indelicacy of costume which would not be tolerated anywhere by cultivated people except in a respectable theater, and not even there if the nudity were of *your* sex, you repay me by wrecking all the furniture you can find to sit down on. And why will you? You damage yourself as much as you do me. You have broken off the end of your spinal column, and littered up the floor with chips of your hams till the place looks like a marble yard. You ought to be ashamed of yourself — you are big enough to know better."

" Well, I will not break any more furniture. But what am I to do? I have not had a chance to sit down for a century." And the tears came into his eyes.

" Poor devil," I said, " I should not have been so harsh with you. And you are an orphan, too, no doubt. But sit down on the floor here — nothing else can stand your weight — and besides, we cannot be sociable with you away up there above me; I want you down where I can perch on this high counting-house stool and gossip with you face to face."

So he sat down on the floor, and lit a pipe which I gave him, threw one of my red blankets over his shoulders, inverted my sitz-bath on his head, helmet fashion, and made himself picturesque and comfort-

able. Then he crossed his ankles, while I renewed
the fire, and exposed the flat, honey-combed bottoms of his prodigious feet to the grateful warmth.

" What is the matter with the bottom of your feet
and the back of your legs, that they are gouged up
so?"

" Infernal chillblains — I caught them clear up to
the back of my head, roosting out there under
Newell's farm. But I love the place; I love it as
one loves his old home. There is no peace for me
like the peace I feel when I am there."

We talked along for half an hour, and then I
noticed that he looked tired, and spoke of it.

" Tired?" he said. " Well, I should think so.
And now I will tell you all about it, since you have
treated me so well. I am the spirit of the Petrified
Man that lies across the street there in the Museum.
I am the ghost of the Cardiff Giant. I can have no
rest, no peace, till they have given that poor body
burial again. Now what was the most natural thing
for me to do, to make men satisfy this wish?
Terrify them into it! — haunt the place where the
body lay! So I haunted the museum night after
night. I even got other spirits to help me. But it
did no good, for nobody ever came to the museum
at midnight. Then it occurred to me to come over
the way and haunt this place a little. I felt that if I
ever got a hearing I must succeed, for I had the
most efficient company that perdition could furnish.
Night after night we have shivered around through

these mildewed halls, dragging chains, groaning, whispering, tramping up and down stairs, till, to tell you the truth, I am almost worn out. But when I saw a light in your room to-night I roused my energies again and went at it with a deal of the old freshness. But I am tired out — entirely fagged out. Give me, I beseech you, give me some hope!"

I lit off my perch in a burst of excitement, and exclaimed:

"This transcends everything! everything that ever did occur! Why you poor blundering old fossil, you have had all your trouble for nothing —you have been haunting a *plaster cast* of yourself — the real Cardiff Giant is in Albany!* Confound it, don't you know your own remains?"

I never saw such an eloquent look of shame, of pitiable humiliation, overspread a countenance before.

The Petrified Man rose slowly to his feet, and said:

" Honestly, *is* that true?"

" As true as I am sitting here."

He took the pipe from his mouth and laid it on the mantel, then stood irresolute a moment (unconsciously, from old habit, thrusting his hands where

---

*A fact. The original fraud was ingeniously and fraudfully duplicated, and exhibited in New York as the "only genuine" Cardiff Giant (to the unspeakable disgust of the owners of the real colossus) at the very same time that the latter was drawing crowds at a museum in Albany.

his pantaloons pockets should have been, and meditatively dropping his chin on his breast), and finally said:

"Well — I *never* felt so absurd before. The Petrified Man has sold everybody else, and now the mean fraud has ended by selling its own ghost! My son, if there is any charity left in your heart for a poor friendless phantom iike me, don't let this get out. Think how *you* would feel if you had made such an ass of yourself."

I heard his stately tramp die away, step by step down the stairs and out into the deserted street, and felt sorry that he was gone, poor fellow — and sorrier still that he had carried off my red blanket and my bath tub.

THE CAPITOLINE VENUS

CHAPTER I.

[Scene — An Artist's Studio in Rome.]

"OH, George, I *do* love you!"

"Bless your dear heart, Mary, I know that — *why* is your father so obdurate?"

"George, he means well, but art is folly to him — he only understands groceries. He thinks you would starve me."

"Confound his wisdom — it savors of inspiration. Why am I not a money-making bowelless grocer, instead of a divinely-gifted sculptor with nothing to eat?"

"Do not despond, Georgy, dear — all his prejudices will fade away as soon as you shall have acquired fifty thousand dol —"

"Fifty thousand demons! Child, I am in arrears for my board!"

CHAPTER II.

[Scene — A Dwelling in Rome.]

"My dear sir, it is useless to talk. I haven't anything against you, but I can't let my daughter marry a hash of love, art, and starvation — I believe you have nothing else to offer."

"Sir, I am poor, I grant you. But is fame nothing? The Hon. Bellamy Foodle of Arkansas says that my new statue of America is a clever piece of sculpture, and he is satisfied that my name will one day be famous."

"Bosh! What does that Arkansas ass know about it? Fame's nothing — the market price of your marble scarecrow is the thing to look at. It took you six months to chisel it, and you can't sell it for a hundred dollars. No, sir! Show me fifty thousand dollars and you can have my daughter — otherwise she marries young Simper. You have just six months to raise the money in. Good morning, sir."

"Alas! Woe is me!"

CHAPTER III.

[Scene — The Studio.]

"Oh, John, friend of my boyhood, I am the unhappiest of men."

"You're a simpleton!"

"I have nothing left to love but my poor statue of America — and see, even she has no sympathy for me in her cold marble countenance — so beautiful and so heartless!"

"You're a dummy!"

"Oh, John!"

" Oh, fudge ! Didn't you say you had six months to raise the money in?"

" Don't deride my agony, John. If I had six centuries what good would it do? How could it help a poor wretch without name, capital, or friends?"

" Idiot! Coward! Baby! Six months to raise the money in — and five will do !"

" Are you insane?"

" Six months — an abundance. Leave it to me. I'll raise it."

" What do you mean, John? How on earth can you raise such a monstrous sum for *me* ?"

" *Will* you let that be *my* business, and not meddle? Will you leave the thing in my hands? Will you swear to submit to whatever I do? Will you pledge me to find no fault with my actions?"

" I am dizzy — bewildered — but I swear."

John took up a hammer and deliberately smashed the nose of America! He made another pass and two of her fingers fell to the floor — another, and part of an ear came away — another, and a row of toes was mangled and dismembered — another, and the left leg, from the knee down, lay a fragmentary ruin !

John put on his hat and departed.

George gazed speechless upon the battered and grotesque nightmare before him for the space of thirty seconds, and then wilted to the floor and went into convulsions.

John returned presently with a carriage, got the broken-hearted artist and the broken-legged statue aboard, and drove off, whistling low and tranquilly. He left the artist at his lodgings, and drove off and disappeared down the *Via Quirinalis* with the statue.

CHAPTER IV.

[Scene — The Studio.]

" The six months will be up at two o'clock to-day! Oh, agony! My life is blighted. I would that I were dead. I had no supper yesterday. I have had no breakfast to-day. I dare not enter an eating-house. And hungry? — don't mention it! My bootmaker duns me to death — my tailor duns me — my landlord haunts me. I am miserable. I haven't seen John since that awful day. *She* smiles on me tenderly when we meet in the great thorough-fares, but her old flint of a father makes her look in the other direction in short order. Now who is knocking at that door? Who is come to persecute me? That malignant villain the bootmaker, I'll warrant. *Come in !*"

" Ah, happiness attend your highness — heaven be propitious to your grace! I have brought my lord's new boots — ah, say nothing about the pay, there is no hurry, none in the world. Shall be proud if my noble lord will continue to honor me with his custom — ah, adieu !''

" Brought the boots himself! Don't want his pay! Takes his leave with a bow and a scrape fit to honor majesty withal! Desires a continuance of my custom! Is the world coming to an end? Of all the — *come in !* "

" Pardon, signor, but I have brought your new suit of clothes for —"

" *Come in ! !* "

" A thousand pardons for this intrusion, your worship! But I have prepared the beautiful suite of rooms below for you — this wretched den is but ill suited to —"

" *Come in ! ! !* "

" I have called to say that your credit at our bank, some time since unfortunately interrupted, is entirely and most satisfactorily restored, and we shall be most happy if you will draw upon us for any —"

" COME IN ! ! ! !"

" My noble boy, she is yours! She'll be here in a moment! Take her — marry her — love her — be happy! — God bless you both! Hip, hip, hur —"

" COME IN ! ! ! ! !"

" Oh, George, my own darling, we are saved!"

" Oh, Mary, my own darling, we *are* saved — but I'll swear I don't know why nor how!"

CHAPTER V.

[*Scene — A Roman Café.*]

One of a group of American gentlemen reads and translates from the weekly edition of *Il Slang-whanger di Roma* as follows:

"WONDERFUL DISCOVERY! — Some six months ago Signor John Smithe, an American gentleman now some years a resident of Rome, purchased for a trifle a small piece of ground in the Campagna, just beyond the tomb of the Scipio family, from the owner, a bankrupt relative of the Princess Borghese. Mr. Smithe afterwards went to the Minister of the Public Records and had the piece of ground transferred to a poor American artist named George Arnold, explaining that he did it as pay-ment and satisfaction for pecuniary damage accidentally done by him long since upon property belonging to Signor Arnold, and further observed that he would make additional satisfaction by improving the ground for Signor A., at his own charge and cost. Four weeks ago, while making some necessary excavations upon the property, Signor Smithe unearthed the most remarkable ancient statue that has ever been added to the opulent art treasures of Rome. It was an exquisite figure of a woman, and though sadly stained by the soil and the mould of ages, no eye can look unmoved upon its ravishing beauty. The nose, the left leg from the knee down, an ear, and also the toes of the right foot and two fingers of one of the hands, were gone, but otherwise the noble figure was in a remarkable state of preservation. The government at once took military possession of the statue, and appointed a commission of art critics, antiquaries, and cardinal princes of the church to assess its value and determine the remuneration that must go to the owner of the ground in which it was found. The whole affair was kept a profound secret until last night. In the meantime the commission sat with closed doors, and deliberated. Last night they decided unanimously that the statue is a Venus, and the work of some unknown but sublimely gifted artist of the third century before Christ. They consider it the most faultless work of art the world has any knowledge of.

"At midnight they held a final conference and decided that the Venus was worth the enormous sum of *ten million francs!* In accord-

ance with Roman law and Roman usage, the government being half
owner in all works of art found in the Campagna, the State has naught
to do but pay five million francs to Mr. Arnold and take permanent
possession of the beautiful statue. This morning the Venus will be
removed to the Capitol, there to remain, and at noon the commission
will wait upon Signor Arnold with His Holiness the Pope's order upon
the Treasury for the princely sum of five million francs in gold!"

Chorus of Voices.—"Luck! It's no name for it!"

Another Voice.—" Gentlemen, I propose that we
immediately form an American joint-stock company
for the purchase of lands and excavations of statues
here, with proper connections in Wall street to bull
and bear the stock."

All.—" Agreed."

CHAPTER VI.

[*Scene — The Roman Capitol Ten Years Later.*]

" Dearest Mary, this is the most celebrated statue
in the world. This is the renowed ' Capitoline
Venus ' you've heard so much about. Here she is
with her little blemishes ' restored ' (that is, patched)
by the most noted Roman artists — and the mere
fact that they did the humble patching of so noble a
creation will make their names illustrious while the
world stands. How strange it seems — this place!
The day before I last stood here, ten happy years
ago, I wasn't a rich man — bless your soul, I hadn't
a cent. And yet I had a good deal to do with
making Rome mistress of this grandest work of
ancient art the world contains."

" The worshiped, the illustrious Capitoline Venus — and what a sum she is valued at! Ten millions of francs!"

" Yes — *now* she is."

" And oh, Georgy, how divinely beautiful she is!"

" Ah, yes — but nothing to what she was before that blessed John Smith broke her leg and battered her nose. Ingenious Smith! — gifted Smith — noble Smith! Author of all our bliss! Hark! Do you know what that wheeze means? Mary, that cub has got the whooping cough. Will you *never* learn to take care of the children!"

THE END.

The Capitoline Venus is still in the Capitol at Rome, and is still the most charming and most illustrious work of ancient art the world can boast of. But if ever it shall be your fortune to stand before it and go into the customary ecstasies over it, don't permit this true and secret history of its origin to mar your bliss — and when you read about a gigantic Petrified Man being dug up near Syracuse, in the State of New York, or near any other place, keep your own counsel — and if the Barnum that buried him there offers to sell to you at an enormous sum, don't you buy. Send him to the Pope!"

Note.— The above sketch was written at the time the famous swindle of the " Petrified Giant " was the sensation of the day in the United States.

SPEECH ON ACCIDENT INSURANCE

DELIVERED IN HARTFORD, AT A DINNER TO CORNELIUS
WALFORD, OF LONDON

GENTLEMEN: I am glad, indeed, to assist in welcoming the distinguished guest of this occasion to a city whose fame as an insurance center has extended to all lands, and given us the name of being a quadruple band of brothers working sweetly hand in hand — the Colt's arms company making the destruction of our race easy and convenient, our life insurance citizens paying for the victims when they pass away, Mr. Batterson perpetuating their memory with his stately monuments, and our fire insurance comrades taking care of their hereafter. I am glad to assist in welcoming our guest — first, because he is an Englishman, and I owe a heavy debt of hospitality to certain of his fellow-countrymen; and secondly, because he is in sympathy with insurance and has been the means of making many other men cast their sympathies in the same direction.

Certainly there is no nobler field for human effort than the insurance line of business — especially acci-

dent insurance. Ever since I have been a director
in an accident insurance company I have felt that I
am a better man. Life has seemed more precious.
Accidents have assumed a kindlier aspect. Distressing special providences have lost half their horror. I
look upon a cripple now with affectionate interest —
as an advertisement. I do not seem to care for
poetry any more. I do not care for politics — even
agriculture does not excite me. But to me now
there is a charm about a railway collision that is
unspeakable.

There is nothing more beneficent than accident
insurance. I have seen an entire family lifted out of
poverty and into affluence by the simple boon of a
broken leg. I have had people come to me on
crutches, with tears in their eyes, to bless this beneficent institution. In all my experience of life, I
have seen nothing so seraphic as the look that comes
into a freshly mutilated man's face when he feels in
his vest pocket with his remaining hand and finds
his accident ticket all right. And I have seen nothing so sad as the look that came into another splin-
tered customer's face, when he found he couldn't
collect on a wooden leg.

I will remark here, by way of advertisement, that
that noble charity which we have named the HART-
FORD ACCIDENT INSURANCE COMPANY,* is an institution which is peculiarly to be depended upon. A
man is bound to prosper who gives it his custom

---

* The speaker is a director of the company named.

No man can take out a policy in it and not get crippled before the year is out. Now there was one indigent man who had been disappointed so often with other companies that he had grown disheartened, his appetite left him, he ceased to smile — said life was but a weariness. Three weeks ago I got him to insure with us, and now he is the brightest, happiest spirit in this land — has a good steady income and a stylish suit of new bandages every day, and travels around on a shutter.

I will say, in conclusion, that my share of the welcome to our guest is none the less hearty because I talk so much nonsense, and I know that I can say the same for the rest of the speakers.

JOHN CHINAMAN IN NEW YORK

AS I passed along by one of those monster American tea stores in New York, I found a Chinaman sitting before it acting in the capacity of a sign. Everybody that passed by gave him a steady stare as long as their heads would twist over their shoulders without dislocating their necks, and a group had stopped to stare deliberately.

Is it not a shame that we, who prate so much about civilization and humanity, are content to degrade a fellow-being to such an office as this? Is it not time for reflection when we find ourselves willing to see in such a being matter for frivolous curiosity instead of regret and grave reflection? Here was a poor creature whom hard fortune had exiled from his natural home beyond the seas, and whose troubles ought to have touched these idle strangers that thronged about him; but did it? Apparently not. Men calling themselves the superior race, the race of culture and of gentle blood, scanned his quaint Chinese hat, with peaked roof and ball on top, and his long queue dangling down his back; his short silken blouse, curiously frogged and figured

(304)

(and, like the rest of his raiment, rusty, dilapidated, and awkwardly put on); his blue cotton, tight-legged pants, tied close around the ankles; and his clumsy blunt-toed shoes with thick cork soles; and having so scanned him from head to foot, cracked some unseemly joke about his outlandish attire or his melancholy face, and passed on. In my heart I pitied the friendless Mongol. I wondered what was passing behind his sad face, and what distant scene his vacant eye was dreaming of. Were his thoughts with his heart, ten thousand miles away, beyond the billowy wastes of the Pacific? among the rice-fields and the plumy palms of China? under the shadows of remembered mountain-peaks, or in groves of bloomy shrubs and strange forest-trees unknown to climes like ours? And now and then, rippling among his visions and his dreams, did he hear familiar laughter and half-forgotten voices, and did he catch fitful glimpses of the friendly faces of a bygone time? A cruel fate it is, I said, that is be-fallen this bronzed wanderer. In order that the group of idlers might be touched at least by the words of the poor fellow, since the appeal of his pauper dress and his dreary exile was lost upon them, I touched him on the shoulder and said:

" Cheer up — don't be down-hearted. It is not America that treats you in this way, it is merely one citizen, whose greed of gain has eaten the humanity out of his heart. America has a broader hospitality for the exiled and oppressed. America

20

and Americans are always ready to help the unfortunate. Money shall be raised — you shall go back to China — you shall see your friends again. What wages do they pay you here?"

" Divil a cint but four dollars a week and find meself; but it's aisy, barrin the troublesome furrin clothes that's so expinsive."

The exile remains at his post. The New York tea merchants who need picturesque signs are not likely to run out of Chinamen.

HOW I EDITED AN AGRICULTURAL PAPER*

I DID not take temporary editorship of an agricultural paper without misgivings. Neither would
a landsman take command of a ship without misgivings. But I was in circumstances that made the
salary an object. The regular editor of the paper
was going off for a holiday, and I accepted the terms
he offered, and took his place.

The sensation of being at work again was luxurious, and I wrought all the week with unflagging
pleasure. We went to press, and I waited a day
with some solicitude to see whether my effort was
going to attract any notice. As I left the office,
toward sundown, a group of men and boys at the
foot of the stairs dispersed with one impulse, and
gave me passageway, and I heard one or two of
them say: " That's him!" I was naturally pleased
by this incident. The next morning I found a
similar group at the foot of the stairs, and scattering couples and individuals standing here and there
in the street, and over the way, watching me with

---

* Written about 1870.

T

(307)

interest. The group separated and fell back as I approached, and I heard a man say, " Look at his eye!" I pretended not to observe the notice I was attracting, but secretly I was pleased with it, and was purposing to write an account of it to my aunt. I went up the short flight of stairs, and heard cheery voices and a ringing laugh as I drew near the door, which I opened, and caught a glimpse of two young rural-looking men, whose faces blanched and lengthened when they saw me, and then they both plunged through the window with a great crash. I was surprised.

In about half an hour an old gentleman, with a flowing beard and a fine but rather austere face, entered, and sat down at my invitation. He seemed to have something on his mind. He took off his hat and set it on the floor, and got out of it a red silk handkerchief and a copy of our paper.

He put the paper on his lap, and while he polished his spectacles with his handkerchief, he said, " Are you the new editor?"

I said I was.

" Have you ever edited an agricultural paper before?"

" No," I said; " this is my first attempt."

" Very likely. Have you had any experience in agriculture practically?"

" No; I believe I have not."

" Some instinct told me so," said the old gentleman, putting on his spectacles, and looking over

I FANCIED HE WAS DISPLEASED

them at me with asperity, while he folded his paper into a convenient shape. " I wish to read you what must have made me have that instinct. It was this editorial. Listen, and see if it was you that wrote it :

"Turnips should never be pulled, it injures them. It is much better to send a boy up and let him shake the tree."

" Now, what do you think of that? — for I really suppose you wrote it?"

" Think of it? Why, I think it is good. I think it is sense. I have no doubt that every year millions and millions of bushels of turnips are spoiled in this township alone by being pulled in a half-ripe condition, when, if they had sent a boy up to shake the tree —"

" Shake your grandmother! Turnips don't grow on trees!"

" Oh, they don't, don't they? Well, who said they did? The language was intended to be figurative, wholly figurative. Anybody that knows anything will know that I meant that the boy should shake the vine."

Then this old person got up and tore his paper all into small shreds, and stamped on them, and broke several things with his cane, and said I did not know as much as a cow; and then went out and banged the door after him, and, in short, acted in such a way that I fancied he was displeased about something. But not knowing what the trouble was, I could not be any help to him.

Pretty soon after this a long cadaverous creature, with lanky locks hanging down to his shoulders, and a week's stubble bristling from the hills and valleys of his face, darted within the door, and halted, motionless, with finger on lip, and head and body bent in listening attitude. No sound was heard. Still he listened. No sound. Then he turned the key in the door, and came elaborately tiptoeing toward me till he was within long reaching distance of me, when he stopped and, after scanning my face with intense interest for a while, drew a folded copy of our paper from his bosom, and said:

" There, you wrote that. Read it to me — quick! Relieve me. I suffer."

I read as follows; and as the sentences fell from my lips I could see the relief come, I could see the drawn muscles relax, and the anxiety go out of the face, and rest and peace steal over the features like the merciful moonlight over a desolate landscape:

" The guano is a fine bird, but great care is necessary in rearing it. It should not be imported earlier than June or later than September. In the winter it should be kept in a warm place, where it can hatch out its young.

" It is evident that we are to have a backward season for grain. Therefore it will be well for the farmer to begin setting out his corn-stalks and planting his buckwheat cakes in July instead of August.

" Concerning the pumpkin. — This berry is a favorite with the natives of the interior of New England, who prefer it to the gooseberry for the making of fruit-cake, and who likewise give it the preference over the raspberry for feeding cows, as being more filling and fully as satisfying. The pumpkin is the only esculent of the orange family that will thrive in the North, except the gourd and one or two varieties of the squash. But the custom of planting it in the front yard with the shrubbery is fast going out of vogue, for it is now generally conceded that the pumpkin as a shade tree is a failure.

"Now, as the warm weather approaches, and the ganders begin to spawn"——

The excited listener sprang toward me to shake hands, and said:

"There, there — that will do. I know I am all right now, because you have read it just as I did, word for word. But, stranger, when I first read it this morning, I said to myself, I never, never believed it before, notwithstanding my friends kept me under watch so strict, but now I believe I *am* crazy; and with that I fetched a howl that you might have heard two miles, and started out to kill somebody — because, you know, I knew it would come to that sooner or later, and so I might as well begin. I read one of them paragraphs over again, so as to be certain, and then I burned my house down and started. I have crippled several people, and have got one fellow up a tree, where I can get him if I want him. But I thought I would call in here as I passed along and make the thing perfectly certain; and now it *is* certain, and I tell you it is lucky for the chap that is in the tree. I should have killed him sure, as I went back. Good-bye, sir, good-bye; you have taken a great load off my mind. My reason has stood the strain of one of your agricultural articles, and I know that nothing can ever unseat it now. *Good*-bye, sir."

I felt a little uncomfortable about the cripplings

and arsons this person had been entertaining himself
with, for I could not help feeling remotely accessory
to them. But these thoughts were quickly banished,
for the regular editor walked in! [I thought to
myself, Now if you had gone to Egypt as I recommended you to, I might have had a chance to get
my hand in; but you wouldn't do it, and here you
are. I sort of expected you.]

The editor was looking sad and perplexed and
dejected.

He surveyed the wreck which that old rioter and
these two young farmers had made, and then said
" This is a sad business — a very sad business.
There is the mucilage bottle broken, and six panes
of glass, and a spittoon, and two candlesticks. But
that is not the worst. The reputation of the paper
is injured — and permanently, I fear. True, there
never was such a call for the paper before, and it
never sold such a large edition or soared to such
celebrity; — but does one want to be famous for
lunacy, and prosper upon the infirmities of his
mind? My friend, as I am an honest man, the
street out here is full of people, and others are
roosting on the fences, waiting to get a glimpse of
you, because they think you are crazy. And well
they might after reading your editorials. They are
a disgrace to journalism. Why, what put it into
your head that you could edit a paper of this nature?
You do not seem to know the first rudiments of
agriculture. You speak of a furrow and a harrow

as being the same thing; you talk of the moulting season for cows; and you recommend the domestication of the pole-cat on account of its playfulness and its excellence as a ratter! Your remark that clams will lie quiet if music be played to them was superfluous — entirely superfluous. Nothing disturbs clams. Clams *always* lie quiet. Clams care nothing whatever about music. Ah, heavens and earth, friend! if you had made the acquiring of ignorance the study of your life, you could not have graduated with higher honor than you could to-day. I never saw anything like it. Your observation that the horse-chestnut as an article of commerce is steadily gaining in favor, is simply calculated to destroy this journal. I want you to throw up your situation and go. I want no more holiday — I could not enjoy it if I had it. Certainly not with you in my chair. I would always stand in dread of what you might be going to recommend next. It makes me lose all patience every time I think of your discussing oyster-beds under the head of 'Landscape Gardening.' I want you to go. Nothing on earth could persuade me to take another holiday. Oh! why didn't you *tell* me you didn't know anything about agriculture?"

" *Tell* you, you cornstalk, you cabbage, you son of a cauliflower? It's the first time I ever heard such an unfeeling remark. I tell you I have been in the editorial business going on fourteen years, and it is the first time I ever heard of a man's

having to know anything in order to edit a newspaper. You turnip! Who write the dramatic criti-
ques for the second-rate papers? Why, a parcel of
promoted shoemakers and apprentice apothecaries,
who know just as much about good acting as I do
about good farming and no more. Who review the
books? People who never wrote one. Who do up
the heavy leaders on finance? Parties who have had
the largest opportunities for knowing nothing about
it. Who criticise the Indian campaigns? Gentlemen
who do not know a war-whoop from a wigwam, and
who never have had to run a foot race with a tomahawk, or pluck arrows out of the several members
of their families to build the evening camp-fire with.
Who write the temperance appeals, and clamor
about the flowing bowl? Folks who will never draw
another sober breath till they do it in the grave.
Who edit the agricultural papers, you — yam?
Men, as a general thing, who fail in the poetry line,
yellow-colored novel line, sensation-drama line, city-
editor line, and finally fall back on agriculture as a
temporary reprieve from the poorhouse. *You* try
to tell *me* anything about the newspaper business!
Sir, I have been through it from Alpha to Omaha,
and I tell you that the less a man knows the bigger
the noise he makes and the higher the salary he
commands. Heaven knows if I had but been ignorant instead of cultivated, and impudent instead of
diffident, I could have made a name for myself in
this cold selfish world. I take my leave, sir. Since

I have been treated as you have treated me, I am perfectly willing to go. But I have done my duty. I have fulfilled my contract as far as I was permitted to do it. I said I could make your paper of interest to all classes — and I have. I said I could run your circulation up to twenty thousand copies, and if I had had two more weeks I'd have done it. And I'd have given you the best class of readers that ever an agricultural paper had — not a farmer in it, nor a solitary individual who could tell a watermelon tree from a peach-vine to save his life. *You* are the loser by this rupture, not me, Pie-plant. Adios."

I then left.

THE PETRIFIED MAN

NOW, to show how really hard it is to foist a
moral or a truth upon an unsuspecting public
through a burlesque without entirely and absurdly
missing one's mark, I will here set down two experiences ot my own in this thing. In the fall of
1862, in Nevada and California, the people got to
running wild about extraordinary petrifications and
other natural marvels. One could scarcely pick up
a paper without finding in it one or two glorified
discoveries of this kind. The mania was becoming
a little ridiculous. I was a bran-new local editor in
Virginia City, and I felt called upon to destroy this
growing evil; we all have our benignant fatherly
moods at one time or another, I suppose. I chose
to kill the petrifaction mania with a delicate, a very
delicate satire. But maybe it was altogether too
delicate, for nobody ever perceived the satire part
of it at all. I put my scheme in the shape of the
discovery of a remarkably petrified man.

I had had a temporary falling out with Mr. ——,
the new coroner and justice of the peace of Humboldt, and thought I might as well touch him up a

(316)

little at the same time and make him ridiculous, and thus combine pleasure with business. So I told, in patient belief-compelling detail, all about the finding of a petrified man at Gravelly Ford (exactly a hundred and twenty miles, over a breakneck mountain trail from where —— lived); how all the savants of the immediate neighborhood had been to examine it (it was notorious that there was not a living creature within fifty miles of there, except a few starving Indians, some crippled grasshoppers, and four or five buzzards out of meat and too feeble to get away); how those savants all pronounced the petrified man to have been in a state of complete petrifaction for over ten generations; and then, with a seriousness that I ought to have been ashamed to assume, I stated that as soon as Mr. —— heard the news he summoned a jury, mounted his mule, and posted off, with noble reverence for official duty, on that awful five days journey, through alkali, sagebrush, peril of body, and imminent starvation, to *hold an inquest* on this man that had been dead and turned to everlasting stone for more than three hundred years! And then, my hand being " in," so to speak, I went on, with the same unflinching gravity, to state that the jury returned a verdict that deceased came to his death from *protracted exposure*. This only moved me to higher flights of imagination, and I said that the jury, with that charity so characteristic of pioneers, then dug a grave, and were about to give the petrified man Christian burial, when they found that for ages a limestone sediment had been trickling down the face of the stone against which he was sitting, and this stuff had run under him and cemented him fast to the " bed-rock"; that the jury (they were all silver miners) canvassed the difficulty a moment, and then got out their powder and fuse, and proceeded to drill a hole under him, in order to *blast him from his position*, when Mr. ————, " with that delicacy so characteristic of him, forbade them, observing that it would be little less than sacrilege to do such a thing."

From beginning to end the " Petrified Man " squib was a string of roaring absurdities, albeit they were told with an unfair pretense of truth that even imposed upon me to some extent, and I was in some danger of believing in my own fraud. But I really had no desire to deceive anybody, and no expectation of doing it. I depended on the way the petrified man was *sitting* to explain to the public that he was a swindle. Yet I purposely mixed that up with other things, hoping to make it obscure — and I did. I would describe the position of one foot, and then say his right thumb was against the side of his nose; then talk about his other foot, and presently come back and say the fingers of his right hand were spread apart; then talk about the back of his head a little, and return and say the left thumb was hooked into the right little finger; then ramble off about something else, and by and by drift back again and remark that the fingers of the left hand were spread like those of the right. But I was too ingenious. I mixed it up rather too much; and so all that description of the attitude, as a key to the humbuggery of the article, was entirely lost, for nobody but me ever discovered and comprehended the peculiar and suggestive position of the petrified man's hands.

As a *satire* on the petrifaction mania, or anything else, my Petrified Man was a disheartening failure; for everybody received him in innocent good faith, and I was stunned to see the creature I had begotten to pull down the wonder-business with, and bring derision upon it, calmly exalted to the grand chief place in the list of the genuine marvels our Nevada had produced. I was so disappointed at the curious miscarriage of my scheme, that at first I was angry, and did not like to think about it; but by and by, when the exchanges began to come in with the Petrified Man copied and guilelessly glorified, I began to feel a soothing secret satisfaction; and as my gentleman's field of travels broadened, and by the exchanges I saw that he steadily and implacably penetrated territory after territory, State after State, and land after land, till he swept the great globe and culminated in sublime and unimpeached legitimacy in the august London *Lancet*, my cup was full, and I said I was glad I had done it. I think that for about eleven months, as nearly as I can remember, Mr. ——'s daily mail-bag continued to be swollen by the addition of half a bushel of newspapers hailing from many climes with the Petrified Man in them, marked around with a prominent belt of ink. I sent them to him. I did it for spite, not for fun. He used to shovel them into his back yard and curse. And every day during all those months the miners, his constituents (for miners never quit joking a person when they get started), would call on him and ask if he could tell them where they could get hold of a paper with the Petrified Man in it. He could have accommodated a continent with them. I hated —— in those days, and these things pacified me and pleased me. I could not have gotten more real comfort out of him without killing him.

MY BLOODY MASSACRE

THE other burlesque I have referred to was my fine satire upon the financial expedients of "cooking dividends," a thing which became shamefully frequent on the Pacific coast for a while. Once more, in my self-complacent simplicity I felt that the time had arrived for me to rise up and be a reformer. I put this reformatory satire in the shape of a fearful "Massacre at Empire City." The San Francisco papers were making a great outcry about the iniquity of the Daney Silver-Mining Company, whose directors had declared a "cooked" or false dividend, for the purpose of increasing the value of their stock, so that they could sell out at a comfortable figure, and then scramble from under the tumbling concern. And while abusing the Daney, those papers did not forget to urge the public to get rid of all their silver stocks and invest in sound and safe San Francisco stocks, such as the Spring Valley Water Company, etc. But right at this unfortunate juncture, behold the Spring Valley cooked a dividend too! And so, under the insidious mask of an invented "bloody massacre," I stole upon the public unawares with my scathing satire upon the dividend-

21   (321)

cooking system. In about half a column of imaginary human carnage I told how a citizen had murdered his wife and nine children, and then committed suicide. And I said slyly, at the bottom, that the sudden madness of which this melancholy massacre was the result, had been brought about by his having allowed himself to be persuaded by the California papers to sell his sound and lucrative Nevada silver stocks, and buy into Spring Valley just in time to get cooked along with that company's fancy dividend, and sink every cent he had in the world.

Ah, it was a deep, deep satire, and most ingeniously contrived. But I made the horrible details so carefully and conscientiously interesting that the public devoured *them* greedily, and wholly overlooked the following distinctly-stated facts, to wit: The murderer was perfectly well known to every creature in the land as a *bachelor*, and consequently he could not murder his wife and nine children; he murdered them " in his splendid dressed-stone mansion just in the edge of the great pine forest between Empire City and Dutch Nick's," when even the very pickled oysters that came on our tables knew that there was not a " dressed-stone mansion " in all Nevada Territory; also that, so far from there being a " great pine forest between Empire City and Dutch Nick's," there wasn't a solitary tree within fifteen miles of either place; and, finally, it was patent and notorious that Empire City and Dutch

Nick's were one and the same place, and contained only six houses anyhow, and consequently there could be no forest *between* them; and on top of all these absurdities I stated that this diabolical murderer, after inflicting a wound upon himself that the reader ought to have seen would kill an elephant in the twinkling of an eye, jumped on his horse and rode *four miles*, waving his wife's reeking scalp in the air, and thus performing entered Carson City with tremendous *éclat*, and dropped dead in front of the chief saloon, the envy and admiration of all beholders.

Well, in all my life I never saw anything like the sensation that little satire created. It was the talk of the town, it was the talk of the Territory. Most of the citizens dropped gently into it at breakfast, and they never finished their meal. There was something about those minutely faithful details that was a sufficing substitute for food. Few people that were able to read took food that morning. Dan and I (Dan was my reportorial associate) took our seats on either side of our customary table in the " Eagle Restaurant," and, as I unfolded the shred they used to call a napkin in that establishment, I saw at the next table two stalwart innocents with that sort of vegetable dandruff sprinkled about their clothing which was the sign and evidence that they were in from the Truckee with a load of hay. The one facing me had the morning paper folded to a long narrow strip, and I knew, without any telling, that

U

that strip represented the column that contained my
pleasant financial satire. From the way he was excitedly mumbling, I saw that the heedless son of a
haymow was skipping with all his might, in order to
get to the bloody details as quickly as possible; and
so he was missing the guideboards I had set up to
warn him that the whole thing was a fraud.
Presently his eyes spread wide open, just as his
jaws swung asunder to take in a potato approaching
it on a fork; the potato halted, the face lit up redly,
and the whole man was on fire with excitement.
Then he broke into a disjointed checking off of the
particulars — his potato cooling in mid-air meantime,
and his mouth making a reach for it occasionally,
but always bringing up suddenly against a new and
still more direful performance of my hero. At last
he looked his stunned and rigid comrade impressively
in the face, and said, with an expression of concen-
trated awe:

" Jim, he b'iled his baby, and he took the old
'oman's skelp. Cuss'd if *I* want any breakfast!"

And he laid his lingering potato reverently down,
and he and his friend departed from the restaurant
empty but satisfied.

He *never got down* to where the satire part of it
began. Nobody ever did. They found the thrilling
particulars sufficient. To drop in with a poor little
moral at the fag-end of such a gorgeous massacre,
was to following the expiring sun with a candle,
and hope to attract the world's attention to it.

The idea that anybody could ever take my massacre for a genuine occurrence never once suggested itself to me, hedged about as it was by all those telltale absurdities and impossibilities concerning the " great pine forest," the " dressed-stone mansion," etc. But I found out then, and never have forgotten since, that we never *read* the dull explanatory surroundings of marvelously exciting things when we have no occasion to suppose that some irresponsible scribbler is trying to defraud us; we skip all that, and hasten to revel in the blood-curdling particulars and be happy.

THE UNDERTAKER'S CHAT

"NOW that corpse," said the undertaker, patting the folded hands of deceased approvingly, "was a brick — every way you took him he was a brick. He was so real accommodating, and so modest-like and simple in his last moments. Friends wanted metallic burial-case — nothing else would do. *I* couldn't get it. There warn't going to be time — anybody could see that.

"Corpse said never mind, shake him up some kind of a box he could stretch out in comfortable, *he* warn't particular 'bout the general style of it. Said he went more on room than style, anyway in a last final container.

"Friends wanted a silver doorplate on the coffin, signifying who he was and wher' he was from. Now *you* know a fellow couldn't roust out such a gaily thing as that in a little country town like this. What did corpse say?

"Corpse said, whitewash his old canoe and dob his address and general destination onto it with a blacking brush and a stencil plate, 'long with a verse from some likely hymn or other, and p'int

him for the tomb, and mark him C. O. D., and just
let him flicker. *He* warn't distressed any more than
you be — on the contrary just as ca'm and collected
as a hearse-horse; said he judged that wher' he was
going to a body would find it considerable better to
attract attention by a picturesque moral character
than a natty burial case with a swell doorplate on it.

" Splendid man, he was. I'd druther do for a
corpse like that 'n any I've tackled in seven year.
There's some satisfaction in buryin' a man like that.
You feel that what you're doing is appreciated.
Lord bless you, so's he got planted before he
sp'iled, he was perfectly satisfied; said his relations
meant well, *per*fectly well, but all them preparations
was bound to delay the thing more or less, and he
didn't wish to be kept layin' around. You never
see such a clear head as what he had — and so ca'm
and so cool. Just a hunk of brains — that is what
he was. Perfectly awful. It was a ripping distance
from one end of that man's head to t'other. Often
and over again he's had brain fever a-raging in one
place, and the rest of the pile didn't know anything
about it — didn't affect it any more than an Injun
insurrection in Arizona affects the Atlantic States.

" Well, the relations they wanted a big funeral,
but corpse said he was down on flummery — didn't
want any procession — fill the hearse full of mourn-
ers, and get out a stern line and tow *him* behind.
He *was* the most down on style of any remains I
ever struck. A beautiful simple-minded creature —

it was what he was, you can depend on that.   He
was just set on having things the way he wanted
them, and he took a solid comfort in laying his little
plans.   He had me measure him and take a whole
raft of directions; then he had the minister stand up
behind a long box with a tablecloth over it, to
represent the coffin, and read his funeral sermon,
saying ' Angcore, angcore!' at the good places, and
making him scratch out every bit of brag about him,
and all the hifalutin; and then he made them trot
out the choir so's he could help them pick out the
tunes for the occasion, and he got them to sing
' Pop Goes the Weasel,' because he'd always liked
that tune when he was down-hearted, and solemn
music made him sad; and when they sung that with
tears in their eyes (because they all loved him), and
his relations grieving around, he just laid there as
happy as a bug, and trying to beat time and showing all over how much he enjoyed it; and presently
he got worked up and excited, and tried to join in,
for, mind you, he was pretty proud of his abilities
in the singing line; but the first time he opened his
mouth and was just going to spread himself his
breath took a walk.

" I never see a man snuffed out so sudden.   Ah,
it was a great loss — a powerful loss to this poor
little one-horse town.   Well, well, well, I hain't got
time to be palavering along here — got to nail on the
lid and mosey along with him; and if you'll just give
me a lift we'll skeet him into the hearse and meander

along. Relations bound to have it so — don't pay
no attention to dying injunctions, minute a corpse's
gone; but, if I had *my* way, if I didn't respect his
last wishes and tow him behind the hearse *I*'ll be
cuss'd. I consider that whatever a corpse wants
done for his comfort is little enough matter, and a
man hain't got no right to deceive him or take advantage of ' ' m; and whatever a corpse trusts me to
do I'm a-going to *do*, you know, even if it's to stuff
him and paint him yaller and keep him for a keep-
sake — you hear *me!*''

He cracked his whip and went lumbering away
with his ancient ruin of a hearse, and I continued
my walk with a valuable lesson learned — that a
healthy and wholesome cheerfulness is not necessarily impossible to *any* occupation. The lesson is
likely to be lasting, for it will take many months to
obliterate the memory of the remarks and circumstances that impressed it.

CONCERNING CHAMBERMAIDS

AGAINST all chambermaids, of whatsoever age or nationality, I launch the curse of bachelordom! Because:

They always put the pillows at the opposite end of the bed from the gas-burner, so that while you read and smoke before sleeping (as is the ancient and honored custom of bachelors), you have to hold your book aloft, in an uncomfortable position, to keep the light from dazzling your eyes.

When they find the pillows removed to the other end of the bed in the morning, they receive not the suggestion in a friendly spirit; but, glorying in their absolute sovereignty, and unpitying your helplessness, they make the bed just as it was originally, and gloat in secret over the pang their tyranny will cause you.

Always after that, when they find you have transposed the pillows, they undo your work, and thus defy and seek to embitter the life that God has given you.

If they cannot get the light in an inconvenient position any other way, they move the bed.

If you pull your trunk out six inches from the wall, so that the lid will stay up when you open it, they always shove that trunk back again. They do it on purpose.

If you want the spittoon in a certain spot, where it will be handy, they don't, and so they move it.

They always put your other boots into inaccessible places. They chiefly enjoy depositing them as far under the bed as the wall will permit. It is because this compels you to get down in an undignified attitude and make wild sweeps for them in the dark with the bootjack, and swear.

They always put the matchbox in some other place. They hunt up a new place for it every day, and put up a bottle, or other perishable glass thing, where the box stood before. This is to cause you to break that glass thing, groping in the dark, and get yourself into trouble.

They are forever and ever moving the furniture. When you come in in the night you can calculate on finding the bureau where the wardrobe was in the morning. And when you go out in the morning, if you leave the slop-bucket by the door and rocking-chair by the window, when you come in at midnight or thereabout, you will fall over that rocking-chair, and you will proceed toward the window and sit down in that slop-tub. This will disgust you. They like that.

No matter where you put anything, they are not going to let it stay there. They will take it and move it the first chance they get. It is their nature. And, besides, it gives them pleasure to be mean and contrary this way. They would die if they couldn't be villains.

They always save up all the old scraps of printed rubbish you throw on the floor, and stack them up carefully on the table, and start the fire with your valuable manuscripts. If there is any one particular old scrap that you are more down on than any other, and which you are gradually wearing your life out trying to get rid of, you may take all the pains you possibly can in that direction, but it won't be of any use, because they will always fetch that old scrap back and put it in the same old place again every time. It does them good.

And they use up more hair-oil than any six men. If charged with purloining the same, they lie about it. What do they care about a hereafter? Absolutely nothing.

If you leave the key in the door for convenience sake, they will carry it down to the office and give it to the clerk. They do this under the vile pretence of trying to protect your property from thieves; but actually they do it because they want to make you tramp back down stairs after it when you come home tired, or put you to the trouble of sending a waiter for it, which waiter will expect you to pay him something. In which case I suppose the degraded creatures divide.

They keep always trying to make your bed before

you get up, thus destroying your rest and inflicting agony upon you; but after you get up, they don't come any more till next day.

They do all the mean things they can think of, and they do them just out of pure cussedness, and nothing else.

Chambermaids are dead to every human instinct.

If I can get a bill through the legislature abolishing chambermaids, I mean to do it.

223

AURELIA'S UNFORTUNATE YOUNG MAN *

THE facts in the following case came to me by letter from a young lady who lives in the beautiful city of San José; she is perfectly unknown to me, and simply signs herself "Aurelia Maria," which may possibly be a fictitious name. But no matter, the poor girl is almost heart-broken by the misfortunes she has undergone, and so confused by the conflicting counsels of misguided friends and insidious enemies, that she does not know what course to pursue in order to extricate herself from the web of difficulties in which she seems almost hopelessly involved. In this dilemma she turns to me for help, and supplicates for my guidance and instruction with a moving eloquence that would touch the heart of a statue. Hear her sad story:

She says that when she was sixteen years old she met and loved, with all the devotion of a passionate nature, a young man from New Jersey, named Williamson Breckinridge Caruthers, who was some six years her senior. They were engaged, with the free consent of their friends and relatives, and for a

---

* Written about 1865.

time it seemed as if their career was destined to be characterized by an immunity from sorrow beyond the usual lot of humanity. But at last the tide of fortune turned; young Caruthers became infected with smallpox of the most virulent type, and when he recovered from his illness his face was pitted like a waffle-mould, and his comeliness gone forever. Aurelia thought to break off the engagement at first, but pity for her unfortunate lover caused her to postpone the marriage-day for a season, and give him another trial.

The very day before the wedding was to have taken place, Breckinridge, while absorbed in watching the flight of a balloon, walked into a well and fractured one of his legs, and it had to be taken off above the knee. Again Aurelia was moved to break the engagement, but again love triumphed, and she set the day forward and gave him another chance to reform.

And again misfortune overtook the unhappy youth. He lost one arm by the premature discharge of a Fourth of July cannon, and within three months he got the other pulled out by a carding-machine. Aurelia's heart was almost crushed by these latter calamities. She could not but be deeply grieved to see her lover passing from her by piecemeal, feeling as she did, that he could not last forever under this disastrous process of reduction, yet knowing of no way to stop its dreadful career, and in her tearful despair she almost regretted, like brokers who hold on and lose, that she had not taken him at first, before he had suffered such an alarming depreciation. Still, her brave soul bore her up, and she resolved to bear with her friend's unnatural disposition yet a little longer.

Again the wedding-day approached, and again disappointment overshadowed it; Caruthers fell ill with the erysipelas, and lost the use of one of his eyes entirely. The friends and relatives of the bride, considering that she had already put up with more than could reasonably be expected of her, now came forward and insisted that the match should be broken off; but after wavering a while, Aurelia, with a generous spirit which did her credit, said she had reflected calmly upon the matter, and could not discover that Breckinridge was to blame.

So she extended the time once more, and he broke his other leg.

It was a sad day for the poor girl when she saw the surgeons reverently bearing away the sack whose uses she had learned by previous experience, and her heart told her the bitter truth that some more of her lover was gone. She felt that the field of her affections was growing more and more circumscribed every day, but once more she frowned down her relatives and renewed her betrothal.

Shortly before the time set for the nuptials another disaster occurred. There was but one man scalped by the Owens River Indians last year. That man was Williamson Breckinridge Caruthers of New

Jersey. He was hurrying home with happiness in his heart, when he lost his hair forever, and in that hour of bitterness he almost cursed the mistaken mercy that had spared his head.

At last Aurelia is in serious perplexity as to what she ought to do. She still loves her Breckinridge, she writes, with truly womanly feeling — she still loves what is left of him — but her parents are bitterly opposed to the match, because he has no property and is disabled from working, and she has not sufficient means to support both comfortably. " Now, what should she do?" she asks with painful and anxious solicitude.

It is a delicate question; it is one which involves the lifelong happiness of a woman, and that of nearly two-thirds of a man, and I feel that it would be assuming too great a responsibility to do more than make a mere suggestion in the case. How would it do to build to him? If Aurelia can afford the expense, let her furnish her mutilated lover with wooden arms and wooden legs, and a glass eye and a wig, and give him another show; give him ninety days, without grace, and if he does not break his neck in the meantime, marry him and take the chances. It does not seem to me that there is much risk, any-way, Aurelia, because if he sticks to his singular propensity for damaging himself every time he sees a good opportunity, his next experiment is bound to finish him, and then you are safe, married or single. If married, the wooden legs and such other

22

valuables as he may possess revert to the widow, and you see you sustain no actual loss save the cherished fragment of a noble but most unfortunate husband, who honestly strove to do right, but whose extraordinary instincts were against him. Try it, Maria. I have thought the matter over carefully and well, and it is the only chance I see for you. It would have been a happy conceit on the part of Caruthers if he had started with his neck and broken that first; but since he has seen fit to choose a different policy and string himself out as long as possible, I do not think we ought to upbraid him for it if he has enjoyed it. We must do the best we can under the circumstances, and try not to feel exasperated at him.

'AFTER" JENKINS

A GRAND affair of a ball — the Pioneers'— came off at the Occidental some time ago. The following notes of the costumes worn by the belles of the occasion may not be uninteresting to the general reader, and Jenkins may get an idea therefrom:

Mrs. W. M. was attired in an elegant *pâté de foie gras*, made expressly for her, and was greatly admired. Miss S. had her hair done up. She was the center of attraction for the gentlemen and the envy of all the ladies. Mrs. G. W. was tastefully dressed in a *tout ensemble*, and was greeted with deafening applause wherever she went. Mrs. C. N. was superbly arrayed in white kid gloves. Her modest and engaging manner accorded well with the unpretending simplicity of her costume and caused her to be regarded with absorbing interest by every one.

The charming Miss M. M. B. appeared in a thrilling waterfall, whose exceeding grace and volume compelled the homage of pioneers and emigrants alike. How beautiful she was!

The queenly Mrs. L. R. was attractively attired in her new and beautiful false teeth, and the *bon jour* effect they naturally produced was heightened by her enchanting and well-sustained smile.

Miss R. P., with that repugnance to ostentation in dress which is so peculiar to her, was attired in a simple white lace collar, fastened with a neat pearl-button solitaire. The fine contrast between the sparkling vivacity of her natural optic, and the steadfast attentiveness of her placid glass eye, was the subject of general and enthusiastic remark.

Miss C. L. B. had her fine nose elegantly enameled, and the easy grace with which she blew it from time to time marked her as a cultivated and accomplished woman of the world; its exquisitely modulated tone excited the admiration of all who had the happiness to hear it.

ABOUT BARBERS

ALL things change except barbers, the ways of barbers, and the surroundings of barbers. These never change. What one experiences in a barber's shop the first time he enters one is what he always experiences in barbers' shops afterward till the end of his days. I got shaved this morning as usual. A man approached the door from Jones street as I approached it from Main — a thing that always happens. I hurried up, but it was of no use; he entered the door one little step ahead of me, and I followed in on his heels and saw him take the only vacant chair, the one presided over by the best barber. It always happens so. I sat down, hoping that I might fall heir to the chair belonging to the better of the remaining two barbers, for he had already begun combing his man's hair, while his comrade was not yet quite done rubbing up and oiling his customer's locks. I watched the probabilities with strong interest. When I saw that No. 2 was gaining on No. 1 my interest grew to solicitude. When No. 1 stopped a moment to make change on a bath ticket for a new comer, and lost ground in

the race, my solicitude rose to anxiety. When No.
1 caught up again, and both he and his comrade
were pulling the towels away and brushing the
powder from their customer's cheeks, and it was
about an even thing which one would say " Next!"
first, my very breath stood still with the suspense.
But when at the culminating moment No. 1 stopped
to pass a comb a couple of times through his
customer's eyebrows, I saw that he had lost the race
by a single instant, and I rose indignant and quitted
the shop, to keep from falling into the hands of No.
2; for I have none of that enviable firmness that
enables a man to look calmly into the eyes of a waiting barber and tell him he will wait for his fellow-
barber's chair.

I stayed out fifteen minutes, and then went back,
hoping for better luck. Of course all the chairs
were occupied now, and four men sat waiting, silent,
unsociable, distraught, and looking bored, as men
always do who are waiting their turn in a barber's
shop. I sat down in one of the iron-armed compartments of an old sofa, and put in the time for a while
reading the framed advertisements of all sorts of
quack nostrums for dyeing and coloring the hair.
Then I read the greasy names on the private bay-
rum bottles; read the names and noted the numbers
on the private shaving cups in the pigeon-holes;
studied the stained and damaged cheap prints on the
walls, of battles, early Presidents, and voluptuous
recumbent sultanas, and the tiresome and everlasting

young girl putting her grandfather's spectacles on;
execrated in my heart the cheerful canary and the
distracting parrot that few barbers' shops are without. Finally, I searched out the least dilapidated of
last year's illustrated papers that littered the foul
center-table, and conned their unjustifiable misrepre-
sentations of old forgotten events.

At last my turn came. A voice said " Next!"
and I surrendered to — No. 2, of course. It always
happens so. I said meekly that I was in a hurry,
and it affected him as strongly as if he had never
heard it. He shoved up my head, and put a napkin
under it. He plowed his fingers into my collar and
fixed a towel there. He explored my hair with his
claws and suggested that it needed trimming. I
said I did not want it trimmed. He explored again
and said it was pretty long for the present style —
better have a little taken off; it needed it behind
especially. I said I had had it cut only a week
before. He yearned over it reflectively a moment,
and then asked with a disparaging manner, who cut
it? I came back at him promptly with a " You
did!" I had him there. Then he fell to stirring
up his lather and regarding himself in the glass,
stopping now and then to get close and examine his
chin critically or inspect a pimple. Then he lathered
one side of my face thoroughly, and was about to
lather the other, when a dog fight attracted his attention, and he ran to the window and stayed and saw
it out, losing two shillings on the result in bets with

the other barbers, a thing which gave me great satisfaction. He finished lathering, and then began to rub in the suds with his hand.

He now began to sharpen his razor on an old suspender, and was delayed a good deal on account of a controversy about a cheap masquerade ball he had figured at the night before, in red cambric and bogus ermine, as some kind of a king. He was so gratified with being chaffed about some damsel whom he had smitten with his charms that he used every means to continue the controversy by pretending to be annoyed at the chaffings of his fellows. This matter begot more surveyings of himself in the glass, and he put down his razor and brushed his hair with elaborate care, plastering an inverted arch of it down on his forehead, accomplishing an accurate " part " behind, and brushing the two wings forward over his ears with nice exactness. In the meantime the lather was drying on my face, and apparently eating into my vitals.

Now he began to shave, digging his fingers into my countenance to stretch the skin and bundling and tumbling my head this way and that as convenience in shaving demanded. As long as he was on the tough sides of my face I did not suffer; but when he began to rake, and rip, and tug at my chin, the tears came. He now made a handle of my nose, to assist him in shaving the corners of my upper lip, and it was by this bit of circumstantial evidence that I discovered that a part of his duties in the shop was to clean the kerosene lamps. I had often wondered in an indolent way whether the barbers did that. or whether it was the boss.

About this time I was amusing myself trying to guess where he would be most likely to cut me this time, but he got ahead of me, and sliced me on the end of the chin before I had got my mind made up. He immediately sharpened his razor — he might have done it before. I do not like a close shave, and would not let him go over me a second time. I tried to get him to put up his razor, dreading that he would make for the side of my chin, my pet tender spot, a place which a razor cannot touch twice without making trouble; but he said he only wanted to just smooth off one little roughness, and in the same moment he slipped his razor along the forbidden ground, and the dreaded pimple-signs of a close shave rose up smarting and answered to the call. Now he soaked his towel in bay rum, and slapped it all over my face nastily; slapped it over as if a human being ever yet washed his face in that way. Then he dried it by slapping with the dry part of the towel, as if a human being ever dried his face in such a fashion; but a barber seldom rubs you like a Christian. Next he poked bay rum into the cut place with his towel, then choked the wound with powered starch, then soaked it with bay rum again, and would have gone on soaking and powdering it forevermore, no doubt, if I had not rebelled and begged off. He powdered my whole face now, straightened me up, and began to plow my hair thoughtfully with his hands. Then he suggested a shampoo, and said my hair needed it badly, very badly. I observed that I shampooed it myself very thoroughly in the bath yesterday. I " had him " again. He next recommended some of " Smith's Hair Glorifier," and offered to sell me a bottle. I declined. He praised the new perfume, " Jones's Delight of the Toilet," and proposed to sell me some of that. I declined again. He tendered me a toothwash atrocity of his own invention, and when I declined offered to trade knives with me.

He returned to business after the miscarriage of this last enterprise, sprinkled me all over, legs and all, greased my hair in defiance of my protest against it, rubbed and scrubbed a good deal of it out by the roots, and combed and brushed the rest, parting it behind, and plastering the eternal inverted arch of hair down on my forehead, and then, while combing my scant eyebrows and defiling them with pomade, strung out an account of the achievements of a six-ounce black and tan terrier of his till I heard the whistles blow for noon, and knew I was five minutes too late for the train. Then he snatched away the towel, brushed it lightly about my face, passed his comb through my eyebrows once more, and gaily sang out " Next!"

This barber fell down and died of apoplexy two hours later. I am waiting over a day for my revenge — I am going to attend his funeral.

"PARTY CRIES" IN IRELAND

BELFAST is a peculiarly religious community. This may be said of the whole of the North of Ireland. About one-half of the people are Protestants and the other half Catholics. Each party does all it can to make its own doctrines popular and draw the affections of the irreligious toward them. One hears constantly of the most touching instances of this zeal. A week ago a vast concourse of Catholics assembled at Armagh to dedicate a new Cathedral; and when they started home again the roadways were lined with groups of meek and lowly Protestants who stoned them till all the region round about was marked with blood. I thought that only Catholics argued in that way, but it seems to be a mistake.

Every man in the community is a missionary and carries a brick to admonish the erring with. The law has tried to break this up, but not with perfect success. It has decreed that irritating " party cries " shall not be indulged in, and that persons uttering them shall be fined forty shillings and costs. And so, in the police court reports every day, one sees

these fines recorded.   Last week a girl twelve years
old was fined the usual forty shillings and costs for
proclaiming in the public streets that she was " a
Protestant." The usual cry is, " To hell with the
Pope !" or " To hell with the Protestants !" according to the utterer's system of salvation.

One of Belfast's local jokes was very good.   It
referred to the uniform and inevitable fine of forty
shillings and costs for uttering a party cry — and it
is no economical fine for a poor man, either, by the
way.   They say that a policeman found a drunken
man lying on the ground, up a dark alley, entertaining himself with shouting, " To *hell* with !"   " To
hell with !" The officer smelt a fine — informers
get half.

" What's that you say ?"

" To *hell* with !"

" To hell with *who* ?   To hell with *what* ?"

" Ah, bedad ye can finish it yourself — it's too
expinsive for me !"

I think the seditious disposition, restrained by the
economical instinct, is finely put in that.

THE FACTS CONCERNING THE RECENT RESIGNATION *

Washington, *Dec. 2, 1867.*

I HAVE resigned. The Government appears to go on much the same, but there is a spoke out of its wheel, nevertheless. I was clerk of the Senate Committee on Conchology, and I have thrown up the position. I could see the plainest disposition on the part of the other members of the Government to debar me from having any voice in the counsels of the nation, and so I could no longer hold office and retain my self-respect. If I were to detail all the outrages that were heaped upon me during the six days that I was connected with the Government in an official capacity, the narrative would fill a volume. They appointed me clerk of that Committee on Conchology, and then allowed me no amanuensis to play billiards with. I would have borne that, lonesome as it was, if I had met with that courtesy from the other members of the Cabinet which was my due. But I did not. Whenever I observed that the head of a department was pursuing a wrong

*Written about 1867.

(348)

course, I laid down everything and went and tried
to set him right, as it was my duty to do; and I
never was thanked for it in a single instance. I
went, with the best intentions in the world, to the
Secretary of the Navy, and said:

" Sir, I cannot see that Admiral Farragut is doing
anything but skirmishing around there in Europe,
having a sort of picnic. Now, that may be all very
well, but it does not exhibit itself to me in that light.
If there is no fighting for him to do, let him come
home. There is no use in a man having a whole
fleet for a pleasure excursion. It is too expensive.
Mind, I do not object to pleasure excursions for
the naval officers — pleasure excursions that are in
reason — pleasure excursions that are economical.
Now they might go down the Mississippi on a
raft —"

You ought to have heard him storm! One would
have supposed I had committed a crime of some
kind. But I didn't mind. I said it was cheap, and
full of republican simplicity, and perfectly safe. I
said that, for a tranquil pleasure excursion, there
was nothing equal to a raft.

Then the Secretary of the Navy asked me who I
was; and when I told him I was connected with the
Government, he wanted to know in what capacity.
I said that, without remarking upon the singularity
of such a question, coming, as it did, from a member of that same Government, I would inform him
that I was clerk of the Senate Committee on Con-

23S

chology. Then there was a fine storm! He finished
by ordering me to leave the premises, and give my
attention strictly to my own business in future. My
first impulse was to get him removed. However,
that would harm others beside himself, and do me
no real good, and so I let him stay.

I went next to the Secretary of War, who was not
inclined to see me at all until he learned that I was
connected with the Government. If I had not been
on important business, I suppose I could not have
got in. I asked him for a light (he was smoking at
the time), and then I told him I had no fault to find
with his defending the parole stipulations of General
Lee and his comrades in arms, but that I could not
approve of his method of fighting the Indians on the
Plains. I said he fought too scattering. He ought
to get the Indians more together — get them together
in some convenient place, where he could have provisions enough for both parties, and then have a
general massacre. I said there was nothing so convincing to an Indian as a general massacre. If he
could not approve of the massacre, I said the next
surest thing for an Indian was soap and education.
Soap and education are not as sudden as a massacre,
but they are more deadly in the long run; because a
half-massacred Indian may recover, but if you educate him and wash him, it is bound to finish him
some time or other. It undermines his constitution;
it strikes at the foundation of his being. "Sir," I
said, "the time has come when blood-curdling

cruelty has become necessary. Inflict soap and a spelling-book on every Indian that ravages the Plains, and let them die!"

The Secretary of War asked me if I was a member of the Cabinet, and I said I was. He inquired what position I held, and I said I was clerk of the Senate Committee on Conchology. I was then ordered under arrest for contempt of court, and restrained of my liberty for the best part of the day.

I almost resolved to be silent thenceforward, and let the Government get along the best way it could. But duty called, and I obeyed. I called on the Secretary of the Treasury. He said:

"What will *you* have?"

The question threw me off my guard. I said, "Rum punch."

He said: "If you have got any business here, sir, state it — and in as few words as possible."

I then said that I was sorry he had seen fit to change the subject so abruptly, because such conduct was very offensive to me; but under the circumstances I would overlook the matter and come to the point. I now went into an earnest expostulation with him upon the extravagant length of his report. I said it was expensive, unnecessary, and awkwardly constructed; there were no descriptive passages in it, no poetry, no sentiment — no heroes, no plot, no pictures — not even woodcuts. Nobody would read it, that was a clear case. I urged him not to ruin his reputation by getting out a thing like that. If he ever hoped to succeed in literature, he must throw more variety into his writings. He must beware of dry detail. I said that the main popularity of the almanac was derived from its poetry and conundrums, and that a few conundrums distributed around through his Treasury report would help the sale of it more than all the internal revenue he could put into it. I said these things in the kindest spirit, and yet the Secretary of the Treasury fell into a violent passion. He even said I was an ass. He abused me in the most vindictive manner, and said that if I came there again meddling with his business, he would throw me out of the window. I said I would take my hat and go, if I could not be treated with the respect due to my office, and I did go. It was just like a new author. They always think they know more than anybody else when they are getting out their first book. Nobody can tell *them* anything.

During the whole time that I was connected with the Government it seemed as if I could not do anything in an official capacity without getting myself into trouble. And yet I did nothing, attempted nothing, but what I conceived to be for the good of my country. The sting of my wrongs may have driven me to unjust and harmful conclusions, but it surely seemed to me that the Secretary of State, the Secretary of War, the Secretary of the Treasury, and others of my *confrères*, had conspired from the very beginning to drive me from the Administration. I never attended but one **Cabinet** meeting while I was connected with the Government. That was sufficient for me. The servant at the White House door did not seem disposed to make way for me until I asked if the other members of the Cabinet had arrived. He said they had, and I entered. They were all there; but nobody offered me a seat. They stared at me as if I had been an intruder. The President said:

" Well, sir, who are *you* ?"

I handed him my card, and he read: " The HON. MARK TWAIN, Clerk of the Senate Committee on Conchology." Then he looked at me from head to foot, as if he had never heard of me before. The Secretary of the Treasury said:

" This is the meddlesome ass that came to recommend me to put poetry and conundrums in my report, as if it were an almanac."

The Secretary of War said: " It is the same visionary that came to me yesterday with a scheme to educate a portion of the Indians to death, and massacre the balance."

The Secretary of the Navy said: " I recognize this youth as the person who has been interfering with my business time and again during the week. He is distressed about Admiral Farragut's using a whole fleet for a pleasure excursion, as he terms it. His proposition about some insane pleasure excursion on a raft is too absurd to repeat."

I said: " Gentlemen, I perceive here a disposition

23

to throw discredit upon every act of my official career; I perceive, also, a disposition to debar me from all voice in the counsels of the nation. No notice whatever was sent to me to-day. It was only by the merest chance that I learned that there was going to be a Cabinet meeting. But let these things pass. All I wish to know is, is this a Cabinet meeting or is it not?"

The President said it was.

"Then," I said, "let us proceed to business at once, and not fritter away valuable time in unbecoming fault-findings with each other's official conduct."

The Secretary of State now spoke up, in his benignant way, and said, "Young man, you are laboring under a mistake. The clerks of the Congressional committees are not members of the Cabinet. Neither are the doorkeepers of the Capitol, strange as it may seem. Therefore, much as we could desire your more than human wisdom in our deliberations, we cannot lawfully avail ourselves of it. The counsels of the nation must proceed without you; if disaster follows, as follow full well it may, be it balm to your sorrowing spirit, that by deed and voice you did what in you lay to avert it. You have my blessing. Farewell."

These gentle words soothed my troubled breast, and I went away. But the servants of a nation can know no peace. I had hardly reached my den in the Capitol, and disposed my feet on the table like a representative, when one of the Senators on the Conchological Committee came in in a passion and said:

"Where have you been all day?"

I observed that, if that was anybody's affair but my own, I had been to a Cabinet meeting.

"To a Cabinet meeting? I would like to know what business you had at a Cabinet meeting?"

I said I went there to consult — allowing for the sake of argument that he was in anywise concerned in the matter. He grew insolent then, and ended by saying he had wanted me for three days past to copy a report on bomb-shells, egg-shells, clam-shells, and I don't know what all, connected with conchology, and nobody had been able to find me.

This was too much. This was the feather that broke the clerical camel's back. I said, "Sir, do you suppose that I am going to *work* for six dollars a day? If that is the idea, let me recommend the Senate Committee on Conchology to hire somebody else. I am the slave of *no* faction! Take back your degrading commission. Give me liberty, or give me death!"

From that hour I was no longer connected with the Government. Snubbed by the department, snubbed by the Cabinet, snubbed at last by the chairman of a committee I was endeavoring to adorn, I yielded to persecution, cast far from me the perils and seductions of my great office, and forsook my bleeding country in the hour of her peril.

W

356 Facts Concerning the Recent Resignation

But I had done the State some service, and I sent
in my bill:

The United States of America in account with
the Hon. Clerk of the Senate Committee on Conchology, Dr.

To consultation with Secretary of War, . . .		$50
To consultation with Secretary of Navy, . . .		50
To consultation with Secretary of the Treasury, . .		50
Cabinet consultation, . . .	No charge.	
To mileage to and from Jerusalem,* *via* Egypt, Algiers, Gibraltar, and Cadiz, 14,000 miles, at 20c. a mile,		2800
To salary as Clerk of Senate Committee on Conchology, six days, at $6 per day, ...		36
Total, ...		$2986

Not an item of this bill has been paid, except that
trifle of thirty-six dollars for clerkship salary. The
Secretary of the Treasury, pursuing me to the last,
drew his pen through all the other items, and simply
marked in the margin "Not allowed." So, the
dread alternative is embraced at last. Repudiation
has begun! The nation is lost.

I am done with official life for the present. Let
those clerks who are willing to be imposed on remain. I know numbers of them in the departments
who are never informed when there is to be a
Cabinet meeting, whose advice is never asked about
war, or finance, or commerce, by the heads of the
nation, any more than if they were not connected
with the Government, and who actually stay in their

---

* Territorial delegates charge mileage both ways, although they
never go back when they get here once. Why my mileage is denied
me is more than I can understand.

offices day after day and work! They know their importance to the nation, and they unconsciously show it in their bearing, and the way they order their sustenance at the restaurant — but they work. I know one who has to paste all sorts of little scraps from the newspaper into a scrapbook — sometimes as many as eight or ten scraps a day. He doesn't do it well, but he does it as well as he can. It is very fatiguing. It is exhausting to the intellect. Yet he only gets eighteen hundred dollars a year. With a brain like his, that young man could amass thousands and thousands of dollars in some other pursuit, if he chose to do it. But no — his heart is with his country, and he will serve her as long as she has got a scrapbook left. And I know clerks that don't know how to write very well, but such knowledge as they possess they nobly lay at the feet of their country, and toil on and suffer for twenty-five hundred dollars a year. What they write has to be written over again by other clerks sometimes; but when a man has done his best for his country, should his country complain? Then there are clerks that have no clerkships, and are waiting, and waiting, and waiting, for a vacancy — waiting patiently for a chance to help their country out — and while they are waiting, they only get barely two thousand dollars a year for it. It is sad — it is very, very sad. When a member of Congress has a friend who is gifted, but has no employment wherein his great powers may be brought to bear, he confers him upon his country, and gives him a clerkship in a department. And there that man has to slave his life out, fighting documents for the benefit of a nation that never thinks of him, never sympathizes with him — and all for two thousand or three thousand dollars a year. When I shall have completed my list of all the clerks in the several departments, with my statement of what they have to do, and what they get for it, you will see that there are not half enough clerks, and that what there are do not get half enough pay.

HISTORY REPEATS ITSELF

THE following I find in a Sandwich Island paper which some friend has sent me from that tranquil far-off retreat. The coincidence between my own experience and that here set down by the late Mr. Benton is so remarkable that I cannot forbear publishing and commenting upon the paragraph. The Sandwich Island paper says:

"How touching is this tribute of the late Hon. T. H. Benton to his mother's influence:—'My mother asked me never to use tobacco; I have never touched it from that time to the present day. She asked me not to gamble, and I have never gambled. I cannot tell who is losing in games that are being played. She admonished me, too, against liquor-drinking, and whatever capacity for endurance I have at present, and whatever usefulness I may have attained through life, I attribute to having complied with her pious and correct wishes. When I was seven years of age she asked me not to drink, and then I made a resolution of total abstinence; and that I have adhered to it through all time I owe to my mother.'"

I never saw anything so curious. It is almost an exact epitome of my own moral career — after simply substituting a grandmother for a mother. How well I remember my grandmother's asking me not to use tobacco, good old soul! She said, "You're at it again, are you, you whelp? Now don't ever let me catch you chewing tobacco before breakfast again, or I lay I'll blacksnake you within an inch of your life!'' I have never touched it at that hour of the morning from that time to the present day.

She asked me not to gamble. She whispered and said, '' Put up those wicked cards this minute! — two pair and a jack, you numskull, and the other fellow's got a flush!''

I never have gambled from that day to this — never once — without a '' cold deck '' in my pocket. I cannot even tell who is going to lose in games that are being played unless I dealt myself.

When I was two years of age she asked me not to drink, and then I made a resolution of total abstinence. That I have adhered to it and enjoyed the beneficent effects of it through all time, I owe to my grandmother. I have never drunk a drop from that day to this of any kind of water.

HONORED AS A CURIOSITY

IF you get into conversation with a stranger in
Honolulu, and experience that natural desire to
know what sort of ground you are treading on by
finding out what manner of man your stranger is,
strike out boldly and address him as " Captain."
Watch him narrowly, and if you see by his countenance that you are on the wrong track, ask him
where he preaches. It is a safe bet that he is either
a missionary or captain of a whaler. I became personally acquainted with seventy-two captains and
ninety-six missionaries. The captains and ministers
form one-half of the population; the third fourth is
composed of common Kanakas and mercantile
foreigners and their families; and the final fourth
is made up of high officers of the Hawaiian Government. And there are just about cats enough for
three apiece all around.

A solemn stranger met me in the suburbs one
day, and said:

" Good morning, your reverence. Preach in the
stone church yonder, no doubt!"

"No, I don't. I'm not a preacher."

"Really, I beg your pardon, captain. I trust you had a good season. How much oil —"

"Oil! Why, what do you take me for? I'm not a whaler."

"Oh! I beg a thousand pardons, your Excellency. Major-General in the household troops, no doubt? Minister of the Interior, likely? Secretary of War? First Gentleman of the Bedchamber? Commissioner of the Royal —"

"Stuff! man. I'm not connected in any way with the Government."

"Bless my life! Then who the mischief are you? what the mischief are you? and how the mischief did you get here? and where in thunder did you come from?"

"I'm only a private personage — an unassuming stranger — lately arrived from America."

"No! Not a missionary! not a whaler! not a member of his Majesty's Government! not even a Secretary of the Navy! Ah! heaven! it is too blissful to be true; alas! I do but dream. And yet that noble, honest countenance — those oblique, ingenuous eyes — that massive head, incapable of — of anything; your hand; give me your hand, bright waif. Excuse these tears. For sixteen weary years I have yearned for a moment like this, and —"

Here his feelings were too much for him, and he swooned away. I pitied this poor creature from the

bottom of my heart. I was deeply moved. I shed
a few tears on him, and kissed him for his mother.
I then took what small change he had, and
" shoved."

FIRST INTERVIEW WITH ARTEMUS WARD*

I HAD never seen him before. He brought letters of introduction from mutual friends in San Francisco, and by invitation I breakfasted with him. It was almost religion, there in the silver mines, to precede such a meal with whisky cocktails. Artemus, with the true cosmopolitan instinct, always deferred to the customs of the country he was in, and so he ordered three of those abominations. Hingston was present. I said I would rather not drink a whisky cocktail. I said it would go right to my head, and confuse me so that I would be in a helpless tangle in ten minutes. I did not want to act like a lunatic before strangers. But Artemus gently insisted, and I drank the treasonable mixture under protest, and felt all the time that I was doing a thing I might be sorry for. In a minute or two I began to imagine that my ideas were clouded. I waited in great anxiety for the conversation to open, with a sort of vague hope that my understanding would prove clear, after all, and my misgivings groundless.

Artemus dropped an unimportant remark or two,

---

* Written about 1870.

and then assumed a look of superhuman earnestness, and made the following astounding speech. He said:

" Now there is one thing I ought to ask you about before I forget it. You have been here in Silverland — here in Nevada — two or three years, and, of course, your position on the daily press has made it necessary for you to go down in the mines and examine them carefully in detail, and therefore you know all about the silver-mining business. Now what I want to get at is — is, well, the way the deposits of ore are made, you know. For instance. Now, as I understand it, the vein which contains the silver is sandwiched in between casings of granite, and runs along the ground, and sticks up like a curbstone. Well, take a vein forty feet thick, for example, or eighty, for that matter, or even a hundred — say you go down on it with a shaft, straight down, you know, or with what you call ' incline,' maybe you go down five hundred feet, or maybe you don't go down but two hundred — anyway you go down, and all the time this vein grows narrower, when the casings come nearer or approach each other, you may say — that is, when they do approach, which, of course, they do not always do, particularly in cases where the nature of the formation is such that they stand apart wider than they otherwise would, and which geology has failed to account for, although everything in that science goes to prove that, all things being equal, it would if it did not, or would not certainly if it did, and then, of course, they are. Do not you think it is?"

I said to myself:

"Now I just knew how it would be — that whisky cocktail has done the business for me; I don't understand any more than a clam."

And then I said aloud:

"I — I — that is — if you don't mind, would you — would you say that over again? I ought —"

"Oh, certainly, certainly! You see I am very unfamiliar with the subject, and perhaps I don't present my case clearly, but I —"

"No, no — no, no — you state it plain enough, but that cocktail has muddled me a little. But I will — no, I do understand for that matter; but I would get the hang of it all the better if you went over it again — and I'll pay better attention this time."

He said, "Why, what I was after was this."

[Here he became even more fearfully impressive than ever, and emphasized each particular point by checking it off on his finger ends.]

"This vein, or lode, or ledge, or whatever you call it, runs along between two layers of granite, just the same as if it were a sandwich. Very well. Now suppose you go down on that, say a thousand feet, or maybe twelve hundred (it don't really matter) before you drift, and then you start your drifts, some of them across the ledge, and others along the length of it, where the sulphurets — I believe they

call them sulphurets, though why they should, considering that, so far as I can see, the main dependence of a miner does not so lie, as some suppose,
but in which it cannot be successfully maintained,
wherein the same should not continue, while part
and parcel of the same ore not committed to either
in the sense referred to, whereas, under different
circumstances, the most inexperienced among us
could not detect it if it were, or might overlook it if
it did, or scorn the very idea of such a thing, even
though it were palpably demonstrated as such.   Am
I not right?"

I said, sorrowfully: " I feel ashamed of myself,
Mr. Ward. I know I ought to understand you perfectly well, but you see that treacherous whisky
cocktail has got into my head, and now I cannot
understand even the simplest proposition. I told
you how it would be."

" Oh, don't mind it, don't mind it; the fault was
my own, no doubt — though I did think it clear
enough for —"

" Don't say a word. Clear! Why, you stated
it as clear as the sun to anybody but an abject idiot;
but it's that confounded cocktail that has played the
mischief."

" No; now don't say that. I'll begin it all over
again, and —"

" Don't now — for goodness' sake, don't do anything of the kind, because I tell you my head is in
such a condition that I don't believe I could under-

stand the most trifling question a man could ask me."

"Now don't you be afraid. I'll put it so plain this time that you can't help but get the hang of it. We will begin at the very beginning." [Leaning far across the table, with determined impressiveness wrought upon his every feature, and fingers prepared to keep tally of each point enumerated; and I, leaning forward with painful interest, resolved to comprehend or perish.] "You know the vein, the ledge, the thing that contains the metal, whereby it constitutes the medium between all other forces, whether of present or remote agencies, so brought to bear in favor of the former against the latter, or the latter against the former or all, or both, or compromising the relative differences existing within the radius whence culminate the several degrees of similarity to which —"

I said: "Oh, hang my wooden head, it ain't any use! — it ain't any use to try — I can't understand anything. The plainer you get it the more I can't get the hang of it."

I heard a suspicious noise behind me, and turned in time to see Hingston dodging behind a newspaper, and quaking with a gentle ecstasy of laughter. I looked at Ward again, and he had thrown off his dread solemnity and was laughing also. Then I saw that I had been sold — that I had been made a victim of a swindle in the way of a string of plausibly worded sentences that didn't mean anything under

the sun.   Artemus Ward was one of the best fellows
in the world, and one of the most companionable.
It has been said that he was not fluent in conversation, but, with the above experience in my mind, I
differ.

CANNIBALISM IN THE CARS *

I VISITED St. Louis lately, and on my way West, after changing cars at Terre Haute, Indiana, a mild, benevolent-looking gentleman of about forty-five, or maybe fifty, came in at one of the way-stations and sat down beside me. We talked together pleasantly on various subjects for an hour, perhaps, and I found him exceedingly intelligent and enter-taining. When he learned that I was from Washing-ton, he immediately began to ask questions about various public men, and about Congressional affairs; and I saw very shortly that I was conversing with a man who was perfectly familiar with the ins and outs of political life at the Capital, even to the ways and manners, and customs of procedure of Senators and Representatives in the Chambers of the National Legislature. Presently two men halted near us for a single moment, and one said to the other:

"Harris, if you'll do that for me, I'll never forget you, my boy."

My new comrade's eye lighted pleasantly. The words had touched upon a happy memory, I

---

* Written about 1867.

thought. Then his face settled into thoughtfulness — almost into gloom. He turned to me and said, " Let me tell you a story; let me give you a secret chapter of my life — a chapter that has never been referred to by me since its events transpired. Listen patiently, and promise that you will not interrupt me."

I said I would not, and he related the following strange adventure, speaking sometimes with animation, sometimes with melancholy, but always with feeling and earnestness.

THE STRANGER'S NARRATIVE.

' On the 19th of December, 1853, I started from St. Louis on the evening train bound for Chicago. There were only twenty-four passengers, all told. There were no ladies and no children. We were in excellent spirits, and pleasant acquaintanceships were soon formed. The journey bade fair to be a happy one; and no individual in the party, I think, had even the vaguest presentiment of the horrors we were soon to undergo.

"At 11 P. M. it began to snow hard. Shortly after leaving the small village of Welden, we entered upon that tremendous prairie solitude that stretches its leagues on leagues of houseless dreariness far away toward the Jubilee Settlements. The winds, unobstructed by trees or hills, or even vagrant rocks, whistled fiercely across the level desert, driving the falling snow before it like spray from the crested

x

waves of a stormy sea. The snow was deepening fast; and we knew, by the diminished speed of the train, that the engine was plowing through it with steadily increasing difficulty. Indeed, it almost came to a dead halt sometimes, in the midst of great drifts that piled themselves like colossal graves across the track. Conversation began to flag. Cheerfulness gave place to grave concern. The possibility of being imprisoned in the snow, on the bleak prairie, fifty miles from any house, presented itself to every mind, and extended its depressing influence over every spirit.

" At two o'clock in the morning I was aroused out of an uneasy slumber by the ceasing of all motion about me. The appalling truth flashed upon me instantly — we were captives in a snow-drift! ' All hands to the rescue !' Every man sprang to obey. Out into the wild night, the pitchy darkness, the billowy snow, the driving storm, every soul leaped, with the consciousness that a moment lost now might bring destruction to us all. Shovels, hands, boards — anything, everything that could displace snow, was brought into instant requisition. It was a weird picture, that small company of frantic men fighting the banking snows, half in the blackest shadow and half in the angry light of the locomotive's reflector.

" One short hour sufficed to prove the utter uselessness of our efforts. The storm barricaded the track with a dozen drifts while we dug one away.

And worse than this, it was discovered that the last grand charge the engine had made upon the enemy had broken the fore-and-aft shaft of the driving-wheel! With a free track before us we should still have been helpless. We entered the car wearied with labor, and very sorrowful. We gathered about the stoves, and gravely canvassed our situation. We had no provisions whatever — in this lay our chief distress. We could not freeze, for there was a good supply of wood in the tender. This was our only comfort. The discussion ended at last in accepting the disheartening decision of the conductor, viz., that it would be death for any man to attempt to travel fifty miles on foot through snow like that. We could not send for help, and even if we could it would not come. We must submit, and await, as patiently as we might, succor or starvation! I think the stoutest heart there felt a momentary chill when those words were uttered.

" Within the hour conversation subsided to a low murmur here and there about the car, caught fitfully between the rising and falling of the blast; the lamps grew dim; and the majority of the castaways settled themselves among the flickering shadows to think — to forget the present, if they could — to sleep, if they might.

" The eternal night — it surely seemed eternal to us — wore its lagging hours away at last, and the cold gray dawn broke in the east. As the light grew stronger the passengers began to stir and give

signs of life, one after another, and each in turn
pushed his slouched hat up from his forehead,
stretched his stiffened limbs, and glanced out at the
windows upon the cheerless prospect. It was cheerless, indeed! — not a living thing visible anywhere,
not a human habitation; nothing but a vast white
desert; uplifted sheets of snow drifting hither and
thither before the wind — a world of eddying flakes
shutting out the firmament above.

"All day we moped about the cars, saying little,
thinking much. Another lingering dreary night —
and hunger.

"Another dawning — another day of silence, sadness, wasting hunger, hopeless watching for succor
that could not come. A night of restless slumber,
filled with dreams of feasting — wakings distressed
with the gnawings of hunger.

"The fourth day came and went — and the fifth!
Five days of dreadful imprisonment! A savage
hunger looked out at every eye. There was in it a
sign of awful import — the foreshadowing of a something that was vaguely shaping itself in every heart—
a something which no tongue dared yet to frame
into words.

"The sixth day passed — the seventh dawned
upon as gaunt and haggard and hopeless a company
of men as ever stood in the shadow of death. It
must out now! That thing which had been growing
up in every heart was ready to leap from every lip
at last! Nature had been taxed to the utmost — she

must yield. RICHARD H. GASTON of Minnesota, tall, cadaverous, and pale, rose up. All knew what was coming. All prepared — every motion, every semblance of excitement was smothered — only a calm, thoughtful seriousness appeared in the eyes that were lately so wild.

" ' Gentlemen: It cannot be delayed longer! The time is at hand! We must determine which of us shall die to furnish food for the rest!'

" MR. JOHN J. WILLIAMS of Illinois rose and said: 'Gentlemen — I nominate the Rev. James Sawyer of Tennessee.'

" MR. WM. R. ADAMS of Indiana said: 'I nominate Mr. Daniel Slote of New York.'

" MR. CHARLES J. LANGDON: 'I nominate Mr. Samuel A. Bowen of St. Louis.'

" MR. SLOTE: 'Gentlemen — I desire to decline in favor of Mr. John A. Van Nostrand, Jun., of New Jersey.'

" MR. GASTON: 'If there be no objection, the gentleman's desire will be acceded to.'

" MR. VAN NOSTRAND objecting, the resignation of Mr. Slote was rejected. The resignations of Messrs. Sawyer and Bowen were also offered, and refused upon the same grounds.

" MR. A. L. BASCOM of Ohio: 'I move that the nominations now close, and that the House proceed to an election by ballot.'

" MR. SAWYER: 'Gentlemen — I protest earnestly against these proceedings. They are, in every way, irregular and unbecoming. I must beg to move that they be dropped at once, and that we elect a chairman of the meeting and proper officers to assist him, and then we can go on with the business before us understandingly.'

"MR. BELL of Iowa: 'Gentlemen — I object. This is no time to stand upon forms and ceremonious observances. For more than seven days we have been without food. Every moment we lose in idle discussion increases our distress. I am satisfied with the nominations that have been made — every gentleman present is, I believe — and I, for one, do not see why we should not proceed at once to elect one or more of them. I wish to offer a resolution —'

"MR. GASTON: 'It would be objected to, and have to lie over one day under the rules, thus bringing about the very delay you wish to avoid. The gentleman from New Jersey —'

"MR. VAN NOSTRAND: 'Gentlemen — I am a stranger among you; I have not sought the distinction that has been conferred upon me, and I feel a delicacy —'

"MR. MORGAN of Alabama (interrupting): 'I move the previous question.'

"The motion was carried, and further debate shut off, of course. The motion to elect officers was passed, and under it Mr. Gaston was chosen chairman, Mr. Blake, secretary, Messrs. Holcomb, Dyer, and Baldwin, a committee on nominations, and Mr.

R. M. Howland, purveyor, to assist the committee in making selections.

" A recess of half an hour was then taken, and some little caucussing followed. At the sound of the gavel the meeting reassembled, and the committee reported in favor of Messrs. George Ferguson of Kentucky, Lucien Herrman of Louisiana, and W. Messick of Colorado as candidates. The report was accepted.

" MR. ROGERS of Missouri: ' Mr. President — The report being properly before the House now, I move to amend it by substituting for the name of Mr. Herrman that of Mr. Lucius Harris of St. Louis, who is well and honorably known to us all. I do not wish to be understood as casting the least reflection upon the high character and standing of the gentleman from Louisiana — far from it. I respect and esteem him as much as any gentleman here present possibly can; but none of us can be blind to the fact that he has lost more flesh during the week that we have lain here than any among us — none of us can be blind to the fact that the committee has been derelict in its duty, either through negligence or a graver fault, in thus offering for our suffrages a gentleman who, however pure his own motives may be, has really less nutriment in him —'

" THE CHAIR: ' The gentleman from Missouri will take his seat. The Chair cannot allow the integrity of the committee to be questioned save by the regular course, under the rules. What action will the House take upon the gentleman's motion?'

"MR. HALLIDAY of Virginia: 'I move to further amend the report by substituting Mr. Harvey Davis of Oregon for Mr. Messick. It may be urged by gentlemen that the hardships and privations of a frontier life have rendered Mr. Davis tough; but, gentlemen, is this a time to cavil at toughness? Is this a time to be fastidious concerning trifles? Is this a time to dispute about matters of paltry significance? No, gentlemen, bulk is what we desire — substance, weight, bulk — these are the supreme requisites now — not talent, not genius, not education. I insist upon my motion.'

"MR. MORGAN (excitedly): 'Mr. Chairman — I do most strenuously object to this amendment. The gentleman from Oregon is old, and furthermore is bulky only in bone — not in flesh. I ask the gentleman from Virginia if it is soup we want instead of solid sustenance? if he would delude us with shadows? if he would mock our suffering with an Oregonian specter? I ask him if he can look upon the anxious faces around him, if he can gaze into our sad eyes, if he can listen to the beating of our expectant hearts, and still thrust this famine-stricken fraud upon us? I ask him if he can think of our desolate state, of our past sorrows, of our dark future, and still unpityingly foist upon us this wreck, this ruin, this tottering swindle, this gnarled and blighted and sapless vagabond from Oregon's inhospitable shores? Never!' [Applause.]

" The amendment was put to vote, after a fiery debate, and lost. Mr. Harris was substituted on the first amendment. The balloting then began. Five ballots were held without a choice. On the sixth, Mr. Harris was elected, all voting for him but himself. It was then moved that his election should be ratified by acclamation, which was lost, in consequence of his again voting against himself.

" Mr. Radway moved that the House now take up the remaining candidates, and go into an election for breakfast. This was carried.

" On the first ballot there was a tie, half the members favoring one candidate on account of his youth, and half favoring the other on account of his superior size. The President gave the casting vote for the latter, Mr. Messick. This decision created considerable dissatisfaction among the friends of Mr. Ferguson, the defeated candidate, and there was some talk of demanding a new ballot; but in the midst of it, a motion to adjourn was carried, and the meeting broke up at once.

" The preparations for supper diverted the attention of the Ferguson faction from the discussion of their grievance for a long time, and then, when they would have taken it up again, the happy announcement that Mr. Harris was ready, drove all thought of it to the winds.

" We improvised tables by propping up the backs

of car-seats, and sat down with hearts full of gratitude to the finest supper that had blessed our vision
for seven torturing days. How changed we were
from what we had been a few short hours before!
Hopeless, sad-eyed misery, hunger, feverish anxiety,
desperation, then — thankfulness, serenity, joy too
deep for utterance now. That I know was the
cheeriest hour of my eventful life. The wind
howled, and blew the snow wildly about our prison-
house, but they were powerless to distress us any
more. I liked Harris. He might have been better
done, perhaps, but I am free to say that no man
ever agreed with me better than Harris, or afforded
me so large a degree of satisfaction. Messick was
very well, though rather high-flavored, but for genuine nutritiousness and delicacy of fiber, give me
Harris. Messick had his good points — I will not
attempt to deny it, nor do I wish to do it — but he
was no more fitted for breakfast than a mummy
would be, sir — not a bit. Lean? — why, bless me!
— and tough? Ah, he was very tough! You could
not imagine it — you could never imagine anything
like it."

"Do you mean to tell me that —"

"Do not interrupt me, please. After breakfast
we elected a man by the name of Walker, from
Detroit, for supper. He was very good. I wrote
his wife so afterwards. He was worthy of all
praise. I shall always remember Walker. He was
a little rare, but very good. And then the next

morning we had Morgan of Alabama for breakfast.
He was one of the finest men I ever sat down to —
handsome, educated, refined, spoke several languages
fluently — a perfect gentleman — he was a perfect
gentleman, and singularly juicy. For supper we
had that Oregon patriarch, and he *was* a fraud,
there is no question about it — old, scraggy, tough,
nobody can picture the reality. I finally said, gentlemen, you can do as you like, but *I* will wait for
another election. And Grimes of Illinois said,
' Gentlemen, *I* will wait also. When you elect a
man that has *something* to recommend him, I shall
be glad to join you again.' It soon became evident
that there was general dissatisfaction with Davis of
Oregon, and so, to preserve the good-will that had
prevailed so pleasantly since we had had Harris, an
election was called, and the result of it was that
Baker of Georgia was chosen. He was splendid!
Well, well — after that we had Doolittle, and Haw-
kins, and McElroy (there was some complaint about
McElroy, because he was uncommonly short and
thin), and Penrod, and two Smiths, and Bailey
(Bailey had a wooden leg, which was clear loss, but
he was otherwise good), and an Indian boy, and an
organ-grinder, and a gentleman by the name of
Buckminster — a poor stick of a vagabond that
wasn't any good for company and no account for
breakfast. We were glad we got him elected before
relief came."

" And so the blessed relief *did* come at last?"

"Yes, it came one bright, sunny morning, just after election. John Murphy was the choice, and there never was a better, I am willing to testify; but John Murphy came home with us, in the train that came to succor us, and lived to marry the widow Harris —"

"Relict of —"

"Relict of our first choice. He married her, and is happy and respected and prosperous yet. Ah, it was like a novel, sir — it was like a romance. This is my stopping-place, sir; I must bid you good-bye. Any time that you can make it convenient to tarry a day or two with me, I shall be glad to have you. I like you, sir; I have conceived an affection for you. I could like you as well as I liked Harris himself, sir. Good day, sir, and a pleasant journey."

He was gone. I never felt so stunned, so distressed, so bewildered in my life. But in my soul I was glad he was gone. With all his gentleness of manner and his soft voice, I shuddered whenever he turned his hungry eye upon me; and when I heard that I had achieved his perilous affection, and that I stood almost with the late Harris in his esteem, my heart fairly stood still!

I was bewildered beyond description. I did not doubt his word; I could not question a single item in a statement so stamped with the earnestness of truth as his; but its dreadful details overpowered me, and threw my thoughts into hopeless confusion.

I saw the conductor looking at me. I said, " Who is that man?"

" He was a member of Congress once, and a good one. But he got caught in a snowdrift in the cars, and like to have been starved to death. He got so frost-bitten and frozen up generally, and used up for want of something to eat, that he was sick and out of his head two or three months afterward. He is all right now, only he is a monomaniac, and when he gets on that old subject he never stops till he has eat up that whole car-load of people he talks about. He would have finished the crowd by this time, only he had to get out here. He has got their names as pat as A B C. When he gets them all eat up but himself, he always says: ' Then the hour for the usual election for breakfast having arrived, and there being no opposition, I was duly elected, after which, there being no objections offered, I resigned. Thus I am here.' "

I felt inexpressibly relieved to know that I had only been listening to the harmless vagaries of a madman instead of the genuine experiences of a bloodthirsty cannibal.

THE KILLING OF JULIUS CÆSAR "LOCALIZED"*

Being the only true and reliable account ever published ; taken from the Roman " Daily Evening Fasces," of the date of that tremendous occurrence.

NOTHING in the world affords a newspaper reporter so much satisfaction as gathering up the details of a bloody and mysterious murder, and writing them up with aggravating circumstantiality. He takes a living delight in this labor of love — for such it is to him, especially if he knows that all the other papers have gone to press, and his will be the only one that will contain the dreadful intelligence. A feeling of regret has often come over me that I was not reporting in Rome when Cæsar was killed — reporting on an evening paper, and the only one in the city, and getting at least twelve hours ahead of the morning-paper boys with this most magnificent " item " that ever fell to the lot of the craft. Other events have happened as startling as this, but

* Written about 1865.

none that possessed so peculiarly all the characteristics of the favorite " item " of the present day,
magnified into grandeur and sublimity by the high
rank, fame, and social and political standing of the
actors in it.

However, as I was not permitted to report Cæsar's
assassination in the regular way, it has at least
afforded me rare satisfaction to translate the following able account of it from the original Latin of the
Roman Daily Evening Fasces of that date — second
edition.

" Our usually quiet city of Rome was thrown into a state of wild
excitement yesterday by the occurrence of one of those bloody affrays
which sicken the heart and fill the soul with fear, while they inspire all
thinking men with forebodings for the future of a city where human life
is held so cheaply, and the gravest laws are so openly set at defiance.
As the result of that affray, it is our painful duty, as public journalists,
to record the death of one of our most esteemed citizens — a man whose
name is known wherever this paper circulates, and whose fame it has
been our pleasure and our privilege to extend, and also to protect from
the tongue of slander and falsehood, to the best of our poor ability.
We refer to Mr. J. Cæsar, the Emperor-elect.

" The facts of the case, as nearly as our reporter could determine them
from the conflicting statements of eye-witnesses, were about as follows:—
The affair was an election row, of course. Nine-tenths of the ghastly
butcheries that disgrace the city now-a-days grow out of the bickerings
and jealousies and animosities engendered by these accursed elections.
Rome would be the gainer by it if her very constables were elected to
serve a century; for in our experience we have never even been able to
choose a dog-pelter without celebrating the event with a dozen knock-
downs and a general cramming of the station-house with drunken vaga-
bonds overnight. It is said that when the immense majority for Cæsar
at the polls in the market was declared the other day, and the crown
was offered to that gentleman, even his amazing unselfishness in refusing
it three times was not sufficient to save him from the whispered insults

25

of such men as Casca, of the Tenth Ward, and other hirelings of the disappointed candidate, hailing mostly from the Eleventh and Thirteenth and other outside districts, who were overheard speaking ironically and contemptuously of Mr. Cæsar's conduct upon that occasion.

"We are further informed that there are many among us who think they are justified in believing that the assassination of Julius Cæsar was a put-up thing—a cut-and-dried arrangement, hatched by Marcus Brutus and a lot of his hired roughs, and carried out only too faithfully according to the programme. Whether there be good grounds for this suspicion or not, we leave to the people to judge for themselves, only asking that they will read the following account of the sad occurrence carefully and dispassionately before they render that judgment.

"The Senate was already in session, and Cæsar was coming down the street towards the capitol, conversing with some personal friends, and followed, as usual, by a large number of citizens. Just as he was passing in front of Demosthenes and Thucydides' drug-store, he was observing casually to a gentleman, who, our informant thinks, is a fortune-teller, that the Ides of March were come. The reply was, 'Yes, they are come, but not gone yet.' At this moment Artemidorus stepped up and passed the time of day, and asked Cæsar to read a schedule or a tract or something of the kind, which he had brought for his perusal. Mr. Decius Brutus also said something about an 'humble suit' which *he* wanted read. Artemidorus begged that attention might be paid to his first, because it was of personal consequence to Cæsar. The latter replied that what concerned himself should be read last, or words to that effect. Artemidorus begged and beseeched him to read the paper instantly.* However, Cæsar shook him off, and refused to read any petition in the street. He then entered the capitol, and the crowd followed him.

"About this time the following conversation was overheard, and we consider that, taken in connection with the events which succeeded it, it bears an appalling significance: Mr. Papilius Lena remarked to George W. Cassius (commonly known as the 'Nobby Boy of the Third Ward'), a bruiser in the pay of the Opposition, that he hoped his

---

* Mark that: It is hinted by William Shakespeare, who saw the beginning and the end of the unfortunate affray, that this "schedule" was simply a note discovering to Cæsar that a plot was brewing to take his life.

enterprise to-day might thrive; and when Cassius asked 'What enterprise?' he only closed his left eye temporarily and said with simulated indifference, 'Fare you well,' and sauntered towards Cæsar. Marcus Brutus, who is suspected of being the ringleader of the band that killed Cæsar, asked what it was that Lena had said. Cassius told him, and added in a low tone, '*I fear our purpose is discovered.*'

"Brutus told his wretched accomplice to keep an eye on Lena, and a moment after Cassius urged that lean and hungry vagrant, Casca, whose reputation here is none of the best, to be sudden for *he feared prevention.* He then turned to Brutus, apparently much excited, and asked what should be done, and swore that either he or Cæsar *should never turn back* — he would kill himself first. At this time Cæsar was talking to some of the back-country members about the approaching fall elections, and paying little attention to what was going on around him. Billy Trebonius got into conversation with the people's friend and Cæsar's — Mark Antony — and under some pretence or other got him away, and Brutus, Decius, Casca, Cinna, Metellus Cimber, and others of the gang of infamous desperadoes that infest Rome at present, closed around the doomed Cæsar. Then Metellus Cimber knelt down and begged that his brother might be recalled from banishment, but Cæsar rebuked him for his fawning conduct, and refused to grant his petition. Immediately, at Cimber's request, first Brutus and then Cassius begged for the return of the banished Publius; but Cæsar still refused. He said he could not be moved; that he was as fixed as the North Star, and proceeded to speak in the most complimentary terms of the firmness of that star and its steady character. Then he said he was like it, and he believed he was the only man in the country that was; therefore, since he was 'constant' that Cimber should be banished, he was also 'constant' that he should stay banished, and he'd be hanged if he didn't keep him so !

"Instantly seizing upon this shallow pretext for a fight, Casca sprang at Cæsar and struck him with a dirk, Cæsar grabbing him by the arm with his right hand, and launching a blow straight from the shoulder with his left, that sent the reptile bleeding to the earth. He then backed up against Pompey's statue, and squared himself to receive his assailants. Cassius and Cimber and Cinna rushed upon him with their daggers drawn, and the former succeeded in inflicting a wound upon his body; but before he could strike again, and before either of the others could strike at all, Cæsar stretched the three miscreants at his feet with as many blows of his powerful fist. By this time the Senate was in an indescribable uproar; the throng of citizens in the lobbies had blockaded the doors in their frantic efforts to escape from the building, the sergeant-at-arms and his assistants were struggling with the assassins, venerable senators had cast aside their encumbering robes, and were leaping over benches and flying down the aisles in wild confusion towards the shelter of the committee-rooms, and a thousand voices were shouting ' Po-lice ! Po-lice !' in discordant tones that rose above the frightful din like shrieking winds above the roaring of a tempest. And amid it all, great Cæsar stood with his back against the statue, like a lion at bay, and fought his assailants weaponless and hand to hand, with the defiant bearing and the unwavering courage which he had shown before on many a bloody field. Billy Trebonius and Caius Legarius struck him with their daggers and fell, as their brother-conspirators before them had fallen. But at last, when Cæsar saw his old friend Brutus step forward armed with a murderous knife, it is said he seemed utterly overpowered with grief and amazement, and dropping his invincible left arm by his side, he hid his face in the folds of his mantle and received the treacherous blow without an effort to stay the hand that gave it. He only said, ' *Et tu, Brute ?* ' and fell lifeless on the marble pavement.

" We learn that the coat deceased had on when he was killed was the same one he wore in his tent on the afternoon of the day he overcame the Nervii, and that when it was removed from the corpse it was found to be cut and gashed in no less than seven different places. There was nothing in the pockets. It will be exhibited at the coroner's inquest, and will be damning proof of the fact of the killing. These latter facts may be relied on, as we get them from Mark Antony, whose position enables him to learn every item of news connected with the one subject of absorbing interest of to-day.

" LATER.— While the coroner was summoning a jury, Mark Antony and other friends of the late Cæsar got hold of the body, and lugged it off to the Forum, and at last accounts Antony and Brutus were making speeches over it and raising such a row among the people that, as we go to press, the chief of police is satisfied there is going to be a riot, and is taking measures accordingly."

THE WIDOW'S PROTEST

ONE of the saddest things that ever came under
my notice (said the banker's clerk) was there
in Corning during the war. Dan Murphy enlisted
as a private, and fought very bravely. The boys all
liked him, and when a wound by and by weakened
him down till carrying a musket was too heavy work
for him, they clubbed together and fixed him up as
a sutler. He made money then, and sent it always
to his wife to bank for him. She was a washer and
ironer, and knew enough by hard experience to keep
money when she got it. She didn't waste a penny.
On the contrary, she began to get miserly as her
bank account grew. She grieved to part with a
cent, poor creature, for twice in her hardworking
life she had known what it was to be hungry, cold,
friendless, sick, and without a dollar in the world,
and she had a haunting dread of suffering so again.
Well, at last Dan died; and the boys, in testimony
of their esteem and respect for him, telegraphed to
Mrs. Murphy to know if she would like to have him
embalmed and sent home; when you know the
usual custom was to dump a poor devil like him

into a shallow hole, and *then* inform his friends what had become of him. Mrs. Murphy jumped to the conclusion that it would only cost two or three dollars to embalm her dead husband, and so she telegraphed " Yes." It was at the " wake " that the bill for embalming arrived and was presented to the widow.

She uttered a wild sad wail that pierced every heart, and said, " Sivinty-foive dollars for stooffin' Dan, blister their sowls ! Did thim divils suppose I was goin' to stairt a Museim, that I'd be dalin' in such expinsive curiassities !"

The banker's clerk said there was not a dry eye in the house.

THE SCRIPTURAL PANORAMIST *

"THERE was a fellow traveling around in that country," said Mr. Nickerson, "with a moral-religious show — a sort of scriptural pano-rama — and he hired a wooden-headed old slab to play the piano for him. After the first night's per-formance the showman says:

"'My friend, you seem to know pretty much all the tunes there are, and you worry along first rate. But then, don't you notice that sometimes last night the piece you happened to be playing was a little rough on the proprieties, so to speak — didn't seem to jibe with the general gait of the picture that was passing at the time, as it were — was a little foreign to the subject, you know — as if you didn't either trump or follow suit, you understand?'

"'Well, no,' the fellow said; 'he hadn't noticed, but it might be; he had played along just as it came handy.'

"So they put it up that the simple old dummy was to keep his eye on the panorama after that, and as soon as a stunning picture was reeled out he was

* Written about 1866.

to fit it to a dot with a piece of music that would help the audience to get the idea of the subject, and warm them up like a camp-meeting revival. That sort of thing would corral their sympathies, the showman said.

" There was a big audience that night — mostly middle-aged and old people who belong to the church, and took a strong interest in Bible matters, and the balance were pretty much young bucks and heifers — they always come out strong on panoramas, you know, because it gives them a chance to taste one another's complexions in the dark.

" Well, the showman began to swell himself up for his lecture, and the old mud-dobber tackled the piano and ran his fingers up and down once or twice to see that she was all right, and the fellows behind the curtain commenced to grind out the panorama. The showman balanced his weight on his right foot, and propped his hands over his hips, and flung his eyes over his shoulder at the scenery, and said:

" ' Ladies and gentlemen, the painting now before you illustrates the beautiful and touching parable of the Prodigal Son. Observe the happy expression just breaking over the features of the poor, suffering youth — so worn and weary with his long march; note also the ecstasy beaming from the uplifted countenance of the aged father, and the joy that sparkles in the eyes of the excited group of youths and maidens, and seems ready to burst into the welcoming chorus from their lips. The lesson, my friends, is as solemn and instructive as the story is tender and beautiful.'

" The mud-dobber was all ready, and when the second speech was finished, struck up:

> " 'Oh, we'll all get blind drunk,
>   When Johnny comes marching home!'

" Some of the people giggled, and some groaned a little. The showman couldn't say a word; he looked at the pianist sharp, but he was all lovely and serene — *he* didn't know there was anything out of gear.

" The panorama moved on, and the showman drummed up his grit and started in fresh.

" ' Ladies and gentlemen, the fine picture now unfolding itself to your gaze exhibits one of the most notable events in Bible history — our Saviour and His disciples upon the Sea of Galilee. How grand, how awe-inspiring are the reflections which the subject invokes! What sublimity of faith is revealed to us in this lesson from the sacred writings! The Saviour rebukes the angry waves, and walks securely upon the bosom of the deep!'

" All around the house they were whispering, ' Oh, how lovely, how beautiful!' and the orchestra let himself out again:

> " 'A life on the ocean wave,
>   And a home on the rolling deep!'

" There was a good deal of honest snickering turned on this time, and considerable groaning, and one or two old deacons got up and went out. The showman grated his teeth, and cursed the piano man to himself; but the fellow sat there like a knot on a log, and seemed to think he was doing first-rate.

"After things got quiet the showman thought he would make one more stagger at it anyway, though his confidence was beginning to get mighty shaky. The supes started the panorama grinding along again, and he says:

"'Ladies and gentlemen, this exquisite painting represents the raising of Lazarus from the dead by our Saviour. The subject has been handled with marvelous skill by the artist, and such touching sweetness and tenderness of expression has he thrown into it that I have known peculiarly sensitive persons to be even affected to tears by looking at it. Observe the half-confused, half-inquiring look upon the countenance of the awakened Lazarus. Observe, also, the attitude and expression of the Saviour, who takes him gently by the sleeve of his shroud with one hand, while He points with the other toward the distant city.

"Before anybody could get off an opinion in the case the innocent old ass at the piano struck up:

> "'Come rise up, William Ri-i-ley,
> And go along with me!'

"Whe-ew! All the solemn old flats got up in a huff to go, and everybody else laughed till the windows rattled.

" The showman went down and grabbed the orchestra and shook him up and says:

" ' That lets you out, you know, you chowder-headed old clam. Go to the doorkeeper and get your money, and cut your stick — vamose the ranche! Ladies and gentlemen, circumstances over which I have no control compel me prematurely to dismiss the house.' '

CURING A COLD*

IT is a good thing, perhaps, to write for the amusement of the public, but it is a far higher and nobler thing to write for their instruction, their profit, their actual and tangible benefit. The latter is the sole object of this article. If it prove the means of restoring to health one solitary sufferer among my race, of lighting up once more the fire of hope and joy in his faded eyes, or bringing back to his dead heart again the quick, generous impulses of other days, I shall be amply rewarded for my labor; my soul will be permeated with the sacred delight a Christian feels when he has done a good, unselfish deed.

Having led a pure and blameless life, I am justified in believing that no man who knows me will reject the suggestions I am about to make, out of fear that I am trying to deceive him. Let the public do itself the honor to read my experience in doctoring a cold, as herein set forth, and then follow in my footsteps.

When the White House was burned in Virginia

* Written about 1864.

City, I lost my home, my happiness, my constitution, and my trunk. The loss of the two first-named articles was a matter of no great consequence, since a home without a mother, or a sister, or a distant young female relative in it, to remind you, by putting your soiled linen out of sight and taking your boots down off the mantel-piece, that there are those who think about you and care for you, is easily obtained. And I cared nothing for the loss of my happiness, because, not being a poet, it could not be possible that melancholy would abide with me long. But to lose a good constitution and a better trunk were serious misfortunes. On the day of the fire my constitution succumbed to a severe cold, caused by undue exertion in getting ready to do something. I suffered to no purpose, too, because the plan I was figuring at for the extinguishing of the fire was so elaborate that I never got it completed until the middle of the following week.

The first time I began to sneeze, a friend told me to go and bathe my feet in hot water and go to bed. I did so. Shortly afterwards, another friend advised me to get up and take a cold shower-bath. I did that also. Within the hour, another friend assured me that it was policy to " feed a cold and starve a fever." I had both. So I thought it best to fill myself up for the cold, and then keep dark and let the fever starve a while.

In a case of this kind, I seldom do things by

halves; I ate pretty heartily; I conferred my custom upon a stranger who had just opened his restaurant that morning; he waited near me in respectful silence until I had finished feeding my cold, when he inquired if the people about Virginia City were much afflicted with colds? I told him I thought they were. He then went out and took in his sign.

I started down toward the office, and on the way encountered another bosom friend, who told me that a quart of salt water, taken warm, would come as near curing a cold as anything in the world. I hardly thought I had room for it, but I tried it anyhow. The result was surprising. I believed I had thrown up my immortal soul.

Now, as I am giving my experience only for the benefit of those who are troubled with the distemper I am writing about, I feel that they will see the propriety of my cautioning them against following such portions of it as proved inefficient with me, and acting upon this conviction, I warn them against warm salt water. It may be a good enough remedy, but I think it is too severe. If I had another cold in the head, and there were no course left me but to take either an earthquake or a quart of warm salt water, I would take my chances on the earthquake.

After the storm which had been raging in my stomach had subsided, and no more good Samaritans happening along, I went on borrowing handkerchiefs again and blowing them to atoms, as had been my custom in the early stages of my cold, until I came across a lady who had just arrived from over the plains, and who said she had lived in a part of the country where doctors were scarce, and had from necessity acquired considerable skill in the treatment of simple " family complaints." I knew she must have had much experience, for she appeared to be a hundred and fifty years old.

She mixed a decoction composed of molasses, aquafortis, turpentine, and various other drugs, and instructed me to take a wine-glass full of it every fifteen minutes. I never took but one dose; that was enough; it robbed me of all moral principle, and awoke every unworthy impulse of my nature. Under its malign influence my brain conceived miracles of meanness, but my hands were too feeble to execute them; at that time, had it not been that my strength had surrendered to a succession of assaults from infallible remedies for my cold, I am satisfied that I would have tried to rob the grave-yard. Like most other people, I often feel mean, and act accordingly; but until I took that medicine I had never revelled in such supernatural depravity, and felt proud of it. At the end of two days I was ready to go to doctoring again. I took a few more unfailing remedies, and finally drove my cold from my head to my lungs.

I got to coughing incessantly, and my voice fell below zero; I conversed in a thundering bass, two octaves below my natural tone; I could only compass my regular nightly repose by coughing myself down to a state of utter exhaustion, and then the moment I began to talk in my sleep, my discordant voice woke me up again.

My case grew more and more serious every day. Plain gin was recommended; I took it. Then gin and molasses; I took that also. Then gin and onions; I added the onions, and took all three. I detected no particular result, however, except that I had acquired a breath like a buzzard's.

I found I had to travel for my health. I went to Lake Bigler with my reportorial comrade, Wilson. It is gratifying to me to reflect that we traveled in considerable style; we went in the Pioneer coach, and my friend took all his baggage with him, consisting of two excellent silk handkerchiefs and a daguerreotype of his grandmother. We sailed and hunted and fished and danced all day, and I doctored my cough all night. By managing in this way, I made out to improve every hour in the twenty-four. But my disease continued to grow worse.

A sheet-bath was recommended. I had never refused a remedy yet, and it seemed poor policy to commence then; therefore I determined to take a sheet-bath, notwithstanding I had no idea what sort of arrangement it was. It was administered at midnight, and the weather was very frosty. My breast and back were bared, and a sheet (there appeared to be a thousand yards of it) soaked in ice-water, was wound around me until I resembled a swab for a Columbiad.

It is a cruel expedient. When the chilly rag touches one's warm flesh, it makes him start with sudden violence, and gasp for breath just as men do in the death agony. It froze the marrow in my bones, and stopped the beating of my heart. I thought my time had come.

Young Wilson said the circumstance reminded him of an anecdote about a negro who was being baptized, and who slipped from the parson's grasp, and came near being drowned. He floundered around, though, and finally rose up out of the water considerably strangled, and furiously angry, and started ashore at once, spouting water like a whale, and remarking, with great asperity, that " one o' dese days some gen'l'man's nigger gwyne to get killed wid jis' such dam foolishness as dis!''

Never take a sheet-bath — never. Next to meeting a lady acquaintance, who, for reasons best known to herself, don't see you when she looks at you, and don't know you when she does see you, it is the most uncomfortable thing in the world.

But, as I was saying, when the sheet-bath failed to cure my cough, a lady friend recommended the application of a mustard plaster to my breast. I believe that would have cured me effectually, if it had not been for young Wilson. When I went to bed, I put my mustard plaster — which was a very gorgeous one, eighteen inches square — where I

26

could reach it when I was ready for it. But young Wilson got hungry in the night, and — here is food for the imagination.

After sojourning a week at Lake Bigler, I went to Steamboat Springs, and, beside the steam baths, I took a lot of the vilest medicines that were ever concocted. They would have cured me, but I had to go back to Virginia City, where, notwithstanding the variety of new remedies I absorbed every day, I managed to aggravate my disease by carelessness and undue exposure.

I finally concluded to visit San Francisco, and the first day I got there, a lady at the hotel told me to drink a quart of whisky every twenty-four hours, and a friend up town recommended precisely the same course. Each advised me to take a quart; that made half a gallon. I did it, and still live.

Now, with the kindest motives in the world, I offer for the consideration of consumptive patients the variegated course of treatment I have lately gone through. Let them try it; if it don't cure, it can't more than kill them.

A CURIOUS PLEASURE EXCURSION *

["We have received the following advertisement, but, inasmuch as it concerns a matter of deep and general interest, we feel fully justified in inserting it in our reading columns. We are confident that our conduct in this regard needs only explanation, not apology.—ED. N. Y. HERALD.]

ADVERTISEMENT

THIS is to inform the public that in connection with Mr. Barnum I have leased the comet for a term of years; and I desire also to solicit the public patronage in favor of a beneficial enterprise which we have in view.

We propose to fit up comfortable, and even luxurious, accommodations in the comet for as many persons as will honor us with their patronage, and make an extended excursion among the heavenly bodies. We shall prepare 1,000,000 staterooms in the tail of the comet (with hot and cold water, gas, looking-glass, parachute, umbrella, etc., in each), and shall construct more if we meet with a sufficiently generous encouragement. We shall have billiard rooms, card rooms, music rooms, bowling

*Published at the time of the "Comet Scare" in the summer of 1874.

alleys and many spacious theaters and free libraries; and on the main deck we propose to have a driving park, with upward of 100,000 miles of roadway in it. We shall publish daily newspapers also.

DEPARTURE OF THE COMET.

The comet will leave New York at 10 P. M. on the 20th inst., and therefore it will be desirable that the passengers be on board by eight at the latest, to avoid confusion in getting under way. It is not known whether passports will be necessary or not, but it is deemed best that passengers provide them, and so guard against all contingencies. No dogs will be allowed on board. This rule has been made in deference to the existing state of feeling regarding these animals, and will be strictly adhered to. The safety of the passengers will in all ways be jealously looked to. A substantial iron railing will be put up all around the comet, and no one will be allowed to go to the edge and look over unless accompanied by either my partner or myself.

THE POSTAL SERVICE

will be of the completest character. Of course the telegraph, and the telegraph only, will be employed; consequently friends occupying staterooms 20,000,000 and even 30,000,000 miles apart, will be able to send a message and receive a reply inside of eleven days. Night messages will be half rate. The whole of this vast postal system will be under the personal superintendence of Mr. Hale of Maine.

Meals served at all hours. Meals served in state-rooms charged extra.

Hostility is not apprehended from any great planet, but we have thought it best to err on the safe side, and therefore have provided a proper number of mortars, siege guns, and boarding pikes. History shows that small, isolated communities, such as the people of remote islands, are prone to be hostile to strangers, and so the same may be the case with

THE INHABITANTS OF STARS

of the tenth or twentieth magnitude. We shall in no case wantonly offend the people of any star, but shall treat all alike with urbanity and kindliness, never conducting ourselves toward an asteroid after a fashion which we could not venture to assume toward Jupiter or Saturn. I repeat that we shall not wantonly offend any star; but at the same time we shall promptly resent any injury that may be done us, or any insolence offered us, by parties or governments residing in any star in the firmament. Although averse to the shedding of blood, we shall still hold this course rigidly and fearlessly, not only toward single stars, but toward constellations. We shall hope to leave a good impression of America behind us in every nation we visit, from Venus to Uranus. And, at all events, if we cannot inspire love we shall at least compel respect for our country wherever we go. We shall take with us, free of charge,

A GREAT FORCE OF MISSIONARIES,

and shed the true light upon all the celestial orbs which, physically aglow, are yet morally in darkness. Sunday-schools will be established wherever practicable. Compulsory education will also be introduced.

The comet will visit Mars first, and proceed to Mercury, Jupiter, Venus, and Saturn. Parties connected with the government of the District of Columbia and with the former city government of New York, who may desire to inspect the rings, will be allowed time and every facility. Every star of prominent magnitude will be visited, and time allowed for excursions to points of interest inland.

THE DOG STAR

has been stricken from the programme. Much time will be spent in the Great Bear, and, indeed, of every constellation of importance. So, also, with the Sun and Moon and the Milky Way, otherwise the Gulf Stream of the skies. Clothing suitable for wear in the sun should be provided. Our programme has been so arranged that we shall seldom go more than 100,000,000 of miles at a time without stopping at some star. This will necessarily make the stoppages frequent and preserve the interest of the tourist. Baggage checked through to any point on the route. Parties desiring to make only a part of the proposed tour, and thus save expense, may stop over at any star they choose and wait for the return voyage.

After visiting all the most celebrated stars and constellations in our system and personally inspecting the remotest sparks that even the most powerful telescope can now detect in the firmament, we shall proceed with good heart upon

A STUPENDOUS VOYAGE

of discovery among the countless whirling worlds that make turmoil in the mighty wastes of space that stretch their solemn solitudes, their unimaginable vastness billions upon billions of miles away beyond the farthest verge of telescopic vision, till by comparison the little sparkling vault we used to gaze at on Earth shall seem like a remembered phosphorescent flash of spangles which some tropical voyager's prow stirred into life for a single instant, and which ten thousand miles of phosphorescent seas and tedious lapse of time had since diminished to an incident utterly trivial in his recollection. Children occupying seats at the first table will be charged full fare.

FIRST CLASS FARE

from the Earth to Uranus, including visits to the Sun and Moon and all the principal planets on the route, will be charged at the low rate of $2 for every 50,000,000 miles of actual travel. A great reduction will be made where parties wish to make the round trip. This comet is new and in thorough repair and is now on her first voyage. She is confessedly the fastest on the line. She makes 20,-

000,000 miles a day, with her present facilities; but, with a picked American crew and good weather, we are confident we can get 40,000,000 out of her. Still, we shall never push her to a dangerous speed, and we shall rigidly prohibit racing with other comets. Passengers desiring to diverge at any point or return will be transferred to other comets. We make close connections at all principal points with all reliable lines. Safety can be depended upon. It is not to be denied that the heavens are infested with

OLD RAMSHACKLE COMETS

that have not been inspected or overhauled in 10,000 years, and which ought long ago to have been destroyed or turned into hail barges, but with these we have no connection whatever. Steerage passengers not allowed abaft the main hatch.

Complimentary round trip tickets have been tendered to General Butler, Mr. Shepherd, Mr. Richardson, and other eminent gentlemen, whose public services have entitled them to the rest and relaxation of a voyage of this kind. Parties desiring to make the round trip will have extra accommodation. The entire voyage will be completed, and the passengers landed in New York again on the 14th of December, 1991. This is, at least, forty years quicker than any other comet can do it in. Nearly all the back pay members contemplate making the round trip with us in case their constituents will allow them a holiday. Every harmless amusement will be allowed on board, but no pools permitted on the run of the comet — no gambling of any kind. All fixed stars will be respected by us, but such stars as seem to need fixing we shall fix. If it makes trouble we shall be sorry, but firm.

Mr. Coggia having leased his comet to us, she will no longer be called by his name but by my partner's. N. B.— Passengers by paying double fare will be entitled to a share in all the new stars, suns, moons, comets, meteors, and magazines of thunder and lightning we may discover. Patent medicine people will take notice that

WE CARRY BULLETIN BOARDS

and a paint brush along for use in the constellations, and are open to terms. Cremationists are reminded that we are going straight to — some hot places — and are open to terms. To other parties our enterprise is a pleasure excursion, but individually we mean business. We shall fly our comet for all it is worth.

FOR FURTHER PARTICULARS,

or for freight or passage, apply on board, or to my partner, but not to me, since I do not take charge of the comet until she is under weigh. It is necessary, at a time like this, that my mind should not be burdened with small business details.

MARK TWAIN.

RUNNING FOR GOVERNOR *

A FEW months ago I was nominated for Governor
of the great State of New York, to run against
Mr. John T. Smith and Mr. Blank J. Blank on an
independent ticket. I somehow felt that I had one
prominent advantage over these gentlemen, and that
was — good character. It was easy to see by the
newspapers that if ever they had known what it was
to bear a good name, that time had gone by. It
was plain that in these latter years they had become
familiar with all manner of shameful crimes. But
at the very moment that I was exalting my advantage and joying in it in secret, there was a muddy
undercurrent of discomfort "riling" the deeps of
my happiness, and that was — the having to hear
my name bandied about in familiar connection with
those of such people. I grew more and more disturbed. Finally I wrote my grandmother about it.
Her answer came quick and sharp. She said:

"You have never done one single thing in all your life to be
ashamed of—not one. Look at the newspapers—look at them and comprehend what sort of characters Messrs. Smith and Blank are, and then

---

* Written about 1870.

see if you are willing to lower yourself to their level and enter a public canvass with them."

It was my very thought! I did not sleep a single moment that night. But after all I could not recede. I was fully committed, and must go on with the fight. As I was looking listlessly over the papers at breakfast I came across this paragraph, and I may truly say I never was so confounded before.

" PERJURY.—Perhaps, now that Mr. Mark Twain is before the people as a candidate for Governor, he will condescend to explain how he came to be convicted of perjury by thirty-four witnesses in Wakawak, Cochin China, in 1863, the intent of which perjury being to rob a poor native widow and her helpless family of a meagre plantain-patch, their only stay and support in their bereavement and desolation. Mr. Twain owes it to himself, as well as to the great people whose suffrages he asks, to clear this matter up. Will he do it?"

I thought I should burst with amazement! Such a cruel, heartless charge. I never had *seen* Cochin China! I never had *heard* of Wakawak! I didn't know a plantain-patch from a kangaroo! I did not know what to do. I was crazed and helpless. I let the day slip away without doing anything at all. The next morning the same paper had this — nothing more :

" SIGNIFICANT.—Mr. Twain, it will be observed, is suggestively silent about the Cochin China perjury."

[*Mem.*— During the rest of the campaign this paper never referred to me in any other way than as " the infamous perjurer Twain."]

Next came the *Gazette*, with this:

" WANTED TO KNOW.—Will the new candidate for Governor deign

to explain to certain of his fellow-citizens (who are suffering to vote for him!) the little circumstance of his cabin-mates in Montana losing small valuables from time to time, until at last, these things having been invariably found on Mr. Twain's person or in his 'trunk' (newspaper he rolled his traps in), they felt compelled to give him a friendly admonition for his own good, and so tarred and feathered him, and rode him on a rail, and then advised him to leave a permanent vacuum in the place he usually occupied in the camp. Will he do this?"

Could anything be more deliberately malicious than that? For I never was in Montana in my life.

[After this, this journal customarily spoke of me as " Twain, the Montana Thief."]

I got to picking up papers apprehensively — much as one would lift a desired blanket which he had some idea might have a rattlesnake under it. One day this met my eye:

"THE LIE NAILED.—By the sworn affidavits of Michael O'Flanagan, Esq., of the Five Points, and Mr. Snub Rafferty and Mr. Catty Mulligan, of Water Street, it is established that Mr. Mark Twain's vile statement that the lamented grandfather of our noble standard-bearer, Blank J. Blank, was hanged for highway robbery, is a brutal and gratuitous LIE, without a shadow of foundation in fact. It is disheartening to virtuous men to see such shameful means resorted to to achieve political success as the attacking of the dead in their graves, and defiling their honored names with slander. When we think of the anguish this miserable falsehood must cause the innocent relatives and friends of the deceased, we are almost driven to incite an outraged and insulted public to summary and unlawful vengeance upon the traducer. But no! let us leave him to the agony of a lacerated conscience (though if passion should get the better of the public, and in its blind fury they should do the traducer bodily injury, it is but too obvious that no jury could convict and no court punish the perpetrators of the deed)."

The ingenious closing sentence had the effect of moving me out of bed with dispatch that night, and out at the back door also, while the " outraged and insulted public " surged in the front way, breaking furniture and windows in their righteous indignation as they came, and taking off such property as they could carry when they went. And yet I can lay my hand upon the Book and say that I never slandered Mr. Blank's grandfather. More: I had never even heard of him or mentioned him up to that day and date.

[I will state, in passing, that the journal above quoted from always referred to me afterward as " Twain, the Body-Snatcher."]

The next newspaper article that attracted my attention was the following:

" A SWEET CANDIDATE.—Mr. Mark Twain, who was to make such a blighting speech at the mass meeting of the Independents last night, didn't come to time! A telegram from his physician stated that he had been knocked down by a runaway team, and his leg broken in two places—sufferer lying in great agony, and so forth, and so forth, and a lot more bosh of the same sort. And the Independents tried hard to swallow the wretched subterfuge, and pretend that they did not know what was the *real* reason of the absence of the abandoned creature whom they denominate their standard-bearer. *A certain man was seen to reel into Mr. Twain's hotel last night in a state of beastly intoxication.* It is the imperative duty of the Independents to prove that this besotted brute was not Mark Twain himself. We have them at last! This is a case that admits of no shirking. The voice of the people demands in thunder-tones, ' WHO WAS THAT MAN? ' "

It was incredible, absolutely incredible, for a moment, that it was really my name that was coupled with this disgraceful suspicion. Three long years had passed over my head since I had tasted ale, beer, wine, or liquor of any kind.

[It shows what effect the times were having on me when I say that I saw myself confidently dubbed "Mr. Delirium Tremens Twain" in the next issue of that journal without a pang — notwithstanding I knew that with monotonous fidelity the paper would go on calling me so to the very end.]

By this time anonymous letters were getting to be an important part of my mail matter. This form was common:

"How about that old woman you kiked of your premisers which was beging.   POL PRY."

And this:

"There is things which you have done which is unbeknowens to any-body but me.   You better trot out a few dols. to yours truly, or you'll hear through the papers from   HANDY ANDY."

This is about the idea.   I could continue them till the reader was surfeited, if desirable.

Shortly the principal Republican journal "convicted" me of wholesale bribery, and the leading Democratic paper "nailed" an aggravated case of blackmailing to me.

[In this way I acquired two additional names: "Twain the Filthy Corruptionist," and "Twain the Loathsome Embracer."]

By this time there had grown to be such a clamor for an "answer" to all the dreadful charges that were laid to me that the editors and leaders of my party said it would be political ruin for me to remain silent any longer. As if to make their appeal

the more imperative, the following appeared in one
of the papers the very next day:

"BEHOLD THE MAN!—The independent candidate still maintains
silence. Because he dare not speak. Every accusation against him has
been amply proved, and they have been endorsed and re-endorsed by
his own eloquent silence, till at this day he stands forever convicted.
Look upon your candidate, Independents! Look upon the Infamous
Perjurer! the Montana Thief! the Body-Snatcher! Contemplate your
incarnate Delirium Tremens! your Filthy Corruptionist! your Loathsome
Embracer! Gaze upon him—ponder him well—and then say if you can
give your honest votes to a creature who has earned this dismal array of
titles by his hideous crimes, and dares not open his mouth in denial of
any one of them!"

There was no possible way of getting out of it,
and so, in deep humiliation, I set about preparing to
"answer" a mass of baseless charges and mean
and wicked falsehoods. But I never finished the
task, for the very next morning a paper came out
with a new horror, a fresh malignity, and seriously
charged me with burning a lunatic asylum with all
its inmates, because it obstructed the view from my
house. This threw me into a sort of panic. Then
came the charge of poisoning my uncle to get his
property, with an imperative demand that the grave
should be opened. This drove me to the verge of
distraction. On top of this I was accused of em-
ploying toothless and incompetent old relatives to
prepare the food for the foundling hospital when I
was warden. I was wavering — wavering. And at
last, as a due and fitting climax to the shameless
persecution that party rancor had inflicted upon me,
nine little toddling children, of all shades of color

and degrees of raggedness, were taught to rush on
to the platform at a public meeting, and clasp me
around the legs and call me PA!

I gave it up. I hauled down my colors and surrendered. I was not equal to the requirements of a
Gubernatorial campaign in the State of New York,
and so I sent in my withdrawal from the candidacy,
and in bitterness of spirit signed it, " Truly yours,
once a decent man, but now

MARK TWAIN, I.P., M.T., B.S., D.T., F.C., and
    L.E."

A MYSTERIOUS VISIT

THE first notice that was taken of me when I " settled down " recently, was by a gentleman who said he was an assessor, and connected with the U. S. Internal Revenue Department. I said I had never heard of his branch of business before, but I was very glad to see him all the same — would he sit down? He sat down. I did not know anything particular to say, and yet I felt that people who have arrived at the dignity of keeping house must be conversational, must be easy and sociable in company. So, in default of anything else to say, I asked him if he was opening his shop in our neighborhood.

He said he was. [I did not wish to appear ignorant, but I *had* hoped he would mention what he had for sale.]

I ventured to ask him " How was trade?" And he said " So-so."

I then said we would drop in, and if we liked his house as well as any other, we would give him our custom.

He said he thought we would like his establishment well enough to confine ourselves to it — said he never saw anybody who would go off and hunt up another man in his line after trading with him once.

That sounded pretty complacent, but barring that natural expression of villainy which we all have, the man looked honest enough.

I do not know how it came about exactly, but gradually we appeared to melt down and run together, conversationally speaking, and then everything went along as comfortably as clockwork.

We talked, and talked, and talked — at least I did; and we laughed, and laughed, and laughed — at least he did. But all the time I had my presence of mind about me — I had my native shrewdness turned on "full head," as the engineers say. I was determined to find out all about his business in spite of his obscure answers — and I was determined I would have it out of him without his suspecting what I was at. I meant to trap him with a deep, deep ruse. I would tell him all about my own business, and he would naturally so warm to me during this seductive burst of confidence that he would forget himself, and tell me all about *his* affairs before he suspected what I was about. I thought to myself, My son, you little know what an old fox you are dealing with. I said:

" Now you never would guess what I made lecturing this winter and last spring?"

" No — don't believe I could, to save me. Let me see — let me see. About two thousand dollars,

maybe? But no; no, sir, I know you couldn't
have made that much. Say seventeen hundred,
maybe?"

" Ha! ha! I knew you couldn't. My lecturing
receipts for last spring and this winter were fourteen
thousand seven hundred and fifty dollars. What do
you think of that?"

" Why, it is amazing — perfectly amazing. I will
make a note of it. And you say even this wasn't
all?"

" All! Why bless you, there was my income
from the *Daily Warwhoop* for four months — about
— about — well, what should you say to about eight
thousand dollars, for instance?"

" Say! Why, I should say I should like to see
myself rolling in just such another ocean of affluence. Eight thousand! I'll make a note of it.
Why man! — and on top of all this I am to understand that you had still more income?"

" Ha! ha! ha! Why, you're only in the suburbs
of it, so to speak. There's my book, ' The Innocents Abroad '— price $3.50 to $5, according to
the binding. Listen to me. Look me in the eye.
During the last four months and a half, saying nothing of sales before that, but just simply during the
four months and a half, we've sold ninety-five thousand copies of that book. Ninety-five thousand!
Think of it. Average four dollars a copy, say. It's
nearly four hundred thousand dollars, my son. I
get half."

AA

"The suffering Moses! I'll set *that* down. Fourteen-seven-fifty — eight — two hundred. Total, say — well, upon my word, the grand total is about two hundred and thirteen or fourteen thousand dollars! *Is* that possible?"

"Possible! If there's any mistake it's the other way. Two hundred and fourteen thousand, cash, is my income for this year if *I* know how to cipher."

Then the gentleman got up to go. It came over me most uncomfortably that maybe I had made my revelations for nothing, besides being flattered into stretching them considerably by the stranger's astonished exclamations. But no; at the last moment the gentleman handed me a large envelope, and said it contained his advertisement; and that I would find out all about his business in it; and that he would be happy to have my custom — would, in fact, be *proud* to have the custom of a man of such prodigious income; and that he used to think there were several wealthy men in the city, but when they came to trade with him, he discovered that they barely had enough to live on; and that, in truth, it had been such a weary, weary age since he had seen a rich man face to face, and talked to him, and touched him with his hands, that he could hardly refrain from embracing me — in fact, would esteem it a great favor if I would *let* him embrace me.

This so pleased me that I did not try to resist, but allowed this simple-hearted stranger to throw his arms about me and weep a few tranquilizing tears down the back of my neck.   Then he went his way.

As soon as he was gone I opened his advertisement. I studied it attentively for four minutes.   I then called up the cook, and said:

"Hold me while I faint! Let Marie turn the griddle-cakes."

By and by, when I came to, I sent down to the rum mill on the corner and hired an artist by the week to sit up nights and curse that stranger, and give me a lift occasionally in the daytime when I came to a hard place.

Ah, what a miscreant he was! His "advertisement" was nothing in the world but a wicked tax-return — a string of impertinent questions about my private affairs, occupying the best part of four foolscap pages of fine print — questions, I may remark, gotten up with such marvelous ingenuity, that the oldest man in the world couldn't understand what the most of them were driving at — questions, too, that were calculated to make a man report about four times his actual income to keep from swearing to a falsehood. I looked for a loophole, but there did not appear to be any. Inquiry No. 1 covered my case as generously and as amply as an umbrella could cover an ant hill:

"What were your profits, during the past year, from any trade, business, or vocation, wherever carried on?"

And that inquiry was backed up by thirteen others of an equally searching nature, the most

modest of which required information as to whether
I had committed any burglary or highway robbery,
or by any arson or other secret source of emolu-
ment had acquired property which was not enumerated in my statement of income as set opposite to
inquiry No. 1.

It was plain that that stranger had enabled me to
make a goose of myself. It was very, very plain;
and so I went out and hired another artist. By
working on my vanity, the stranger had seduced me
into declaring an income of $214,000. By law,
$1,000 of this was exempt from income tax — the
only relief I could see, and it was only a drop in the
ocean. At the legal five per cent., I must pay to
the Government the sum of ten thousand six hundred and fifty dollars, income tax!

[I may remark, in this place, that I did not do it.]

I am acquainted with a very opulent man, whose
house is a palace, whose table is regal, whose out-
lays are enormous, yet a man who has no income,
as I have often noticed by the revenue returns; and
to him I went for advice in my distress. He took
my dreadful exhibition of receipts, he put on his
glasses, he took his pen, and presto! — I was a
pauper! It was the neatest thing that ever was.
He did it simply by deftly manipulating the bill of
" DEDUCTIONS." He set down my " State, national,
and municipal taxes " at so much; my " losses by
shipwreck, fire, etc.," at so much; my " losses on
sales of real estate "— on " live stock sold "— on

" payments for rent of homestead "— on " repairs, improvements, interest "— on " previously taxed salary as an officer of the United States army, navy, revenue service," and other things. He got astonishing " deductions " out of each and every one of these matters — each and every one of them. And when he was done he handed me the paper, and I saw at a glance that during the year my income, in the way of profits, had been *one thousand two hundred and fifty dollars and forty cents.*

" Now," said he, " the thousand dollars is exempt by law. What you want to do is to go and swear this document in and pay tax on the two hundred and fifty dollars."

[While he was making this speech his little boy Willie lifted a two dollar greenback out of his vest pocket and vanished with it, and I would wager anything that if my stranger were to call on that little boy to-morrow he would make a false return of his income.]

" Do you," said I, " do you always work up the ' deductions ' after this fashion in your own case, sir?"

" Well, I should say so! If it weren't for those eleven saving clauses under the head of ' Deduction ' I should be beggared every year to support this hateful and wicked, this extortionate and tyrannical government."

This gentleman stands away up among the very best of the solid men of the city — the men of moral weight, of commercial integrity, of unimpeachable social spotlessness — and so I bowed to his example. I went down to the revenue office, and under the accusing eyes of my old visitor I stood up and swore to lie after lie, fraud after fraud, villainy after villainy, till my soul was coated inches and inches thick with perjury, and my self-respect gone forever and ever.

But what of it? It is nothing more than thousands of the richest and proudest, and most respected, honored, and courted men in America do every year. And so I don't care. I am not ashamed. I shall simply, for the present, talk little, and eschew fire-proof gloves, lest I fall into certain dreadful habits irrevocably.

THE END.